GCSE OCR 21st Century
Additional Science
The Revision Guide

This book is for anyone doing **GCSE OCR 21st Century Additional Science** at higher level.

GCSE Science is all about **understanding how science works**.
And not only that — understanding it well enough to be able to **question**
what you hear on TV and read in the papers.

But you can't do that without a fair chunk of **background knowledge**. Hmm, tricky.

Happily this CGP book includes all the **science facts** you need to learn,
and shows you how they work in the **real world**. And in true CGP style,
we've explained it all as **clearly and concisely** as possible.

It's also got some daft bits in to try and make the whole
experience at least vaguely entertaining for you.

What CGP is all about

Our sole aim here at CGP is to produce the highest
quality books — carefully written, immaculately presented
and dangerously close to being funny.

Then we work our socks off to get them out to you — at the cheapest possible prices.

Contents

Published by Coordination Group Publications Ltd.

From original material by Richard Parsons.

Editors:

Amy Boutal, Ellen Bowness, Tom Cain, Katherine Craig, Sarah Hilton,
Kate Houghton, Rose Parkin, Ami Snelling, Laurence Stamford, Jane Towle,
Julie Wakeling, Sarah Williams.

Contributors:

Michael Aicken, Mike Bossart, John Duffy, James Foster, Jason Howell,
Barbara Mascetti, John Myers, Andy Rankin, Philip Rushworth, Mike Thompson,
Jim Wilson.

ISBN: 978 1 84762 000 2

With thanks to Jeremy Cooper, Ian Francis, Sue Hocking and Glenn Rogers for the proofreading.

Groovy website: www.cgpbooks.co.uk

Printed by Elanders Hindson Ltd, Newcastle upon Tyne.
Jolly bits of clipart from CorelDRAW®

The Basics of Homeostasis

Homeostasis is a fancy word, but it covers lots of things, so maybe that's fair enough.
It's about how your body keeps its internal environment constant.

Homeostasis — Maintaining a Constant Internal Environment

The conditions inside your body need to be kept <u>steady</u>, even when the <u>external environment changes</u>.
This is really important because your <u>cells</u> need the <u>right conditions</u> in order to <u>function properly</u>.
Homeostasis is all about balancing <u>inputs</u> (stuff going into your body) with <u>outputs</u> (stuff leaving)
to <u>maintain a constant internal environment</u>. For example...

1) <u>Water content</u> — you need to keep a <u>balance</u> between the water you gain
   (in food, drink and from respiration) and the water you pee, sweat and
   breathe out. This is regulated by the kidneys (see pages 8-9 for more details).

   Respiration is the chemical reactions that release energy from food.

2) <u>Body temperature</u> — you need to get rid of <u>excess</u> body heat when you're hot but
   <u>retain</u> heat when your environment is cold. Your body has several ways it can do this,
   see page 6 for more details. So, whether its boiling hot or freezing cold
   outside, your body is kept at a relatively constant temperature (around 37 °C).

You have loads of <u>automatic control systems</u> in your body that regulate your internal environment.
There's a control system that maintains your <u>water content</u> (see pages 8-9) and one that maintains
your <u>body temperature</u> (see page 6).

Exercise and Climate can Affect Homeostasis

There are several things that can affect your internal environment.
You need to know about the effects of <u>strenuous exercise</u> and <u>extreme climates</u> on homeostasis:

1) <u>Strenuous exercise</u> changes some conditions in your body, including...
   * <u>temperature</u> — when you exercise you <u>generate heat</u>, so your body temperature <u>increases</u>.
   * <u>water content</u> (hydration) — during exercise more water is lost in <u>sweat</u> through the skin as you
     get hotter and more <u>water vapour</u> is lost from your lungs as your <u>breathing rate increases</u>.
   * <u>salt levels</u> — <u>sweat</u> contains salt, so if you sweat a lot the level in your body will <u>decrease</u>.
2) <u>Extreme climates</u> can play havoc with your internal environment too.
   * <u>hot climates</u> — generally have the same effect as strenuous exercise.
   * <u>cold climates</u> — can cause your <u>body temperature</u> to <u>decrease rapidly</u>.

All these changes sound a bit scary, but don't worry — your body works overtime to combat them.
You need to know how the following activities affect homeostasis:

MOUNTAIN CLIMBING

Mountaineering involves both strenuous
exercise and a cold climate. Climbing to <u>high
altitudes</u> also affects your <u>blood oxygen level</u>.
Higher up, the pressure is <u>lower</u>, which means
there's <u>less oxygen available</u> for you to breathe.
This can lead to a low blood oxygen levels and
contribute to <u>altitude sickness</u>.

SCUBA-DIVING

A scuba diver's <u>temperature</u> will drop in <u>cold
water</u>. Diving deep can affect your <u>blood oxygen
level</u> too. As you go deeper more oxygen is
'pushed' into your blood because of the <u>higher</u>
pressure. If <u>too much oxygen</u> is pushed into the
blood, divers can develop a dangerous condition
called <u>oxygen toxicity</u>.

My sister never goes out — she's got homeostasis...

Mountain climbers aren't usually at high altitudes for long, but their bodies can <u>acclimatise</u> by producing
more red blood cells (which carry oxygen around the body) to make sure their muscles get enough oxygen.

Negative Feedback

Now you know what homeostasis is you need to learn how it's controlled... What fun.

Negative Feedback Counteracts Changes

A mechanism called negative feedback helps to keep your internal environment constant. When the level of something (e.g. water or temperature) gets too high or too low, your body uses negative feedback to bring it back to normal. All homeostatic control systems are made up of three main components, which work together to maintain a steady condition:

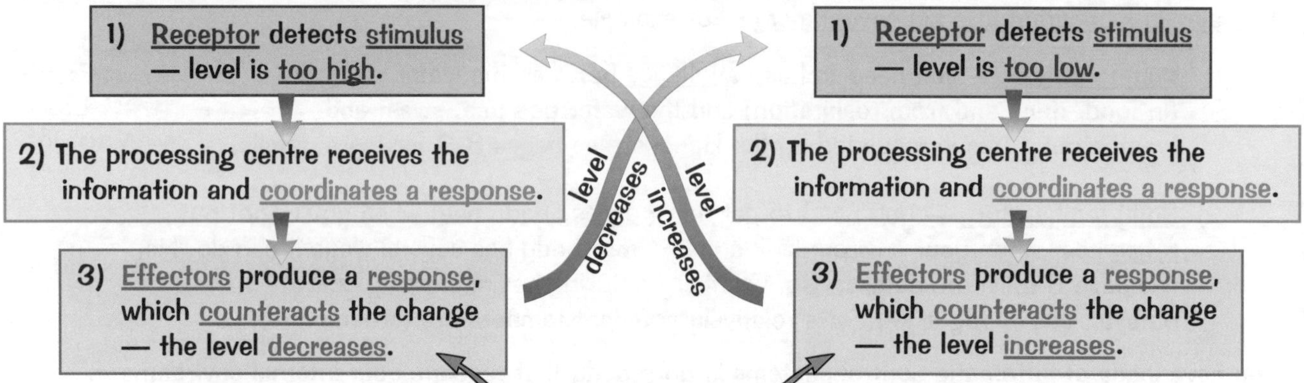

The effectors will just carry on producing the responses for as long as they're stimulated by the processing centre. This might cause the opposite problem — making the level change too much (away from the ideal). Luckily the receptor detects if the level becomes too different and negative feedback starts again.

This process happens without you thinking about it — it's all automatic.

Some Artificial Systems Function Like Body Control Systems

Some artificial systems, like incubators, work in a similar way to your body's control systems — using negative feedback. Incubators are used in hospitals to provide an environment with the correct temperature for premature babies. Incubators have a thermostat that can detect temperature changes, and a heater to correct the change by either heating or not heating...

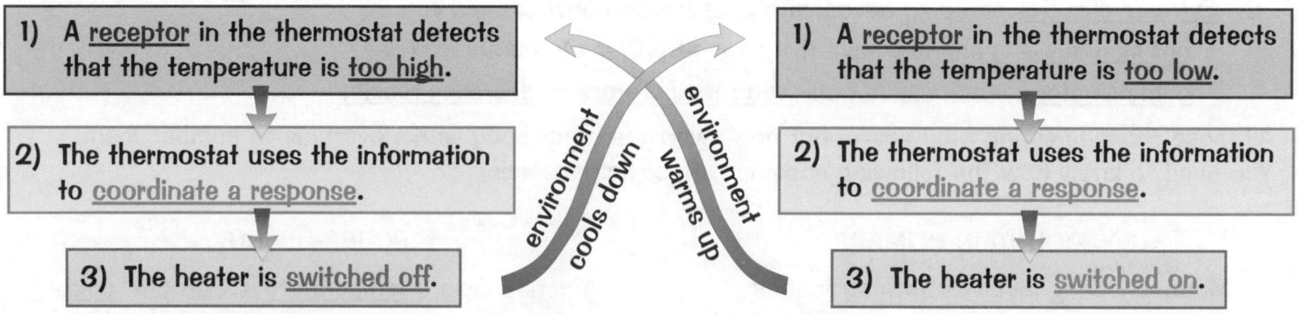

Your internal temperature control isn't too different to this — see page 6.

Some Effectors Work Antagonistically

Some effectors work antagonistically, e.g. one effector heats and another cools — they'll work at the same time to achieve a very precise temperature. This mechanism allows a more sensitive response.

If you do enough revision, you can avoid negative feedback...

Negative feedback isn't too hard to understand once you've got the basics. The response produced has the opposite (negative) effect to the change detected — it counteracts the change.

Diffusion

Your body is pretty fussy — the levels of certain chemicals need to be controlled in order for it to function properly. Some of these substances can move around by diffusion, so you've got to learn about it...

Don't be Put Off by the Fancy Word

"Diffusion" is simple. It's just the gradual movement of particles from places where there are lots of them to places where there are fewer of them. That's all it is — just the natural tendency for stuff to spread out. Unfortunately you also have to learn the fancy way of saying the same thing, which is this:

> **DIFFUSION is the passive overall movement of particles from a region of their HIGHER CONCENTRATION to a region of their LOWER CONCENTRATION.**

1) The particles are moving about randomly, so they go both ways — but if there are a lot more particles in one area, there's a net (overall) movement from that side.

2) Diffusion happens in both liquids and gases — that's because the particles in these substances are free to move about randomly. The simplest type is when different gases diffuse through each other. This is what's happening when the smell of perfume diffuses through a room:

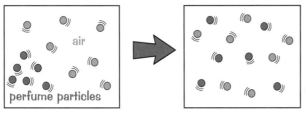

The bigger the difference in concentration, the faster the diffusion rate.

smell diffused in the air

Some Chemicals can Move In and Out of Cells by Diffusion

Some chemicals can diffuse across cell membranes — from an area of higher concentration to an area of lower concentration. Diffusion across cell membranes is important as it's one way our cells can obtain the things they need to function.

1) Cells produce carbon dioxide, which means that there is always a higher concentration of CO_2 in the cells than in the blood. So, CO_2 will move out of the cells and into the blood by diffusion to be carried away.

2) Cells need oxygen and dissolved food (e.g. glucose) to function. There is a lower concentration of these in the cells than in the blood, so oxygen and dissolved food diffuse out of the blood into the cells.

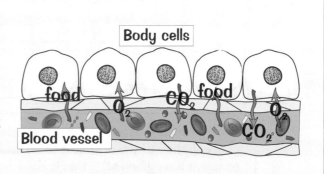

Revision by diffusion — you wish...

Wouldn't that be great — if all the ideas in this book would just gradually drift across into your mind, from an area of high concentration (in the book) to an area of low concentration (in your mind — no offence). Actually, that probably will happen if you read it again. Why don't you give it a go...

Osmosis and Active Transport

Osmosis is <u>diffusion</u> of <u>water</u>, so its pretty important in the control of water levels in your cells.

Osmosis is a Specific Case of Diffusion, That's All

Osmosis is a type of <u>diffusion</u> — the passive movement of water molecules from an area of higher concentration to an area of lower concentration.

> <u>Osmosis</u> is the overall <u>movement of water</u> from a <u>DILUTE</u> to a <u>MORE CONCENTRATED</u> solution through a <u>partially permeable membrane</u>.

1) A <u>partially permeable</u> membrane is just one that <u>only allows certain substances</u> to <u>diffuse</u> through it. For example, it may only allow small molecules like <u>water</u> to pass through and not larger molecules like <u>sucrose</u>.

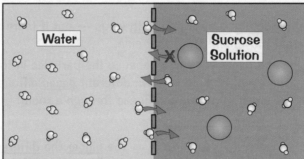

Water | Sucrose Solution

Net movement of water molecules

A cell membrane is partially permeable.

2) The <u>concentrated</u> starch solution gets more <u>dilute</u> as more water moves in. The water acts like it's trying to '<u>even up</u>' the concentration either side of the membrane.

Animals Must Regulate Their Water Content

1) Animal cells <u>can't withstand big changes</u> in the <u>amount of water</u> they contain.
2) If too much water <u>moves into</u> an animal cell by osmosis, it can <u>rupture</u> (burst), killing the cell.
3) If too much water <u>moves out</u> of an animal cell, it shrivels up and <u>can't function properly</u>.

Some Chemicals can be Moved by Active Transport

> Sometimes chemicals, e.g. glucose, need to be moved from an area with a <u>lower</u> concentration of the chemical to an area with a <u>higher</u> concentration (against the concentration gradient). This is done by a process called <u>active transport</u>. <u>Glucose</u> is reabsorbed in the <u>kidneys</u> by active transport (see page 8).

Osmosis — it stops you from bursting, like a big fat balloon...

So, if <u>osmosis</u> is the <u>same</u> as <u>diffusion</u> but with <u>water</u>, why don't they just call it water diffusion... It isn't even a good word — how can you possibly <u>make a joke</u> using osmosis. Not even my panel of specially trained, professional joke thinker-uppers can come up with anything remotely amusing about it.

Enzymes

Enzymes are a great example of why it's so important to maintain a constant internal environment. They won't work if they don't have the right conditions, and without enzymes your body won't function properly.

Enzymes **are Catalysts Produced by Living Things**

1) Living things have thousands of different chemical reactions going on inside them all the time.

2) These reactions need to be carefully controlled — to get the right amounts of substances.

3) So... living things produce enzymes which act as biological catalysts. These speed up the useful chemical reactions in the body.

> **ENZYMES** are proteins that **SPEED UP CHEMICAL REACTIONS** in cells.

Enzymes **are Very Specific**

1) Chemical reactions usually involve things either being split apart or joined together.

2) A substrate is a molecule that is changed in a reaction.

3) Every enzyme molecule has an active site — the part where a substrate joins on to the enzyme.

4) Enzymes are really picky — they usually only speed up one reaction.

5) This is because, for an enzyme to work, a substrate has to be the correct shape to fit into the active site. If a substrate's shape doesn't match the active site's shape, then the reaction won't be catalysed. This is called the 'lock and key' model, because the substrate fits into the enzyme just like a key fits into a lock.

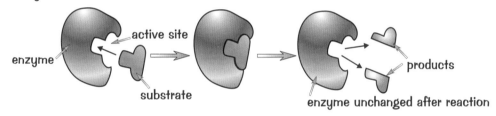

Enzymes **Need the Right Temperature and pH**

Enzymes need to be at a specific constant temperature to work at their optimum.

1) Changing the temperature changes the rate of an enzyme-catalysed reaction.

2) Like with any reaction, a higher temperature increases the rate at first. This is because it increases the frequency and energy of collisions between an enzyme and its substrate. But, if it gets too hot, some of the bonds holding the enzyme together break. This changes the shape of the enzyme's active site and so the substrate will no longer fit and the enzyme won't work any more. It's said to be denatured.

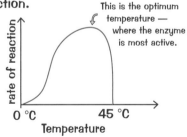

This is the optimum temperature — where the enzyme is most active.

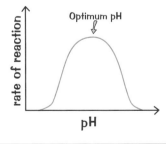

3) The pH also affects enzymes. If it's too high or too low, the pH interferes with the bonds holding the enzyme together. This changes the shape of the active site and denatures the enzyme.

4) All enzymes have an optimum pH that they work best at. It's often neutral pH 7, but not always — e.g. pepsin is an enzyme used to break down proteins in the stomach. It works best at pH 2, which means it's well-suited to the acidic conditions there.

If only enzymes could speed up revision...

Just like you've got to have the correct key for a lock, enzymes have got to have the right substrate. If a substrate doesn't fit, the enzyme won't catalyse the reaction...

Controlling Body Temperature

Now you know that enzymes need a specific constant temperature — here's how your body maintains it...

Body Temperature Must be Kept Constant

1) The reactions in your body work best at about 37 °C. This means that you need to keep your core body temperature around this value — within 1 or 2 °C of it.

Core body temperature is the temperature inside your body, where your organs are.

2) So the amount of heat energy gained and lost by the body must be balanced to keep it at a constant temperature.

3) Temperature receptors in the skin detect the external temperature, and receptors in the hypothalamus (a part of the brain) detect the temperature of the blood.

4) The nervous system (see page 61) helps to control body temperature, using the following negative feedback mechanism (see page 2)...

1) Temperature receptors detect that core body temperature is too high.	1) Temperature receptors detect that core body temperature is too low.
2) The hypothalamus acts as a processing centre — it receives information from the temperature receptors and triggers the effectors automatically.	2) The hypothalamus acts as a processing centre — it receives information from the temperature receptors and triggers the effectors automatically.
3) Effectors, e.g. sweat glands, produce a response and counteract the change.	3) Effectors, e.g. muscles, produce a response and counteract the change.

body cools down / body warms up

The Body has Some Nifty Tricks for Altering its Temperature

Different responses are produced by effectors to counteract an increase or decrease in body temperature.

When You're TOO HOT:

1) Blood vessels close to the skin's surface get bigger in diameter — this is called vasodilation. This means that more blood gets to the surface of the skin. The warm blood then loses more of its heat to the surroundings.

2) Your sweat glands produce more sweat — when the water in the sweat evaporates heat is used, which cools the body.

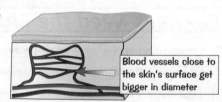
Blood vessels close to the skin's surface get bigger in diameter

When You're TOO COLD:

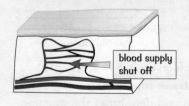
blood supply shut off

1) Blood vessels close to the skin's surface get smaller in diameter — this is called vasoconstriction. This means that less blood gets to the surface of the skin, which stops the blood losing as much heat to the surroundings.

2) You shiver — your muscles contract rapidly. This increases the rate of respiration and warms the tissue surrounding the muscles.

The extremities of your body (like your fingers and toes) tend to be cooler than your core body temperature — you've probably already noticed. When blood reaches these cooler parts heat energy is transferred from the blood to the tissues, helping to keep them warm. Handy really.

Sweaty and red — I'm so attractive in the heat...

So, your body is pretty good at regulating its temperature in everyday situations. Make sure you learn where the temperature receptors are and the effectors involved in the negative feedback mechanism.

Controlling Body Temperature

Extreme external temperatures are pretty dangerous because they can cause your core body temperature to change dramatically. If you're crazy enough to go swanning around in extreme environments your body might find it all a bit too much...

Big Changes in Body Temperature can be Dangerous

High Temperatures can Cause Heat Stroke

1) Heat stroke is caused by an uncontrolled increase in body temperature.
2) This increase in body temperature can be caused by a hot climate, physical exertion or extensive burns.

Body temperatures above 40 °C are life-threatening.

> **SYMPTOMS**
> Symptoms can include headaches, dizziness, nausea, vomiting, loss of appetite, confusion, disorientation and visual hallucinations.

> **INITIAL TREATMENT**
> Treatment involves attempting to cool the patient down, by making sure the room is ventilated, giving the patient water and cooling down the body with water.

3) When you're exposed to very hot temperatures you naturally produce more sweat. Sweat can help you cool down, however the water loss may cause you to become dehydrated. This can cause a worse state of affairs — a reduction in sweating and a further increase in body temperature.
4) When you get too hot (your core body temperature becomes too high) the normal mechanisms for controlling body temperature can break down.

Low Temperatures can Cause Hypothermia

1) Hypothermia occurs when the core body temperature falls below 35 °C. It occurs when body heat can't be replaced as fast as it's being lost.
2) This decrease in body temperature can be caused by exposure to a very cold climate. You can also get hypothermia if you go out in the wind and rain for ages and don't get dry properly afterwards.

> **SYMPTOMS**
> Symptoms can include shivering, low energy, confusion and feeling fearful, loss of control of the hands, feet and limbs, memory loss and unconsciousness.

> **INITIAL TREATMENT**
> Treatment involves trying to warm the patient up. This should be done slowly by moving them somewhere warmer (e.g. indoors or out of the wind if there is no indoors), providing them with warm, dry clothes and wrapping them in insulating blankets.

Shiver me timbers — it's a wee bit nippy in here...

Heat stroke can cause people to have quite vivid hallucinations — just like in films when the sweaty but handsome traveller lost in the desert sees a pool of fresh water and lots of beautiful ladies appear before him. I'm sure it's not as nice as it sounds... especially when you realise it's not there.

Module B4 — Homeostasis

Controlling Water Content

The kidneys are really important in this whole homeostasis thing — they help regulate water content.

Balancing Water Level is Really Important

As you learnt on page 4, the water level in your cells is very important — the body must maintain this level for the cells to function. So your body needs to <u>balance</u> the <u>inputs</u> and the <u>outputs</u>...

1) <u>Inputs</u> — water can be gained from drinks, food and respiration.
2) <u>Outputs</u> — water can be lost through sweating, breathing, in faeces and in urine.

Kidneys Help Balance Substances in the Body

The kidneys are pretty useful organs as they play a vital role in <u>removing waste urea</u> from the blood and in <u>balancing levels</u> of other chemicals in the body. To balance these levels of chemicals the kidneys do the following things...

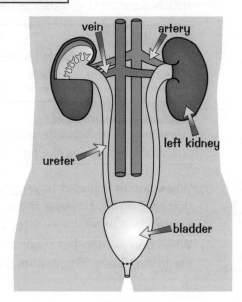

vein   artery

left kidney

ureter

bladder

1) They <u>filter small molecules</u> from the <u>blood</u>, including <u>water</u>, <u>sugar</u>, <u>salt</u> and <u>urea</u>.

2) They <u>reabsorb</u> various things...
   • All the <u>sugar</u> — this is by active transport (see p.4).
   • As much <u>salt</u> and <u>water</u> as the body requires. Water absorption is controlled by the level of the hormone ADH (see next page).

3) Whatever isn't reabsorbed forms <u>urine</u>, which is excreted by the kidneys and stored in the <u>bladder</u>.

Blood plasma is a liquid that carries blood cells and dissolved substances.

Your Urine isn't Always the Same

The kidneys balance water levels by producing <u>dilute</u> or <u>concentrated</u> urine. The concentration of the urine depends on the <u>concentration of the blood plasma</u>, which can vary with the external temperature, exercise level, and the intake of fluids and salt.

1) External temperature

Temperature affects the amount you sweat. Sweat contains water so sweating causes <u>water loss</u>. This means when it's hot the kidneys will <u>reabsorb</u> more water back into the blood. This leaves only a small amount of water — so only a <u>small amount</u> of quite <u>concentrated</u> urine will be produced.

See page 6 for more on sweating.

2) Exercise

Exercise makes you <u>hotter</u>, so you <u>sweat</u> to cool down. This produces the same effect as heat — a <u>concentrated</u>, <u>small volume</u> of urine.

3) Intake of fluids and salts

Not drinking enough water or eating too much salt will produce <u>concentrated</u> urine (since there'll be little excess water to 'dilute' the other wastes). Drinking lots of water will produce <u>lots</u> of <u>dilute</u> urine.

Reabsorb those facts and excrete the excess...

On average, the kidneys filter 180 litres of blood a day (you only have 4-6 litres of blood in your body — it just goes through the kidneys about <u>40 times</u>). And the kidneys excrete 1.5 litres of urine a day. So that's 547.5 litres of wee a year... that's five baths full... not that I'm suggesting you put it there.

Controlling Water Content

Waste disposal isn't the easiest or most interesting topic in the world, I admit.

The Concentration of Urine is Controlled by a Hormone

1) The concentration of urine is controlled by a hormone called anti-diuretic hormone (ADH). This is released into the bloodstream by the pituitary gland.

2) The brain monitors the water content of the blood and instructs the pituitary gland to release ADH into the blood according to how much is needed.

3) The whole process of water content regulation is controlled by negative feedback (see page 2). This means that if the water content gets too high or too low a mechanism will be triggered that brings it back to normal.

1) A receptor in the brain detects that the water content is too high.	1) A receptor in the brain detects that the water content is too low.
2) The processing centre in the brain receives the information and coordinates a response.	2) The processing centre in the brain receives the information and coordinates a response.
3) The pituitary gland releases less ADH, so the kidneys reabsorb less water.	3) The pituitary gland releases more ADH, so the kidneys reabsorb more water.

water content decreases / *water content increases*

So, using negative feedback the amount of water in your body can be closely regulated.
Your body needs to maintain the concentration of its cell contents at the correct level for cell activity.
Don't forget that the more water your kidneys reabsorb, the less water will pass out as urine.

ADH Production can be Affected by Drugs

ADH production is usually regulated by the negative feedback mechanism. However, some drugs can interfere with the natural state of affairs — affecting your urine. Nice.

Alcohol Suppresses ADH Production

1) Drinking alcohol can result in a larger amount of more dilute urine (than normal) being produced.
2) Alcohol causes the production of ADH to decrease, so the kidneys will reabsorb less water.
3) This means more water passes out of the body as urine — this can cause dehydration.

Ecstasy Increases ADH Production

1) Ecstasy is an illegal recreational drug. Taking ecstasy can result in a smaller amount of more concentrated urine (than normal) being produced. It can produce lots of other, more horrible effects on your body too.
2) Ecstasy causes the production of ADH to increase, so the kidneys will reabsorb more water.
3) This means that less water can pass out of the body as urine.

Bet you didn't realise wee is so exciting...

Scientists have made a machine that can do the kidney's job for us — a kidney dialysis machine.
People with kidney failure have to use it for 3-4 hours, 3 times a week. Unfortunately it's not something you can carry around in your back pocket, which makes life difficult for people with kidney failure.

Revision Summary for Module B4

You've probably got the idea by now — this module is all about keeping things constant in your body. Body temperature and water content are the main things it focuses on.

Have a bash at the questions, go back and check anything you're not sure about, then try again. Practise until you can answer all these questions really easily without having to look back at the section. I know you want to look at the section again, right now, as it is so exciting and so beautifully made. But you can't — not until you've had a go at these equally thrilling questions...

1) What is homeostasis?
2) Name two things in your body that automatic control systems regulate.
3) Describe how strenuous exercise can affect homeostasis.
4) How might climbing to a high altitude affect your blood oxygen level?
5) Name the three main stages involved in negative feedback.
6) What is the advantage of effectors that work antagonistically?
7) Give a definition of diffusion.
8) Give two examples of chemicals that can move into cells by diffusion.
9) What is osmosis?
10) Why is it important for animal cells to regulate their water content?
11) How does active transport differ from diffusion?
12) Give a definition of an enzyme.
13) Describe the 'lock and key' model.
14) What is the name of the part of an enzyme where a substrate binds?
15) What is a denatured enzyme?
16) What is the average human core body temperature?
17) Name the area of the brain that detects the temperature of the blood.
18) Name two responses the body has to high body temperature.
19) Give an example of an effector involved in increasing body temperature.
20) What is vasoconstriction?
21) How does blood help to keep the extremities of the body warm?
22) Name two symptoms of heat stroke.
23) What is hypothermia?
24) Give two ways that water is gained by the body.
25) Describe how the kidneys balance levels of some chemicals in the body.
26) What factors can affect the concentration of urine produced by the kidneys?
27) Which organ releases ADH?
28) If there is an increase in water content in the body will more or less ADH be released?
29) What effect does alcohol have on urine production?

Atoms

Atoms are the building blocks of <u>everything</u> — and I mean everything. They're <u>amazingly tiny</u> — you can only see them with an incredibly powerful electron microscope.

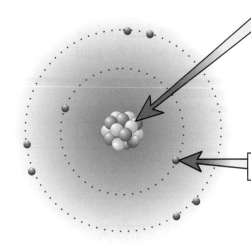

The Nucleus

1) It's in the <u>middle</u> of the atom.
2) It contains <u>protons</u> and <u>neutrons</u>.
3) It has a <u>positive charge</u> because of the protons.
4) Almost the <u>whole</u> mass of the atom is <u>concentrated</u> in the nucleus.
5) But size-wise it's <u>tiny</u> compared to the rest of the atom.

The Electrons

1) Move <u>around</u> the nucleus.
2) They're <u>negatively charged</u>.
3) They're <u>tiny</u>, but they cover <u>a lot of space</u>.
4) The <u>volume</u> of their orbits determines how big the atom is.
5) They have virtually <u>no</u> mass.
6) They're arranged in <u>shells</u> around the nucleus.
7) These shells explain <u>the whole of Chemistry</u>.

Know Your Particles...

1) <u>Protons</u> are <u>heavy</u> and <u>positively charged</u>.
2) <u>Neutrons</u> are <u>heavy</u> and <u>neutral</u>.
3) <u>Electrons</u> are <u>tiny</u> and <u>negatively charged</u>.

PARTICLE	MASS	CHARGE
Proton	1	+1
Neutron	1	0
Electron	0.0005	-1

(<u>Electron mass</u> is often taken as <u>zero</u>.)

Number of Protons Equals Number of Electrons

1) Neutral atoms have <u>no charge</u> overall.
2) The <u>charge</u> on the electrons is the <u>same</u> size as the charge on the <u>protons</u> — but <u>opposite</u>.
3) This means the <u>number</u> of <u>protons</u> always equals the <u>number</u> of <u>electrons</u> in a <u>neutral atom</u>.
4) If some electrons are <u>added or removed</u>, the atom becomes <u>charged</u> and is then an <u>ion</u>.
5) The number of <u>neutrons</u> isn't fixed but is usually about the same as the number of <u>protons</u>.

Each Element has a Different Number of Protons

1) It's the <u>number of protons</u> in an atom that decides what element it is.
   For example, any atom of the element <u>helium</u> will have <u>2 protons</u> — and any atom with <u>2 protons</u> will be a <u>helium</u> atom.

Atoms of the <u>same</u> element all have the <u>same</u> number of <u>protons</u>
— and atoms of <u>different</u> elements will have <u>different</u> numbers of <u>protons</u>.

2) Elements all have <u>different properties</u> from each other due to differences in their atomic structure.

Number of protons = number of electrons...

This stuff might seem a bit useless at first, but it should be permanently engraved into your mind. If you don't know these basic facts, you've got no chance of understanding the rest of Chemistry. So <u>learn it now</u>, and watch as the Universe unfolds and reveals its timeless mysteries to you...

Balancing Equations

Every time you write an equation you need to make sure it balances rather than skate over it.

Atoms aren't Lost or Made in Chemical Reactions

1) During chemical reactions, things don't appear out of nowhere and things don't just disappear.

2) You still have the same atoms at the end of a chemical reaction as you had at the start. They're just arranged in different ways.

3) Balanced symbol equations show the atoms at the start (the reactant atoms) and the atoms at the end (the product atoms) and how they're arranged. For example:

Word equation: sodium + chlorine → sodium chloride

Balanced symbol equation: $2Na$ + Cl_2 → $2NaCl$

Na Na   Cl Cl   Na Cl   Na Cl

Balancing the Equation — Match Them Up One by One

1) There must always be the same number of atoms on both sides — they can't just disappear.

2) You balance the equation by putting numbers in front of the formulas where needed. For example...

$$Na + H_2O \rightarrow NaOH + H_2$$

The formulas are all correct but the numbers of some atoms don't match up on both sides. You can't change formulas like H_2O to H_3O. You can only put numbers in front of them:

Method: Balance Just ONE Type of Atom at a Time

The more you practise, the quicker you'll get, but all you do is this:

1) Find an element that doesn't balance and pencil in a number to try and sort it out.
2) See where it gets you. It may create another imbalance — if so, just pencil in another number and see where that gets you.
3) Carry on chasing unbalanced elements and it'll sort itself out pretty quickly.

I'll show you. In the equation above you'll soon notice we're short of H atoms on the LHS (Left-Hand Side).

1) The only thing you can do about that is make it $2H_2O$ instead of just H_2O:
$$Na + 2H_2O \rightarrow NaOH + H_2$$

2) But that now causes too many H atoms and O atoms on the LHS, so to balance that up you could try putting $2NaOH$ on the RHS (Right-Hand Side). You'll then need to put 2 in front of the Na on the LHS to balance the number of Na atoms:
$$2Na + 2H_2O \rightarrow 2NaOH + H_2$$

3) And suddenly there it is! Everything balances.

State Symbols Tell You What Physical State It's In

These are easy enough, so make sure you know them — especially aq (aqueous).

(s) — Solid   (l) — Liquid   (g) — Gas   (aq) — Dissolved in water

E.g. $2K_{(s)} + Cl_{2(g)} \rightarrow 2KCl_{(s)}$

Balancing equations — weigh it up in your mind...

Remember what those numbers mean: A number in front of a formula applies to the entire formula. So, $3Na_2SO_4$ means three lots of Na_2SO_4. The little numbers in the middle or at the end of a formula only apply to the atom or brackets immediately before. So the 4 in Na_2SO_4 just means 4 O's, not 4 S's.

Line Spectrums

Colour isn't just to do with art — you've got to learn about it in Chemistry too.

Some Elements Emit Distinctive Colours When Heated

1) When heated, some elements produce <u>flames</u> with a <u>distinctive colour</u>.
   For example:

> (i)   <u>Lithium</u>, Li, produces a red flame.
> (ii)   <u>Sodium</u>, Na, produces a yellow/orange flame.
> (iii)   <u>Potassium</u>, K, produces a lilac flame.

2) All the different colours seen in <u>fireworks</u> are due to the colours produced by <u>different elements</u> — it's a great bit of chemistry.

3) What's more... these colours also help chemists to <u>identify</u> a metal in a compound. Just put a little bit of the substance into a blue <u>Bunsen flame</u>, and see what colour's produced.

Each Element Gives a Characteristic Line Spectrum

See page 83 for more on wavelength.

1) When <u>heated</u>, the <u>electrons</u> in an atom are <u>excited</u>, and <u>release energy as light</u>.
2) The wavelengths emitted can be <u>recorded</u> as a <u>line spectrum</u>.
3) <u>Different elements</u> emit <u>different wavelengths</u> of light. This is due to each element having a different <u>electron arrangement</u> (see p.15).
4) So each element has a <u>different pattern</u> of wavelengths, and a different line spectrum.
5) This means that line spectrums can be used to <u>identify elements</u>.
6) The practical technique used to produce line spectrums is called <u>spectroscopy</u>.

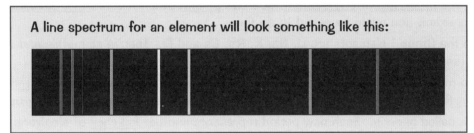

A line spectrum for an element will look something like this:

Line Spectrums Have Identified New Elements

New practical techniques (e.g. spectroscopy) have allowed scientists to <u>discover new elements</u>. Some of these elements simply wouldn't have been discovered without the development of these <u>techniques</u>.

> • <u>Caesium</u> and <u>rubidium</u> were both discovered by their line spectrum.
> • <u>Helium</u> was discovered in the line spectrum of the Sun.

Spectroscopy — it's a flaming useful technique...

These are quite nifty ways of <u>identifying</u> elements. Maybe more importantly, we've been able to <u>discover</u> elements that otherwise might still be unknown to us using these techniques. I know it's a bit tricky, but make sure you understand the details on this page.

The Periodic Table

The periodic table is a chemist's bestest friend — start getting to know it now... seriously...

The Periodic Table Puts Elements with Similar Properties Together

1) There are <u>100ish elements</u>, which all materials are made of. If it wasn't for the periodic table <u>organising everything</u>, you'd have a <u>heck of a job</u> remembering all those properties. It's <u>ace</u>.

2) It's laid out in order of <u>increasing proton number</u>.

3) It's a handy tool for working out which elements are <u>metals</u> and which are <u>non-metals</u>. Metals are found to the <u>left</u> and non-metals to the <u>right</u>.

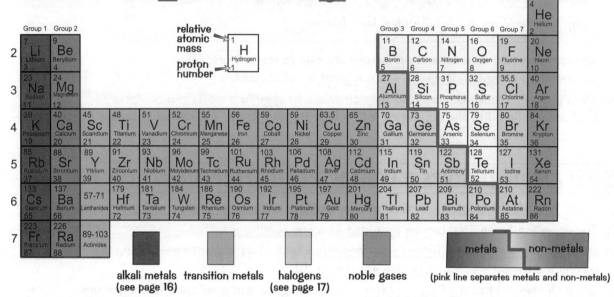

alkali metals (see page 16)   transition metals   halogens (see page 17)   noble gases   (pink line separates metals and non-metals)

4) Elements with <u>similar properties</u> form <u>columns</u>.

5) These <u>vertical columns</u> are called <u>groups</u> and Roman numerals are often (but not always) used for them.

6) If you know the <u>properties</u> of <u>one element</u>, you can <u>predict</u> properties of <u>other elements</u> in that group — and in the exam, you might be asked to do this.

7) For example the <u>Group 1</u> elements are Li, Na, K, Rb, Cs and Fr. They're all <u>metals</u> and they <u>react in a similar way</u> (see page 16).

8) You can also make predictions about <u>reactivity</u>. E.g. in Group 1, the elements react <u>more vigorously</u> as you go <u>down</u> the group. And in Group 7, <u>reactivity decreases</u> as you go down the group.

9) The <u>rows</u> are called <u>periods</u>. Each new period represents another <u>full shell</u> of electrons (see page 15).

You Can Get Loads of Information from the Periodic Table

By looking at the table, you can immediately find out:

1) The <u>name</u> and <u>symbol</u> of each element.

2) The <u>proton number</u> of each element — this tells you <u>how many protons</u> there are in the nucleus.

3) The <u>relative atomic mass</u> of each element — this tells you the <u>total number of protons and neutrons</u> there are in the nucleus.

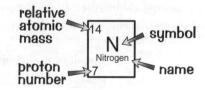

I'm in a chemistry band — I play the symbols...

Scientists keep making <u>new elements</u> and feeling well chuffed with themselves. The trouble is, these new elements only last for <u>a fraction of a second</u> before falling apart. You <u>don't</u> need to know the properties of each group of the periodic table, but if you're told, for example, that fluorine (Group 7) forms <u>two-atom molecules</u>, it's a fair guess that chlorine, bromine, iodine and astatine <u>do too</u>.

Electron Shells

Electron shells... the orbits electrons zoom about in.

Electron Shell Rules:

1) Electrons always occupy <u>shells</u> (sometimes called <u>energy levels</u>).

2) The <u>lowest</u> energy levels are <u>always filled first</u>.

3) Only <u>a certain number</u> of electrons are allowed in each shell:
   <u>1st shell</u>: 2   <u>2nd Shell</u>: 8   <u>3rd Shell</u>: 8

4) Atoms are much <u>happier</u> when they have <u>full electron shells</u>.

5) In most atoms the <u>outer shell</u> is <u>not full</u> and this makes the atom want to <u>react</u>.

6) An element's <u>electron arrangement</u> determines its chemical <u>properties</u>. (See pages 16 and 17.)

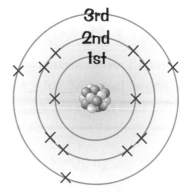

3rd shell still filling

Working Out Electron Configurations

You need to know the <u>electron configurations</u> for the first <u>20</u> elements in the periodic table.
They're shown in the diagram below — but they're not hard to work out.
For a quick example, take nitrogen. <u>Follow the steps</u>...

1) The periodic table tells you that nitrogen has <u>seven</u> protons... so it must have <u>seven</u> electrons.

2) Follow the 'Electron Shell Rules' above. The <u>first</u> shell can only take 2 electrons and the <u>second</u> shell can take a <u>maximum</u> of 8 electrons.

3) So the electron configuration for nitrogen must be 2, 5 — easy peasy.

4) Now <u>you</u> try it for argon.

Each shell <u>fills</u> across a row of the periodic table.

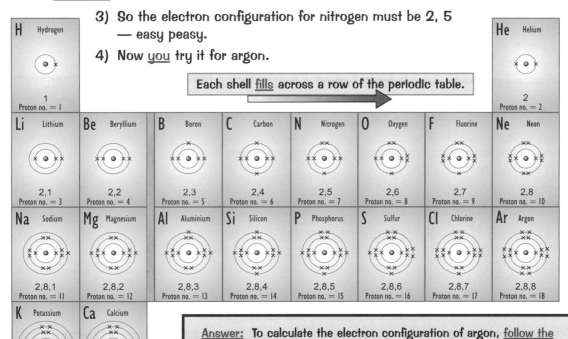

Answer: To calculate the electron configuration of argon, <u>follow the rules</u>. It's got 18 protons, so it <u>must</u> have 18 electrons. The first shell must have <u>2</u> electrons, the second shell must have <u>8</u>, and so the third shell must have <u>8</u> as well. It's as easy as <u>2, 8, 8</u>.

One little duck and two fat ladies — 2, 8, 8...

You need to know enough about electron shells to draw out that <u>whole diagram</u> at the bottom of the page without looking at it. Obviously, you don't have to learn each element separately — just <u>learn the pattern</u>. Cover the page: using a periodic table, find the atom with the electron configuration 2, 8, 6.

Group 1 — Alkali Metals

Alkali metals are all members of the same group — Group 1.
So, yes, you've got it — that means they'll all have similar properties.

Group 1 Metals are Known as the 'Alkali Metals'

1) Group 1 metals include <u>lithium</u>, <u>sodium</u> and <u>potassium</u>... know these names really well.

2) They all have <u>ONE outer electron</u>. This makes them <u>very reactive</u> and gives them all <u>similar properties</u>.

3) The alkali metals are <u>shiny</u> when freshly cut, but quickly <u>tarnish</u> in <u>moist air</u>.

As you go <u>DOWN</u> Group 1, the alkali metals:

1) become <u>MORE REACTIVE</u> (see below)

...because the outer electron is <u>more easily lost</u>, because it's <u>further</u> from the nucleus.

2) have a <u>HIGHER DENSITY</u>

...because the atoms have <u>more mass</u>.

3) have a <u>LOWER MELTING POINT</u>

4) have a <u>LOWER BOILING POINT</u>

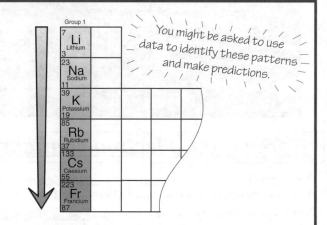

You might be asked to use data to identify these patterns and make predictions.

Reaction with Cold Water Produces Hydrogen Gas

1) When <u>lithium</u>, <u>sodium</u> or <u>potassium</u> are put in <u>water</u>, they react very <u>vigorously</u>.

2) They <u>move</u> around the surface, <u>fizzing</u> furiously.

3) They produce <u>hydrogen</u>. Potassium gets hot enough to <u>ignite</u> it. If it hasn't already been ignited by the reaction, a lighted splint will <u>indicate</u> hydrogen by producing the notorious "<u>squeaky pop</u>" as it ignites.

4) The reaction makes an <u>alkaline solution</u> — this is why Group 1 is known as the <u>alkali</u> metals.

5) A <u>hydroxide</u> of the metal forms, e.g. sodium hydroxide (NaOH), potassium hydroxide (KOH) or lithium hydroxide (LiOH).

$$2Na_{(s)} + 2H_2O_{(l)} \rightarrow 2NaOH_{(aq)} + H_{2(g)}$$

$$2K_{(s)} + 2H_2O_{(l)} \rightarrow 2KOH_{(aq)} + H_{2(g)}$$

Squeaky pop!!

6) This experiment shows the <u>relative reactivities</u> of the alkali metals. The <u>more violent</u> the reaction, the <u>more reactive</u> the alkali metal is.

Reaction with Chlorine Produces Salts

1) Alkali metals react vigorously with <u>chlorine</u>.

2) The reaction produces <u>colourless crystalline salts</u>, e.g. lithium chloride (LiCl), sodium chloride (NaCl) and potassium chloride (KCl).

$$2Na_{(s)} + Cl_{2(g)} \rightarrow 2NaCl_{(s)}$$

$$2K_{(s)} + Cl_{2(g)} \rightarrow 2KCl_{(s)}$$

Notorious Squeaky Pop — a.k.a. the Justin Timberlake test...

Alkali metals are ace. They're <u>so reactive</u> you have to store them in <u>oil</u> — because otherwise they'd react with the water vapour in the air. AND they <u>fizz</u> in water and <u>explode</u> and everything. <u>Cool</u>.

Group 7 — Halogens

The 'trend thing' happens in Group 7 as well — no surprise there.

Group 7 Elements are Known as the Halogens

1) Group 7 elements include chlorine, bromine and iodine... remember these names.

2) They all have SEVEN outer electrons. This makes them very reactive and gives them similar properties.

3) Chlorine's good because it kills bacteria. It's used in bleach and swimming pools. The other halogens act in a similar way.

As you go DOWN Group 7, the halogens:

1) become LESS REACTIVE (see below)

...because the outer electrons are further from the nucleus and so additional electrons are attracted less strongly.

2) have a HIGHER MELTING POINT

3) have a HIGHER BOILING POINT

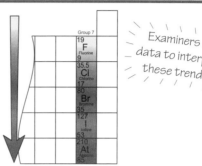

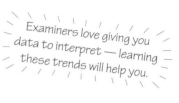

Examiners love giving you data to interpret — learning these trends will help you.

The Halogens are All Non-metals with Coloured Vapours

Fluorine is a very reactive, poisonous yellow gas at room temperature.

Chlorine is a fairly reactive, poisonous dense green gas at room temperature.

Bromine is a dense, poisonous, red-brown volatile liquid at room temperature and forms a red-brown gas.

Iodine is a dark grey crystalline solid at room temperature or a purple vapour.

The halogens go from gases to solids down the group — this shows the trend in melting and boiling points.

They All Form Diatomic Molecules Which are Pairs of Atoms:

Cl_2  Br_2  I_2

More Reactive Halogens Will Displace Less Reactive Ones

A displacement reaction is where a more reactive element 'pushes out' (displaces) a less reactive element from a compound.

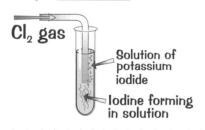

Cl₂ gas

Solution of potassium iodide

Iodine forming in solution

These displacement reactions can be used to determine the relative reactivity of the halogens.

Chlorine is more reactive than iodine. So chlorine reacts with potassium iodide solution to form potassium chloride, and the iodine is left in solution.

Chlorine can also displace bromine from solutions of bromides.

Bromine will displace iodine because of the trend in reactivity.

$$Cl_{2(g)} + 2KI_{(aq)} \rightarrow I_{2(aq)} + 2KCl_{(aq)}$$

$$Cl_{2(g)} + 2KBr_{(aq)} \rightarrow Br_{2(aq)} + 2KCl_{(aq)}$$

They're great, the halogens — you have to hand it to them...

The halogens are another group from the periodic table, and just like the alkali metals (p.16) you've got to learn their trends and the equations on this page. Learn them, cover up the page, scribble, check.

Laboratory Safety

You Need to Learn the Common Hazard Symbols...

Lots of chemicals can be bad for you or dangerous in some way.
These hazard symbols might just save your skin...

Oxidising
Provides oxygen which allows other materials to burn more fiercely.
Example: Liquid oxygen.

Harmful
Like toxic but not quite as dangerous.
Example: Copper sulfate.

Highly Flammable
Catches fire easily.
Example: Petrol.

Irritant
Not corrosive but can cause reddening or blistering of the skin.
Examples: Bleach, children, etc.

Toxic
Can cause death either by swallowing, breathing in, or absorption through the skin.
Example: Hydrogen cyanide.

Corrosive
Attacks and destroys living tissues, including eyes and skin.
Example: Concentrated sulfuric acid.

... And Know How to Work Safely with Dangerous Chemicals

Some of the elements you've come across so far in this section, like the alkali metals (see p.16) and the halogens (see p.17), are pretty dangerous. There are certain safety precautions that need to be followed when using these chemicals. The usual 'wear safety specs' goes without saying...

Alkali Metals

1) The Group 1 elements are really reactive and can combust spontaneously.

2) If they come into contact with water vapour in the air there can be a violent reaction, depending on how much alkali metal is present — so they're stored under oil to prevent this. Make sure there's a fire extinguisher handy...

3) Alkali metals should never be touched with bare hands — the sweat on your skin is enough to cause a reaction that will produce lots of heat and a corrosive hydroxide. Not pleasant.

4) Every piece of apparatus used in an experiment needs to be kept completely dry.

5) The alkaline solutions they form are corrosive and may cause blistering
— it's important they don't touch the eyes or the skin.

Halogens

1) The Group 7 elements are also harmful. Chlorine and iodine are both very toxic.

2) Fluorine is the most reactive halogen — it's too dangerous to use inside the lab.

3) Liquid bromine is corrosive and so contact with the skin must be avoided.

4) Halogens have poisonous vapours that irritate the respiratory system and the eyes. They must be used inside a fume cupboard so that you don't breathe in the fumes.

No, it means 'oxidising' — not a guy with a wacky hairstyle...

The stuff on this page is all pretty important, not just for passing your exam but also for when you're doing experiments with chemicals in the lab. Make sure you know what the hazard symbols that appear on the containers of chemicals mean — they're not just there to look pretty...

Ionic Bonding

This stuff's a bit tricky, but keep at it and you'll be bonding with it in no time...

Ionic Bonding — Transferring Electrons

In ionic bonding, atoms lose or gain electrons to form charged particles (called ions) which are then strongly attracted to one another (because of the attraction of opposite charges, + and –).

A Shell with Just One Electron is Well Keen to Get Rid...

All the atoms over at the left-hand side of the periodic table, e.g. sodium, potassium, calcium etc., have just one or two electrons in their outer shell. And they're pretty keen to get shot of them, because then they'll only have full shells left, which is how they like it. So given half a chance they do get rid, and that leaves the atom as an ion instead. Now ions aren't the kind of things that sit around quietly watching the world go by. They tend to leap at the first passing ion with an opposite charge and stick to it like glue.

A Nearly Full Shell is Well Keen to Get That Extra Electron...

On the other side of the periodic table, the elements in Group 6 and Group 7, such as oxygen and chlorine, have outer shells that are nearly full. They're obviously pretty keen to gain that extra one or two electrons to fill the shell up. When they do of course they become ions (you know, not the kind of things to sit around) and before you know it, pop, they've latched onto the atom (ion) that gave up the electron a moment earlier. The reaction of sodium and chlorine is a classic case:

The sodium atom gives up its outer electron and becomes an Na^+ ion.

The chlorine atom picks up the spare electron and becomes a Cl^- ion.

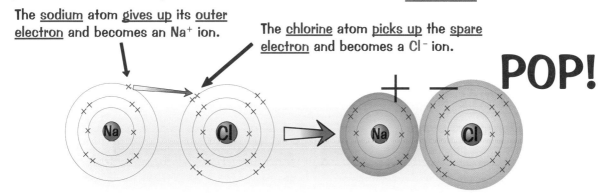

POP!

Groups 1 and 7 are the Most Likely to Form Ions

1) Ions are charged particles — they can be made from single atoms (e.g. the Cl^- ion) or groups of atoms (e.g. the NO_3^- ion).

2) When atoms lose or gain electrons to form ions, all they're trying to do is get a full outer shell. Atoms like full outer shells — it's atom heaven.

3) Group 1 elements are metals and they lose electrons to form positive ions.

4) Group 7 elements are non-metals. They gain electrons to form negative ions.

5) When an element from Group 1 reacts with an element from Group 7, they form an ionic compound, which you can find out about on page 42. In fact, take a look at them NOW.

6) Molten ionic compounds conduct electricity. This is evidence that they're made up of ions.

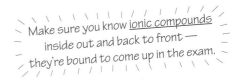
Make sure you know ionic compounds inside out and back to front — they're bound to come up in the exam.

Forming ions — seems like the trendy thing to do...

Remember, the +ve and –ve charges we talk about, e.g. Na^+ for sodium, just tell you what type of ion the atom WILL FORM in a chemical reaction. In sodium metal there are only neutral sodium atoms, Na. The Na^+ ions will only appear if the sodium metal reacts with something like water or chlorine.

Ions and Formulas

Once the positive and negative ions have been identified you can work out the formula. Lucky you.

The Charges in an Ionic Compound Add Up to Zero

Different ions have <u>different charges</u>, shown in the table:

Some metals (like iron, copper and tin) can form ions with <u>different charges</u>. The number <u>in brackets</u> after the name tells you the <u>size</u> of the <u>positive charge</u> on the ion — and luckily for us, this makes the charge really easy to remember. E.g. an iron(II) ion has a charge of 2+, so it's Fe^{2+}.

The main thing to remember is that in compounds the <u>total charge must always add up to zero</u>.

Positive Ions		Negative Ions	
Sodium	Na^+	Chloride	Cl^-
Potassium	K^+	Fluoride	Fl^-
Calcium	Ca^{2+}	Bromide	Br^-
Iron(II)	Fe^{2+}	Carbonate	CO_3^{2-}
Iron(III)	Fe^{3+}	Sulfate	SO_4^{2-}

The Easy Ones

If the ions in the compound have the <u>same size charge</u> then it's easy.

EXAMPLE: Find the formula for <u>lithium fluoride</u>.
Find the charges on a lithium ion and a fluoride ion.
A lithium ion is Li^+ and a fluoride ion is F^-.
To balance the total charge you need one lithium ion to every one fluoride ion.
So the formula of lithium fluoride must be: **LiF**

EXAMPLE: Find the formula for <u>sodium chloride</u>.
Find the charges on a sodium ion and a chloride ion.
A sodium ion is Na^+ and a chloride ion is Cl^-.
To balance the total charge you need one sodium ion to every one chloride ion.
So the formula of sodium chloride must be: **NaCl**

The Harder Ones

If the ions have <u>different</u> size charges, you need to put in some numbers to balance things up.

EXAMPLE: Find the formula for <u>calcium chloride</u>.
Find the charges on a calcium ion and a chloride ion.
A calcium ion is Ca^{2+} and a chloride ion is Cl^-.
To balance the total charge you need two chloride ions to every one calcium ion.
So the formula of calcium chloride must be: $CaCl_2$

EXAMPLE: Find the formula for <u>iron(III) sulfate</u>.
Find the charges on an iron(III) ion and a sulfate ion.
An iron(III) ion is Fe^{3+} and a sulfate ion is SO_4^{2-}.
To balance the total charge you need two iron(III) ions to every three sulfate ions.
So the formula of iron(III) sulfate must be: $Fe_2(SO_4)_3$

You Can Also Work Out the Charges on Ions

If you know the <u>formula</u> of a salt and the <u>charge</u> on one of the ions, you can work out the <u>charge</u> on the other ion:

EXAMPLE: Find the charge on the <u>lithium ion</u> in LiBr if the charge on the bromide ion is <u>1−</u>.
There is one bromide ion (1−) and the charges must balance, so the charge on the lithium ion must be 1+.

EXAMPLE: Find the charge on the <u>oxide ion</u> in K_2O if the charge on the potassium ion is <u>1+</u>.
There are two potassium ions (2 × 1+) = 2+. The charges always balance, so the charge on the oxygen ion must be 2−.

Any old ion, any old ion — any, any, any old ion...
* Answers on p.100.
After all those examples, I'm sure you could work out the formula to any ionic compound. And just to test that theory here are a few for you to try: a) magnesium oxide, b) lithium oxide, c) sodium sulfate.*

Revision Summary for Module C4

Okay, if you were just about to turn the page without doing these revision summary questions, then stop. What kind of an attitude is that... Is that really the way you want to live your life... running, playing and having fun... Of course not. That's right. Do the questions. It's for the best all round.

1) What does the nucleus of an atom contain?
2) What is the mass and charge of a neutron?
3)* Balance these equations:
   a) $Na + Cl_2 \rightarrow NaCl$
   b) $K + H_2O \rightarrow KOH + H_2$
4) Write the state symbols for each physical state.
5) A forensic scientist carries out a flame test to identify a metal. The scientist sees a lilac flame. Which metal does this result indicate?
6) Why does each element produce a different line spectrum?
7) What can line spectrums be used for?
8) What feature of atoms determines the order of the periodic table?
9) What are the rows in the periodic table known as?
10) What is significant about the properties of elements in the same group?
11)* Oxygen can be written as $^{16}_{8}O$. How many protons does one atom of oxygen contain?
12) How many electrons can the first shell of any atom hold?
13) Draw the electron configuration of carbon.
14) Which group are the alkali metals?
15) As you go down the group of alkali metals, do they become more or less reactive?
16) Give details of the reactions of the alkali metals with water.
17) Write a balanced equation for the reaction between lithium and chlorine.
18) Describe how the reactivity of the Group 7 elements changes as you go down the group.
19) Atoms of Group 7 elements tend to go round in pairs. What word describes this type of molecule?
20) Describe the appearance of chlorine at room temperature.
21) Describe an experiment that could be used to determine the relative reactivity of the halogens.
22) What does this hazard symbol mean?
   Give an example of a substance that would need this symbol on its label.
23) What precautions need to be taken when working with Group 7 elements? Why?
24) What is ionic bonding?
25) What kind of atoms like to do ionic bonding? Why is this?
26)* The formula of magnesium bromide is $MgBr_2$. The charge on the bromide ion is 1–. What is the charge on the magnesium ion?
27)* Use the table to help you find the formula for:
   a) iron(II) oxide
   b) iron(III) chloride
   c) calcium oxide
   d) sodium carbonate

Positive ions		Negative ions	
sodium	Na^+	chloride	Cl^-
calcium	Ca^{2+}	oxide	O^{2-}
iron(II)	Fe^{2+}	carbonate	CO_3^{2-}
iron(III)	Fe^{3+}		

* Answers on page 100.

Module C4 — Chemical Patterns

Speed

This whole speed thing's pretty easy really — just make sure you've had lots of practice at <u>calculating speeds</u>, <u>distances</u> and <u>times</u>, and you'll have it sorted.

Speed *is Just the* Distance *Travelled in a Certain* Time

1) To find the <u>speed</u> of an object (in <u>metres per second</u>, m/s), you need to know the <u>distance</u> it travels (in metres) and the <u>time</u> it takes (in seconds).

2) You really ought to get <u>pretty slick</u> with this <u>very easy formula</u>:

$$\text{Speed} = \frac{\text{Distance}}{\text{Time}}$$

1) A <u>formula triangle</u> can help with calculations, <u>especially</u> if you need to find the <u>distance</u> or <u>time</u> rather than the speed...

2) You just <u>cover up</u> the thing you're trying to find, and the triangle magically tells you how to calculate it:

<u>Distance</u> is speed × time...

 ...and <u>time</u> is distance ÷ speed

So now you just need to try and think up some interesting word for remembering the <u>order</u> of the <u>letters</u> in the triangle, s^dt.   Errm... sedit, perhaps... well, I'm sure you can think up something better...

<u>EXAMPLE:</u>   A cat skulks 20 metres in 40 seconds.
          Find: a) its speed,   b) how long it will take to skulk 75 m.

<u>ANSWER:</u>   Using the formula triangle: a) s = d/t = 20/40 = <u>0.5 m/s</u>
          b) t = d/s = 75/0.5 = 150 s = <u>2 min 30 s</u>

The Speed of an Object Normally Changes...

1) In real life, it's <u>pretty rare</u> for an object to go at <u>exactly</u> the same speed for a <u>long period</u> of time. <u>Cars</u>, for example, have to start off at <u>0 m/s</u>, then <u>accelerate</u> up to speed. Even if you're on the motorway, you'll have to <u>alter</u> your speed depending on <u>other traffic</u>, etc.

2) So it's usually more <u>useful</u> to know <u>average</u> speed, and that's what the speed formula will normally tell you — the skulking cat <u>averaged</u> 0.57 m/s over its journey.

3) Sometimes though, it's handy to know something's '<u>instantaneous</u>' speed. <u>Speed cameras</u>, for instance, use lines painted on the road to measure the <u>distance</u> travelled by a vehicle in a <u>set time</u> — the police want to know how fast you're going <u>right now</u>, not your average. (So here 'instantaneous' speed is still an average, just an average over a <u>really short</u> time period...)

Don't speed through this page — learn it properly...

Calculating speed is <u>easy</u> — you know the units are <u>m/s</u>, so it's pretty obviously <u>metres</u> ÷ <u>seconds</u>...

Speed and Velocity

One way to look at the movement of an object is to draw a lovely old distance-time graph...

Distance-Time Graphs

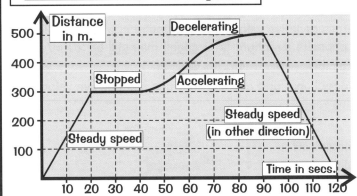

Very Important Notes:

1) GRADIENT = SPEED.
2) Flat sections are where it's stopped.
3) The steeper the graph, the faster it's going.
4) 'Downhill' sections mean it's coming back toward its starting point.
5) Curves represent acceleration or deceleration.
6) A steepening curve means it's speeding up (increasing gradient).
7) A levelling off curve means it's slowing down (decreasing gradient).

Speed is the Gradient of a Distance-Time Graph

Examiners love to ask you to calculate speed from a distance-time graph. It's pretty easy...
For example, for the first section of the graph:

Don't worry too much about curved bits of the graph — you need to know what they mean, but you don't need to calculate anything from them.

$$\underline{Speed} = \underline{gradient} = \frac{vertical}{horizontal} = \frac{300}{20} = \underline{15 \text{ m/s}}$$

Don't forget that you have to use the scales of the axes to work out the gradient. Don't measure in cm.

Distances can be Positive or Negative

1) You might see distances referred to as either positive or negative.
2) All this means is that an object can be going in one direction or in the opposite direction.
3) For example, imagine that Wayne and Garth are at point A. When they leave, Garth heads towards point B, and Wayne heads in the opposite direction, to point C.
4) So at the end of their journeys, Garth is 40 m from A and Wayne is −35 m from point A.

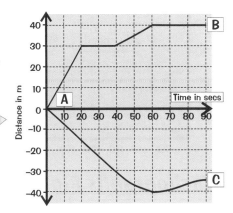

Speed is Just a Number, but Velocity Has Direction Too

1) The speed of an object is just how fast it's going — the direction isn't important. E.g. speed = 30 mph.
2) Velocity is sometimes a more useful measure of motion, because it describes both the speed and direction. E.g. velocity = 30 mph due north.
3) A quantity like speed, that has only a size, is called a scalar quantity. A quantity like velocity, that has direction as well, is a vector quantity.

Scalar quantities:
mass, temperature, time, length etc.

Vector quantities:
force, acceleration, momentum etc.

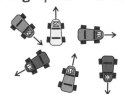

All speeds = 0.5 m/s
Velocities = completely different

Distance-time graphs — almost as fun as Antiques Roadshow...

OK, so these graphs aren't exactly exciting, but you need to be really comfortable with calculating things from them. As for velocity, that's a trickier concept, but there's more fun on the next page...

Velocity

Yearning for more things to <u>mysteriously</u> become <u>negative</u>? Desperate for <u>another graph</u> of something plotted against <u>time</u>? You've come to the right place...

Velocity can be Positive or Negative

1) Just like negative directions, you'll also come across <u>negative velocities</u> — if you're in a car travelling at <u>20 m/s</u> but then you <u>turn around</u> and go in the opposite direction, your <u>speed</u> may <u>still</u> be 20 m/s but your <u>velocity</u>'s changed from 20 m/s to <u>–20 m/s</u>. (Remember, velocity has <u>direction</u>...)

2) Likewise, if <u>two objects</u> are heading in opposite directions, you can say that <u>one</u> has positive velocity and <u>the other</u> has negative velocity...

<u>EXAMPLE:</u>

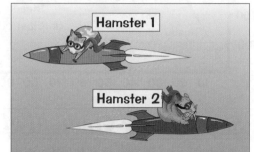

1) Two hamsters strap themselves to rockets and set off to the North and South Pole to escape global warming.

2) Hamster 1 has a velocity of 200 m/s due north, whereas Hamster 2 has a velocity of 230 m/s due south.

3) Another way of saying this is that Hamster 1's velocity is <u>+200 m/s</u> and Hamster 2's is <u>–230 m/s</u>.

Velocity-Time Graphs

You might be asked to draw a graph of <u>velocity</u> against <u>time</u>, or to answer <u>questions</u> about a graph you're given.

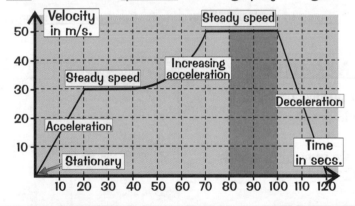

Very Important Notes:

1) <u>Gradient = acceleration</u>.
2) <u>Flat</u> sections represent <u>steady</u> speed.
3) The <u>steeper</u> the graph, the <u>greater</u> the <u>acceleration</u> or deceleration.
4) <u>Uphill</u> sections (/) are <u>acceleration</u>.
5) <u>Downhill</u> sections (\) are <u>deceleration</u>.
6) The <u>area</u> under any section of the graph (or all of it) is equal to the <u>distance</u> travelled in that <u>time</u> interval.
7) A <u>curve</u> means <u>changing acceleration</u>.

Tachographs Plot Speed Against Time

1) Sometimes <u>direction</u> isn't all that important, so instead of worrying about <u>velocity</u>, you can just plot <u>speed</u> against time.

2) All delivery and haulage businesses have to have devices that produce speed-time graphs installed in their <u>lorries</u> — they call them <u>tachographs</u>.

3) With a tachograph installed, drivers can't be <u>forced</u> to drive for <u>long periods</u> without a <u>break</u>, since it'll show up on the graph. You can also tell if they've been <u>speeding</u>...

4) So on this tachograph, the driver was travelling constantly at about <u>110 km/h</u> between <u>12.00</u> and <u>13.15</u>.

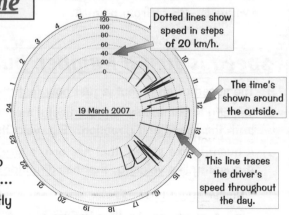

I wish I had a rocket hamster. I'd call him Rockster...

Whatever other mistakes you make in life, don't get velocity-time and distance-time graphs muddled up. On a v-t graph <u>steady speed</u> is shown by <u>flat lines</u> (on a d-t graph that'd be a sloping straight line). <u>Steadily changing speed</u> is shown by <u>straight, sloping lines</u> (not curves, as on d-t graphs).

Forces and Friction

A <u>force</u> is just a <u>push</u> or a <u>pull</u>, but they never come on their own — there's always <u>at least one</u> force in the <u>opposite direction</u>, just to keep you on your toes.

Forces Occur When Two Objects Interact

When an <u>object</u> exerts a <u>force</u> on another object, it always experiences a force <u>in return</u>. These two forces are sometimes called an '<u>interaction pair</u>'. Because there are two of them. And they interact...

1) That means if you <u>push</u> against a wall, the wall will <u>push back</u> against you, <u>just as hard</u>.

2) And as soon as you <u>stop</u> pushing, <u>so does the wall</u>. Kinda clever really.

3) If you think about it, there must be an <u>opposing force</u> when you push (or lean) against a wall — otherwise you (and the wall) would <u>fall over</u>.

4) Likewise, if you <u>pull</u> a cart, whatever force <u>you exert</u> on the rope, the rope exerts the <u>exact opposite</u> pull on <u>you</u>...

5) ...and if you put a book on a table, the <u>weight</u> of the book acts <u>downwards</u> on the table — and the table exerts an <u>equal and opposite</u> force <u>upwards</u> on the book.

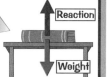

6) This upward force is called a <u>reaction force</u> — because it's the table's '<u>response</u>' to the <u>weight</u> of the book. If the book weighs <u>10 N</u> then the table's reaction force will be <u>10 N</u>.

> The interaction pairs shown above are examples of **Newton's Third Law** — if object A exerts a force on object B, then object B exerts an <u>equal and opposite force</u> on object A.
>
> It's pretty obvious when you think about it — if someone <u>leans</u> on you with a force of <u>200 N</u>, you have to <u>push back</u> with a force of <u>200 N</u>, or you'll both <u>fall over</u>.

Moving Objects Normally Experience Friction

1) When an object is <u>moving</u> relative to another one, both objects experience a <u>force</u> in the direction that <u>opposes the movement</u> — this is called <u>friction</u>.

2) There are <u>three types of friction</u> you should know about:

| a) FRICTION **BETWEEN SOLID SURFACES** **WHICH ARE** <u>GRIPPING</u> | (static friction) |

This is the kind of friction you find in the <u>Earth's crust</u> — great big sections of <u>rock</u> trying to <u>slide</u> past each other, but friction forcing them to <u>stay put</u> (until the sliding force finally gets <u>too strong</u> and they shift <u>suddenly</u>, causing an earthquake...)

| b) FRICTION **BETWEEN SOLID SURFACES** **WHICH ARE SLIDING** PAST EACH OTHER |

E.g. the moving bits and pieces in a car engine.

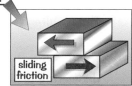

You can <u>reduce</u> sliding friction and gripping friction by putting a <u>lubricant</u> like <u>oil</u> or <u>grease</u> between the surfaces.

| c) RESISTANCE **OR "DRAG"** FROM FLUIDS (LIQUIDS **OR GASES, E.G. AIR**) |

It might seem a bit <u>different</u> from the other types of friction, but drag's basically <u>just the same</u> — an object moving through a fluid has to force its way <u>past</u> all the <u>molecules</u> in that fluid, and that causes <u>friction</u>. Obviously, a <u>big, squarish</u> object like a lorry experiences more air resistance than a <u>streamlined</u> object like a sports car.

Don't think there'll <u>always</u> be friction acting on a moving object though — it <u>only happens</u> if the object is moving <u>through a fluid</u> (i.e. air, water, ketchup). So there's <u>no friction in space</u> (it's a vacuum, so there's no fluid to move through).

Forces and Motion

It's all very well knowing that there are forces acting all over the place, but you need to be able to show where and when they're acting too...

Arrows Show the Size and Direction of Forces

When it comes to the exam, you might be given a diagram of an object and asked to draw arrows showing the forces acting on it. (Once you've done three or four of these, they're all pretty easy...)

1) The length of the arrow shows the size of the force.

2) The direction of the arrow shows the direction of the force (didn't see that one coming, did you...).

3) So if the arrows come in opposite pairs, and they're all the same size, then the forces are balanced...

1) The Reaction of a Surface — Balanced Forces

1) If an object's resting on a surface, its weight is pushing downwards (because of gravity).

2) This causes an equal reaction force from the surface pushing up on the object.

3) The two forces are the same size, so the arrows on the diagram are the same size.

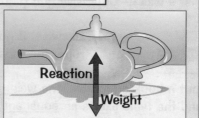

2) Steady Speed — Balanced Forces

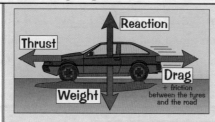

1) If an object is moving with a steady speed the forces must be in balance.

2) Just because something's moving doesn't mean that there's an overall force acting on it — unless it's changing speed or direction, the overall force is zero.

You can apply these ideas to lots of other objects...

EXAMPLE: A jet aircraft is moving at a steady speed and at a constant altitude. The forces acting on it must therefore be balanced. So if its weight is 250,000 N, the force pushing it upwards (i.e. the lift it generates) must also be 250,000 N. If its jets produce a force of 300,000 N, the drag must also be 300,000 N. Easy peasy...

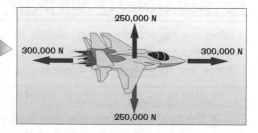

Resultant Force is Really Important

In many real situations the forces acting on an object are not all the same size — they're unbalanced.

1) The resultant force is the overall force acting on an object — the force you get when you take into account all the individual forces and their directions.

2) It's this force that decides the motion of the object — whether it will accelerate, decelerate or stay at a steady speed.

3) Remember that 'accelerate' just means change velocity — and since velocity has both speed and direction, accelerating doesn't necessarily mean changing speed — it might just mean changing direction. For example, a car going round a corner is changing its velocity (and therefore accelerating), even if it stays at a steady speed.

4) So if there's a resultant force acting on an object, its speed or direction (or both) changes.

Resultant force... I'm pretty sure that's a Steven Seagal film...

So unless there's an overall force acting on an object, it won't accelerate. Simple.

Forces and Motion

"But my forces are unbalanced! What will become of me?!", I hear you scream...
Don't worry my friend, this page has a kangaroo on it.

Acceleration — Unbalanced Forces

1) If a car's engine exerts a bigger force (forwards) than the drag force (backwards), the car will accelerate.

2) That's what's happening in this diagram — the thrust arrow is bigger than the drag arrow, so there's a resultant force in the forward direction.

3) The bigger this resultant force, the greater the acceleration.

4) Note that the forces in the other directions (up and down) are still balanced.

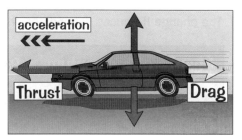

You can use these ideas to describe the forces acting on a rocket...
A rocket taking off accelerates away from the ground, so the upward force provided by burning all that fuel must be greater than the downward forces slowing it down. In this case, there are two downward forces — gravity and drag (from friction between the rocket and the air).

Momentum = Mass × Velocity

Momentum is mainly about how much 'oomph' an object has — how hard it'd be to stop it moving. The heavier an object is, and the faster it's moving, the harder it is to stop. Something to bear in mind next time you stand in the way of a six-foot, 16-stone rugby player...

1) The greater the mass of an object and the greater its velocity, the more momentum the object has. Here's a nice easy equation:

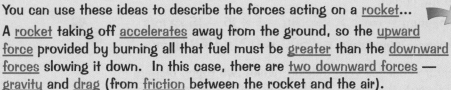

$$\text{Momentum} = \text{Mass} \times \text{Velocity}$$
$$\text{(kg m/s)} \qquad \text{(kg)} \qquad \text{(m/s)}$$

2) Momentum is a vector quantity — it has size and direction (like velocity, but not speed).

Example: A 65 kg kangaroo is moving in a straight line at 10 m/s.
Calculate its momentum.

Answer: Momentum = mass × velocity
= 65 × 10
= 650 kg m/s

Easy stuff... You can do that with your eyes closed.
As long as you can smell the speed of kangaroos.

3) A resultant force of zero means that a stationary object will stay still.
If the object was moving, it stays at the same speed in the same direction.

4) If the resultant force on an object is not zero, its momentum changes in the direction of the force (see the next page).

Accelerate your learning — force yourself to revise...

OK so there's another equation of doom for you to learn, but it's a fairly simple one. In fact, if you remember the units of momentum (kg m/s), then it's pretty obvious that momentum = kg × m/s...

Forces and Motion

The Change in Momentum Depends on the Force

1) When a <u>resultant force</u> acts on an object, it causes a <u>change</u> in momentum.

2) The change it causes depends on the <u>size</u> of the force and the <u>time</u> it acts for.

Change of momentum	= Resultant Force	× Time for which the force acts
(kg m/s)	(N)	(s)

<u>Example:</u> A rock with mass 1 kg is travelling through space at 15 m/s. A comet hits the rock, giving it a resultant force of 2500 N for 0.7 seconds. Calculate the rock's initial momentum, then calculate the change in its momentum resulting from the impact with the comet.

<u>Answer:</u> Momentum = mass × velocity = 1 × 15 = 15 kg m/s
Change of momentum = 2500 × 0.7 = 1750 kg m/s

3) If someone's momentum changes <u>very quickly</u> (when two <u>rugby players</u> crash into each other, say), the <u>forces</u> on the body will be very <u>large</u>, and more likely to cause <u>injury</u>.

Car Safety Features Reduce Forces

1) If your momentum changes <u>slowly</u>, like in nice controlled braking, the <u>forces</u> acting on your body are <u>small</u> and you're unlikely to be <u>hurt</u>. (If you rearrange the equation above, you get force = change in momentum ÷ time, so the <u>greater</u> the <u>time</u>, the <u>smaller</u> the <u>force</u>.)

2) In a collision, you <u>can't really affect</u> the <u>change in momentum</u> — whatever you do, the car's <u>mass</u> and its <u>change in velocity</u> stay <u>the same</u>. However, the average <u>force</u> on an object can be lowered by <u>slowing the object down</u> over a <u>longer time</u>.

3) <u>Safety features</u> in a car <u>increase the collision time</u> to <u>reduce the forces</u> on the passengers.

<u>CRUMPLE ZONES</u> crumple on impact, <u>increasing the time</u> taken for the car to stop.

<u>CYCLE AND MOTORCYCLE HELMETS</u> provide padding that <u>increases the time</u> taken for your head to come to a stop if it <u>hits something hard</u>.

<u>AIR BAGS</u> also slow you down more <u>gradually</u>.

<u>SEAT BELTS</u> stretch slightly, <u>increasing the time</u> taken for the wearer to stop. This <u>reduces the forces</u> acting on the chest.

Learn this stuff — it'll only take a moment... um...

<u>Momentum</u>'s a pretty <u>fundamental</u> bit of physics — so make sure you <u>learn it properly</u>. There are a few equations to cover in this section, but none of them are too hard, so keep <u>practising</u> different questions and Robert's your <u>mother's brother</u>. And never forget to stick the <u>units</u> on the end of your answers...

Work

In Physics, "<u>work done</u>" means something special — it's got its own formula and everything.

"Work Done" is Just "Energy Transferred"

When a <u>force</u> moves an <u>object</u>, <u>energy is transferred</u> and <u>work is done</u>.

That statement sounds far more complicated than it needs to. Try this:

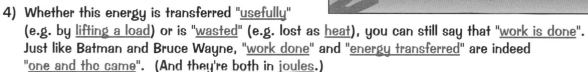

1) Whenever something <u>moves</u>, something else is providing some sort of "<u>effort</u>" to move it.

2) The thing putting the <u>effort</u> in needs a <u>supply</u> of energy (like <u>fuel</u> or <u>food</u> or <u>electricity</u> etc.).

3) It then does "<u>work</u>" by <u>moving</u> the object — and one way or another it <u>transfers</u> the energy it receives (as fuel) into <u>other forms</u>.

4) Whether this energy is transferred "<u>usefully</u>" (e.g. by <u>lifting a load</u>) or is "<u>wasted</u>" (e.g. lost as <u>heat</u>), you can still say that "<u>work is done</u>". Just like Batman and Bruce Wayne, "<u>work done</u>" and "<u>energy transferred</u>" are indeed "<u>one and the same</u>". (And they're both in <u>joules</u>.)

5) And if energy is transferred, then the <u>object doing the work loses energy</u>:

> Change in energy (J) = Work done (J)

6) In the picture above, the guy doing the sweeping is <u>doing work</u> on the <u>rubbish</u>, so he loses energy — if he does <u>500 J of work</u>, then he loses <u>500 J of energy</u>. The rubbish is having <u>work done</u> on it, so it <u>gains</u> energy (though not the full 500 J — some will be lost as <u>noise</u> and <u>heat</u>).

And Another Formula to Learn...

This formula only works if the force is in exactly the same direction as the movement.

Work Done (J) = Force (N) × Distance (m)

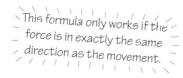

To find how much <u>work</u> has been <u>done</u> (in joules), you just multiply the <u>force in newtons</u> by the <u>distance moved in metres</u>. Easy as that. I'll show you...

> <u>Example:</u> Some hooligan kids drag an old tractor tyre 5 m over flat ground. They pull with a total force of 340 N. Find the work done.
>
> <u>Answer:</u> W = F × d = 340 × 5 = <u>1700 J</u>.

Revise work done — what else...

So, <u>work</u> is just <u>energy transferred</u>. Learn the formula, then have a go at this question: A <u>gorilla</u> finds himself with nothing to do on a Sunday evening, so he does <u>1050 J</u> of work pushing a log <u>3 m</u> across the forest floor. What is the average <u>force</u> he exerts on the log?

Answer: force = work done ÷ distance = 1050 ÷ 3 = 350 N

Kinetic Energy

<u>Work done</u> always involves <u>movement</u>. That's where this whole <u>kinetic energy business</u> comes in...

Kinetic Energy is Energy of Movement

1) Anything that's <u>moving</u> has <u>kinetic energy</u> (KE).

2) The <u>kinetic energy</u> of something depends both on its <u>mass</u> and <u>speed</u>. The <u>greater its mass</u> and the <u>faster</u> it's going, the <u>bigger</u> its kinetic energy.

3) There's a <u>slightly tricky</u> formula for it, so you have to concentrate <u>a little bit harder</u> for this one:

$$\text{Kinetic Energy} = \tfrac{1}{2} \times \text{mass} \times \text{velocity}^2$$

K.E.
$$\tfrac{1}{2} \times m \times v^2$$

<u>Example</u>: A car of mass 2450 kg is travelling at 38 m/s. Calculate its kinetic energy.

<u>Answer</u>: It's pretty easy. You just plug the numbers into the formula — but watch the "v^2".

KE = $\tfrac{1}{2}mv^2$ = $\tfrac{1}{2} \times 2450 \times 38^2$ = <u>1 768 900 J</u> (<u>joules</u> because it's <u>energy</u>)

(If the car suddenly brakes to a stop, all this energy is dissipated as heat at the brakes — that's a lot of heat.)

4) To increase something's <u>kinetic energy</u>, you need to increase its <u>speed</u>, and the only way to increase something's speed is to apply a <u>force</u> to it...

5) ...and if you're applying a force to something, you're <u>doing work</u> on it. It doesn't matter what kind of work this is — it could be a <u>person</u> pushing a <u>trolley</u>, a <u>jet engine</u> providing thrust to an <u>aeroplane</u>, a <u>golf club</u> hitting a <u>golf ball</u>. If object A is causing object B's <u>velocity</u> to increase by exerting a <u>force</u> on it, then it's <u>doing work</u> and increasing object B's <u>kinetic energy</u>.

6) On the other hand, kinetic energy is just <u>movement energy</u>, so if you do work on an object but it doesn't <u>accelerate</u>, then you haven't increased its KE.

Increase in KE = Work Done. Just About...

1) OK, so if <u>work is done</u> on an object, then <u>energy is transferred</u> to that object, which is probably going to make it <u>start moving</u> or <u>move faster</u>.

2) Now then, a really <u>important concept</u> in physics is the idea that <u>energy is always conserved</u>. What that means is that you can't <u>create</u> or <u>destroy</u> energy — it just gets <u>transformed</u> from one kind of energy to another. E.g. a <u>light bulb</u> transforms <u>electrical</u> energy into <u>light</u> and <u>heat</u> energy.

3) So if <u>energy is conserved</u>, then you'd expect the <u>increase</u> in an object's <u>kinetic energy</u> to be <u>equal</u> to the <u>amount of work</u> that's been done on it.

4) The problem is, some of the energy that's transferred gets '<u>wasted</u>' as <u>heat</u> because of <u>friction</u> and <u>air resistance</u>. If you do <u>30 J</u> of work hitting a stationary ball, the ball's kinetic energy will be a bit <u>less than 30 J</u> because air resistance creates <u>heat</u> (OK, so the ball won't get <u>hot</u>, but it'll be a <u>tiny bit hotter</u> than it would be if there was no air resistance). So...

The increase in an object's <u>KE</u> is normally <u>a bit less</u> than the amount of <u>work done</u> on it.

That's some <u>pretty important stuff</u>, so don't forget it.

After doing all this work you should be bouncing around...

The kinetic energy equation's the <u>hardest</u> one in this section — make sure you've got it <u>nailed</u>.

Gravitational Potential Energy

It's the last page of this section... and it's got roller coasters on it. Two more reasons to rejoice.

G.P.E. is 'Height Energy'

Gravitational potential energy (G.P.E.) is the energy stored in an object when you raise it to a height against the force of gravity.

You can think of G.P.E. as a way of storing kinetic energy. You have to lift something to increase its gravitational potential energy, and that energy is only released when the object falls (movement again).

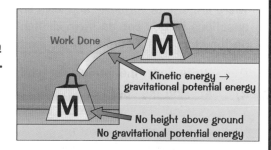

Change in G.P.E. (J) = Weight (N) × Change in Height (m)

Example: A 4000 N cow walks onto a geyser, and is propelled 10 m upwards. Calculate its change in G.P.E.

Answer: Weight × change in height = 4000 × 10 = 40,000 J (or 40 kJ)

Falling Objects Convert G.P.E. into K.E.

1) When something falls, its gravitational potential energy is converted into kinetic energy. So the further it falls, the faster it goes.

2) In practice, some of the G.P.E. will be dissipated as heat due to air resistance, but in exam questions they'll likely say you can ignore air resistance, in which case you'll just need to remember this simple and really quite obvious formula:

Kinetic energy gained = Potential energy lost

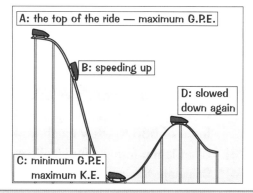

3) For example, the roller coaster to the right will lose G.P.E. and gain K.E. as it falls between points A and C.

4) If you ignore friction (between the tracks and the wheels) and air resistance, the amount of K.E. it gains will be the same as the amount of G.P.E. it loses.

5) Between C and D, it's gaining height, so some of that K.E. is converted back to G.P.E. again.

Example: The carriage in the diagram has a weight of 5000 N (a mass of about 500 kg), and the height difference between A and C is 20 m.

    a) Ignoring friction and air resistance, how much K.E. is gained by the carriage in moving from A to C?

    b) Assuming the roller coaster was stationary at A, calculate its speed at C.

Answer: a) Gain in K.E. = Loss in G.P.E. = Weight × change in height = 5000 × 20 = 100,000 J

    b) At C it has 100,000 J of K.E. You know that K.E. = ½mv², so...

$$\frac{1}{2}mv^2 = 100,000$$
$$v^2 = 100,000 \div \frac{1}{2}m = 100,000 \div (\frac{1}{2} \times 500) = 400$$
$$v = \sqrt{400} = 20 \text{ m/s}$$

Revise roller coasters — don't let your thoughts wander off into oblivion...

Roller coasters are constantly transferring between potential and kinetic energy. In reality, energy will be lost due to friction, air resistance and even as sound. But in exams you can usually ignore these.

Revision Summary for Module P4

Yay — revision summary! I know these are your favourite bits of the book, all those jolly questions. There are lots of formulas and laws and picky little details to learn in this section. So, practise these questions till you can do them all standing on one leg with your arms behind your back while being tickled on the nose with a purple ostrich feather. Or something.

1) Write down the formula for working out speed.

2)* a) Find the speed of a partly chewed mouse which hobbles 3.2 metres in 35 seconds.
   b) Find how far he would go in 25 minutes.

3)* A speed camera is set up in a 30 mph (13.3 m/s) zone. It takes two photographs 0.5 s apart. A car travels 6.3 m between the two photographs. Was the car breaking the speed limit?

4) What does the gradient of a distance-time graph tell you?

5) What's the difference between speed and velocity?

6) Sketch a typical velocity-time graph and point out all the important points.

7) Explain how to find acceleration and distance travelled from a velocity-time graph.

8) Give two reasons why tachographs are used in lorries.

9) What is an interaction pair?

10) A man leans on a wall with a force of 50 N. What can you say about the force exerted by the wall?

11) Define friction.

12) What could you do to reduce the friction between two surfaces?

13) Do all moving objects experience friction?

14) Explain what the 'reaction' of a surface is.

15) Give two scenarios where forces are balanced. Draw diagrams.

16) Describe the forces acting when a jet plane flies horizontally at a steady speed.

17) What is meant by resultant force?

18) If an object has zero resultant force on it, can it be moving? Can it be accelerating?

19)* Write down the formula for momentum. Find the momentum of a 78 kg sheep moving at 5 m/s.

20) Write down a formula for change of momentum.

21) Explain how air bags, seat belts and crumple zones reduce the risk of serious injury in a car crash.

22)* A crazy dog dragged a big branch 12 m over the next-door neighbour's front lawn, pulling with a force of 535 N. How much work was done on the branch?

23) What is the formula for kinetic energy (K.E.)?

24)* Calculate the increase in gravitational potential energy when a box of weight 120 N is raised through 4.5 m.

25)* At the top of a roller coaster ride when it is stationary, a carriage has 150 kJ of gravitational potential energy (G.P.E.). Ignoring friction, how much kinetic energy must the carriage have at the bottom (when G.P.E. = 0)?

26)* A 600 kg (6000 N) roller coaster carriage is travelling at 40 m/s. What is the maximum height it could climb if all its kinetic energy is transferred to gravitational potential energy?

27)* A trolley is stationary at the top of a hill. The trolley weighs 200 N (mass 20 kg), and the hill is 50 m high. Assuming all of its G.P.E. is converted into K.E., how fast will the trolley be going when it reaches the bottom of the hill?

Answers on page 100.

DNA — Making Proteins

This module's about <u>growth and development</u> in plants and animals, including you. All the instructions for how to grow and develop are contained in your DNA. DNA molecules contain a <u>genetic code</u>, which is basically a long list of instructions for how to make <u>all the proteins</u> in your body.

DNA *is a* Double Helix *of* Paired Bases

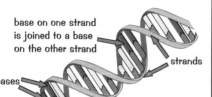

base on one strand
is joined to a base
on the other strand

strands

bases

1) A DNA molecule has <u>two strands</u> coiled together in the shape of a <u>double helix</u> (two spirals).

2) Each strand is made up of lots of small groups called "<u>nucleotides</u>".

3) Each <u>nucleotide</u> contains a small molecule called a "<u>base</u>". DNA has just <u>four</u> different bases — <u>adenine</u> (A), <u>cytosine</u> (C), <u>guanine</u> (G) and <u>thymine</u> (T).

4) The two strands are <u>held together</u> by the bases, which always <u>pair up</u> in the same way — it's always A-T and C-G. This is called <u>base pairing</u>.

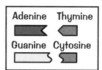

Adenine Thymine

Guanine Cytosine

DNA *Controls the* Production *of* Proteins *in a* Cell

1) A <u>gene</u> is a <u>section of DNA</u> that contains the instructions for <u>one</u> particular <u>protein</u>.

2) Cells make <u>proteins</u> by joining <u>amino acids</u> together in a particular order.

3) It's the order of the <u>bases</u> in a gene that <u>tells the cell</u> in what order to put the <u>amino acids</u> together.

4) Each set of <u>three bases</u> (called a <u>triplet</u>) <u>codes</u> for one <u>amino acid</u>.

5) DNA also determines which genes are <u>switched on or off</u> — and so which <u>proteins</u> the cell <u>produces</u>, e.g. keratin or haemoglobin. That in turn determines what <u>type of cell</u> it is, e.g. a skin cell.

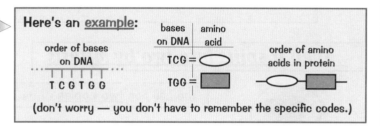

Here's an <u>example</u>:

order of bases on DNA	bases on DNA	amino acid	order of amino acids in protein
	TCG =	◯	
T C G T G G	TGG =	▢	◯—▢

(don't worry — you don't have to remember the specific codes.)

Proteins *are* Made *by* Ribosomes

Organelles are parts of cells, e.g. nucleus, chloroplasts.

Proteins are made in the cell <u>cytoplasm</u> by <u>organelles</u> called <u>ribosomes</u>. DNA is found in the cell <u>nucleus</u> and can't move out of it because it's really big. The cell needs to get the information from the DNA to the ribosome. A <u>copy</u> of the DNA is made using a molecule called <u>RNA</u>, which is very similar to DNA but it's much shorter and only a single strand. RNA is like a <u>messenger</u> between the DNA in the nucleus and the ribosome in the cytoplasm. Here's how it's done:

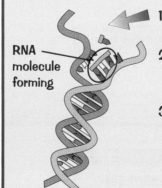

RNA molecule forming

1) The two DNA strands <u>unzip</u>. A molecule of <u>RNA</u> is made using one strand of the DNA as a <u>template</u>. Base pairing ensures it's an exact match.

2) The RNA molecule <u>moves out</u> of the nucleus and <u>joins</u> with a ribosome in the cytoplasm.

3) The job of the ribosome is to <u>stick amino acids together</u> in a chain to make a <u>protein</u>, following the order of bases in the RNA.

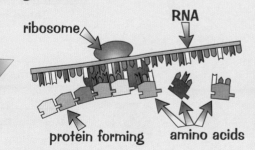

ribosome

RNA

protein forming   amino acids

What do DNA and a game of rounders have in common?

...they both have four bases. Genes <u>control</u> what <u>proteins</u> are made. And proteins are essential things — all your body's enzymes are proteins and enzymes control the making of your other, non-protein bits.

Cell Division — Mitosis

Your cells have to be able to <u>divide</u> for your body to <u>grow</u>. And that means your <u>DNA</u> has to be copied...

New Cells are Needed for Growth and Repair

The cells of your body <u>divide</u> to <u>produce more cells</u>, so your body can <u>grow</u> and <u>replace</u> damaged cells. Of course, cell division doesn't just happen in humans — animals and plants do it too. There are two stages...

First the cell physically grows and duplicates its contents...

The cell has to <u>copy everything</u> it contains so that when it <u>splits</u> in half the two new cells will contain the right amount of material.

Chromosomes are long lengths of coiled DNA. Genes are short sections of DNA on chromosomes.

1) The <u>number</u> of <u>organelles increases</u> during cell growth.

2) The <u>chromosomes</u> are <u>copied</u>, so that the cell has <u>two copies</u> of its DNA:

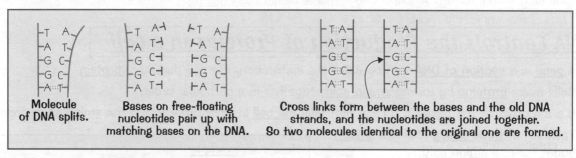

Molecule of DNA splits.

Bases on free-floating nucleotides pair up with matching bases on the DNA.

Cross links form between the bases and the old DNA strands, and the nucleotides are joined together. So two molecules identical to the original one are formed.

...then it splits into two by Mitosis

The cell has <u>two copies</u> of its DNA all spread out in <u>long strings</u>.

Before the cell <u>divides</u>, the DNA forms <u>X-shaped</u> chromosomes. Each 'arm' of a chromosome is an <u>exact duplicate</u> of the other.

The left arm has the same DNA as the right arm of the chromosome.

The chromosomes then <u>line up</u> at the centre of the cell and <u>cell fibres</u> pull them apart. The <u>two arms</u> of each chromosome go to <u>opposite ends</u> of the cell.

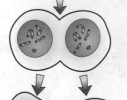

<u>Membranes</u> form around each of the sets of chromosomes. These become the <u>nuclei</u> of the two new cells.

Lastly, the <u>cytoplasm</u> divides.

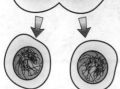

You now have <u>two new cells</u> containing exactly the same DNA — they're <u>identical</u> to <u>each other</u> and to the <u>parent cell</u>.

A cell's favourite computer game — divide and conquer...

This can seem tricky at first. But don't worry — just go through it <u>slowly</u>, one step at a time. This type of division produces identical cells, but there's another type which doesn't... (see next page)

Module B5 — Growth and Development

Cell Division — Meiosis

All the cells in your body divide by mitosis <u>except</u> cells in your reproductive organs
— they divide by <u>meiosis</u> to form sperm or egg cells (<u>gametes</u>).

Gametes Have Half the Usual Number of Chromosomes

1) During <u>sexual reproduction</u>, an egg and a sperm
combine to form a new cell, called a <u>zygote</u>.

2) All human body cells have <u>two copies</u> of the 23
chromosomes (so <u>46 in total</u>). But gametes only have
<u>one copy</u> of each chromosome (<u>23 in total</u>).

3) So when the egg and sperm combine the zygote will contain
<u>46 chromosomes</u> — one <u>set of 23</u> from <u>each parent</u>.

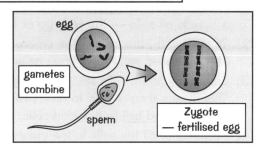

Gametes are Produced by Meiosis

Meiosis involves <u>TWO divisions</u>. It produces new cells that only have <u>half</u> the original number
of chromosomes. In humans it <u>only</u> happens in the ovaries and testes (reproductive organs).

"<u>MEIOSIS</u> produces cells which have <u>half</u> the normal number of chromosomes."

chromosome
pair

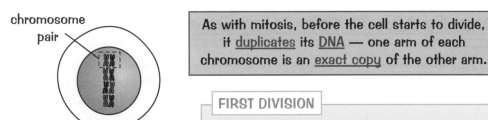

As with mitosis, before the cell starts to divide,
it <u>duplicates</u> its <u>DNA</u> — one arm of each
chromosome is an <u>exact copy</u> of the other arm.

FIRST DIVISION

In the <u>first division</u> in meiosis (there are two divisions)
the chromosome pairs <u>line up</u> in the oentre of the cell.

The <u>pairs</u> are then <u>pulled apart</u>, so each new cell only
has one copy of each chromosome. <u>Some</u> of the father's
chromosomes (shown in blue) and <u>some</u> of the mother's
chromosomes (shown in red) go into each new cell.

SECOND DIVISION

In the <u>second division</u> the chromosomes <u>line up</u>
again in the centre of the cell. It's a lot like mitosis.
The <u>arms</u> of the chromosomes are <u>pulled apart</u>.

You get four gametes each with only a
<u>single set</u> of chromosomes in it.

After two gametes join at fertilisation, the
zygote grows by repeatedly dividing by <u>mitosis</u>.

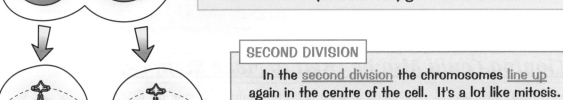

Now that I have your undivided attention...

Remember — in humans, meiosis only occurs in <u>reproductive organs</u>, where gametes are being made.

Development from a Single Cell

You've seen how you get a zygote, so now you can learn how that <u>single cell develops</u> into a homework-dodging, pizza-lovin' student...

Cells in an Early Embryo Can Turn into Any Type of Cell

1) A fertilised egg (<u>zygote</u>) divides by mitosis to produce a bundle of cells — the <u>embryo</u> of the new organism.

2) To start with, the cells in the embryo are <u>all the same</u>. They're called <u>embryonic stem cells</u>.

3) Embryonic stem cells are <u>undifferentiated</u>. This means they're able to divide to produce <u>any type</u> of <u>specialised cell</u> (e.g. blood cells, nerve cells).

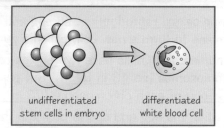

undifferentiated stem cells in embryo → differentiated white blood cell

4) In <u>humans</u>, all the cells in the embryo are undifferentiated up to the <u>eight cell</u> stage.

5) The process of stem cells <u>becoming specialised</u> is called <u>differentiation</u>. As the cells start to <u>differentiate</u> the embryo begins to develop <u>tissues</u> and <u>organs</u>.

6) <u>All cells</u> contain the <u>same genes</u> but not all genes are <u>active</u> (<u>turned on</u>) in each cell type. What <u>type</u> of cell a stem cell differentiates into depends on what <u>genes are active</u> in that cell — and so what <u>proteins</u> that cell produces.

7) <u>Adult</u> humans only have <u>stem cells</u> in certain places like the <u>bone marrow</u>. These stem cells <u>aren't as versatile</u> as the stem cells in embryos — they can only differentiate into certain types of cell.

Stem Cells May be Able to Cure Many Diseases

ADULT STEM CELLS

<u>Adult stem cells</u> are already used to cure disease. For example, people with some <u>blood diseases</u> (e.g. <u>sickle-cell anaemia</u>) can be treated by <u>bone marrow transplants</u>. Bone marrow contains <u>stem cells</u> that can turn into <u>new blood cells</u> to replace the faulty old ones.

EMBRYONIC STEM CELLS

<u>Embryonic stem cells</u> can be extracted from very early human embryos. These could then be controlled to differentiate into specific cells to <u>replace faulty cells</u> in sick people — <u>heart muscle cells</u> for people with <u>heart disease</u>, <u>nerve cells</u> for people <u>paralysed by spinal injuries</u>, and so on.

To get cultures of <u>one specific type</u> of cell, scientists try to <u>control</u> differentiation of the stem cells by <u>altering the conditions</u> to <u>activate certain genes</u>. It's a bit tricky and more <u>research</u> is needed.

Cloning Could Also be Used to Make Stem Cells

1) <u>Human adult cell cloning</u> could also be used to produce tissues for disease sufferers that wouldn't be rejected by the sufferer's immune system.

2) A <u>cloned embryo</u> is created that is genetically identical to the sufferer.

3) Basically, you take an <u>egg cell</u> and remove its <u>genetic material</u>. A <u>complete set</u> of <u>chromosomes</u> from the cell of the <u>adult</u> you're cloning is then inserted into the 'empty' egg cell. If the <u>conditions are right</u>, <u>inactive genes</u> are <u>reactivated</u> and an <u>embryo</u> grows.

4) <u>Embryonic stem cells</u> that can become any cell in the body are then extracted from it.

Develop — birds do it, bees do it, even educated fleas do it...

The potential use of stem cells is huge — but it's early days yet. Some people are <u>against</u> embryonic stem cell research so some researchers have been looking at getting stem cells from alternative sources.

Growth in Plants

Plant growth is different from animal growth — plants can <u>regenerate</u> (grow new parts) and can <u>grow almost continuously</u> throughout their life.

Animals *Stop* Growing, Plants Can Grow *Continuously*

1) Animals grow while they're <u>young</u>, and then they reach <u>full growth</u> and <u>stop</u> growing. Plants can grow <u>continuously</u> — even really old trees will keep putting out <u>new branches</u>.
2) In animals, growth happens by <u>cell division</u>, but in plants, growth in height is mainly due to <u>cell enlargement</u> (elongation) — cell <u>division</u> usually just happens in the <u>tips</u> of the <u>roots</u> and <u>shoots</u>.

Meristems *Contain* Plant Stem Cells

1) Some plant tissues (called <u>meristems</u>) contain <u>unspecialised cells</u> that are able to divide and form <u>any cell type</u> in the plant — they act like <u>embryonic stem cells</u>. But unlike human stem cells, these cells can <u>divide</u> to generate any type of cell <u>for as long as the plant lives</u>.
2) If <u>hormone conditions</u> are right, the unspecialised cells can <u>differentiate</u> into:
   - plant <u>tissues</u> — e.g. xylem and phloem (the water and food transport tissues),
   - plant <u>organs</u> — e.g. leaves, roots and flowers.
3) As with human cells, all the cells contain exactly the <u>same DNA</u> — differentiation is a matter of <u>switching</u> certain genes <u>on or off</u>.
4) Meristem tissue is found in the areas of a plant that are <u>growing</u> — such as the <u>roots and shoots</u>.
5) The dividing meristems produce cells that <u>increase</u> the plants <u>height</u>, <u>girth</u> and <u>length</u> of the roots.

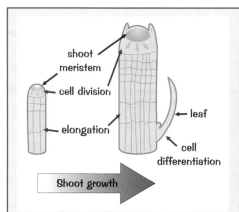

You don't need to learn the diagram — just understand how growth happens in plants.

Cells in the <u>meristem</u> divide to produce more cells, increasing the <u>height and girth</u> of the shoot.

In the area behind the shoot meristem, cells <u>elongate</u>, increasing the height of the shoot even more.

If conditions are right, unspecialised cells will <u>differentiate</u> — creating tissues and organs, e.g. leaves and flowers.

Clones *of Plants* Can be Produced *from* Cuttings

A <u>cutting</u> is part of a plant that has been <u>cut off it</u>, like the end of a branch with a few leaves on it. Gardeners are familiar with taking <u>cuttings</u> from good parent plants, and then planting them in soil with rooting powder (see next page), to produce <u>identical copies</u> (clones) of the parent plant. Cuttings will contain unspecialised meristem cells which can <u>differentiate</u> to make any cell. This means a whole new plant can grow from the cutting.

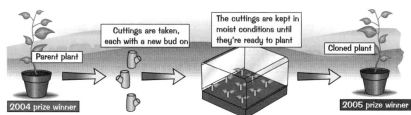

Cheery cells those Merry-stems...

So some plant cells can make <u>any cell</u> in the plant and for the whole time that the plant is alive. Nice.

Module B5 — Growth and Development

Growth in Plants

Plants <u>don't</u> grow randomly. Plant hormones make sure they grow in a <u>useful direction</u> (e.g. toward light).

Phototropism *is* Movement *in Response to Light*

1) Some parts of a plant, e.g. roots and shoots, can <u>move</u> in response to <u>light</u> — this is called <u>phototropism</u>.
2) Shoots are <u>positively phototropic</u> — they grow <u>towards</u> light.
3) Roots are <u>negatively phototropic</u> — they grow <u>away</u> from light.
4) The <u>movement</u> of the shoots and roots in response to light helps plants to <u>survive</u>:

> ### Positive Phototropism
> Plants need <u>sunlight</u> for <u>photosynthesis</u>. Without sunlight, plants can't photosynthesise and don't produce the food they need for <u>energy and growth</u>. Photosynthesis occurs <u>mainly</u> in the <u>leaves</u>, so it's important for plant shoots, which will grow leaves, to grow <u>towards light</u>.

> ### Negative Phototropism
> Plants need <u>nutrients and water</u> from the <u>soil</u> to grow. Phototropism means roots grow <u>away</u> from light, <u>down into the soil</u> where they can <u>absorb</u> the water and nutrients the plant needs for <u>healthy growth</u>.

Auxins *are Plant* Growth Hormones

1) <u>Auxins</u> are <u>chemicals</u> that control <u>growth</u> near the <u>tips</u> of <u>shoots</u> and <u>roots</u>.
2) Auxin is produced in the <u>tips</u> and <u>diffuses backwards</u> to stimulate the <u>cell elongation (enlargement) process</u>, which occurs in the cells <u>just behind</u> the tips.
3) If the tip of a shoot is <u>removed</u>, no auxin is available and the shoot may <u>stop growing</u>.
4) Auxins are involved in the responses of plants to <u>light</u>, <u>gravity</u> and <u>water</u>.

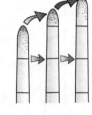

> ### Auxins make shoots grow towards light
> 1) When a <u>shoot tip</u> is exposed to <u>light</u>, <u>more auxin</u> accumulates on the side that's in the <u>shade</u> than the side that's in the light.
> 2) This makes the cells grow (elongate) <u>faster</u> on the <u>shaded side</u>, so the shoot bends <u>towards</u> the light.

Auxins *Help* Cuttings *Grow into a Complete Plant*

1) If you stick cuttings in the soil they <u>won't always grow</u>.
2) If you add <u>rooting powder</u>, which contains the plant hormone <u>auxin</u>, they'll <u>produce roots</u> rapidly and start growing as <u>new plants</u>.
3) This helps growers to produce lots of <u>clones</u> (exact copies) of a really good plant <u>very quickly</u>.

boring old soil

rooting compound — containing auxin

A plant auxin to a bar — 'ouch'...
Learn the page. Learn the <u>whole darn page</u>. There's no getting out of it folks.

Revision Summary for Module B5

Well done — you've finished another topic. And what an incredibly tricky topic it was — especially all the ins and outs of mitosis and meiosis. Award yourself a gold star, relax, get a cup of tea, and take a leisurely glance through these beautiful revision summary questions. Once you've glanced through them, you'll have to answer them. And then you'll have to check your answers and go back and revise any bits you got wrong. And then do the questions again. In fact, it's not really a matter of relaxing at all. More a matter of knuckling down to lots of hard work. Oops. Sorry.

1) How many different bases does DNA have?
2) What are proteins made of?
3) What is a gene?
4) Where in the cell are genes found?
5) Where in the cell are proteins made?
6) During cell growth does the number of chromosomes double or halve?
7) The table below compares mitosis and meiosis. Complete the table using crosses (✗) and ticks (✓) to show whether the statements are true for mitosis or meiosis. The first row's been filled in for you.

	Mitosis	Meiosis
Its purpose is to provide new cells for growth and repair.	✓	✗
Its purpose is to create gametes (sex cells).		
The cells produced are genetically identical.		
Four cells are produced.		
It happens in the reproductive organs.		

8) What is the name of the cell produced when two gametes combine?
9) Do gametes have half or twice the usual number of chromosomes?
10) What is meant by the term 'undifferentiated'?
11) In a human embryo, all the cells are undifferentiated until what stage?
12) What determines the type of cell a stem cell becomes?
13) How are the stem cells in an embryo different from the stem cells in an adult?
14) Name one place in a human adult that stem cells are found.
15) What are plant stem cells called?
16) Name two things plant stem cells can differentiate into.
17) Why can cuttings of plants grow into new complete plants?
18) In which parts of plants does cell elongation and division usually happen?
19) What does 'phototropism' mean?
20) Are roots negatively or positively phototropic?
21) Explain how auxins cause plant shoots to grow towards light.
22) What is added to soil to encourage cuttings to grow?

Chemicals in the Atmosphere

Welcome to the next section of wonderful Chemistry. Let's kick off with the atmosphere.

Dry Air is a Mixture of Gases

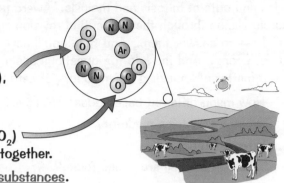

1) The Earth's atmosphere contains many gases.

2) Some of these gases are elements, e.g. oxygen (O_2), nitrogen (N_2) and argon (Ar) — they contain only one type of atom.

3) Other gases are compounds, e.g. carbon dioxide (CO_2) — they contain more than one type of atom joined together.

4) Most of the gases in the atmosphere are molecular substances.

Molecular Substances Have Low Melting and Boiling Points

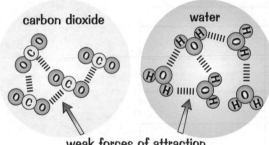

carbon dioxide   water

weak forces of attraction

1) Molecular substances usually exist as small molecules, like CO_2 and H_2O.

2) The atoms within the molecules are held together by very strong covalent bonds (see next page).

3) In contrast, the forces of attraction between these molecules are very weak.

4) You only need a little bit of energy to overcome the weak forces between the molecules — so molecular substances have low melting and boiling points.

5) This means that they're usually gases and liquids at room temperature.

6) Pure molecular substances don't conduct electricity, simply because their molecules aren't charged. There are no free electrons or ions.

7) Most non-metal elements and most compounds formed from non-metal elements are molecular.

You Have to be Able to Interpret Data

There's loads of opportunity in this module for examiners to test your ability to interpret data. Here's a nice example on molecular substances.

Example:

Which of the molecular substances in the table is a liquid at room temperature (25 °C)?

	melting point	boiling point
oxygen	-219 °C	-183 °C
nitrogen	-210 °C	-196 °C
bromine	-7 °C	59 °C
argon	-189 °C	-186 °C

There's only one substance that fits the bill here — bromine. It melts (turns to a liquid) at -7 °C and boils (turns to a gas) at 59 °C. So, it'll be a liquid at room temperature. Oxygen, nitrogen and argon will be gases at room temperature.

Stop gassing about it — and get learning...

So, the key things here are those covalent bonds within molecules, and the weaker forces that join the separate molecules together. It's these things that give covalent compounds their properties and make them likely to be liquids and gases at room temperature.

Covalent Bonding

Some elements bond ionically (see page 19), but others form strong covalent bonds.

Covalent Bonds — Sharing Electrons

1) Sometimes atoms make covalent bonds by sharing electrons with other atoms.
2) This way both atoms feel that they have a full outer shell, and that makes them happy.
3) Each covalent bond provides one extra shared electron for each atom.
4) Each atom involved has to make enough covalent bonds to fill up its outer shell.
5) The atoms bond due to the electrostatic attraction between the positive nuclei and the negative electrons shared between them.

E.g. Hydrogen, H₂

Hydrogen needs just one extra electron to fill its outer shell.

So, two hydrogen atoms share their outer electron so that they each have a full shell, and a covalent bond is formed.

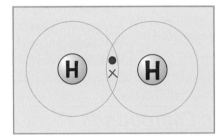

E.g. Carbon Dioxide, CO₂

Carbon needs four more electrons to fill it up.
Oxygen needs two.
So two double covalent bonds are formed.
A double covalent bond has two shared pairs of electrons.

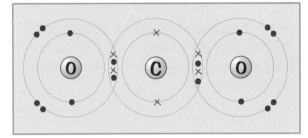

2-D Drawings Don't Always Tell the Whole Story

1) The shape of a molecule is often important, especially with organic (carbon-based) molecules. A simple molecule like methane is often drawn looking flat, but it really has a different shape:

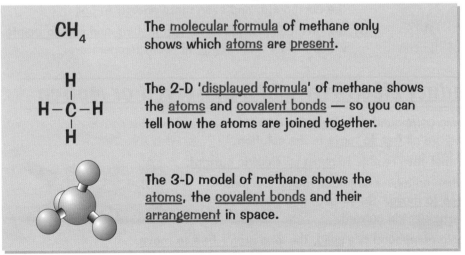

CH₄ — The molecular formula of methane only shows which atoms are present.

H–C–H (with H above and below) — The 2-D 'displayed formula' of methane shows the atoms and covalent bonds — so you can tell how the atoms are joined together.

The 3-D model of methane shows the atoms, the covalent bonds and their arrangement in space.

2) Computers are often used to produce 3-D models of molecules.

Covalent bonding — it's good to share...

3-D models are especially important when it comes to studying enzymes and some drugs. With enzymes (see p.5), it's their three-dimensional shape rather than their molecular formula that lets them do their job. There are different types of 3-D model that show you different things about molecules.

Chemicals in the Hydrosphere

The oceans are packed with fish, whales, jellyfish and also plenty of chemicals. Read and learn...

The Earth's Hydrosphere is the Oceans

1) The Earth's hydrosphere consists of all the water in the oceans, seas, lakes, rivers, puddles and so on...
2) It also contains any compounds that are dissolved in the water.
3) Many of these compounds are ionic compounds called salts — that's why sea water is 'salty'.
4) Examples of salts are sodium chloride (NaCl), magnesium chloride ($MgCl_2$) and potassium bromide (KBr).

You need to be able to work out the chemical formulas of salts — here's an example, but flick back to page 20 if you need a recap.

EXAMPLE: Find the formula for magnesium sulfate.
Find the charges on a magnesium ion and a sulfate ion.
A magnesium ion is Mg^{2+} and a sulfate ion is SO_4^{2-}.
To balance the total charge you need one sulfate ion to every one magnesium ion.
So the formula of magnesium sulfate must be: $MgSO_4$

You'll be given a table of charges on ions in the exam.

Solid Ionic Compounds Form Crystals

1) Ionic compounds are made of charged particles called ions.
2) Ions with opposite charges are strongly attracted to one another. You get a massive giant lattice of ions built up.
3) There are very strong chemical bonds called ionic bonds between all the ions.
4) A single crystal of salt is one giant ionic lattice, which is why salt crystals tend to be cuboid in shape.

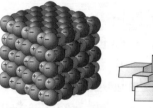

Ionic Compounds Have High Melting and Boiling Points

strong forces of attraction

1) The forces of attraction between the ions are very strong.
2) It takes a lot of energy to overcome these forces and melt the compound, and even more energy to boil it.
3) So ionic compounds have high melting and boiling points, which makes them solids at room temperature.

They Conduct Electricity When Dissolved or Molten

1) When an ionic compound dissolves, the ions separate and are all free to move in the solution.
2) This means that they're able to carry an electric current.
3) Similarly, when an ionic compound melts, the ions are again free to move. So — yep, you guessed it — they'll carry electric current.
4) When an ionic compound is a solid, the ions aren't free to move, and so an electrical current can't pass through the substance.

Not all ionic compounds will dissolve in water.

Solid

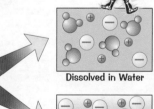
Dissolved in Water

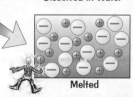
Melted

Giant ionic lattices — all over your chips...

Because they conduct electricity when they're dissolved in water, ionic compounds are used to make some types of battery. In the olden days, most batteries had actual liquid in, so they tended to leak all over the place. Now they've come up with a sort of paste that doesn't leak but still conducts. Clever.

Chemicals in the Lithosphere

So, we've done the skies and the seas. Now it's on to the hard stuff (the land, not the work...).

The Earth's Lithosphere is Made Up of a Mixture of Minerals

1) The lithosphere is the Earth's rigid outer layer — the crust and part of the mantle below it.

2) It's made up of a mixture of minerals, often containing silicon, oxygen and aluminium.

3) Most of the silicon and oxygen in the Earth's crust exists as the compound silicon dioxide.

Different types of rock contain different minerals and different elements. For example, limestone contains a lot of calcium, whereas sandstone contains a lot of silicon.

You might have to interpret data on the abundance of elements in rocks. Don't panic — you'll be given all the information you need.

Silicon Dioxide Forms a Giant Covalent Structure

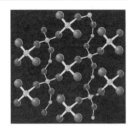

1) Giant covalent structures, like silicon dioxide, contain no charged ions.

2) All the atoms are bonded to each other by strong covalent bonds. This gives it a rigid structure, which makes the substance hard.

3) They have very high melting and boiling points.

4) They don't conduct electricity — not even when molten.

5) They're usually insoluble in water.

Silicon Dioxide

This is what sand is made of. Each grain of sand is one giant structure of silicon and oxygen.
It's also called silica.
Silicon dioxide is the main constituent of sandstone, and it's also found as quartz in granite.

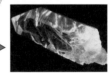

Interpreting data could sneak its way into this section of the exam too...

Example: Diamond has a giant covalent structure.
Suggest why it's often used in industrial drill tips.

All the atoms in diamond are bonded to each other by strong covalent bonds, making it an incredibly hard substance — so hard that it can drill through just about any material.

Some Minerals are Very Valuable Gemstones

1) There are a lot of different minerals in the Earth. Some are worth more than others.

2) Some minerals are very rare, which can make them valuable. Gems like diamond, ruby and sapphire are examples of this.

3) Gemstones are very hard. This is all down to their giant covalent structures.

4) They're also pretty and sparkly, which makes them attractive and useful for making jewellery.

Don't forget your minerals — and your vitamins too...

So, all that stuff beneath your feet is packed full of minerals. Some of them are really abundant, but others are quite rare, which can make them pretty valuable. But that doesn't mean you should go off and start digging up your back garden to look for diamonds — right now you need to be learning this.

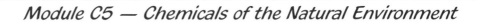

Chemicals in the Biosphere

The biosphere is anything that's alive, or comes from living things. Again, it's made of chemicals.

Living Things All Share the Same Building Blocks

1) All living things are formed from compounds made up of the same basic elements.

2) The main elements are carbon, hydrogen, oxygen and nitrogen, along with small amounts of phosphorus and sulfur.

3) These elements make up molecules vital for life, such as carbohydrates, proteins, fats and DNA.

> It's possible to recognise molecules by the elements they contain.
>
> 1) DNA always contains phosphorus and nitrogen.
>
> 2) Proteins always contain nitrogen and may also contain sulfur.
>
> 3) Fats and carbohydrates only contain carbon, hydrogen and oxygen... you can tell them apart as fats contain a greater percentage of carbon.

This is another 'interpret data' topic, so make sure you know what makes up each molecule.

4) Don't forget, carbohydrates, proteins and DNA are all molecular — there are no ions involved.

You Can Write Formulas by Counting Elements

For example, the carbohydrate glucose looks like this:

CH₂OH

C — O
H   H
H
C   C
OH   OH H   OH
C — C
H   OH

The diagram shows that it only contains carbon, hydrogen and oxygen atoms.

There are 6 carbon atoms, 12 hydrogen atoms and 6 oxygen atoms, so you can work out that glucose's formula is $C_6H_{12}O_6$.

Flow Charts Show Changes Between Spheres

1) Elements are constantly moving between the atmosphere, biosphere, hydrosphere and lithosphere.

2) Flow charts can be used to summarise chemical changes between the spheres.

> 1) Arrows show the direction of change.
>
> 2) Boxes represent the various stages.

☐ atmosphere
☐ lithosphere
☐ biosphere

carbon dioxide in the atmosphere

burning

coal, oil and natural gas

burial   burial

The diagram shows part of the carbon cycle.

Carbon in the atmosphere (carbon dioxide) is captured by green plants and converted into other carbon compounds, like carbohydrates. Animals graze on plants, taking in the carbon compounds they contain. The plants and animals die and some are buried. Over millions of years these form coal and oil, which, when burnt, will return the carbon dioxide to the atmosphere.

compounds in animals   compounds in plants

grazing

ONE carbon atom — ah, ah, ah, ah...

Examiners love to ask you to interpret information like flow charts and molecule data. Don't panic if it's something you don't know about. You won't be asked questions about specific facts — you just need to be able to understand what the data means. So take a deep breath and use your common sense.

Module C5 — Chemicals of the Natural Environment

Metals from Minerals

Ores Contain Enough Metal to Make Extraction Worthwhile

1) Rocks are made of minerals. Minerals are just solid elements and compounds.

2) Metal ores are rocks that contain varying amounts of minerals from which metals can be extracted.

3) In many cases the ore is an oxide of the metal. Here are a few examples of ores:

Chalcopyrite

   a) A type of iron ore is called haematite. This is iron(III) oxide (Fe_2O_3).
   b) A type of copper ore is called chalcopyrite. This is copper iron sulfide ($CuFeS_2$).

4) For some metals, large amounts of ore need to be mined just to obtain small percentages of valuable minerals. A good example of this is copper mining — copper ores typically contain about 1% copper.

You may be asked to calculate the mass of a metal that can be extracted from a certain mass of mineral given its formula (see below) or an equation (see p.75).

Example: How much copper can be extracted from 800 g of copper oxide (CuO)?

Step 1: Calculate the proportion of copper in copper oxide $= \dfrac{A_r \times \text{no. of atoms}}{M_r} = \dfrac{63.5 \times 1}{79.5} = 0.79874$

See p.74 for more about A_r and M_r.

Step 2: Multiply your answer by the mass of copper oxide $= 0.79874 \times 800 = \underline{639 \text{ g}}$

More Reactive Metals are Harder to Get

1) A few unreactive metals like gold are found in the Earth as the metal itself, rather than as a compound.

2) But most metals need to be extracted from their ores using a chemical reaction.

3) More reactive metals, like sodium, are harder to extract — that's why it took longer to discover them.

Some Metals can be Extracted by Reduction with Carbon

1) Electrolysis (splitting with electricity) is one way of extracting a metal from its ore (see next page). The other common way is chemical reduction using carbon or carbon monoxide.

2) When an ore is reduced, oxygen is removed from it, e.g.

$Fe_2O_3(s)$	+	$3CO(g)$	→	$2Fe(s)$	+	$3CO_2(g)$
iron(III) oxide	+	carbon monoxide	→	iron	+	carbon dioxide

3) When a metal oxide loses its oxygen it is REDUCED. The carbon gains the oxygen and is OXIDISED.

The position of a metal in the reactivity series determines whether it can be extracted by reduction with carbon or carbon monoxide.

   a) Metals higher than carbon in the reactivity series have to be extracted using electrolysis, which is expensive.

   b) Metals below carbon in the reactivity series can be extracted by reduction using carbon.
   This is because carbon can only take the oxygen away from metals which are less reactive than carbon itself is.

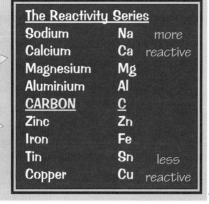

The Reactivity Series
Sodium   Na   more reactive
Calcium   Ca
Magnesium Mg
Aluminium Al
CARBON   C
Zinc   Zn
Iron   Fe
Tin   Sn   less reactive
Copper   Cu

Miners — they always have to stick their ore in...

Extracting metals isn't cheap. You have to pay for special equipment, energy and labour. Then there's the cost of getting the ore to the extraction plant. If there's a choice of extraction methods, a company always picks the cheapest, unless there's a good reason not to. They're not extracting it for fun.

Electrolysis

Electrolysis is a useful way of extracting <u>reactive metals</u> from their ores.

Electrolysis Means 'Splitting Up with Electricity'

1) <u>Electrolysis</u> is the <u>decomposition</u> (breaking down) of a substance using <u>electricity</u>.
2) It needs a <u>liquid</u> to <u>conduct</u> the electricity — called the <u>electrolyte</u>. Electrolytes are usually <u>free ions dissolved in water</u> (e.g. <u>dissolved salts</u>) or <u>molten ionic compounds</u>.
3) It's the <u>free ions</u> that <u>conduct</u> the electricity and allow the whole thing to work.
4) For an electrical circuit to be complete, there's got to be a <u>flow of electrons</u>. In electrolysis, <u>electrons</u> are taken <u>away from</u> ions at the <u>positive electrode</u> and <u>given to</u> other ions at the <u>negative electrode</u>. As ions gain or lose electrons they become atoms or molecules.

NaCl dissolved

Molten NaCl
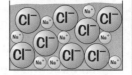

Electrolysis Removes Aluminium from Its Ore

1) The main ore of aluminium is <u>bauxite</u>, which contains aluminium oxide, Al_2O_3.
2) <u>Molten</u> aluminium oxide contains <u>free ions</u> — so it'll <u>conduct electricity</u>.
3) The <u>positive Al^{3+} ions</u> are attracted to the <u>negative electrode</u> where they <u>each pick up three electrons</u> and "zup", they turn into neutral <u>aluminium atoms</u>. These then <u>sink</u> to the bottom.
4) The <u>negative O^{2-} ions</u> are attracted to the <u>positive electrode</u> where they <u>each lose two electrons</u>. The neutral oxygen atoms will then <u>combine</u> to form <u>O_2</u> molecules.

<u>Metals</u> form <u>positive ions</u>, so they're attracted to the <u>negative electrode</u>.

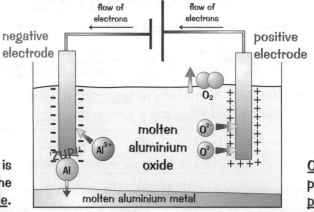
molten aluminium oxide / molten aluminium metal

<u>Non-metals</u> form <u>negative ions</u>, so they're attracted to the <u>positive electrode</u>.

<u>Aluminium</u> is produced at the <u>negative electrode</u>.

<u>Oxygen</u> is produced at the <u>positive electrode</u>.

At the Negative Electrode:
$$Al^{3+} + 3e^- \rightarrow Al$$
Reduction — a gain of electrons

At the Positive Electrode:
$$2O^{2-} \rightarrow O_2 + 4e^-$$
Oxidation — a loss of electrons

So, the complete equation for the decomposition of <u>aluminium oxide</u> is:

aluminium oxide → aluminium + oxygen
$$2Al_2O_{3(l)} \rightarrow 4Al_{(l)} + 3O_{2(g)}$$

Always remember state symbols when writing symbol equations.

Faster shopping at Tesco — use Electrolleys...

Electrolysis ain't cheap — it takes a lot of <u>electricity</u>, which costs <u>money</u>. It's the only way of extracting some metals from their ores though, so it's <u>worth it</u>. This isn't such a bad page to learn — try writing a <u>mini-essay</u> about it. Don't forget to have a go at drawing the diagram <u>from memory</u> too.

Metals

Who'd have thought you'd find metals lurking about in rocks...
Now you've seen how to extract them, it's time to learn all about metals and their properties, yay!

Metal Properties *are All Due to the* Sea of Free Electrons

1) Metals consist of a giant structure.

2) Metallic bonds involve the all-important 'free electrons', which produce all the properties of metals.

3) These free electrons come from the outer shell of every metal atom in the structure.

4) The positively charged metal ions are held together by these electrons.

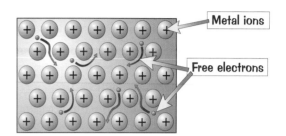

1) They're Good Conductors of Heat and Electricity

The free electrons carry both heat and electrical current through the material, so metals are good conductors of heat and electricity.

> Metals are ideal if you want to make something that heat needs to travel through, like a saucepan base.
> Their electrical conductivity makes them great for making things like electrical wires.

2) Most Metals are Strong and Malleable

Metals have a high tensile strength — in other words they're strong and hard to break.

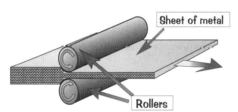

The layers of atoms in a metal can slide over each other, making metals malleable — they can be hammered or rolled into flat sheets.

> Metals' strength and 'bendability' makes them handy for making into things like bridges and car bodies.

3) They Generally Have High Melting and Boiling Points

Metallic bonds are very strong, so it takes a lot of energy to break them — you have to get the metal pretty hot to melt it (except for mercury, which is a bit weird), e.g. copper melts at 1085 °C and tungsten melts at 3422 °C.

> Metals' high melting and boiling points make them handy — you don't want your saucepan to melt when you're cooking, or bridges to melt in hot weather.

Someone robbed your metal? — call a copper...

The skin of the Statue of Liberty is made of copper — about 80 tonnes of it in fact. Its surface reacts with gases in the air to form copper carbonate — which is why it's that pretty shade of green. It was a present from France to the United States — I wonder if they found any wrapping paper big enough?

Module C5 — Chemicals of the Natural Environment

Environmental Impact

Metals are definitely a big part of modern life. Once they're finished with, it's far better to recycle them than to dig up more ore and extract fresh metal.

Ores are Finite Resources

1) This means that there's a limited amount of them — eventually, they'll run out.

2) People have to balance the social, economic and environmental effects of mining the ores.

3) So, mining metal ores is good because useful products can be made. It also provides local people with jobs and brings money into the area. This means services such as transport and health can be improved.

4) But mining ores is bad for the environment as it uses loads of energy, scars the landscape and destroys habitats. Also, noise, dust and pollution are caused by an increase in traffic.

5) Deep mine shafts can also be dangerous for a long time after the mine has been abandoned.

Recycling Metals is Important

1) Mining and extracting metals takes lots of energy, most of which comes from burning fossil fuels.

2) Fossil fuels are running out so it's important to conserve them. Not only this, but burning them contributes to acid rain, global dimming and climate change.

3) Recycling metals only uses a small fraction of the energy needed to mine and extract new metal. E.g. recycling copper only takes 15% of the energy that's needed to mine and extract new copper.

4) Energy doesn't come cheap, so recycling saves money too.

5) As there's a finite amount of each metal in the Earth, recycling conserves these resources.

6) Recycling metal cuts down on the amount of rubbish that gets sent to landfill. Landfill takes up space and pollutes the surroundings. If all the aluminium cans in the UK were recycled, there'd be 14 million fewer dustbins of waste each year.

For example...

1) If you didn't recycle, say, aluminium, you'd have to mine more aluminium ore — 4 tonnes for every 1 tonne of aluminium you need. But mining makes a mess of the landscape (and these mines are often in rainforests). The ore then needs to be transported, and the aluminium extracted (which uses loads of electricity). And don't forget the cost of sending your used aluminium to landfill.

2) So it's a complex calculation, but for every 1 kg of aluminium cans you recycle, you save:

- 95% or so of the energy needed to mine and extract 'fresh' aluminium,
- 4 kg of aluminium ore,
- a lot of waste.

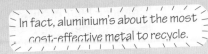
In fact, aluminium's about the most cost-effective metal to recycle.

Recycling — do the Tour de France twice...

Recycling metal saves natural resources and money and reduces environmental problems. It's great. There's no limit to the number of times metals like aluminium, copper and steel can be recycled. So your humble little drink can may one day form part of a powerful robot who takes over the galaxy.

Module C5 — Chemicals of the Natural Environment

Revision Summary for Module C5

Here are some questions for you to get your teeth into. Have a go at them. If there are any you can't do, go back to the section and do a bit more learning, then try again. It's not fun, but it's the best way to make sure you know everything. Hop to it.

1) Name a gas in dry air that is a compound. Give the formula of this gas.
2) Explain why most molecular substances are gases.
3) Why don't molecular compounds conduct electricity?
4) What is covalent bonding?
5)* Ethane can be represented by the molecular formula C_2H_6. Draw a 2-D diagram of its structure.
6) What is the Earth's hydrosphere?
7) What makes sea water 'salty'?
8) Why do solid ionic compounds form crystals?
9) Do solid ionic compounds have low or high boiling points? Explain why.
10) Why can ionic compounds conduct electricity when dissolved in water but not when they're solid?
11) What is the Earth's lithosphere?
12) Name three abundant elements in the Earth's lithosphere.
13) What type of structure does silicon dioxide have?
14) Give two chemical properties of silicon dioxide.
15) Why are some minerals considered to be valuable gemstones?
16) From the table, which molecule is more likely to be a fat, and which is more likely to be a carbohydrate?

element	molecule A	molecule B
carbon	40%	75%
hydrogen	6%	13%
oxygen	54%	12%

17) In a flowchart, what do: a) the arrows represent? b) the boxes represent?
18) What is an ore?
19)* Calculate how much aluminium can be extracted from 400 g of aluminium oxide.
20) Name a metal that can be extracted by heating its oxide with carbon.
21) Why can't some metal oxides be reduced using carbon?
22) What is electrolysis?
23) Why can a molten ionic crystal act as an electrolyte?
24) During electrolysis, do metals form at the negative electrode or at the positive electrode?
25) Describe what happens at the electrodes during the electrolysis of molten aluminium oxide.
26) What do the terms 'reduced' and 'oxidised' mean?
27) Why are metals able to conduct electricity?
28) Why have metals got high melting and boiling points?
29) Give one impact on the environment for each of the following:
    a) extracting metals,
    b) disposing of metals.
30) Give two reasons why it's a good idea to recycle metals.

* Answers on page 100.

Static Electricity

Static electricity's all about <u>charges</u> which are <u>not free to move</u>. This causes them to build up in one place — and lead to <u>sparks</u> or <u>shocks</u> when they finally do move — <u>crackling</u> when you take a jumper off, say.

Build-up of Static is Caused by Friction

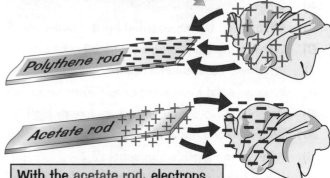

1) When two <u>insulating</u> materials are <u>rubbed</u> together, electrons are <u>scraped off one</u> and <u>dumped</u> on the other.

> With the <u>polythene rod</u>, electrons move <u>from the duster</u> to the rod.

2) This leaves a <u>positive</u> static charge on one and a <u>negative</u> static charge on the other.

3) <u>Which way</u> the electrons are transferred <u>depends</u> on the <u>two materials</u> involved.

4) Electrically charged objects <u>attract</u> small objects placed near them.
(Try this: rub a balloon on a woolly pully — then put it near tiddly bits of paper and watch them jump.)

5) The classic examples are <u>polythene</u> and <u>acetate</u> rods being rubbed with a <u>cloth duster</u>, as shown in the diagrams.

> With the <u>acetate rod</u>, electrons move <u>from the rod</u> to the duster.

Only Electrons Move — Never the Positive Charges

Both +ve and –ve electrostatic charges are only ever produced by the movement of <u>electrons</u> — the <u>negatively</u> charged particles. The positive charges <u>definitely do not move</u>! A positive static charge is always caused by electrons <u>moving</u> away elsewhere, as shown above. Don't forget!

Like Charges Repel, Opposite Charges Attract

Two things with <u>opposite</u> electric charges are <u>attracted</u> to each other.
Two things with the <u>same</u> electric charge will <u>repel</u> each other.

When you rub two <u>insulating</u> materials together a whole load of <u>electrons</u> get dumped <u>together</u>. They try to <u>repel</u> each other, but <u>can't move</u> apart because their positions are fixed. The patch of charge that results is <u>static electricity</u>.

Static Electricity can be a Little Joker

Static electricity is responsible for some of life's little annoyances...

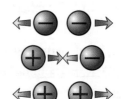

1) Attracting Dust

<u>Dust particles</u> are really tiny and lightweight and are easily <u>attracted</u> to anything that's <u>charged</u>. Unfortunately, many objects around the house are made of <u>insulating</u> materials (e.g. glass, wood, plastic) that get <u>easily charged</u> and attract the dust particles — this makes cleaning a <u>nightmare</u>. (Have a look at how dusty your TV screen is.)

2) Clinging Clothes and Crackles

When <u>synthetic clothes</u> are <u>dragged</u> over each other (like in a <u>tumble drier</u>) or over your <u>head</u>, electrons get scraped off, leaving <u>static charges</u> on both parts, and that leads to the inevitable — <u>attraction</u> (they stick together and cling to you) and little <u>sparks</u> or <u>shocks</u> as the charges <u>rearrange themselves</u>.

Static caravans — where electrons go on holiday...

Static electricity's great fun. You must have tried it — rubbing a balloon against your jumper and trying to get it to stick to the ceiling. It really works... well, sometimes. <u>Bad hair days</u> are caused by static too — it builds up on your hair, giving each strand the same charge — so they repel each other.

Electric Current

Static electricity's all well and good, but things get much more interesting when the charge can <u>move</u>.
<u>Moving charge</u> is called <u>current</u> — you can use it to <u>power</u> all sorts of toys and gadgets. It's great stuff.

Electric Current is a Flow of Charge Round a Circuit

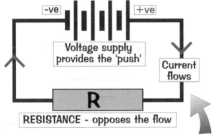

1) Electric <u>current</u> is the <u>flow of charge</u>. Its <u>units</u> are <u>amperes</u>, <u>A</u>.
2) In an electrical <u>circuit</u> the components and wires are <u>full of charges</u> that can <u>move</u>.
3) Circuit wires are usually <u>metal</u> with a <u>plastic</u> cover. Electric <u>charge flows</u> in a <u>metal conductor</u> because there are lots of <u>electrons</u> that are <u>free</u> to move around. Current can't flow in an <u>insulator</u> (like <u>plastic</u>) because the <u>electrons</u> are <u>fixed</u>.
4) The <u>circuit</u> shown is <u>complete</u> — the <u>loop</u> between one side of the <u>battery</u> and the other is <u>continuous</u>.
5) In a <u>complete</u> circuit, the <u>battery pushes charge</u> through the wires. The charge flows <u>all the way</u> round the circuit and <u>back</u> to the battery — it's <u>not used up</u> and doesn't disappear or anything funny.

Current Depends on Voltage and Resistance

1) <u>Current</u> will <u>only flow</u> through a component if there's a <u>voltage</u> across that component.
2) <u>Voltage</u> is the <u>driving force</u> that pushes the current round. Its <u>units</u> are <u>volts</u>, <u>V</u>.
3) <u>Resistance</u> is anything in the circuit which <u>slows the flow down</u>. Its <u>units</u> are <u>ohms</u>, Ω.
4) There's a <u>balance</u>: the <u>voltage</u> is trying to <u>push</u> the current round the circuit, and the <u>resistance</u> is <u>opposing</u> it — the <u>relative sizes</u> of the voltage and resistance decide <u>how big</u> the current will be:

> If you <u>increase the voltage</u> — then <u>more current</u> will flow.
> If you <u>increase the resistance</u> — then <u>less current</u> will flow.

It's Just Like the Flow of Water Round a Set of Pipes

1) The <u>current</u> is simply like the <u>flow of water</u>. The <u>pipes</u> are full of <u>water</u> that's free to move around, just like the <u>wires</u> of a circuit are full of <u>charge</u> that is free to <u>move</u>.
2) <u>Voltage</u> is like the <u>pressure</u> provided by a <u>pump</u> (or <u>battery</u>), which pushes the water (<u>charge</u>) round and round <u>without it being used up</u>.

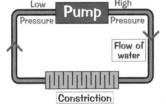

3) <u>Resistance</u> is like any sort of <u>constriction</u> in the flow (or a <u>resistor</u>, <u>lamp</u> or <u>motor</u>), which is what the pressure has to <u>work against</u>.
4) If you <u>turn up the pump</u> (battery) and provide more <u>pressure</u> (or "<u>voltage</u>"), the flow will <u>increase</u>.
5) If you put in more <u>constrictions</u> ("<u>resistance</u>"), the flow will <u>decrease</u>.

Electrons Flow the Opposite Way to Conventional Current

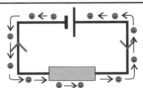

We <u>normally</u> say that current in a circuit flows from <u>positive to negative</u> (shown by red arrows on the diagram). Alas, electrons were discovered long after that was decided and they turned out to be <u>negatively charged</u> — <u>unlucky</u>. This means they <u>actually flow</u> from –ve to +ve, <u>opposite</u> to the flow of "<u>conventional current</u>".

A recipe for electrifying fruit cake — just add current...

Remember — <u>current</u> is the <u>flow of electrons</u>, voltage is what pushes the current and resistance is what slows it down. If you understand that, it should make sense that the amount of <u>current</u> you get depends on the <u>voltage</u> of the power supply and the <u>resistance</u> of the appliance you're running.

52

Circuits — The Basics

Electric current only flows when there's a complete circuit — no circuit = no current.

Circuit Symbols You Should Know:

Circuit diagrams can look a little scary at first — all those squiggly pictures. You'll come across these symbols over the next few pages. If you learn what they mean it'll make a whole lot more sense later on...

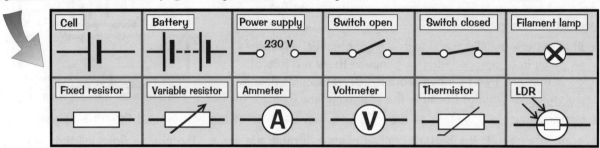

| Cell | Battery | Power supply 230 V | Switch open | Switch closed | Filament lamp |
| Fixed resistor | Variable resistor | Ammeter | Voltmeter | Thermistor | LDR |

The Standard Test Circuit

This is without doubt the most totally bog-standard circuit the world has ever known. So know it.

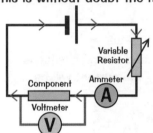

1) This very basic circuit is used for testing components.

2) The component, the ammeter and the variable resistor are all in series, which means they can be put in any order in the main circuit.

3) The voltmeter, on the other hand, can only be placed in parallel around the component under test, as shown. Anywhere else is a definite no-no.

4) Varying the variable resistor alters the current flowing through the circuit.

A Voltmeter Measures Potential Difference Between Two Points

1) Potential difference tells you how much energy is transferred to or from a unit of charge as it moves between two points.

2) The battery transfers energy to the charge as it passes — that's the "push" that moves the charge round the circuit.

3) Components transfer energy away from the charge as it passes — e.g. to use as light in a lamp or sound in a buzzer.

4) A voltmeter is used to measure the potential difference (the proper name for voltage) between two points.

5) A voltmeter must be placed in parallel (see p.55) with a component so it can compare the energy the charge has before and after passing through the component.

The battery transfers energy to the charge as it passes.

The lamp transfers the same amount of energy from the charge as it passes (and converts it to light and heat).

Measure gymnastics — use a vaultmeter...

An interesting fact — voltage is named after Count Alessandro Volta, an Italian physicist. I heard once that potential difference was named after his cousin — Baron Potentialo Differenché. I'm not so sure if it's true... What is true and very important is that voltage and potential difference are the same thing.

Module P5 — Electric Circuits

Resistance

Resistance resists the flow of current — simple. Resistors come in all shapes and sizes — and some have fixed resistance while others can change their resistance.

The Slope of a Voltage-Current Graph Shows Resistance

V-I graphs show how the current in a circuit varies as you change the voltage.

1) The current through a resistor (at constant temperature) is proportional to the voltage.
2) Different resistors have different resistances — the steeper the slope the lower the resistance.
3) The wires in an electric circuit have such a small resistance that it's usually ignored.

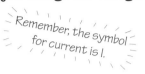
Remember, the symbol for current is I.

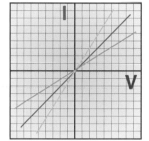

Calculating Resistance: R = V/I (or R = "1/gradient")

At constant temperature the resistance of a component is steady and is equal to the inverse of the gradient of the line, or "1/gradient". In other words, the steeper the graph the lower the resistance. Alternatively, you can take any pair of values (V, I) and stick them in the formula R = V/I.

$$\text{Resistance} = \frac{\text{Potential Difference}}{\text{Current}}$$

Resistors Get Hot When Current Passes Through Them

When electrons move through a resistor they collide with stationary particles in the resistor. These collisions cause the resistor to heat up, which changes its resistance. A filament lamp contains a piece of wire with a really high resistance. When current passes through it its temperature increases so much that it glows — which is the light you see.

Light-Dependent Resistor or "LDR" to You

A light-dependent resistor or LDR is a special type of resistor that changes its resistance depending on how much light there is:

1) In bright light, the resistance falls.
2) In darkness, the resistance is highest.

This makes it a useful device for various electronic circuits, e.g. automatic night lights, burglar detectors.

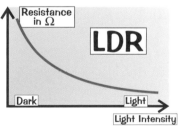

Thermistor (Temperature-Dependent Resistor)

A thermistor is like an LDR — but its resistance depends on temperature.

1) In hot conditions, the resistance drops.
2) In cool conditions, the resistance goes up.

Thermistors make useful temperature detectors, e.g. car engine temperature sensors and electronic thermostats.

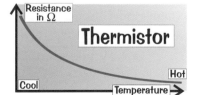

In the end you'll have to learn this — resistance is futile...

This page is packed full of useful stuff. You have to be able to interpret those voltage-current graphs. Remember — the steeper the slope, the lower the resistance. That equation's important too — make sure you learn it. You'll need to rearrange it later, too — I didn't put that formula triangle in for fun.

Series Circuits

You need to be able to tell the difference between series and parallel circuits <u>just by looking at them</u>. You also need to know the <u>rules</u> about what happens with both types. Read on.

Series Circuits — All or Nothing

1) In <u>series circuits</u>, the different components are connected <u>in a line</u>, <u>end to end</u>, between the +ve and –ve of the power supply (except for <u>voltmeters</u>, which are always connected <u>in parallel</u>, but they don't count as part of the circuit).

2) If you remove or disconnect <u>one</u> component, the circuit is <u>broken</u> and they all <u>stop working</u>.

3) This is generally <u>not very handy</u>, and in practice <u>very few things</u> are connected in series.

Potential Difference is Shared:

1) In series circuits the <u>total P.D.</u> of the <u>supply</u> is <u>shared</u> between the various <u>components</u>. So the <u>voltages</u> round a series circuit always <u>add up</u> to equal the <u>source voltage</u>:

$$V = V_1 + V_2$$

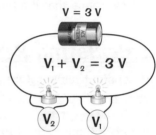

2) This means that the <u>energy</u> transferred <u>to</u> the charge by the battery is the <u>same</u> as the <u>total energy</u> transferred <u>from</u> the charge to the components.

Current is the Same Everywhere:

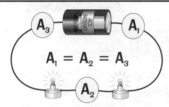

1) In series circuits the <u>same current</u> flows through <u>all parts</u> of the circuit:

$$A_1 = A_2 = A_3$$

2) The <u>size</u> of the current is determined by the <u>total P.D.</u> of the cells and the <u>total resistance</u> of the circuit: i.e. I = V/R. This means <u>all</u> the <u>components</u> get the same <u>current</u>.

Resistance Adds Up:

1) In series circuits the <u>total resistance</u> is just the <u>sum</u> of the individual resistances:

$$R = R_1 + R_2 + R_3$$

2) The resistance of <u>two</u> (or more) resistors in <u>series</u> is <u>bigger</u> than the resistance of just one of the resistors on its own because the <u>battery</u> has to <u>push charge</u> through <u>all</u> of them.

3) The <u>bigger</u> the <u>resistance</u> of a component, the bigger its <u>share</u> of the <u>total P.D.</u>, because more <u>energy is transferred</u> when the resistance is high.

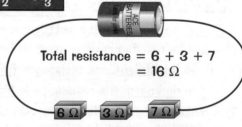

Total resistance = 6 + 3 + 7 = 16 Ω

Cell Voltages Add Up:

1) If you connect <u>several cells in series</u>, <u>all the same way</u> (+ to –) you get a <u>bigger total voltage</u> — because each charge in the circuit passes though all the cells and gets a 'push' from each cell in turn.

2) So <u>two 1.5 V</u> cells <u>in series</u> would supply <u>3 V in total</u>.

3) Cell voltages <u>don't</u> add up like that for cells connected <u>in parallel</u>. Here, each charge can only go through (and get a 'push' from) one cell.

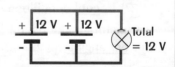

Series circuits — they're no laughing matter...

If you connect a lamp to a battery, it lights up with a certain brightness. If you then add more identical lamps in series with the first one, they'll all light up <u>less brightly</u> than before. That's because in a series circuit the voltage is <u>shared out</u> between all the components. That doesn't happen in parallel circuits...

Parallel Circuits

Parallel circuits are much more <u>sensible</u> than series circuits so they're much more <u>common</u> in <u>real life</u>.

Parallel Circuits — Independence and Isolation

1) In <u>parallel circuits</u>, each component is <u>separately</u> connected to the +ve and −ve of the <u>supply</u>.
2) If you remove or disconnect <u>one</u> of them, it will often <u>hardly affect</u> the others at all.
3) This is <u>obviously</u> how <u>most</u> things must be connected, for example in <u>cars</u> and in <u>household electrics</u>. You have to be able to switch everything on and off <u>separately</u>.

P.D. is the Same Across All Components:

1) In parallel circuits <u>all</u> components get the <u>full source P.D.</u>, so the voltage is the <u>same</u> across all components:

$$V_1 = V_2 = V_3$$

2) This means that <u>identical bulbs</u> connected in parallel will all be at the <u>same brightness</u>.

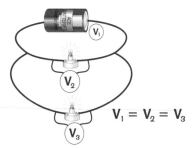

$V_1 = V_2 = V_3$

Current is Shared Between Branches:

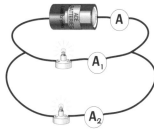

$A = A_1 + A_2$

1) In all circuits the <u>current</u> flowing <u>from</u> the battery is the <u>same</u> as the current flowing <u>back</u> to it — there's nowhere else for the charge to go.
2) In parallel circuits the <u>current</u> flowing from the battery is <u>shared</u> between the branches. So the <u>total current</u> leaving the battery is equal to the <u>total</u> of the currents in the <u>separate branches</u>.

$$A = A_1 + A_2$$

3) In a parallel circuit, there are <u>junctions</u> where the current <u>splits</u> or <u>rejoins</u>. The total current going <u>into</u> a junction equals the total current <u>leaving</u>.

Resistance Is Tricky:

1) The <u>total resistance</u> of a parallel circuit is <u>tricky to work out</u>, but it's always <u>less</u> than that of the branch with the <u>smallest</u> resistance.
2) The resistance is lower because the <u>current</u> has more than one branch to take — only <u>some</u> of the current will flow along each branch.
3) A circuit with <u>two</u> resistors in <u>parallel</u> will have a <u>lower</u> resistance than a circuit with either of the resistors <u>by themselves</u> — which means the <u>parallel</u> circuit will have a <u>higher current</u>.

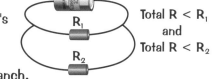

Total R < R_1
and
Total R < R_2

The Current Through a Component Depends on its Resistance

1) Each <u>component</u> in a parallel circuit is <u>separately</u> connected to the <u>battery</u>. This means the <u>current</u> through each component is the <u>same</u> as if that component was the <u>only</u> one in the circuit.
2) The <u>resistance</u> of a component <u>controls</u> how much <u>current</u> the <u>voltage</u> is able to push through it.
3) In a parallel circuit all the components have the <u>same</u> p.d. across them, so the component with the <u>most</u> resistance has the <u>lowest</u> current and the component with the <u>least</u> resistance has the <u>highest</u> current.

*A current shared — is a current halved...**

Parallel circuits might look a bit scarier than series ones, but they're much more useful. Remember: each branch has the <u>same voltage</u> across it, the <u>current</u> is <u>shared</u> between branches, the <u>total resistance</u> is <u>lower</u> than that of the least resistant branch, and <u>components</u> work as if they were on their <u>own</u>.

* Conditions may apply. CGP takes no responsibility for the accuracy of this proverb.

Module P5 — Electric Circuits

Mains Electricity

Parallel circuits aren't just crusty old science — all the electrics in your home will use them.

Mains Supply is AC, Battery Supply is DC

1) The UK mains supply is approximately <u>230 volts</u>.
2) It's produced by <u>generators</u> using a process called <u>electromagnetic induction</u>.
3) It's an <u>AC supply</u> (alternating current), which means the current is constantly <u>changing direction</u>.
4) Batteries supply <u>direct current</u> (DC). This just means the current always flows in the <u>same direction</u>.
5) AC is used for mains electricity because it's <u>easy</u> to generate and can be <u>distributed</u> more efficiently.

Moving a Magnet in a Coil of Wire Induces a Voltage

1) You can create a <u>voltage</u> and maybe a <u>current</u> in a conductor by <u>moving a magnet</u> in or near a <u>coil of wire</u>. This is called <u>electromagnetic induction</u>.
2) As you <u>move</u> the magnet, the <u>magnetic field</u> through the <u>coil</u> changes — this <u>change</u> in the magnetic field induces (creates) a <u>voltage</u>, and a <u>current</u> flows in the wire (if it's part of a <u>complete</u> circuit).
3) The <u>direction</u> of the voltage depends on which way you move the magnet:

If you <u>move</u> the magnet <u>into</u> the coil the voltage is induced in the <u>opposite</u> direction from when you move it <u>out</u> of the coil.

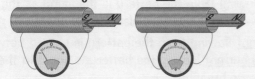

If you <u>reverse</u> the magnet's North-South polarity — so that the opposite <u>pole</u> points into the coil, the voltage is induced in the <u>opposite</u> direction.

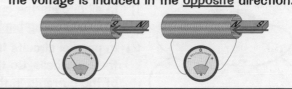

AC Generators — Just Turn the Magnet and There's a Current

Generators <u>generate electricity</u>. You didn't see that one coming did you...

1) In a generator a <u>magnet rotates</u> in a coil of wire. As the magnet <u>turns</u>, the <u>magnetic field</u> through the <u>coil</u> changes — this <u>change</u> in the magnetic field induces a <u>voltage</u>, which makes a <u>current</u> flow in the coil.

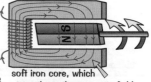

soft iron core, which strengthens the magnetic field

2) When the magnet is turned through half a turn, the <u>direction</u> of the <u>magnetic field</u> through the coil <u>reverses</u>. When this happens, the <u>voltage reverses</u>, so the <u>current</u> flows in the <u>opposite direction</u> around the coil of wire.

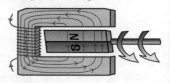

3) If the magnet keeps turning in the <u>same direction</u> — clockwise, say — then the voltage keeps on reversing every half turn and you get an <u>AC current</u>.

Three Factors Affect the Size of the Induced Voltage

1) If you want a <u>bigger</u> peak voltage (and current) you could <u>increase</u> one or more of these three things ... or add an <u>iron core</u> inside the coil.

2) To <u>reduce</u> the voltage, you would <u>reduce</u> one of these factors, obviously, or take the iron core out.

1) The <u>STRENGTH</u> of the <u>MAGNET</u>
2) The <u>SPEED</u> of movement
3) The <u>number of TURNS</u> on the <u>COIL</u>

faster turns

3) Note — if you <u>move</u> the magnet <u>faster</u>, you'll get a higher peak voltage, but also a <u>higher frequency</u> — because the magnetic field is reversing more frequently.

So THAT's how they make electricity — I always wondered...

Generators are mostly powered by <u>burning things</u> to make <u>steam</u>, to turn a turbine, to turn the magnet. You can get portable generators too, to use in places without mains electricity — like in refugee camps.

Mains Electricity

So you've generated your electricity, but it's not the right voltage — what do you need? A transformer.

Transformers Change the Voltage — but Only AC Voltages

Transformers use electromagnetic induction to 'step up' or 'step down' the voltage. They have two coils of wire, the primary and the secondary, wound around an iron core.

STEP-UP TRANSFORMERS step the voltage up. They have more turns on the secondary coil than the primary coil.

STEP-DOWN TRANSFORMERS step the voltage down. They have more turns on the primary coil than the secondary.

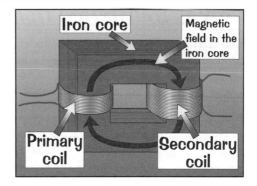

Transformers Work by Electromagnetic Induction

1) The primary coil produces a magnetic field which stays within the iron core.

2) Because there's alternating current (AC) in the primary coil, the magnetic field in the iron core constantly changes direction (100 times a second if it's at 50 Hz) — i.e. it's a changing magnetic field.

3) This changing magnetic field induces an alternating voltage in the secondary coil (with the same frequency as the alternating current in the primary) — electromagnetic induction of a voltage in fact.

4) The relative number of turns on the two coils determines whether the voltage induced in the secondary coil is greater or less than the voltage in the primary (see below).

5) If you supplied DC to the primary coil, you'd get nothing out of the secondary at all. Sure, there'd still be a magnetic field in the iron core, but it wouldn't be constantly changing, so there'd be no induction in the secondary coil — because you need a changing field to induce a voltage. Don't you. So don't forget it — transformers only work with AC. They won't work with DC at all.

The Transformer Equation — Use It Either Way Up

You can calculate the output voltage from a transformer if you know the input voltage and the number of turns on each coil.

$$\frac{\text{Primary Voltage}}{\text{Secondary Voltage}} = \frac{\text{Number of turns on Primary}}{\text{Number of turns on Secondary}}$$

$$\frac{V_P}{V_S} = \frac{N_P}{N_S}$$

or

$$\frac{V_S}{V_P} = \frac{N_S}{N_P}$$

Well, it's just another formula. You stick in the numbers you've got and work out the one that's left. And you can write the formula either way up — you should always put the thing you're trying to find on the top.

EXAMPLE: A transformer has 40 turns on the primary and 800 on the secondary. If the input voltage is 1000 V, find the output voltage.

ANSWER: The question asks you to find V_S, so put it on the top: $\frac{V_S}{V_P} = \frac{N_S}{N_P}$

Substitute the values: $\frac{V_S}{1000} = \frac{800}{40}$, $V_S = 1000 \times \frac{800}{40} = \underline{20\ 000\ V}$

Which transformer do you need to enslave the Universe — Megatron...

You'll need to practise with those tricky equations. They're unusual because they can't be put into formula triangles, but other than that the method is the same — stick in the numbers. Just practise.

Electrical Energy

You can look at <u>electrical circuits</u> in <u>two ways</u>. The first is in terms of a voltage <u>pushing the current</u> round and the resistances opposing the flow, as on p.51. The <u>other way</u> of looking at circuits is in terms of <u>energy transfer</u>. Learn them <u>both</u> and be ready to tackle questions about <u>either</u>.

Energy is Transferred from Cells and Other Sources

Anything that <u>supplies electricity</u> is also supplying <u>energy</u>. So cells, batteries, generators etc. all <u>transfer energy</u> to the charge, which then transfers it to the <u>components</u> in the circuit:

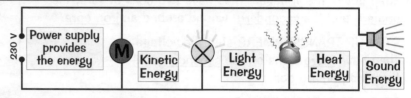

Power is the Rate of Energy Transfer

The <u>power</u> of an appliance tells you <u>how fast</u> it <u>transfers energy</u> from the charge passing through it. <u>Power</u> is usually measured in <u>watts</u>, W, or <u>kilowatts</u>, kW. (<u>1 kW = 1000 W</u>)

 A light bulb converts <u>electrical energy</u> into <u>light</u> energy and heat energy. A power rating of 100 W means it transfers <u>100 joules of energy every second</u>.

A kettle converts <u>electrical energy</u> into <u>heat</u> energy. If it has a power rating of 2.5 kW, it transfers <u>2500 joules every second</u>.

The total energy transferred by an appliance depends on <u>how long</u> the appliance is on and its <u>power rating</u>. The formula is:

$$\text{ENERGY TRANSFERRED} = \text{POWER} \times \text{TIME}$$
$$\text{(in joules)} \qquad\qquad \text{(in W)} \qquad \text{(in s)}$$

EXAMPLE 1: How much energy is transferred by a 2.5 kW kettle left on for 5 minutes?

ANSWER: Energy (in J) = Power (in W) × Time (in s) = **2500 W × 300 s** (300 s = 5 minutes)
= <u>750 000 J</u>

EXAMPLE 2: What is the power of a light bulb that transfers 54 000 J in 15 minutes?

ANSWER: Power = Energy ÷ Time = 54 000 J ÷ 900 s = <u>60 W</u>

Kilowatt-hours (kWh) are "UNITS" of Energy

Energy is usually measured in joules. The trouble is, <u>one joule</u> is a <u>tiny</u>, tiny amount of electrical energy — so your electricity meter records how much <u>energy</u> you use in units of <u>kilowatt-hours</u>, or <u>kWh</u>.

A <u>KILOWATT-HOUR</u> is the amount of electrical energy converted by a <u>1 kW appliance</u> left on for <u>1 HOUR</u>.

Using kilowatt-hours, the energy transfer equation above becomes:

Energy transferred	=	Power	×	Time
(in KILOWATT-HOURS)		(in KILOWATTS)		(in HOURS)

This is still the <u>same</u> equation — so you can use the same formula triangle.

The <u>higher</u> the <u>power rating</u> of an appliance, and the <u>longer</u> you leave it on, the more energy it transfers — and the more it costs...

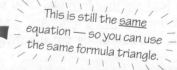

$$\text{COST} = \text{NUMBER OF kWh} \times \text{COST PER kWh}$$

EXAMPLE: Find the cost of leaving a 60 W light bulb on for 30 minutes if one kWh costs 10p.

ANSWER: Energy (in kWh) = Power (in kW) × Time (in hours) = 0.06 kW × ½ hr = <u>0.03 kWh</u>
Cost = number of kWh × price per kWh = 0.03 × 10p = <u>0.3p</u>

Kilo-what? hours — exactly, well almost...

You've got to be careful with your units in this topic — <u>power</u> is in <u>kilowatts</u>, <u>energy</u> is in <u>kilowatt-hours</u>. Kilowatt-hours can also remind you of the equation for electrical energy — <u>power × time</u>.

Electrical Energy

Electrical <u>appliances</u> transfer <u>energy</u> from the charge passing through them (to do whatever they're designed to do), but not all of the energy is used <u>usefully</u> — some always gets <u>wasted</u>.

Power Ratings of Appliances

An appliance with a <u>high</u> power rating transfers a <u>lot</u> of <u>energy</u> in a <u>short time</u>. This energy comes from the <u>current</u> flowing through it. This means that an appliance with a <u>high power rating</u> will draw a <u>large current</u> from the supply.

1) The formula for <u>electrical power</u> is: **POWER = VOLTAGE × CURRENT** (P = V × I)

2) So to find the power of a component in a circuit you'd measure the <u>voltage</u> across it and the <u>current</u> flowing through it, then <u>multiply</u> them together. Simple.

3) Most electrical goods show their <u>power rating</u> and <u>voltage rating</u>. To work out the <u>current</u> that the item will normally draw you need to rearrange the equation:

> <u>Example</u>: A hairdrier is rated at 230 V, 1 kW. Find the current it draws.
>
> <u>ANSWER</u>: Rearranging, I = P/V = 1000 ÷ 230 = 4.3 A.

More Efficient Machines Waste Less Energy

Appliances <u>convert</u> electrical <u>energy</u> taken from the charge passing through them to other forms. Some of these forms will be <u>useful</u>, but some are not wanted so are <u>wasted</u> (often as heat or sound). The <u>efficiency</u> of a machine is defined as:

$$\text{Efficiency} = \frac{\text{ENERGY USEFULLY TRANSFERRED}}{\text{TOTAL ENERGY SUPPLIED}} \times 100\%$$

1) To work out the efficiency of a machine, first find out the <u>total energy supplied</u> — the energy input.

2) Then find how much <u>useful energy</u> the machine <u>transfers</u>. The question might tell you this directly, or it might tell you how much energy is <u>wasted</u> as heat/sound.

3) Then just <u>divide</u> the <u>smaller number</u> by the <u>bigger one</u> to get a value for <u>efficiency</u> somewhere between <u>0 and 1</u>. Easy. If your number is bigger than 1, you've done the division upside down.

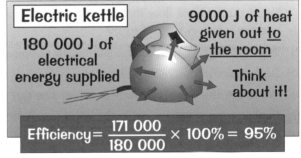

Electric kettle

180 000 J of electrical energy supplied

9000 J of heat given out <u>to</u> the room

Think about it!

$$\text{Efficiency} = \frac{171\ 000}{180\ 000} \times 100\% = 95\%$$

4) Then convert the efficiency to a <u>percentage</u>, by multiplying it by 100. E.g. 0.6 = 60%.

5) In the exam you might be told the <u>efficiency</u> and asked to work out the <u>total energy supplied</u>, the <u>energy usefully transferred</u> or the <u>energy wasted</u>. So you need to be able to <u>rearrange</u> the formula.

<u>EXAMPLE</u>: An ordinary light bulb is 5% efficient. If 1000 J of light energy is given out, how much energy is wasted?

<u>ANSWER</u>: Total Energy Supplied $= \dfrac{\text{Energy Usefully Transferred}}{\text{Efficiency}}$

$= \dfrac{1000 \text{ J}}{0.05} = 20\ 000 \text{ J}$

so Energy Wasted = 20 000 − 1000 = <u>19 000 J</u>

Shockingly inefficient, those ordinary light bulbs. Low-energy light bulbs are roughly 4 times more efficient, and last about 8 times as long. They're more expensive to buy though.

Efficiency = pages learned ÷ cups of tea made...

Some new appliances (like washing machines and fridges) come with a sticker with a letter from A to H on, to show how <u>energy efficient</u> they are. A really <u>well-insulated fridge</u> might have an 'A' rating. But if you put it right next to the oven, or never defrost it, it will run much less efficiently than it should.

Revision Summary for Module P5

There's some pretty heavy physics in this section. But just take it one page at a time and it's not so bad. When you think you know it all, try these questions and see how you're getting on. If there are any you can't do, look back at the right bit of the section, learn it, then come back here and try again.

1)   What causes the build-up of static electricity? Which particles move when static builds up?

2)   Describe the forces between objects with: a) like charges,   b) opposite charges.

3)   Explain how static electricity can make synthetic clothes crackle when you take them off.

4)   Explain why metals are good conductors of electricity.

5)   Explain what current, voltage and resistance are in an electric circuit.

6)   What happens to the amount of current in a circuit if the voltage of the battery is increased?

7)   Sketch a diagram of a circuit containing a cell, filament lamp, switch and fixed resistor.

8)   Add an ammeter and voltmeter to your circuit, connected sensibly.

9)   What is another name for potential difference? What is it a measure of?

10) Sketch a typical voltage-current graph for a resistor at a constant temperature.

11)* Calculate the resistance of a wire if the voltage across it is 12 V and the current through it is 2.5 A.

12) Describe how the resistance of an LDR varies with light intensity. Give an application of an LDR.

13)* Find each unknown voltage, current or resistance in the circuit shown.

14) What happens to the voltage when cells are added to a series circuit?

15) Explain, in terms of energy, why P.D. is shared out in a series circuit.

16) Why are parallel circuits generally more useful than series ones?

17) Two circuits each contain a 2 Ω and a 4 Ω resistor — in one circuit they're in series, in the other they're in parallel. Which circuit will have the <u>higher</u> total resistance? Why?

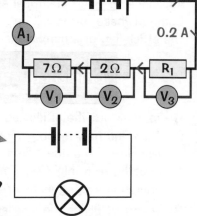

18)* A current of 0.4 A flows through the filament lamp in this circuit. What current will flow through this lamp if another, identical lamp is connected in parallel to it?

19) What voltage is U.K. mains electricity supplied at? Why is A.C. used?

20) Define electromagnetic induction.

21) What are the four factors that affect the size of the induced voltage produced by a generator?

22) Explain how a generator works — use a sketch if it helps.

23) Write down the transformer equation.

24)* A transformer has 20 turns on the primary coil and 600 on the secondary coil. If the input voltage is 9 V, find the output voltage.

25) What does the power of an appliance measure?

26) Give possible units for: a) power,   b) energy.

27)* Calculate the energy used by a 2.1 kW kettle if it's on for 1½ minutes.

28)* A light bulb is rated at 0.1 kW. If one unit of electricity costs 8p, how much will it cost if the bulb is left on for 1 hour and 50 minutes?

29) Write down the formula linking voltage, current and power.

30)* Calculate the efficiency of a motor that converts 100 J of electrical energy into 70 J of useful kinetic energy.

Answers on page 100.

The Nervous System

The environment around you is constantly changing. A change in the environment of an organism is called a stimulus. Humans and other animals need to respond to stimuli to keep themselves in favourable conditions, e.g. out of danger and where food is plentiful. Larger animals, like humans, have a complex nervous system that allows them to detect and react to what's going on around them. Simple animals only use reflexes to respond to stimuli (see p.63).

The Nervous System Detects and Reacts to Stimuli

The Nervous System is made up of Different Parts

Central Nervous System (CNS)

Consists of the brain and spinal cord only. The CNS is connected to the body by sensory neurones and motor neurones — these make up the peripheral nervous system.

Sensory Neurones

The neurones that carry impulses from the receptors to the CNS.

Motor Neurones

The neurones that carry impulses from the CNS to effectors.

Effectors

All your muscles and glands, which respond to nervous impulses.

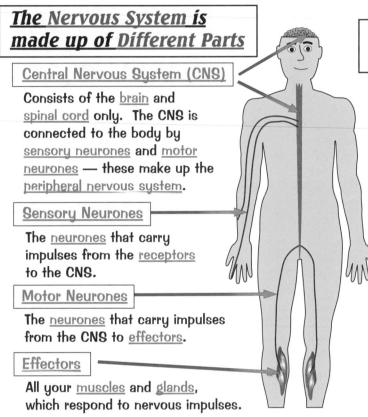

Receptors and Effectors can form part of Complex Organs

1) Receptors are the cells that detect stimuli.

2) There are many different types of receptors, such as taste receptors on the tongue and sound receptors in the ears.

3) Receptors can form part of larger, complex organs, e.g. the retina of the eye is covered in light receptor cells.

4) Effectors respond to nervous impulses and bring about a change. Effectors can also form part of complex organs.

5) There are two types of effector. Muscle cells — which make up muscles. And hormone secreting cells — which are found in glands, e.g. cells that secrete the hormone ADH are found in the pituitary gland (see p.9).

The Central Nervous System (CNS) Coordinates the Response

The CNS collects all of the information from the receptors and then decides what to do about it.

...for example, a small bird is eating some seed...

1) When, out of the corner of its eye, it spots a cat skulking towards it (this is the stimulus).

2) The receptors in the bird's eye are stimulated. Sensory neurones carry the information from the receptors to the CNS.

3) The CNS decides what to do about it.

4) The CNS sends information to the muscles in the bird's wings (the effectors) along motor neurones. The muscles contract and the bird flies away to safety.

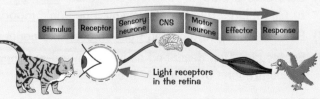

Stimulus → Receptor → Sensory neurone → CNS → Motor neurone → Effector → Response

Light receptors in the retina

Don't let the thought of exams play on your nerves...

Don't forget that it's only large animals like mammals and birds that have complex nervous systems. Simple animals like jellyfish don't — everything they do is a reflex response (see p.63).

The Nervous System

When a stimulus is <u>detected</u>, information needs to be passed from <u>receptor cells</u> to <u>effector cells</u>. The way it's done is basically the same in any organism with a nervous system, whether <u>simple</u> or <u>complex</u>, brain or no brain.

Information *is* Transmitted *Around the Body by* Neurones

When stimulated, <u>neurones</u> (nerve cells) transmit information around the body as <u>electrical impulses</u>.

1) The <u>electrical impulses</u> pass along the <u>axon</u> of the nerve cells.

2) <u>Axons</u> are made from the nerve cell's <u>cytoplasm</u> stretched out into a <u>long fibre</u> and surrounded by a <u>cell membrane</u>.

3) Some axons are also surrounded by a <u>fatty sheath</u> that acts as an <u>electrical insulator</u>, shielding the neurone from neighbouring cells and <u>speeding up</u> the electrical impulse.

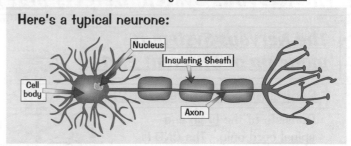

Here's a typical neurone:

The Gap Between Two Neurones is Called a Synapse

There are billions of neurones in the body, which connect up to form pathways. Neurones <u>aren't attached</u> to each other though — there's a <u>tiny gap</u> between them called the <u>synapse</u>. Information in one neurone needs to be <u>transmitted</u> across the synapse to the <u>next neurone</u>. This is done using <u>transmitter chemicals</u>:

1) When an electrical impulse reaches the <u>end</u> of a <u>neurone</u> it triggers the <u>release</u> of <u>transmitter chemicals</u> into the <u>synapse</u>.

2) The transmitter chemicals <u>diffuse</u> across the gap and <u>bind</u> to <u>receptor molecules</u> on the membrane of the <u>next neurone</u>.

3) The transmitter chemicals can only bind to certain <u>receptor molecules</u> on the neurone.

4) When the chemicals bind to the right receptors they trigger a <u>new electrical impulse</u> in the next <u>neurone</u>.

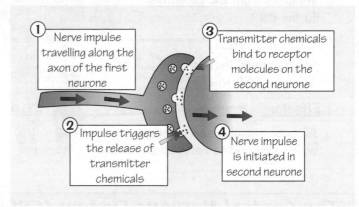

Some Drugs Affect Transmission Across Synapses

Many <u>drugs</u> and <u>toxins</u> can <u>interfere</u> with the <u>transmission</u> of impulses across a synapse.

1) One way in which the drug <u>ecstasy</u> (also known as MDMA) works is to <u>block sites</u> in the brain's synapses where the transmitter chemical <u>serotonin</u> is <u>removed</u>.

2) Serotonin is thought to affect things like <u>pain</u>, <u>aggression</u> and <u>appetite</u>. It's also thought to play a large role in determining a person's <u>mood</u>.

3) Because the serotonin <u>can't be removed</u> the <u>concentration increases</u> — which affects a person's mood.

4) Ecstasy is often described as having <u>mood-enhancing effects</u> because of the increased concentrations of serotonin it causes.

Neurones transmit information from this book to your brain...

Ecstasy may make some people who take it feel <u>happy</u> but it's not without <u>risks</u> and the long-term <u>side effects</u> aren't fully understood. Ecstasy isn't the only drug that affects the <u>nervous system</u>, e.g. <u>alcohol</u> slows down <u>reactions</u>, which is why you're not allowed to <u>drink and drive</u> — though at your age you shouldn't be doing either, let alone thinking of combining them.

Reflexes

Sometimes waiting for your brain to make a decision is <u>too slow</u> — that's why you're <u>born</u> with <u>reflexes</u>. And if you're a simple animal without a brain, reflexes are pretty much all you can rely on.

Reflexes <u>are</u> Involuntary Responses

1) <u>Reflexes</u> are <u>rapid</u>, <u>automatic</u> responses to certain stimuli.

2) Reflexes are <u>quick</u> because you <u>don't think</u> about them — they're <u>involuntary</u>.

3) Many reflexes are there to <u>protect you</u> from damage, e.g. pulling your hand off a hot object. Many animals also depend on reflexes for things like <u>finding food</u> or a <u>mate</u> (see below).

4) The route taken by the information in a reflex (from receptor to effector) is called a <u>reflex arc</u>.

The <u>Reflex</u> Arc <u>Goes</u> Through <u>the</u> Central Nervous System

1) The neurones in reflex arcs go through the <u>spinal cord</u> or through an <u>unconscious part of the brain</u>.

2) When a <u>stimulus</u> (e.g. a painful bee sting) is detected by receptors, an impulse is sent along a <u>sensory neurone</u> to the CNS.

3) In the CNS the sensory neurone passes on the message to another type of neurone — a <u>relay neurone</u>.

4) Relay neurones <u>relay</u> the impulse to a <u>motor neurone</u>.

5) The impulse then travels along the motor neurone to the <u>effector</u> (in this example it's a muscle).

6) The <u>muscle</u> then <u>contracts</u> and moves your hand away from the bee.

7) Because you don't think about the response (which takes time), it's <u>quicker</u> than normal responses.

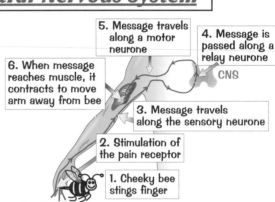

5. Message travels along a motor neurone

4. Message is passed along a relay neurone

CNS

6. When message reaches muscle, it contracts to move arm away from bee

3. Message travels along the sensory neurone

2. Stimulation of the pain receptor

1. Cheeky bee stings finger

Simple Reflexes Improve <u>the Chance of</u> Survival

<u>Simple reflexes</u> cause animals to respond to some <u>stimuli</u> in a way that <u>helps them survive</u>, e.g.:

<u>Finding food:</u> e.g. sea anemones wave their tentacles more when stimulated by chemicals emitted by their prey.

<u>Sheltering from predators:</u> e.g. molluscs (things like mussels and clams) close their shells when they detect a predator. Hedgehogs roll into a ball as a defence mechanism — this is also a reflex.

<u>Finding a mate:</u> e.g. some courtship displays in birds — making their feathers stand on end is a reflex.

<u>Humans</u> also have simple reflexes that protect them or help them survive.

1) Very bright <u>light</u> can <u>damage</u> the <u>eye</u> — so there's a reflex to protect it. In very bright light muscles in the eye <u>contract</u> making the <u>pupil smaller</u>, allowing less light into the eye.

2) <u>Newborn babies</u> will <u>suckle</u> from their mothers — suckling can be stimulated by touching the lips or skin around the mouth.

Some simple animals only have simple reflexes

<u>Simple animals</u>, such as jellyfish, have <u>no brain</u> — they rely <u>entirely</u> on reflex actions.

1) They can sense <u>movement</u> using their <u>tentacles</u>, which allows them to <u>trap prey</u>.

2) They also have <u>light receptors</u> that help them figure out whether to swim up or down.

3) Animals like jellyfish can <u>respond</u> to their normal environment. But the big <u>disadvantage</u> is that they <u>can't learn new things</u> — they have difficulty responding to <u>new situations</u>.

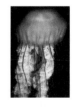

Don't get all twitchy — just learn it...

You <u>don't think about reflexes</u> — they just happen. This can come in quite handy if you're a jellyfish.

Learning and Modifying Reflexes

Reflexes are pretty handy, but it doesn't stop there — you can <u>modify</u> some of the reflexes you're born with if you need to and you can even <u>learn new ones</u>.

Reflex Responses can be Modified by the Brain

In some cases it's possible to <u>modify</u> a natural <u>reflex response</u>. Here's an example:

1) When you pick up a <u>hot object</u> such as a hot dinner plate you'll want to <u>drop</u> the plate — this is a <u>reflex response</u> to protect your skin from damage.

2) Dropping the plate might not be the best idea (you'd be left without any tea for one), but luckily reflex responses can be <u>modified</u>.

3) The response can be <u>overridden</u> by a <u>neurone</u> between the <u>brain</u> and the <u>motor neurone</u> of the <u>reflex arc</u> — the result is a little bit of pain but at least you've saved your dinner.

Reflex Responses can Also be Learned

A stimulus causes a particular reflex response, but animals can <u>learn</u> to produce the same response to a <u>new stimulus</u>. The new reflex is called a <u>conditioned reflex</u>. The best example of this is <u>Pavlov's dogs</u>:

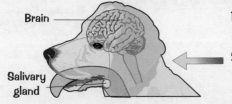

1) Pavlov studied the behaviour of dogs and noticed that they would <u>salivate</u> (drool) every time they smelt food.

2) This is a <u>simple reflex</u> in response to a <u>primary stimulus</u> (the smell of food).

3) He experimented by ringing a <u>bell</u> just before the dogs were given their food.

4) After a while he found that the dogs <u>salivated</u> when the bell was rung — even if they couldn't smell food.

5) This is a <u>conditioned reflex</u> in response to a <u>secondary stimulus</u> (the bell).

In a conditioned reflex, the final <u>response</u> (drooling) has <u>no direct connection</u> to the <u>primary stimulus</u>.

Conditioned Reflexes can Increase Chances of Survival

Dogs drooling every time a bell rings doesn't really sound that useful — but that's not always the case. Some <u>conditioned reflexes</u> can <u>increase</u> an animal's chances of <u>survival</u>. Here's an example:

1) Instead of being camouflaged to match their surroundings, some insects are <u>brightly coloured</u> so that they <u>stand out</u>. This may sound a bit odd but there's a very good reason...

2) Insects with <u>bright colouring</u> are often <u>poisonous</u> — their bright colours act as a <u>warning</u> to predators (such as birds) that they'll probably taste pretty <u>horrible</u> and could even cause some <u>harm</u>.

3) The predators develop a <u>conditioned reflex</u> to the <u>primary stimulus</u> (i.e. the colour of the insects).

4) For example, a bird spots a <u>brightly coloured caterpillar</u>. When the bird eats the caterpillar it notices that it doesn't taste too good and makes the bird feel <u>ill</u>. The bird <u>associates</u> the <u>bad taste</u> and <u>illness</u> with the <u>colour</u> and the next time it spots a caterpillar with that colouring, it <u>avoids it</u>.

5) By avoiding the <u>poisonous insects</u>, the birds are <u>increasing</u> their own <u>chances of survival</u>. Clever.

I condition my hair to make it lie down...

If this stuff pops up in the exam they might not necessarily give you the classic <u>Pavlov</u> example. You just have to apply what you know to the situation, identifying the <u>simple</u> and <u>conditioned reflexes</u>.

Brain Development and Learning

You can learn more than just reflexes though. That great big spongy mass in your conk helps you <u>learn useful things</u> like how to walk and talk, and not so useful things like how to play snap and do handstands. Learning in animals with brains happens in the same way as it does in humans.

The Brain is Pretty Complex

The brain is basically a big bunch of <u>neurones</u> all <u>interconnected</u> — it contains <u>billions</u> of the things. This means that it can do clever things like:

- modify behaviour as a result of experience — i.e. <u>learn stuff</u>.
- coordinate complicated behaviour, e.g. <u>social behaviour</u> (interacting with other members of the group).

The Environment can Affect Brain Development and Learning

The brain develops at an early age

1) The brain of a <u>newborn baby</u> is only <u>partly developed</u> — most of the <u>neurone connections</u> are <u>not yet formed</u>. It becomes more and more developed with every <u>new experience</u>.

2) <u>Connections form</u> as the child <u>experiences new things</u> — when a neurone is stimulated by the experience it <u>branches out</u>, connecting cells that were <u>previously unconnected</u>.

3) By the age of about <u>three</u> most of the connections that will <u>ever</u> form have been formed — making a huge <u>network of neurones</u> with trillions of possible routes for nerve impulses to travel down. The number of connections remains <u>constant</u> until about age <u>ten</u>.

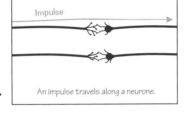
An impulse travels along a neurone.

The neurone responds by branching out.

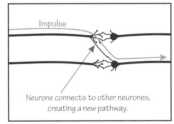
Neurone connects to other neurones, creating a new pathway.

You learn throughout your life

1) When experiences are <u>repeated</u> over and over again the <u>pathways</u> that the nerve impulses travel down become <u>strengthened</u>.

2) Strengthened pathways are <u>more likely</u> to <u>transmit impulses</u> than others.

3) This is why playing the piano is easier if you've practised a lot.

4) After the age of about ten the pathways that aren't used as often <u>die off</u> — that's why it's <u>harder</u> for older people to learn new things like a <u>foreign language</u> or how to use a <u>computer</u> (though new neurones and connections can still form in adults, which is why they <u>can learn</u>).

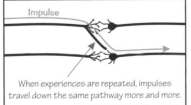
When experiences are repeated, impulses travel down the same pathway more and more.

This strengthens the connection

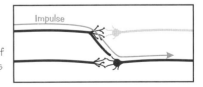
At around the age of ten the connections that are no longer used are deleted.

Strengthening pathways — usually done with tarmac...

This stuff is pretty complicated but you need to get your head round it. When you're really young you <u>connect</u> all your neurones, then the ones you use the most are <u>strengthened</u> and the others are <u>pruned</u>.

Learning Skills and Behaviour

Despite what you might think, <u>learning</u> is a <u>good thing</u> — without it you'd still be trying to figure out who that strange woman is that keeps making baby-faces at you...

Being Able to Learn Means You can Adapt to New Situations

1) Complex animals are incredibly <u>adaptable</u> — they're able to <u>cope</u> with whatever the <u>environment</u> throws at them.

2) They're adaptable because of the <u>variety</u> of <u>potential pathways</u> in the brain — there are <u>trillions</u>.

3) <u>Simpler animals</u> (like worms and insects) have <u>less flexible</u> nervous systems — they don't have anything like as many <u>pathways</u>, making their behaviour <u>more predictable</u> and much <u>less adaptable</u>.

Some Skills Only Develop at Certain Ages

Most scientists believe that there are definite <u>stages</u> in the <u>development</u> of a child's brain — some nerve pathways need to be strengthened at a <u>particular age</u>, otherwise it's <u>too late</u>. Here's an example:

1) The ability to <u>communicate</u> by <u>language</u> (talk) depends on a child <u>hearing other people speak</u>.

2) It is thought that they must hear this during a certain <u>critical period</u>. If children haven't learnt to talk by around the age of <u>ten</u> then they probably won't ever be able to.

3) Evidence to back this up comes from studies of <u>feral children</u> (children who have been raised by animals <u>without</u> any <u>human contact</u>, just like in the Jungle Book).

> A famous case was the <u>wild boy of Aveyron</u>, who was discovered around 200 years ago. He grew up in a <u>forest</u> in France. It's believed he was raised by <u>wolves</u>. He was about <u>12 years old</u> when he was discovered and although he showed signs of <u>intelligence</u>, he <u>never</u> learned to <u>speak</u>.

4) Similar children, discovered at a <u>younger age</u>, <u>have</u> been able to learn to talk. This evidence <u>supports</u> the idea of a critical period.

> One girl was discovered at the age of <u>eight</u>, <u>unable to speak</u>. After a short time with doctors she started to pick up <u>new words</u>. Although she never understood things like <u>grammar</u> she did develop a <u>vocabulary</u> of several hundred words.

Different Parts of the Brain Process Different Information

The brain is a pretty <u>complex organ</u> — luckily the only part you need to know about is the <u>cerebral cortex</u>.

1) The cerebral cortex is the <u>outer part</u> of the brain.

2) It has a folded structure — this makes the brain look <u>wrinkled</u>.

3) The cerebral cortex plays a pretty big role in things like <u>intelligence</u>, <u>memory</u>, <u>language</u> and <u>consciousness</u>.

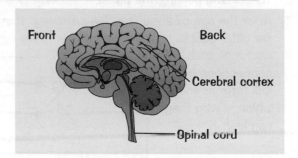

My sister looks like she was raised by wolves...

Okay so maybe it isn't "just like in the jungle book". When Mowgli meets the girl at the end, if he's missed the <u>critical period</u> chances are she isn't going to be too impressed by his <u>grunts</u>. Oh and don't get me started on the talking animals that dress up in grass skirts and dance just to befriend monkeys.

Studying the Brain

Scientists know a bit about the <u>brain</u> but <u>not as much</u> as they'd like to. Their knowledge is improving with the invention of new <u>gadgetry</u> that helps them study the brain. And as usual there are <u>different theories</u> about some of the brain's more <u>mysterious functions</u>... du du du du, du du du du...

Scientists Use a Range of Methods to Study the Brain

Knowing what the <u>different parts of the cortex do</u> can be pretty useful — it helps in the <u>diagnosis</u> and <u>treatment</u> of people with <u>brain disorders</u> (e.g. Alzheimer's disease) and <u>brain damage</u> (e.g. from a stroke). Scientists use a few different methods to study the brain and figure out <u>which bits do what</u>:

1) **Studying patients with brain damage** If a <u>small</u> part of the brain has been <u>damaged</u> the <u>effect</u> this has on the patient can tell you a lot about what the damaged part of the brain does. E.g. if an area at the back of the brain was damaged by a stroke and the patient went <u>blind</u> you know that that area has something to do with <u>vision</u>.

2) **Electrically stimulating the brain** The brain can be <u>stimulated electrically</u> by pushing a tiny <u>electrode</u> into the tissue and giving it a small zap of electricity. By observing what stimulating <u>different parts</u> of the brain does, it's possible to get an idea of what those parts do. E.g. when a certain part of the brain (know as the <u>motor area</u>) is stimulated, it causes <u>muscle contraction</u> and <u>movement</u>.

3) **MRI Scans** A <u>magnetic resonance imaging (MRI) scanner</u> is a big fancy tube-like machine that can produce a very <u>detailed picture</u> of the brain. Scientists use it to find out what areas of the brain are active when people are doing things like listening to music or trying to recall a memory.

Memory is the Storage and Retrieval of Information

To <u>remember</u> something first you have to <u>store</u> the information (i.e. <u>learn it</u>) and then you have to <u>retrieve</u> it. There are two main types of memory — <u>long-term</u> and <u>short-term</u>.

1) <u>Short-term memory</u> lasts for anything from a few <u>seconds</u> to a few <u>hours</u>.
   It's used for information that you're thinking about <u>at the moment</u>, e.g.:
   • input from the <u>senses</u> (things that you hear, smell, see, etc.)
   • longer-term memories that have been <u>recalled</u> (e.g. thinking back to the good old days).

2) <u>Long-term memories</u> are memories that were stored <u>days</u>, <u>months</u> or even <u>years</u> ago.

Humans are <u>more likely</u> to <u>remember</u> things when they can see a <u>pattern</u> (or impose a pattern) in the information, e.g. remembering the phone number 123123 is a lot easier than remembering 638294. You're also more likely to remember things if the information is associated with <u>strong stimuli</u>, like bright lights and colours, strong smells or noises. It also helps if the information is <u>repeated</u>, especially if it's over a <u>long time</u>.

The problem with memory is that nobody knows for sure <u>how it works</u>. There are loads of different <u>models</u> that try to explain it. For example, some scientists believe that information is <u>temporarily</u> held in <u>short-term</u> memory before being <u>transferred</u> to <u>long-term</u> memory. Others believe that the long-term memory <u>doesn't</u> involve short-term memory at all. So far no model has provided a <u>satisfactory explanation</u> of human memory.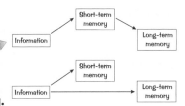

Memory's just like knitting — all you need is a good pattern...

Hopefully this should give you some handy <u>revision tips</u>. <u>Repeating</u> things helps lodge them in your <u>long-term memory</u> and using <u>bright colours</u> means you associate <u>facts</u> with a <u>strong stimulus</u>. Simple.

Revision Summary for Module B6

Hmm... so this whole behaviour and brain malarkey — I'll admit it's not the easiest topic in the world, but it's pretty interesting I reckon. And now you know why the only way to get stuff into your long-term memory for your exam is to repeat it over and over and over and over and over again... and on that note here's some questions to see whether any of the information you've just read has made it into your long-term storage space.

1) Name the two organs that make up the CNS.
2) What is the role of the CNS?
3) Where do motor neurones carry signals to and from?
4) What do sensory neurones do?
5) Draw a diagram to show the pathway between a stimulus and a response.
6) Draw a typical neurone, labelling all the bits.
7) What is the function of the fatty sheath surrounding some axons?
8) What is a synapse?
9) Describe how impulses are transmitted across a synapse.
10) Describe one of the effects of the drug ecstasy on synapses.
11) What is a reflex?
12) Draw a diagram to show a reflex arc.
13) Give three ways that simple reflexes increase an animal's chance of survival.
14) Give one example of a human behaviour that relies on reflexes.
15) Give one example of a reflex that protects humans from damage.
16) Give one disadvantage of relying on reflexes for all behaviour.
17) How are reflexes modified?
18) Give an example of when it would be advantageous to modify a reflex.
19) a) Briefly describe the experiment carried out by Ivan Pavlov on reflexes.
    b) What name is given to this type of reflex?
20) Describe how a learned reflex can increase an animal's chances of survival.
21) How can new experiences increase the number of connections in the brain?
22) What happens to pathways when activities are repeated?
23) Why is it harder for older people to learn new things?
24) Why are complex animals better at adapting to new situations than simple animals?
25) What is meant by the 'critical period' in terms of learning how to communicate? Use an example of a feral child to explain your answer.
26) Name two things that the cerebral cortex of the brain is important for.
27) Give three methods used by scientists to study the brain.
28) What is memory?
29) Explain what is meant by short-term and long-term memory.

Industrial Chemical Synthesis

Chemical synthesis is the term used by those in the know to describe the process of making complex chemical compounds from simpler ones. That's what this section is all about — some of the methods chemists use to make and purify chemicals, the calculations they carry out and how they control the reactions to make the maximum amount of product and ultimately the maximum amount of money.

The Chemical Industry Makes Useful Products

Chemicals aren't just found in the laboratory. Most of the products you come across in your day-to-day life will have been carefully researched, formulated and tested by chemists. Here are a few examples...

1) Food additives — the chemical industry produces additives like preservatives, colourings and flavourings for food producers.

2) Cleaning and decorating products — things like paints contain loads of different pigments and dyes, all of which have been developed by chemists. Cleaning products like bleach, oven cleaner and washing-up liquid will all have been developed by chemists.

3) Drugs — the pharmaceutical industry is huge (see below). Whenever you have a headache or an upset tummy the drugs you take will have gone through loads of development and testing before you get to use them.

4) Fertilisers — we use about a million tonnes of fertiliser every year. Amongst other things fertilisers contain loads of ammonia, all of which has to be produced by the chemical industry.

As well as figuring out how to make chemicals, chemists must also figure out how to make them in the way that produces the highest yield (p.76) — they do this by controlling the rate of the reaction (p.79). They must also think about the environment, choosing processes with a low impact.

The Chemical Industry is Huge

It's absolutely massive, in terms of both the amount of chemicals it produces and the money it generates.

Scale — chemicals can be produced on a large or small scale.

1) Some chemicals are produced on a massive scale — for example, over 150 million tonnes of sulfuric acid are produced around the world every year.

2) Sulfuric acid has loads of different uses, for example in car batteries and fertiliser production.

3) Other chemicals, e.g. pharmaceuticals, are produced on a smaller scale, but this doesn't make them any less important — we just need less of them.

Sectors — there are loads of different sectors within the chemical industry.

1) In the UK, the chemical industry makes up a significant chunk of the economy.

2) In the UK alone, there are over 200 000 people employed in the chemical industry.

3) Some chemicals are sold directly to consumers, while others are sold to other industries as raw materials for other products.

4) The pharmaceutical industry has the largest share of the industry.

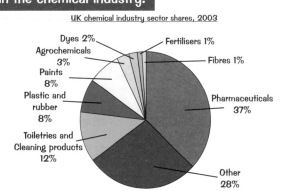

UK chemical industry sector shares, 2003

Dyes 2%
Agrochemicals 3%
Paints 8%
Plastic and rubber 8%
Toiletries and Cleaning products 12%
Fertilisers 1%
Fibres 1%
Pharmaceuticals 37%
Other 28%

You'd need a big fish to make all those chemicals on a scale...

You don't need to remember all the figures on the pie chart but they may ask you to interpret a similar one in the exam. Don't worry though — everything you'll need to answer the questions will be there.

Acids and Alkalis

You'll find <u>acids</u> and <u>alkalis</u> at <u>home</u>, in the <u>lab</u> and in <u>industry</u> — they're an important set of chemicals.

Substances can be Acidic, Alkaline or Neutral

There's a <u>sliding scale</u> from very strong <u>acid</u> (pH 0) to very strong <u>alkali</u> (pH 14).

These are the colours you get when you add universal indicator to an acid or an alkali.

pH numbers
0 1 2 3 4 5 6 7 8 9 10 11 12 13 14

← ACIDS — NEUTRAL — ALKALIS →

<u>Pure acidic compounds</u> can be <u>solids</u> (e.g. <u>citric acid</u>, which is used as a food additive, and <u>tartaric acid</u>), <u>liquids</u> (e.g. <u>sulfuric acid</u>, <u>nitric acid</u> and <u>ethanoic acid</u>, which is the acid in vinegar) or <u>gases</u> (e.g. <u>hydrogen chloride</u>).

<u>Common alkalis</u> include <u>sodium hydroxide</u> (which is used to make cleaning products like bleach), <u>potassium hydroxide</u> (used in alkaline batteries) and <u>calcium hydroxide</u> (which can be used to neutralise acidic soils).

Indicators and pH Meters can be Used to Determine pH

1) Indicators contain a dye that <u>changes colour</u> depending on whether it's <u>above</u> or <u>below</u> a certain pH.

2) <u>Universal indicator</u> is a very useful <u>combination of dyes</u>, which gives the colours shown above. It's useful for <u>estimating</u> the pH of a solution.

3) <u>pH meters</u> can also be used to measure the pH of a substance. These usually consist of a <u>probe</u>, which is dipped into the substance, and a <u>meter</u>, which gives a reading of the pH.

4) pH meters are <u>more accurate</u> than indicators.

Neutralisation Reactions Between Acids and Alkalis Make Salts

An <u>ACID</u> is a substance with a pH of less than 7.
Acidic compounds form <u>aqueous hydrogen ions</u>, H^+(aq), in <u>water</u>.
An <u>ALKALI</u> is a substance with a pH of greater than 7.
Alkaline compounds form <u>aqueous hydroxide ions</u>, OH^-(aq), in <u>water</u>.

An acid and an alkali <u>react together</u> to form a <u>salt</u> and <u>water</u>. The products of the reaction aren't acidic or alkaline — they're <u>neutral</u>. So it's called a <u>neutralisation reaction</u>.
The general equation is the same for <u>any neutralisation reaction</u>, so make sure you learn it:

$$\text{acid} + \text{alkali} \rightarrow \text{salt} + \text{water}$$

Neutralisation can also be seen in terms of H^+ and OH^- <u>ions</u>. The <u>hydrogen ions</u> from the <u>acid</u> react with the <u>hydroxide ions</u> from the <u>alkali</u> to make <u>water</u> (which is neutral).

$$H^+_{(aq)} + OH^-_{(aq)} \rightarrow H_2O_{(l)}$$

All my indicators are orange...

There's no getting away from acids and alkalis in Chemistry, or even in real life. They're everywhere — acids are found in loads of <u>foods</u>, either naturally like in fruit, or as <u>flavourings</u> and <u>preservatives</u>, whilst alkalis (particularly sodium hydroxide) are used to help make all sorts of things from <u>soaps</u> to <u>ceramics</u>.

Acids Reacting with Metals

Not only do you need to know about how <u>acids</u> react with <u>alkalis</u> but also how they react with <u>metals</u>.

Acid + Metal → Salt + Hydrogen

That's written big 'cos it's kinda worth remembering. Here's the <u>typical experiment</u>:

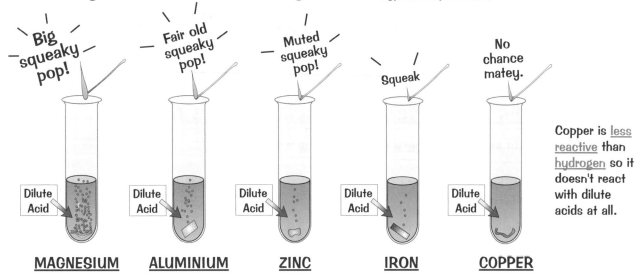

Big squeaky pop! — MAGNESIUM
Fair old squeaky pop! — ALUMINIUM
Muted squeaky pop! — ZINC
Squeak — IRON
No chance matey. — COPPER

Copper is <u>less reactive</u> than <u>hydrogen</u> so it doesn't react with dilute acids at all.

1) The more <u>reactive</u> the metal, the <u>faster</u> the reaction will go — very reactive metals (e.g. sodium) react <u>explosively</u>.
2) <u>Copper</u> does <u>not</u> react with dilute acids <u>at all</u> — because it's <u>less</u> reactive than <u>hydrogen</u>.
3) The <u>speed</u> of reaction is indicated by the <u>rate</u> at which the <u>bubbles</u> of hydrogen are given off.
4) The <u>hydrogen</u> is confirmed by the <u>burning splint test</u> giving the notorious 'squeaky pop'.
5) The <u>name</u> of the <u>salt</u> produced depends on which <u>metal</u> is used, and which <u>acid</u> is used:

Hydrochloric Acid Will Always Produce Chloride Salts:

$2HCl_{(aq)} + Mg_{(s)} \rightarrow MgCl_{2(aq)} + H_{2(g)}$ (Magnesium chloride)
$6HCl_{(aq)} + 2Al_{(s)} \rightarrow 2AlCl_{3(aq)} + 3H_{2(g)}$ (Aluminium chloride)
$2HCl_{(aq)} + Zn_{(s)} \rightarrow ZnCl_{2(aq)} + H_{2(g)}$ (Zinc chloride)

You need to be able to write balanced symbol equations — see p.12 for more.

Sulfuric Acid Will Always Produce Sulfate Salts:

$H_2SO_{4(aq)} + Mg_{(s)} \rightarrow MgSO_{4(aq)} + H_{2(g)}$ (Magnesium sulfate)
$3H_2SO_{4(aq)} + 2Al_{(s)} \rightarrow Al_2(SO_4)_{3(aq)} + 3H_{2(g)}$ (Aluminium sulfate)
$H_2SO_{4(aq)} + Zn_{(s)} \rightarrow ZnSO_{4(aq)} + H_{2(g)}$ (Zinc sulfate)

Remember to include state symbols. Chloride and sulfate salts are generally <u>soluble in water</u> so they get an aqueous (aq) state symbol (the main exceptions are lead chloride, lead sulfate and silver chloride, which are insoluble).

Nitric Acid Produces Nitrate Salts When NEUTRALISED, But...

Nitric acid (HNO_3) reacts fine with alkalis, to produce nitrates, but it can play silly devils with metals and produce nitrogen oxides instead, so we'll ignore it here. Chemistry's a real messy subject sometimes.

Nitric acid, tut — there's always one...

Some of these reactions are really useful, and some are just for fun (who said Chemistry was dull). Try writing equations for <u>different combinations</u> of <u>acids</u> and <u>metals</u>. Balance them. Cover the page and scribble all the equations down. If you make any mistakes just try again...

Oxides, Hydroxides and Carbonates

Here's more stuff on <u>neutralisation</u> reactions — mixing <u>acids</u> with various <u>alkalis</u> and <u>carbonates</u>.

Metal Oxides and Metal Hydroxides React with Acids

All metal oxides and hydroxides <u>react with acids</u> to form <u>a salt</u> and <u>water</u>.

> Acid + Metal Oxide → Salt + Water

> Acid + Metal Hydroxide → Salt + Water

These are neutralisation reactions.

The Combination of Metal and Acid Decides the Salt

Here are a couple of examples of <u>metal oxides</u> reacting with acids:

Here the copper ion is Cu^{2+}, so it needs two Cl^- ions.

| hydrochloric acid | + | copper oxide | → | copper chloride | + | water |
| 2HCl(aq) | + | CuO(s) | → | $CuCl_2$(aq) | + | H_2O(l) |

| sulfuric acid | + | zinc oxide | → | zinc sulfate | + | water |
| H_2SO_4(aq) | + | ZnO(s) | → | $ZnSO_4$(aq) | + | H_2O(l) |

And here are a couple of examples of <u>metal hydroxides</u> reacting with acids:

| hydrochloric acid | + | sodium hydroxide | → | sodium chloride | + | water |
| HCl(aq) | + | NaOH(aq) | → | NaCl(aq) | + | H_2O(l) |

| sulfuric acid | + | calcium hydroxide | → | calcium sulfate | + | water |
| H_2SO_4(aq) | + | $Ca(OH)_2$(aq) | → | $CaSO_4$(aq) | + | $2H_2O$(l) |

The sulfate ion is SO_4^{2-}, so it needs two H^+ ions.

The calcium ion is Ca^{2+}, so it needs two OH^- ions.

See p.20 for more on finding formulas.

Metal Carbonates Give Salt + Water + Carbon Dioxide

More gripping reactions involving acids. At least there are some <u>bubbles</u> involved here.

> Acid + Metal Carbonate → Salt + Water + Carbon Dioxide

The reaction is the same as any other neutralisation reaction EXCEPT that <u>carbonates</u> give off <u>carbon dioxide</u> as well. <u>Practise</u> writing the following equations out <u>from memory</u> — it'll do you no harm at all.

| hydrochloric acid + sodium carbonate | → | sodium chloride + water + carbon dioxide |
| 2HCl(aq) + Na_2CO_3(s) | → | 2NaCl(aq) + H_2O(l) + CO_2(g) |

Here's another example. (Notice how the equation's quite similar.)

| hydrochloric acid + calcium carbonate | → | calcium chloride + water + carbon dioxide |
| 2HCl(aq) + $CaCO_3$(s) | → | $CaCl_2$(aq) + H_2O(l) + CO_2(g) |

Someone threw some NaCl at me — I said, "Hey that's a salt"...

The acid + carbonate reaction is one you might have to do at home. If you live in a <u>hard water</u> area, you'll get insoluble $MgCO_3$ and $CaCO_3$ 'furring up' your kettle. You can get rid of this with 'descaler', which is dilute <u>acid</u> (often citric acid) — this reacts with the <u>insoluble carbonates</u> to make <u>soluble salts</u>.

Synthesising Compounds

As I'm sure you know, the chemical industry is really important. Without it we'd be without loads of everyday chemicals. When it comes to making these chemicals it's not just a case of throwing everything into a bucket — oh no, there are quite a few stages to the process — seven, to be precise.

There are Seven Stages Involved in Chemical Synthesis

① CHOOSING THE REACTION

Chemists need to choose the reaction (or series of reactions) to make the product. For example:
* neutralisation (see p.70) — an acid and an alkali react to produce a salt.
* thermal decomposition — heat is used to break up a compound into simpler substances.
* precipitation — an insoluble solid is formed when two solutions are mixed.

② RISK ASSESSMENT

This is an assessment of anything in the process that could cause injury (see p.18)
It involves: • identifying hazards
• assessing who might be harmed
• deciding what action can be taken to reduce the risk.

③ CALCULATING THE QUANTITIES OF REACTANTS

This includes a lot of maths and a balanced symbol equation (p.12). Using the equation chemists can calculate how much of each reactant is needed to produce a certain amount of product. This is particularly important in industry because you need to know how much of each raw material is needed so there's no waste — waste costs money.

④ CHOOSING THE APPARATUS AND CONDITIONS

The reaction needs to be carried out using suitable apparatus and in the right conditions. The apparatus needs to be the correct size (for the amount of product and reactants) and strength (for the type of reaction being carried out, e.g. if it is explosive or gives out a lot of heat). Chemists need to decide what temperature the reaction should be carried out at, what concentrations of reactants should be used, and whether or not to use a catalyst (see p.80).

⑤ ISOLATING THE PRODUCT

After the reaction is finished the products may need to be separated from the reaction mixture. This could involve evaporation (if the product is dissolved in the reaction mixture), filtration (if the product is an insoluble solid) and drying (to remove any water) see p.76.

⑥ PURIFICATION

Isolating the product and purification go together like peas and carrots. As you're isolating the product you're also helping to purify it. Crystallisation can be useful in the purification process.

⑦ MEASURING YIELD AND PURITY

The yield tells you about the overall success of the process. It compares what you think you should get with what you get in practice (see p.76). The purity of the chemical also needs to be measured (p.78).

It's just like Snow White — but with chemical synthesis steps...

It's important that none of these stages are missed out. It'd be pointless if you weren't able to separate the product from the reaction mixture and even worse if the process caused injury or death. Be safe.

Relative Formula Mass

One of the most important stages in chemical synthesis is deciding the mass of reactants needed. Careful calculations mean less waste, and less waste means more profit. But to do all that you'll need to understand <u>relative atomic mass</u> and <u>relative formula mass</u>. It's not as bad as is sounds...

Relative Atomic Mass, A_r — Easy Peasy

1) This is just a way of saying how <u>heavy</u> different atoms are <u>compared</u> with the mass of an atom of carbon-12. So carbon-12 has an A_r of <u>exactly 12</u>.
2) You can work out an element's the <u>relative atomic mass</u> by looking at the periodic table.
3) In the periodic table, the elements all have <u>two</u> numbers. The <u>bigger one</u> is the <u>relative atomic mass</u> — for more on this see p14.

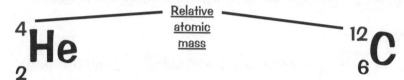

Relative atomic mass

^4_2He $^{12}_6C$

Helium has A_r = 4. Carbon has A_r = 12. Chlorine has A_r = 35.5.

Relative Formula Mass, M_r — Also Easy Peasy

If you have a compound like $MgCl_2$ then it has a <u>relative formula mass</u>, M_r, which is just all the relative atomic masses <u>added together</u>.
For $MgCl_2$ it would be:

$MgCl_2$

24 + (35.5 × 2) = 95

So the M_r for $MgCl_2$ is simply <u>95</u>.

You can easily get the A_r for any element from the periodic table (see p14).
I'll tell you what, since it's nearly Christmas I'll run through another example for you:

Compounds with Brackets in...

Find the relative formula mass for magnesium hydroxide, $Mg(OH)_2$.

<u>ANSWER:</u> The <u>small number 2</u> after the bracket in the formula $Mg(OH)_2$ means that <u>there's two of everything inside the brackets</u>. But that doesn't make the question any harder really.

The brackets in the sum are in the same place as the brackets in the chemical formula.

$Mg(OH)_2$

So the relative formula mass for $Mg(OH)_2$ is <u>58</u>.

(1 × 24) + [(16 + 1) × 2] = 58

And that's all it is. A big fancy name like <u>relative formula mass</u> and all it means is "<u>add up all the relative atomic masses</u>". What a swizz, eh? You'd have thought it'd be something a bit juicier than that, wouldn't you. Still, that's life — it's all a big disappointment in the end. Sigh.

Numbers? — and you thought you were doing chemistry...

Learn the definitions of relative atomic mass and relative formula mass, then have a go at these:
1) Use the periodic table to find the relative atomic mass of these elements: Cu, K, Kr, Cl
2) Also find the relative formula mass of these compounds: NaOH, HNO_3, KCl, $CaCO_3$

Answers on page 100.

Calculating Masses in Reactions

Once you've mastered relative formula masses you can calculate the masses in reactions.

The Three Important Steps — Not to be Missed...

(Miss one out and it'll all go horribly wrong, believe me.)

> 1) Write out the balanced equation.
> 2) Work out M_r — just for the two bits you want.
> 3) Apply the rule: Divide to get one, then multiply to get all.
>   (But you have to apply this first to the substance they give information about, and then the other one!)

Don't worry — these steps should all make sense when you look at the example below.

Example: What mass of magnesium is needed to produce 100 g of magnesium oxide?

Answer:

1) Write out the balanced equation:

$$2Mg + O_2 \rightarrow 2MgO$$

See page 12 for how to write a balanced equation.

2) Work out the relative formula masses:
   (don't do the oxygen — you don't need it)

$$2 \times 24 \rightarrow 2 \times (24 + 16)$$
$$48 \rightarrow 80$$

3) Apply the rule: Divide to get one, then multiply to get all.
   The two numbers, 48 and 80, tell us that 48 g of Mg react to give 80 g of MgO.
   Here's the tricky bit. You've now got to be able to write this down:

> 48 g of Mg ......reacts to give.....80 g of MgO
>
> ? g of Mg ......reacts to give.....1 g of MgO
>
> ? g of Mg .....reacts to give......100 g of MgO

The big clue is that in the question they've said that 100 g of magnesium oxide is produced, i.e. they've told us how much magnesium oxide to have, and that's how you know to fill in the right-hand side of the box first, because:

We'll first need to ÷ by 80 to get 1 g of MgO
and then need to × by 100 to get 100 g of MgO.

Then you can work out the numbers on the other side (shown in red below) by realising that you must divide both sides by 80 and then multiply both sides by 100. It's tricky.

÷80 48 g of Mg .... 80 g of MgO ÷80
     0.6 g of Mg .... 1 g of MgO
×100 60 g of Mg .... 100 g of MgO ×100

The mass of product is called the yield of a reaction. Masses you calculate in this way are called THEORETICAL YIELDS. In practice you never get 100% of the yield, so the amount of product will be less than calculated (see next page).

This tells us that 60 g of magnesium is needed to produce 100 g of magnesium oxide. If the question had said, "What mass of magnesium oxide is produced when 60 g of magnesium is burned in air", you'd fill in the Mg side first instead, because that's the one you'd have the information about.

Reaction mass calculations — no worries, matey...

The only way to get good at these is to practise. So make sure you can do the example, then try these:
1) Find the mass of calcium which gives 30 g of calcium oxide (CaO) when burnt in air.
2) What mass of fluorine fully reacts with potassium to make 116 g of potassium fluoride (KF)?

Answers on page 100.

Isolating the Product and Measuring Yield

Once all the <u>boring maths</u> has been done, chemists can crack on with making, <u>isolating</u> and <u>purifying</u> the product. Maths is never far away though — they then have to <u>calculate the yield</u>.

Isolating the Product and Purification Use Similar Techniques

The product needs to be <u>isolated</u> from the <u>reaction mixture</u> and <u>purified</u>. Here's where the real fun starts.

FILTRATION — used to separate an <u>insoluble solid from a liquid</u>.

Filter paper folded into a cone shape — the solid is left in the filter paper.

1) Filtration can be used if the <u>product</u> is an <u>insoluble solid</u> that needs to be separated from a <u>liquid reaction mixture</u>, e.g. in the pharmaceutical industry it's used to separate out <u>aspirin</u>.

2) It can be used in <u>purification</u> as well. For example <u>solid impurities</u> in the reaction mixture can be separated out using <u>filtration</u>.

EVAPORATION and CRYSTALLISATION — used to separate a <u>soluble solid from solution</u>.

1) Heating up the solution causes the solute to <u>evaporate</u>, leaving behind <u>solid crystals</u> of the product.

2) This is also useful for <u>purifying</u> the product. The crystals have a <u>regular structure</u> that the <u>impurities</u> can't fit into.

3) This process is often <u>repeated</u> over and over again to <u>improve the purity</u>. Products are <u>dissolved</u> and then <u>crystallised</u> again, which is called <u>recrystallisation</u>.

evaporating dish

HEAT

DRYING — used to dry the product by removing <u>excess liquid</u>.

1) The product can be <u>dried</u> in a <u>drying oven</u>. Some simply <u>heat</u> the sample, but others are more like <u>hairdriers</u> — they blow <u>hot</u>, <u>dry air</u> over the product.

2) Products are also dried using <u>desiccators</u>. These are containers that contain <u>chemicals</u> like <u>silica gel</u> that <u>remove water</u> from their surroundings. They help to keep the product <u>dry</u>.

Percentage Yield Compares Actual and Theoretical Yield

You need to understand the <u>difference</u> between the <u>actual yield</u>, the <u>theoretical yield</u> and the <u>percentage yield</u> of a product:

1) <u>ACTUAL YIELD</u> — this is the <u>mass</u> of <u>pure</u>, <u>dry product</u>. It depends on the amount of reactants you started with. The actual yield is calculated by weighing the dried product.

2) <u>THEORETICAL YIELD</u> — this is the <u>maximum possible mass</u> of pure product that <u>could</u> have been made using the amounts of reactants you started with. It's calculated from the balanced symbol equation and the maths you learnt on the previous page.

3) <u>PERCENTAGE YIELD</u> — this is the <u>actual yield</u> of the product as a <u>percentage</u> of the <u>theoretical yield</u>.

$$\text{percentage yield} = \frac{\text{actual yield (grams)}}{\text{theoretical yield (grams)}} \times 100$$

The percentage yield will <u>always be less than 100%</u>. That's because some product will be lost along the way, e.g. during purification and drying.

It can all be quite dull — like watching chemicals dry...

Unfortunately, no matter how careful you are, you're not going to get a 100% yield in any reaction. You'll <u>always</u> get a little loss of product. In industry, people work very hard to keep waste as <u>low</u> as possible — so <u>reactants</u> that don't react first time are <u>collected</u> and <u>recycled</u> whenever possible.

Titrations

Titrations have a bad reputation — but they're not as bad as they're made out to be.

Titrations are Carried Out Using a Burette

Titrations can be used to check the purity of acidic or alkaline products (see next page). They work using neutralisation reactions (see p.70).

1) Add a known volume of alkali to a titration flask, along with two or three drops of indicator.
2) Fill a burette with the acid. A burette is a nice fancy bit of kit:

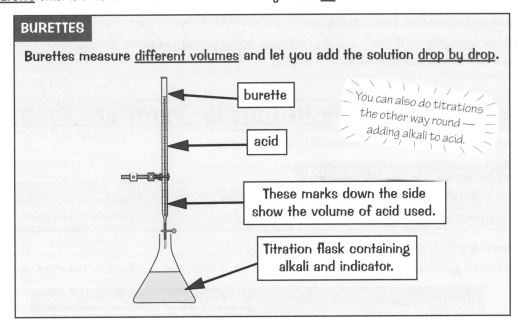

BURETTES

Burettes measure different volumes and let you add the solution drop by drop.

burette

acid

These marks down the side show the volume of acid used.

Titration flask containing alkali and indicator.

You can also do titrations the other way round — adding alkali to acid.

3) Using the burette, add the acid to the alkali a bit at a time — giving the conical flask a regular swirl. Go slow when you think the end-point (colour change) is about to be reached.
4) The indicator changes colour when all the alkali has been neutralised.
5) Record the volume of acid used to neutralise the alkali.

Solids are Weighed Out into a Titration Flask

Titrations can't be carried out with solids — only liquids. So any solid product being tested needs to be made into a solution.

1) If the product is a solid lump, it can help to first crush it into a powder.
2) Put a titration flask onto a balance.
3) Carefully weigh some of the powder into the flask. (The amount of solid used will differ from product to product.)
4) Add a solvent, e.g. water or ethanol, to dissolve the powder. (Again the solvent used and the amount will depend on what is being tested.)
5) Finally, swirl the titration flask until all of the solid has dissolved.

How do you get lean molecules? Feed them titrations...

Before the end of this module you'll be a dab hand at titrations — whether you want to be or not. They're not too tricky really — you just need to make as sure as you can that your results are accurate, which means going slowly near the end-point.

Purity

It's all very well making a product, but how do you know if it's any good or not...

Some Products Need to be Very Pure

1) The purity of a product will improve as it's being isolated. But to get a really pure product earlier stages (such as filtration, evaporation and crystallisation) will often need to be repeated.

2) Purifying and measuring the purity of a product are particularly important steps in the chemical industry. For example, in the production of...

...pharmaceuticals — it's really important to ensure drugs intended for human consumption are free from impurities — these could do more harm than good.

...petrochemicals — if there are impurities or contaminants in petrol products they could cause damage to a car's engine.

Titrations Can be Used to Measure the Purity of a Substance

The purity of a compound can be calculated using a titration:

Example — Determining the Purity of Aspirin

Say you start off with 0.2 g of impure aspirin dissolved in 25 cm³ of ethanol in your conical flask. You find from your titration that it takes 9.5 cm³ of 4 g/dm³ NaOH to neutralise the aspirin solution.

Step 1: Work out the concentration of the aspirin solution.
You'll be given a formula, so all you have to do is stick the numbers in the right places.

$$\text{conc. of aspirin solution} = 4.5 \times \frac{\text{conc. of NaOH} \times \text{vol. of NaOH}}{\text{vol. of aspirin solution}}$$

This number will change depending on which acid and alkali are used.

$$= 4.5 \times \frac{4 \times (9.5 / 1000)}{25 / 1000} = \underline{6.84 \text{ g/dm}^3}$$

The volumes need to be in dm³, not cm³, so you need to divide by 1000 to convert it.

1 dm³ = 1000 cm³

Step 2: Work out the mass of the aspirin. You'll need to use another formula:

$$\text{mass} = \text{concentration} \times \text{volume}$$

$$= 6.84 \times 25 / 1000 = \underline{0.171 \text{ g}}$$

This is the concentration of the aspirin solution.

In the 0.2 g that you started with, 0.171 g was aspirin.

Step 3: Calculate the purity, using the formula:

$$\% \text{ purity} = \frac{\text{calculated mass of substance}}{\text{mass of impure substance at start}} \times 100$$

$$= 0.171 \div 0.2 \times 100 = \underline{85.5\%}$$

This is the percentage purity of the aspirin.

This is the mass of aspirin that reacted in the titration.

This is the mass of impure aspirin you started with.

Concentrate when doing titrations...

This is all pretty complicated stuff, but don't worry about it too much. If you get asked to do it in the exam they'll give you all the information you need — like the formulas, concentrations and volumes.

Rates of Reaction

There's an old saying in the <u>chemical industry</u> — the <u>faster</u> you make <u>chemicals</u> the <u>faster</u> you make <u>money</u>. For this reason it's important to know what <u>factors</u> affect the rate of a <u>chemical reaction</u>.

Reactions Can Go at All Sorts of _Different Rates_

The <u>rate</u> of a chemical reaction is how fast the <u>reactants</u> are <u>changed</u> into <u>products</u>.

1) One of the <u>slowest</u> is the <u>rusting</u> of iron (it's not slow enough though — what about my little MGB).

2) Other slow reactions include <u>chemical weathering</u> — like acid rain damage to limestone buildings.

3) An example of a <u>moderate speed</u> reaction is a <u>metal</u> (e.g. magnesium) reacting with <u>acid</u> to produce a <u>gentle stream of bubbles</u>.

4) <u>Burning</u> is a <u>fast</u> reaction, but <u>explosions</u> are even <u>faster</u> and release a lot of gas. Explosive reactions are all over in a <u>fraction of a second</u>.

Controlling the _Rate of Reaction_ is Important in Industry

In <u>industry</u>, it's important to <u>control</u> the rate of a chemical reaction for <u>two</u> main reasons:

1) <u>Safety</u> — if the reaction is <u>too fast</u> it could cause an <u>explosion</u>, which can be a bit <u>dangerous</u>.

2) <u>Economic reasons</u> — changing the conditions can be <u>costly</u>. For example, using very high <u>temperatures</u> means there'll be bigger <u>fuel bills</u>, so the cost of production is pushed up. But, a <u>faster rate</u> means that <u>more product</u> will be produced in <u>less time</u>. Companies often have to choose optimum conditions that give <u>low production costs</u>, but this may mean compromising on the <u>rate of production</u>, or the <u>yield</u>.

In the exam they could ask you to <u>interpret information</u> about rates of reaction in <u>chemical synthesis</u>. You might be given a <u>load of info</u> and asked to pick the <u>best process</u>. You'll have to think about what the <u>optimum conditions</u> would be — look for reactions that will give the <u>best yield</u> and <u>rate of production</u> for the <u>lowest cost</u>. You'll also need to think about <u>environmental issues</u> (like poisonous gases) and how <u>dangerous</u> the reactions are.

Typical Graphs for Rate of Reaction

The plot below shows how the <u>speed</u> of a particular reaction <u>varies</u> under <u>different conditions</u>. The quickest reactions have the <u>steepest lines</u> and become <u>flat</u> in the <u>least time</u>.

Make sure you understand the graphs — you might be given data to interpret in the exam.

1) Graph 1 represents the <u>original reaction</u>.

2) Graph 2 represents the reaction taking place <u>quicker</u>, but with the same initial amounts. The <u>same amount</u> of product is produced overall — just at a quicker rate.

3) The <u>increased rate</u> could be due to <u>any</u> of these:

> a) increase in <u>temperature</u>
> b) increase in <u>concentration</u>
> c) <u>catalyst</u> added
> d) solid reactant crushed up into <u>smaller bits</u>.

Amount of product evolved

④ faster, and more reactants

Flat lines show the reaction has finished.

③ much faster reaction

② faster reaction

① original reaction

Time

4) <u>Graph 4</u> shows <u>more product</u> as well as a <u>faster</u> reaction. This can <u>only</u> happen if <u>more reactant(s)</u> are added at the start. <u>Graphs 1, 2 and 3</u> all converge at the same level, showing that they all produce the same amount of product, although they take <u>different</u> times to produce it.

Get a fast, furious reaction — tickle your teacher...

First off... remember that the <u>amount of product</u> you get depends only on the <u>amount of reactants</u> you start with. So all this stuff about the <u>rate of a reaction</u> is only talking about <u>how quickly</u> your products form — <u>not</u> how much you get. It's an important difference — so get your head round it ASAP.

Collision Theory

Reaction rates are explained perfectly by collision theory. It's really simple.

It just says that the rate of a reaction simply depends on how often and how hard the reacting particles collide with each other. The basic idea is that particles have to collide in order to react, and they have to collide hard enough (with enough energy).

The Rate of Reaction Depends on Four Things:

1) Temperature   2) Concentration
3) Catalyst   4) Size of 'lumps' (or surface area)

LEARN THEM!

More Collisions Increases the Rate of Reaction

All four methods of increasing the rate of a reaction can be explained in terms of increasing the number of successful collisions between the reacting particles:

Increasing the TEMPERATURE Increases the Rate of Reaction

1) When the temperature is increased the particles all move faster.
2) If they're moving faster, they're going to have more collisions.
3) Also the faster they move the more energy they have, so more of the collisions will have enough energy to make the reaction happen.

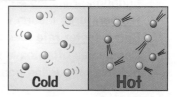

Increasing the CONCENTRATION Increases the Rate of Reaction

1) If a solution is made more concentrated it means there are more particles of reactant knocking about in the same volume of water (or other solvent).
2) This makes collisions between the reactant particles more likely.

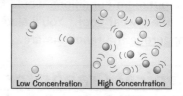

SMALLER SOLID PARTICLES (or MORE SURFACE AREA) Increases the Rate of Reaction

1) If one of the reactants is a solid then breaking it up into smaller pieces will increase its surface area.
2) This means the particles around it will have more area to work on so there'll be more collisions.
3) For example, soluble painkillers dissolve faster when they're broken into bits.

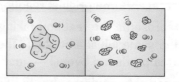

Using a CATALYST Increases the Rate of Reaction

1) A catalyst is a substance which increases the speed of a reaction, without being changed or used up in the reaction.
2) A catalyst works by giving the reacting particles a surface to stick to where they can bump into each other — increasing the number of successful collisions.

Collision theory — it's always the other driver...

Industries that use chemical reactions to make their products have to think carefully about reaction rates. Ideally, they want to speed up the reaction to get the products quickly, but high temperatures and pressures are expensive. So they compromise — they use a slower reaction but a cheaper one.

Module C6 — Chemical Synthesis

Measuring Rates of Reaction

Three Ways to Measure the Speed of a Reaction

The <u>speed of a reaction</u> can be observed <u>either</u> by how quickly the reactants are used up or how quickly the products are formed. It's usually a lot easier to measure <u>products forming</u>.

The rate of reaction can be calculated using the following equation:

$$\text{Rate of Reaction} = \frac{\text{Amount of reactant used or amount of product formed}}{\text{Time}}$$

There are different ways that the speed of a reaction can be <u>measured</u>. Learn these three:

1) Precipitation

1) This is when the product of the reaction is a <u>precipitate</u> which <u>clouds</u> the solution.
2) Observe a <u>mark</u> through the solution and measure how long it takes for it to <u>disappear</u>.
3) The <u>faster</u> the mark disappears, the <u>quicker</u> the reaction.
4) This only works for reactions where the initial solution is <u>see-through</u>.
5) The result is very <u>subjective</u> — <u>different people</u> might not agree over the <u>exact</u> point when the mark 'disappears'.

2) Change in Mass (Usually Gas Given Off)

1) Measuring the speed of a reaction that <u>produces a gas</u> can be carried out using a <u>mass balance</u>.
2) As the gas is released the mass <u>disappearing</u> is easily measured on the balance.
3) The <u>quicker</u> the reading on the balance <u>drops</u>, the <u>faster</u> the reaction.
4) <u>Rate of reaction graphs</u> are particularly easy to plot using the results from this method.
5) This is the <u>most accurate</u> of the three methods described on this page because the mass balance is very accurate. But it has the <u>disadvantage</u> of releasing the gas straight into the room.

3) The Volume of Gas Given Off

1) This involves the use of a <u>gas syringe</u> to measure the <u>volume</u> of gas given off.
2) The <u>more</u> gas given off during a given <u>time interval</u>, the <u>faster</u> the reaction.
3) A graph of <u>gas volume</u> against <u>time</u> could be plotted to give a rate of reaction graph.
4) Gas syringes usually give volumes accurate to the <u>nearest cm^3</u>, so they're quite accurate. You have to be quite careful though — if the reaction is too <u>vigorous</u>, you can easily blow the plunger out of the end of the syringe!

OK, have you got your stopwatch ready... *BANG!* — oh...

Each method has its <u>pros and cons</u>. The mass balance method is only accurate as long as the flask isn't too hot, otherwise you lose mass by evaporation as well as by the reaction. The first method isn't very accurate, but if you're not producing a gas you can't use either of the other two. Ah well.

Revision Summary for Module C6

And that's it... the end of another section. Which means it's time for some more questions. There's no point in trying to duck out of these — they're the best way of testing that you've learned everything in this topic. If you can't answer any of them, look back in the book. If you can't do all this now, you won't be able to in the exam either.

1) Name two chemicals that you might come across in everyday life.

2) Give an example of one chemical that is produced on a small scale and one chemical that is produced on a large scale.

3) State whether substances with the following pH are acid, alkali or neutral:
   a) pH 2   b) pH 13   c) pH 0   d) pH 7

4) Give an example of a pure acidic compound that is a liquid.

5) Name two ways of measuring the pH of a substance.

6) What types of ions are always present in: a) acids, and b) alkalis dissolved in water?

7) Write the equation for neutralisation in terms of the ions you named in question 6.

8) Why is it dangerous to add potassium to an acid?

9) Write balanced symbol equations and name the salts formed in the following reactions:
   a) hydrochloric acid with: i) magnesium, ii) aluminium and iii) zinc,
   b) sulfuric acid with: i) magnesium, ii) aluminium and iii) zinc.

10) Name the salts formed and write a balanced equation for the reaction between:
   a) hydrochloric acid and copper oxide.
   b) hydrochloric acid and calcium hydroxide.

11) When designing a chemical process why is it important to carry out a risk assessment?

12) Why is it important to choose the right apparatus for a chemical process?

13) What does calculating the yield tell you about a reaction?

14)* Find A_r or M_r for each of these (use the periodic table):
   a) Ca   b) Ag   c) CO_2 d) $MgCO_3$ e) $Al(OH)_3$
   f) ZnO   g) Na_2CO_3 h) sodium chloride

15)* Write down the method for calculating reacting masses.
   a) What mass of magnesium oxide is produced when 112.1 g of magnesium burns in air?
   b) What mass of sodium is needed to produce 108.2 g of sodium oxide?

16) How would you separate an insoluble product from a liquid reaction mixture?

17) Name two stages in the synthesis of a chemical where evaporation can be useful.

18) Give two methods used to dry a product.

19) What is the formula for percentage yield? How does it differ from actual yield?

20) Why is purification of a product important?

21) Describe how to carry out a titration.

22)* Calculate the purity of a 0.5 g aspirin tablet that contains 0.479 g of aspirin.

23) What four things affect the rate of a reaction?

24) Give two reasons why it is important to control the rate of a chemical reaction in industry.

25)* Magnesium metal was placed into a solution of 0.1 M hydrochloric acid. The reaction produced 50 cm³ of hydrogen. Would you expect the same reaction with 0.2 M hydrochloric acid to be faster or slower? Explain why.

26) Describe three different ways of measuring the rate of a reaction.
   Give one advantage and one disadvantage of each method.

* Answers on page 100.

Waves — The Basics

Waves transfer <u>energy</u> from one place to another without transferring any <u>matter</u> (stuff).

Waves Have Amplitude, Wavelength and Frequency

1) The <u>amplitude</u> is the displacement from the <u>rest position</u> to the <u>crest</u> (NOT from a trough to a crest).

2) The <u>wavelength</u> is the length of a <u>full cycle</u> of the wave, e.g. from <u>crest to crest</u>.

3) <u>Frequency</u> is the <u>number of complete waves</u> passing a certain point <u>per second</u> OR the <u>number of waves</u> produced by a source <u>each second</u>. Frequency is measured in hertz (Hz). 1 Hz is <u>1 wave per second</u>.

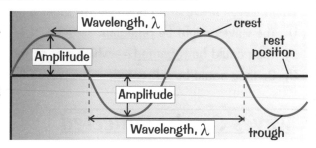

Transverse Waves Have Sideways Vibrations

<u>Most waves</u> are <u>transverse</u>:

1) <u>Light</u> and <u>all other EM waves</u>.
2) <u>Ripples</u> on water.
3) <u>Waves</u> on <u>strings</u>.
4) A <u>slinky spring</u> wiggled up and down.

> In **<u>TRANSVERSE</u>** waves the vibrations are at **<u>90°</u>** to the **<u>DIRECTION OF TRAVEL</u>** of the wave.

Longitudinal Waves Have Vibrations Along the Same Line

Examples of <u>longitudinal waves</u> are:
1) <u>Sound waves</u> and <u>ultrasound</u>.
2) <u>Shock waves</u>, e.g. seismic waves.
3) A <u>slinky spring</u> when you <u>push</u> the end.

Oscilloscopes show even longitudinal waves as transverse — just so you can see what's going on.

> In **<u>LONGITUDINAL</u>** waves the vibrations are along the **<u>SAME DIRECTION</u>** as the wave is travelling.

Wave Speed = Frequency × Wavelength

You need to learn this equation — and <u>practise using it</u>.

> Speed = Frequency × Wavelength
> (m/s)   (Hz)   (m)

OR

> $v = f\lambda$

Speed (v is for <u>velocity</u>)

Wavelength (that's the Greek letter 'lambda')

Frequency

<u>EXAMPLE</u>: A radio wave has a frequency of 92.2×10^6 Hz. Find its wavelength. (The speed of all EM waves is 3×10^8 m/s.)

<u>ANSWER</u>: You're trying to find λ using f and v, so you've got to rearrange the equation. So $\lambda = v \div f = 3 \times 10^8 \div 9.22 \times 10^7 = \underline{3.25\ m}$.

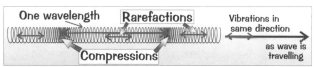

The <u>speed</u> of a wave is <u>usually independent</u> of the <u>frequency</u> or <u>amplitude</u> of the wave. Changes in speed are linked to changes in wavelength, as you'll find out on the next page...

Waves — dig the vibes, man...

The first thing to learn is that diagram at the top of the page. Then get that <u>v = fλ</u> business <u>imprinted</u> on your brain. When you've done <u>that</u>, try this question: A sound wave travelling in a solid has a frequency of <u>1.9×10^4 Hz</u> and a wavelength of <u>12.5 cm</u>. Find its speed.*

Wave Properties

Waves don't always trundle along at the same speed. They can do all sorts of weird and wonderful things...

All Waves Can be Reflected, Refracted and Diffracted

When waves arrive at an obstacle (or meet a new material), their direction of travel can be changed...
1) The waves might be reflected.
2) They could be refracted — which means they go through the new material but change direction.
3) Or they could be diffracted — the waves 'bend round' obstacles, causing the waves to spread out.

Waves Can be Reflected

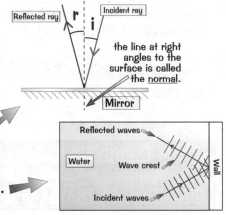

1) When waves hit a boundary between one medium and another, they are partially reflected.
2) The angle of reflection, r, of the waves is the same as the angle of incidence, i (the angle at which the waves hit the boundary). These angles are always measured from the normal.
3) You can draw the reflection using a ray diagram, e.g. for light reflected by a flat mirror (a 'plane reflector'). You can also draw the reflection by showing the crests of the waves, e.g. water waves being reflected by a swimming pool wall.

Refraction — Waves Change Speed and Direction

1) Waves travel at different speeds in substances which have different densities. For example, light waves travel more slowly in denser media (usually). Sound waves travel faster in denser substances.
2) So when a wave crosses a boundary between two substances (from glass to air, say) it changes speed:

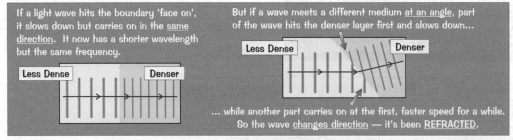

3) When light shines on a glass window pane, some of the light is reflected, but a lot of it passes through the glass and gets refracted as it does so:

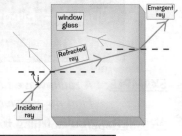

4) As the light passes from the air into the glass (a denser medium), it slows down. This causes the light ray to bend ('refract') towards the normal.
5) When the light reaches the 'glass to air' boundary on the other side of the window, it speeds up and bends (refracts) away from the normal.
6) Water waves travel faster in deeper water, causing refraction when waves hit a boundary (between two depths) at an angle. There's a change in direction and a change in wavelength.

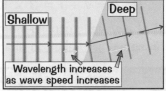

7) All the waves will have the same change in speed and the same change in wavelength — so there is NO change in frequency.

Reflect on this...

Waves often reach the beach with their crests parallel to the shore — because the waves get refracted as the sea gets shallower. Have a look next time you're at the seaside with your bucket and spade...

Wave Properties

Ah... some more properties of waves... let the fun continue.

Total Internal Reflection Happens Above the Critical Angle

1) When a light wave travels <u>from a dense substance</u> like glass or water <u>into a less dense</u> substance like air, its <u>angle of refraction</u> is <u>greater</u> than the angle of incidence.

2) If the angle of incidence is <u>big enough</u>, the angle of refraction gets <u>above 90°</u> and that makes <u>strange</u> things happen. 'Big enough' means bigger than what's called the '<u>critical angle</u>':

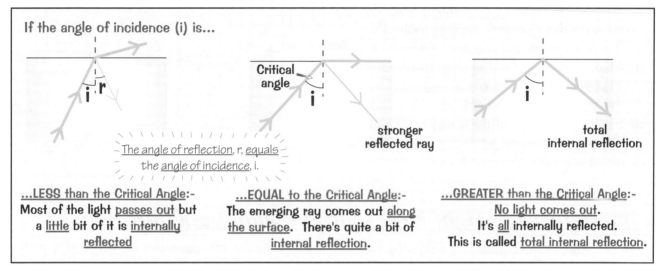

If the angle of incidence (i) is...

The angle of reflection, r, equals the angle of incidence, i.

stronger reflected ray

total internal reflection

...LESS than the Critical Angle:-
Most of the light <u>passes out</u> but a <u>little</u> bit of it is <u>internally reflected</u>

...EQUAL to the Critical Angle:-
The emerging ray comes out <u>along the surface</u>. There's quite a bit of <u>internal reflection</u>.

...GREATER than the Critical Angle:-
No light comes out.
It's <u>all</u> internally reflected.
This is called <u>total internal reflection</u>.

3) <u>Total internal reflection</u> only happens when the wave would <u>speed up</u> at a boundary. And it only happens if the angle of incidence is bigger than the critical angle.

4) Different materials have different critical angles. The critical angle for light at a <u>glass/air boundary</u> is about 42°.

5) <u>Optical fibres</u> work by total internal reflection — by bouncing waves off the sides of a thin <u>inner core</u> of glass or plastic using total internal reflection. The wave enters one end of the fibre and is reflected repeatedly until it emerges at the other end.

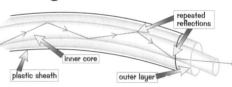

repeated reflections

inner core

plastic sheath

outer layer

Diffraction — Waves Spreading Out

1) All waves <u>spread out</u> ('<u>diffract</u>') at the edges when they pass through a <u>gap</u> or <u>past an object</u>.

2) The amount of diffraction depends on the size of the gap relative to the wavelength of the wave. The <u>narrower the gap</u>, or the <u>longer the wavelength</u>, the <u>more</u> the wave spreads out.

3) A <u>narrow gap</u> is one about the same size as the <u>wavelength</u> of the wave.

So whether a gap counts as narrow or not depends on the wave in question.

4) <u>Light</u> has a very <u>small wavelength</u> (about 0.0005 mm), so it can be diffracted but it needs a <u>really small gap</u>.

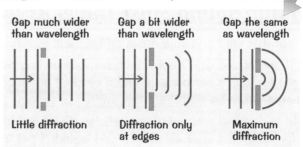

Gap much wider than wavelength

Gap a bit wider than wavelength

Gap the same as wavelength

Little diffraction

Diffraction only at edges

Maximum diffraction

Concentrate — don't get diffracted...

Remember (deep breath) — total internal reflection happens when light waves hit a 'dense/less dense' boundary at an angle <u>greater</u> than the critical angle. Diffraction is where waves spread out when they travel through a gap — the <u>narrower</u> the gap, the <u>more</u> they spread. Strange but true.

Wave Interference

Interference — not just what you have to deal with from your parents... waves do it too.

When Waves Meet They Cause a Disturbance   (just like teenagers)

1) All waves cause some kind of <u>disturbance</u> — water waves disturb water, sound waves disturb air (or whatever they're travelling through), light waves disturb electric and magnetic fields.

2) When <u>two waves meet</u>, they both cause their own disturbances and their effects <u>combine</u>. This is called <u>interference</u>.

3) When waves arrive '<u>in step</u>' they disturb in the same direction and <u>reinforce</u> each other. This is known as <u>constructive</u> interference.

4) Where waves meet <u>out of step</u>, they disturb in opposite directions and <u>cancel out</u>. This is <u>destructive</u> interference.

5) The <u>total amplitude</u> of the waves at a point is the <u>sum</u> of the <u>individual displacements</u> at that point, taking direction into account.

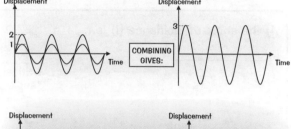

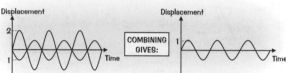

Interference of Light Makes 'Bright' and 'Dark' Bits

You can <u>observe interference</u> by diffracting two identical light beams through a pair of <u>narrow slits</u> just a <u>fraction of a millimetre</u> apart. If you do this experiment in a <u>dark room</u> with a <u>screen</u> you'll see an <u>interference pattern</u> — several bands of light and dark on the screen. Here's why it happens:

1) At certain points on the screen, light waves arrive from the two slits <u>in phase</u> — here you get <u>constructive interference</u>. The <u>amplitude</u> of the waves is <u>doubled</u>, so you get a <u>bright</u> band of light.

2) These points occur where the <u>distance travelled</u> by the waves from both slits is either the <u>same</u> or different by a <u>whole number of wavelengths</u>.

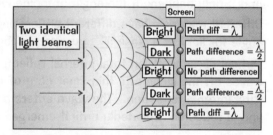

3) At certain other points the light waves will be exactly <u>out of phase</u> — here you get <u>destructive interference</u>. The waves <u>cancel out</u> and you see a <u>dark</u> band on the screen.

4) These out-of-phase points occur where the difference in the <u>distance travelled</u> by the waves (the "<u>path difference</u>") is ½ wavelength, 1½ wavelengths, 2½ wavelengths, etc.

Light and Sound Must Travel as Waves

1) The fact that light and sound can <u>diffract</u> and <u>interfere</u> shows that they have <u>wave properties</u>.

2) If light and sound didn't act like waves, but as tiny particles, the particles would just pass <u>straight through</u> a narrow gap, and if blocked by an object wouldn't be able to 'bend' around it — they'd either be <u>absorbed</u>, <u>transmitted</u> or <u>reflected</u> back.

3) If light and sound just acted as particles, there wouldn't be any positive or negative <u>disturbances</u> to <u>interfere</u> with one another, and so you wouldn't get interference patterns either.

Destructive interference — too many cooks spoil the wave...

It's weird, isn't it... I mean, constructive interference makes <u>perfect sense</u> — two waves, bigger sound... it's just <u>destructive</u> interference that gets me. I know I've just drawn the diagrams — I know WHY it happens... but I still find it <u>weird</u>. Just one of the Universe's little quirks I suppose. (Like <u>peanut butter</u>.)

Electromagnetic Radiation

Electromagnetic waves are things like radio waves, microwaves and X-rays. They're a bit odd, frankly.

There are Seven Types of Electromagnetic (EM) Waves

Good old light is just one type of electromagnetic (EM) radiation. EM radiation occurs at many different wavelengths. In fact, there is a continuous spectrum of different wavelengths, but waves with similar wavelengths tend to have similar properties. Electromagnetic radiation is normally split into seven types of waves:

| RADIO WAVES | MICRO- WAVES | INFRA- RED | VISIBLE LIGHT | ULTRA- VIOLET | X-RAYS | GAMMA RAYS |

Increasing Frequency

Increasing Wavelength

1) All types of electromagnetic radiation travel at exactly the same speed through space, which is a vacuum. That speed is very high — about 300 million m/s.
2) This means that waves with a shorter wavelength have a higher frequency (see p.83).
3) Even in the visible light part of the spectrum each colour of light has a different frequency (and wavelength). For example, blue has a wavelength of about 475 nm, and red is around 700 nm.

$1\,nm = 1 \times 10^{-9}\,m$

Sound Waves Can't Travel Through a Vacuum

Sound waves are quite different from EM waves. For a start, they're transmitted by vibrating particles — so they can't travel through a vacuum.

This is nicely demonstrated by the jolly old bell jar experiment.
As air is removed by the vacuum pump, the sound gets quieter and quieter.
(The bell has to be mounted on something like foam to stop the sound from it travelling through the solid surface and making the base vibrate, because you'd hear that instead.)

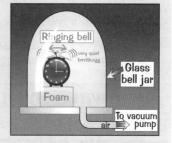

The Energy of a Photon Depends on Frequency of EM waves

1) All EM radiation transfers energy, but it's a bit weird...
2) EM radiation doesn't just act like waves — it can also act like it's made up of lots of really tiny particles. These particles are tiny packets of energy called photons.
3) The energy delivered by each photon in a beam of electromagnetic radiation depends on the frequency of the electromagnetic waves.

> The higher the frequency, the higher the energy the photon delivers.

Intensity Depends on the Number of Photons per Second

1) The intensity of a beam of radiation is the amount of energy it delivers per second.
2) In a beam of EM radiation of a particular frequency, each photon carries the same amount of energy — this amount of energy depends on the frequency of the radiation.
3) This means that the intensity of a radiation beam depends on the number of photons that arrive each second, and the energy of the photons in the beam.

That was intense man...

The fact that stuff like light, heat, radio and gamma radiation are all the same thing is completely insane in my opinion. I mean, you're reading this page by detecting the visible EM waves bouncing off it, but if the frequency of those waves changed, they could melt your face... it's mental.

Uses of EM waves

You use EM waves for all sorts of stuff — your satellite TV (and your terrestrial TV), your radio, your microwave, your pet dog Jimbo... OK maybe not that last bit.

Radio Waves are Used Mainly for Communications

1) Radio waves and microwaves are good at transmitting information over long distances.
2) This is because they don't get absorbed by the Earth's atmosphere as much as most waves in the middle of the EM spectrum (like heat), or those at the high-frequency end of the spectrum (e.g. gamma rays or X-rays).

You couldn't use high-frequency waves anyway — they'd be far too dangerous.

3) The radio waves used for TV and FM radio transmissions have very short wavelengths compared to most radio waves. Microwaves used for mobile phone communications have very long wavelengths compared to most microwaves, but are still titchy compared to radio waves.

Microwaves are Used for Satellite Communication...

1) Communication to and from satellites (including for satellite TV and phones) uses microwaves that can pass easily through the atmosphere.
2) For satellite TV, the signal from a transmitter is transmitted into space...
3) ... where it's absorbed by the satellite receiver dish orbiting thousands of kilometres above the Earth. The satellite transmits the signal back to Earth in a different direction...
4) ... where it's received by a satellite dish on the ground.
5) These dishes are made of metal — metal reflects microwaves well, so the dish can focus the waves onto its receiver, rather than just absorbing them.

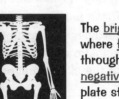

Microwaves reflected by metal dish to receiver

microwaves

clouds and water vapour

Microwave Ovens Use a Different Wavelength from Satellites

1) Microwaves used for communications need to pass through the Earth's watery atmosphere, but the microwaves used in microwave ovens have a different wavelength.
2) These microwaves are actually absorbed by the water molecules in the food. They penetrate up to a few centimetres into the food before being absorbed by water molecules, increasing the molecules' kinetic energy. The extra energy is then conducted or convected to other parts of the food.

X-Rays are Used to Identify Fractures

1) Radiographers in hospitals take X-ray 'photographs' of people to see if they have any broken bones.
2) X-rays pass easily through flesh but not so easily through denser material like bones or metal. So it's the varying amount of radiation that's absorbed (or not absorbed, really) that makes an X-ray image.
3) X-ray imaging is also used in airports to check the contents of passengers' bags.

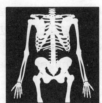

The brighter bits are where fewer X-rays get through. This is a negative image. The plate starts off all white.

Infrared and Light are Used in Optical Fibres

Light and infrared are great for transmitting information along optical fibres — the signal doesn't weaken too much as it travels along. (See p.85 for more on optical fibres.)

EM waves? Plastic cups and string, that's all we had in my day...

It's pretty logical really that EM waves with different wavelengths have quite different properties and completely different uses. I mean, you wouldn't try and cook your tea using X-rays would you...

Adding Information to Waves

OK, so there are <u>lots</u> of ways to send <u>signals</u>, whether it's through <u>the atmosphere</u> (like radio waves and microwaves) or along <u>optical fibres</u> (like light or infrared). But how do waves <u>carry</u> your <u>information</u>?

Information is Converted into Signals

<u>Information</u> is being transmitted everywhere all the time.

1) Whatever kind of information you're sending (text, sound, pictures...) is converted into <u>electrical signals</u> before it's transmitted...

2) It's then sent long distances down <u>telephone wires</u> or carried on <u>EM waves</u>.

3) There are <u>two ways</u> you can send information as waves — <u>AM</u> and <u>FM</u>.

AM Radio Waves *Have Varying Amplitude*

1) An <u>AM radio transmitter</u> sends out a continuous <u>carrier wave</u>.

2) The <u>signal</u> (e.g. music) is <u>superimposed</u> on the carrier wave using <u>amplitude modulation</u>:

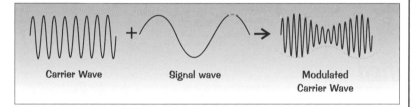

Carrier Wave   Signal wave   Modulated
                                           Carrier Wave

AM — Amplitude Modulation

The <u>sound wave</u> from the music 'modulates' or <u>changes</u> the <u>carrier wave</u> by changing its <u>amplitude</u>. The two waves <u>combine</u> so that the information is carried by the pattern of the final wave's variation.

FM Radio Waves *Have Varying Frequency*

FM radio (<u>frequency modulation</u>) is exactly the <u>same idea</u> as AM, but instead of changing the carrier wave's <u>amplitude</u>, you change its <u>frequency</u>:

FM — Frequency Modulation

Where there's a <u>peak</u> in the <u>signal wave</u>, the frequency of the modulated wave is <u>decreased</u>. Where there's a <u>trough</u> in the signal wave, the frequency is <u>increased</u>. Or vice versa.

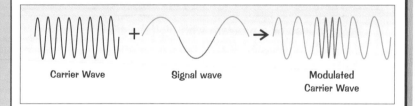

Carrier Wave   Signal wave   Modulated
                                           Carrier Wave

So when it comes to modulation, an <u>AM transmission</u> has <u>changing amplitude</u> (but constant frequency), and an <u>FM transmission</u> has <u>changing frequency</u> (but constant amplitude). Easy peasy.

Receivers Recover the Original Signal

When a <u>receiver</u> detects a modulated wave, it <u>ignores</u> the <u>carrier</u> part of the wave and <u>extracts</u> the <u>original signal</u> from the pattern of the wave's variation. That way, Terry Wogan comes through loud and clear when you're sitting by the fire listening to your wireless.

That's all very fancy — but who listens to AM radio any more?!

Some of this stuff might seem pretty <u>old fashioned</u> (AM was invented in the 1870s...), but I think you'll agree it's <u>not the easiest</u> thing to get your head around. So make sure you can tell which of those wave diagrams is which <u>without reading the text</u> — is it the <u>frequency</u> or the <u>amplitude</u> that's changing?

Analogue and Digital Signals

Digital technology is gradually taking over. By 2012, you won't be able to watch TV unless you've got a digital version — that's when the Government's planning to switch off the last analogue signal.

Analogue Signals Vary but Digital's Either On or Off

1) The amplitude or frequency of an analogue signal vary continuously. An analogue signal can take any value in a particular range.

2) Dimmer switches, thermometers, speedometers and old-fashioned watches are all analogue devices.

3) Digital signals can only take two values — they're made up of 'pulses' (the two values sometimes get different names, but the key thing is that there are only two of them): on or off, true or false, 0 or 1...

4) A digital receiver will decode these pulses to get a copy of the original signal (Terry's words of wisdom — loud and clear).

5) On/off switches and the displays on digital clocks and meters are all digital devices.

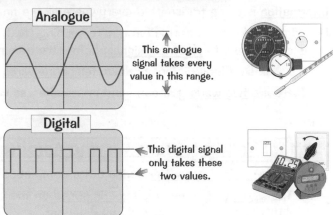

Analogue

This analogue signal takes every value in this range.

Digital

This digital signal only takes these two values.

Signals Have to be Amplified

Both digital and analogue signals weaken as they travel, so they may need to be amplified along their route.

They also pick up interference or noise from electrical disturbances or other signals.

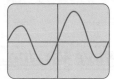
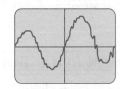

A nice smooth analogue signal   The same signal with noise

Digital Signals are Far Better Quality

1) Noise is less of a problem with digital signals than with analogue. If you receive a 'noisy' digital signal, it's pretty obvious what it's supposed to be. So it's easy to 'clean up' the signal — the noise doesn't get amplified.

2) But if you receive a noisy analogue signal, it's difficult to know what the original signal would have looked like. And if you amplify a noisy analogue signal, you amplify the noise as well.

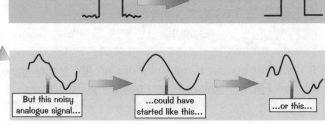

This noisy digital signal...   ...is obviously supposed to be this.

But this noisy analogue signal...   ...could have started like this...   ...or this...

3) This is why digital signals are much higher quality — the information received is the same as the original.

4) Digital signals are also easy to process using computers, since computers are digital devices too.

5) And another advantage of digital technology is you can transmit several signals at once using just one cable or EM wave — so you can send more information (in a given time) than using analogue signals.

I've got loads of digital stuff — watch, radio, fingers...

Digital signals are great — unless you live in a part of the country which currently has poor reception of digital broadcasts, in which case you get no benefit at all. This is because if you don't get spot-on reception of digital signals in your area, you won't get a grainy but watchable picture (as with analogue signals) — you'll get nothing at all. Except snow.

Revision Summary for Module P6

Try these lovely questions. Go on — you know you want to. It'll be nice.

1)   Draw a diagram of a wave and label a crest and a trough, and the wavelength and amplitude.
2)   How do transverse waves differ from longitudinal waves?
3)   What formula connects the speed, frequency and wavelength of a wave?
4)*   Find the speed of a wave with frequency 50 kHz and wavelength 0.3 cm.
5)   'The angle of reflection is always twice the angle of incidence.' True or false?
6)   Do light waves generally travel faster in less dense or more dense substances?
7)   Do sound waves generally travel faster in less dense or more dense substances?
8)   Do water waves travel faster in shallower or deeper water?
9)   Explain what is meant by: a) refraction, b) total internal reflection.
10)* In which of the cases A to D below would the ray of light be totally internally reflected?
      (The critical angle for glass is approximately 42°.)

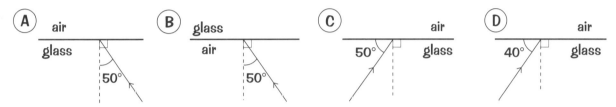

11)   Draw diagrams showing the diffraction of a wave as it passes through: a) a small gap, b) a big gap.
12)   Describe what might happen when two waves with very similar frequencies meet.
13)   What evidence is there that light and sound can be thought of as waves?
14)   Electromagnetic waves don't transfer any matter. What <u>do</u> they transfer?
15)   Sketch the EM spectrum, with all the details you've learned. Put the lowest frequency waves first.
16)   What is it about EM waves that determines their differing properties?
17)   How is the frequency of EM radiation related to the energy carried by its photons?
18)   Define the 'intensity' of a beam of EM radiation.
19)   Why are radio waves good at transmitting information over long distances?
20)   Describe two uses of microwaves.
21)   What are satellite dishes made of? Why?
22)   Explain how X-rays can be useful in hospitals.
23)   Explain how you can tell the difference between an AM signal and an FM signal.
24)   Draw diagrams illustrating analogue and digital signals. What advantages do digital signals have?
25)   'Analogue signals weaken as they travel whereas digital signals do not.' True or false?

* Answers on page 100.

Dealing With Tricky Questions

So, the end of the book is nigh (all good things come to an end). Sadly though, nobody but me will take your word for it that you know loads of stuff now — they tend to <u>check up on you</u> — with <u>exams</u>.

The Exams for Units 1, 2 and 3 are Fairly Straightforward

Most of the questions you'll get in the exam will be pretty straightforward, as long as you've learned your stuff. But there are a few things you need to be aware of that could <u>catch you out</u>...

A Lot of Questions Will be Based on Real-Life Situations...

...so learn to live with it.

All they do is ask you how <u>the science</u> you've learned fits into the <u>real world</u> — that's all.

<u>That chemical reaction</u> you learned <u>still balances</u>... and <u>that graph</u> is still the <u>same shape</u>.

<u>Don't</u> worry that the <u>theory you've learned might not apply</u> in different situations. <u>IT WILL</u>. For example...

> 3. The paper manufacturing industry uses a lot of hydrogen peroxide solution, which is harmful and corrosive.
>
> Describe the safety precautions that should be taken when handling hydrogen peroxide solution.

It doesn't matter if all you know about paper is that it's for writing on. You don't even have to know about hydrogen peroxide. The important bit is what you know about <u>hazard terms</u> and <u>safety measures</u>.

There are Quite a Few Tick-the-Box Questions

The examiners seem fairly keen on questions where you have to choose from <u>options</u> by <u>ticking boxes</u>.

<u>First things first</u> — is it 'TICK' or 'TICK<u>S</u>'?
Check whether you can tick more than one box...
Then look through your options and <u>use what you know</u> to rule out the wrong 'uns.

You're looking for <u>all the statements</u> that are true.

If the thrust force (upwards) equals the weight (acting downwards) there's <u>no resultant force</u> so the shuttle stays stationary — <u>so this can't be right</u>.

The <u>thrust</u> force comes from the shuttle's <u>rockets</u> — you're told this in the question — it's nothing to do with the ground.

This one's <u>true</u> — the resultant force during take-off must be upwards, so the thrust force must be upwards.

This statement is a correct version of the first one — it's <u>true</u>.

> 4. A NASA space shuttle together with its launch rockets weighs 20 300 000 N.
>
> Which of the following statements correctly describe the thrust force that must be supplied by the shuttle's rockets to achieve take-off?
>
> Put ticks in the boxes next to any correct statements.
>
> The rockets must supply 20 300 000 N of thrust. ☐
>
> The thrust force is the reaction of the ground to the shuttle's weight. ☐
>
> The thrust force must act in the opposite direction to the shuttle's weight. ☑
>
> The rockets must supply more than 20 300 000 N of thrust. ☑

If at first you don't succeed — come back to it later...

The questions aren't <u>all</u> multi-choice — you'll have to write answers from scratch for some. But this advice applies to both types — do the straightforward questions first, then come back to the <u>tricky</u> ones.*

Extract Questions

There might be a question in the exam where you have to answer questions about a <u>chunk of text</u>.
If there is, here's what to do....

Questions with Extracts can be Tricky

1) Nowadays, the examiners want you to be able to <u>apply</u> your scientific knowledge, not just recite a load of facts you've learnt. Sneaky.

2) But <u>don't panic</u> — you won't be expected to know stuff you've not been taught.

3) The chunk of text will contain <u>extra info</u> — about real-life applications of science, or details that you haven't been taught. That stuff is there for a reason — <u>for you to use</u> when you're answering the questions.

Here's an idea of what to expect come exam time. Read the article and have a go at the questions.*

Underlining or making notes of the main bits as you read is a good idea.

only power source is a battery

10% of electrical energy (from battery) is wasted

The graph will give you all the information you need, but read the axes carefully — it's a speed-time graph, not distance-time. And remember — 'describe fully' means you should give all the details you can.

For this one you need to apply what you know about motion and forces. Think logically — how many different forces are acting? Are there any balanced pairs of forces?

Some modern electric cars now have better efficiency and performance than conventional models.

The Cumbria-based manufacturer 'Westmoreland' has produced an electric car, the *Joule*, that can accelerate from <u>0 to 100 km/h (28 m/s) in four</u> seconds and has a <u>top speed of about 215 km/h (60 m/s)</u>. The graph below shows its performance during part of a test.

The *Joule* weighs just <u>9800 N</u>. It's powered by an <u>electric motor</u> — so there's no fuel tank, just a <u>rechargeable battery</u>.

The <u>200 kW motor</u> in this latest model is approximately <u>90% efficient</u>. This means that the car can travel almost <u>400 km</u> before the battery needs to be recharged.

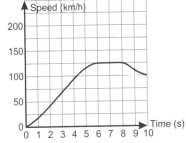

1 Using the graph above, describe fully the car's motion:
   a) between 0 and 6 seconds
   b) between 6 and 10 seconds

2 a) At its top speed, how long would the *Joule* take to travel 1 km?
   b) With the motor working at full power, how much electrical energy would be transferred from the car's battery in this time?

3 The car is driven up a ramp so that it is 10 m vertically above the ground. It is then allowed to roll, from stationary, down the ramp.
   a) Ignoring friction and air resistance, calculate how fast the car will be travelling when it reaches the bottom of the ramp. The car's mass is 980 kg.
   b) On reaching the bottom of the ramp the car gradually slows to a stop. Draw a labelled diagram using arrows to illustrate **all** the forces acting on the car **as it slows down**.

Thinking in an exam — it's not like the old days... *Answers on page 100.

It's scary when they expect you to <u>think</u> in the exam. But questions like this often have some of the answers <u>hidden</u> in the text, which is always a bonus. Just make sure you read <u>carefully</u> and take your <u>time</u>.

Mathematical Skills

Calculation questions are bound to crop up — especially in the physicsy bits of your exams.
So you need to be able to handle formulas, units and standard form...

Formula Triangles Make Rearranging Equations a Doddle

You'll be given some formulas, but not as triangles — so it makes sense to learn how to put formulas into triangles for yourself. There are two easy rules:

1) If the formula is "A = B×C" then A goes on the top and B×C goes on the bottom.
2) If the formula is "A = B/C" then B must go on the top (because that's the only way it'll give "B divided by something") — and so pretty obviously A and C must go on the bottom.

So...

$V = I \times R$
turns into: $\dfrac{V}{I \times R}$

$W = F \times d$
turns into: $\dfrac{W}{F \times d}$

$V = E/Q$
turns into: $\dfrac{E}{V \times Q}$

HOW TO USE THEM: Cover up the thing you want to find and write down what's left showing.
Example: To find Q from the last one, cover up Q and you get E/V left showing, so "Q = E/V".

Standard Form is Great for Very Big and Very Small Numbers

Standard form is a convenient way of writing very big and very small numbers, e.g.

56 000 000 would be written as 5.6×10^7.
0.000 000 56 would be written as 5.6×10^{-7}.

You need to be able to read and write any number in standard form for your exam.

A number in standard form is always written as:

A is a number between 1 and 10 (though not 10 itself). → $A \times 10^n$ ← n is the number of places the decimal point moves. n is positive if the number is big, and negative if the number is small.

EXAMPLE: Write "35 000 N" in standard form.

Write the number out with its decimal point (in this case 35 000.0).
Move the decimal point until you get a number between 1 and 10 (in this case, 3.5).
The decimal point moves 4 places, so n = 4. 35 000 is a big number, so n is positive.
So 35 000 N = 3.5×10^4 N (the units stay the same).

Unit Prefixes are Often Used Instead of Standard Form

In science, numbers will often have units attached.
So, instead of using standard form, you can add a prefix to your unit.

The prefixes you need to know are:

Prefix	milli-	centi-	kilo-	mega-
Symbol	m	c	k	M
Meaning	one thousandth ($\times 10^{-3}$)	one hundredth ($\times 10^{-2}$)	one thousand ($\times 10^3$)	one million ($\times 10^6$)

So, 23 000 Hz could be written as 23 kHz (just divide the number by 1000).
0.0054 s could be written as 5.4 ms (multiply by 1000).
48 500 000 J could be written as 48.5 MJ (divide by 1 000 000).

Drawing and Interpreting Graphs

You'll probably get at least one question in the exam where you have to <u>draw</u> or <u>interpret a graph</u>, e.g. read off some values. This kind of thing can be <u>easy marks</u>, but only if you <u>pay attention</u> to the details.

Look at the <u>Axes and Scales</u> When You're <u>Reading Graphs...</u>

When you're confronted with a graph and you have to answer questions about it, make sure you do all these things:

1) This might seem obvious, but <u>read the question</u> and be sure you know <u>what the graph's about</u>.

2) Jot down or highlight <u>what you're finding out</u>.

3) Read the <u>labels</u> on the axes, including any <u>units</u>. The units can be really important if you have to do <u>calculations</u>.

4) Look at the <u>scales</u> — does each little square stand for 10 units, 0.5 units or what? And <u>don't assume</u> that both axes will have the same scale — they probably <u>won't</u>.

5) Now do the questions... and make sure you <u>show your working</u>. For instance, if you drew lines on the graph to work something out, leave them in.

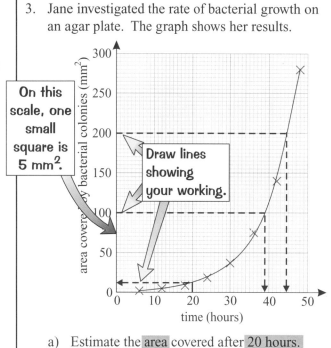

3. Jane investigated the rate of bacterial growth on an agar plate. The graph shows her results.

On this scale, one small square is 5 mm².

Draw lines showing your working.

a) Estimate the area covered after 20 hours.
b) How long does it take the bacteria population to double?

...And <u>Choose Them Sensibly</u> When You <u>Draw Graphs</u>

You might be given some data and asked to draw a graph. Don't rush — read the instructions carefully.

1) You might have to <u>pick your own</u> axes and scales. Remember these pointers:

- Always put the <u>thing that's being investigated</u> on the <u>vertical axis</u> (see the example above).
- <u>Label</u> both axes and give the right <u>units</u>.
- Make your graph as <u>big</u> as possible...
- But <u>don't</u> choose a weird scale like 3 units per square — it'll be a nightmare to plot points.

2) Now you can <u>plot the points</u> as <u>crosses</u>, using a <u>sharp pencil</u>.

3) Think whether any of your points look <u>dodgy</u>. If so, have you made a mistake plotting them — <u>check</u>. Or might they have been caused by experimental error...?

4) ...in which case you can ignore them when you're drawing a <u>line of best fit</u> or a <u>smooth curve</u>. (Don't rub dodgy points out — just ignore them when you're thinking where to put the line or curve).

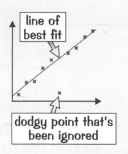

line of best fit

dodgy point that's been ignored

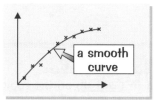

a smooth curve

5) Remember, for graphs in science you <u>don't</u> <u>have to go through all the points</u>. But you <u>do</u> have to use a <u>pencil</u>. And unless you're a fan of <u>throwing away marks for no good</u> <u>reason at all</u>, use a <u>ruler</u> for straight lines.

Exam Skills — Paper Four

Paper Four is known as 'Ideas In Context'. It's a bit odd — but no odder than, say, beetroot.

You'll be Given Some Material in Advance

Before the exam you'll be given a booklet containing some articles that you'll be examined on. Don't just stuff it in the bottom of your bag with your PE kit — start working on it straight away.

The articles could be on any science topic that's related to the material on the specification. They could well be about something that's been in the news recently, or you could get an article about how scientific understanding has developed over time.

So, don't be surprised if some of them seem a bit wacky — they will be related to the stuff you've learned — it might just take you a while to figure out how...

Start work as soon as you get the booklet

1) Read all the articles carefully and slowly
   — take your time and make sure you understand everything.

2) Look up any words that you don't know.

3) If there are any graphs, tables or figures in the articles then study them carefully. Identify any trends and make sure you know what they show.

4) You don't need to do any extra research on the topics but if you're struggling with the material then a bit of extra reading might help you to understand it — try textbooks and internet searches. Don't get too carried away though — you shouldn't need any extra knowledge to answer the questions.

5) Although you don't need to do research you do need to make sure you've revised the topics that the articles are about. So if there's one about running marathons in hot climates, make sure you've revised homeostasis really thoroughly, in all its glorious detail.

6) Remember to do all of the above for all of the articles — you'll have to answer questions on all of them in the exam.

7) It's a good idea to highlight important things in the booklet and make some notes as you go along, but remember that you can't take the booklet into the exam.

There'll be a mixture of questions in the exam

When you get to the exam you'll be given another copy of the articles, and some questions to go with them.

1) For some of the questions you'll need to extract information from the articles (see page 93).

2) Other questions will be about analysing data or information in the articles (see pages 93-95).

3) Other questions will ask you about related topics from the specification — but you won't be expected to know anything that isn't on the specification or in the article.

I'd prefer an exam where you get the questions in advance...

Paper 4 should hold no fears, providing you've used the time before the exam to swot up on the topics that are covered in the articles. If you're the type who watches the news and stuff then chances are you'll be familiar with some of the issues before you even get the booklet. Even so, get swotting...

Index

Index

F

fats 44
feedback mechanism 2, 6
fertilisers 69
filtration 76
fizzing 16
flame tests 13
fluorine 17
FM (frequency modulation) 89
food 3
forces 25-31
formula triangles 94
fossil fuels 48
frequency 83, 84, 87-90
friction 25, 50

G

gametes 35
gas syringes 81
generators 56
genes 33, 36, 37
global dimming 48
graphs, drawing and interpreting 95
gravitational potential energy (G.P.E.) 31
Group 1 14, 16
Group 7 14, 17
groups in the periodic table 14
guanine 33

H

haematite 45
hallucinations 7
halogens 14, 17
hazard symbols 18
heat energy 6
heat stroke 7
homeostasis 1
hormones 9, 61
hot climates 1
hydrochloric acid 71
hydrogen 16, 71
hydrosphere 42
hydroxides 16
hypothalamus 6
hypothermia 7

I

incubators 2
indicators, pH 16, 70, 77
induced voltage 56
infrared 88
intensity 87
interaction pairs 25
interference 86, 90
iodine 17
ionic bonding 19, 42
ionic compounds 42
   formulas 20
ions 11, 19, 20, 40, 42, 43, 46, 47
iron 79
iron core 56, 57

J

Jimbo 88
joules (J) 29-31, 58, 59

K

kidneys 1, 4, 8, 9
kilowatt-hours 58
kilowatts 58
kinetic energy 30, 31

L

landfill 48
language development 66
LDR (light-dependent resistor) 53
learning 63-67
light 83, 85-88
line of best fit 95
line spectrums 13
lithium 13
lithosphere 43
lock and key model 5
longitudinal waves 83

M

magnets 56
mains electricity 56, 57
malleability 47
mass 27, 28, 30
meiosis 35

measuring rates of reaction 81
melting points 16, 17, 40, 42, 43
membranes, cell 34
memory 66, 67
meristems 37
metals 14, 16, 45-48, 71, 72
   metal hydroxides 72
   metallic bonds 47
   metal oxides 72
microwave ovens 88
microwaves 88
minerals 43, 45
mitosis 34, 35
molecular substances 40
momentum 27, 28
motion 26, 28
motorcycle helmets 28
motor neurons 61, 63
mountain climbing 1
MRI (magnetic resonance imaging) scans 67

N

naming salts 71
negative feedback 2, 6, 9
nervous system 61-66
neurones 61-63, 65
neutralisation 70-72, 77
neutrons 11, 14
newborn babies 63
nitrate salts 71
nitric acid 71
nitrogen oxides 71
noble gases 14
noise, in a signal 90
nucleotides 33, 34
nucleus 11, 33

O

optical fibres 85
orbits, of electrons 11, 15
organelles 33, 34
osmosis 4
oxygen 1, 3, 40, 44, 46

Index

Index

Answers

Bottom of page 20

a) MgO

b) Li_2O

c) Na_2SO_4

Revision Summary for Module C4 (page 21)

3) a) $2Na + Cl_2 \rightarrow 2NaCl$

b) $2K + 2H_2O \rightarrow 2KOH + H_2$

11) 8

26) 2+

27) a) FeO

b) $FeCl_3$

c) CaO

d) Na_2CO_3

Revision Summary for Module P4 (page 32)

2) a) $3.2 \div 35 = 0.091$ m/s (to 3 d.p.)

b) $0.091 \times 25 \times 60 = 137$ m

3) $6.3 \div 0.5 = 12.6$ m/s

The car wasn't breaking the speed limit.

19) Momentum = mass $\times$ velocity

$= 78 \times 5 = 390$ kg m/s

22) $535 \times 12 = 6420$ J

24) $120 \times 4.5 = 540$ J

25) 150 kJ

26) K.E. $= 0.5 \times 600 \times 40^2 = 480\ 000$ J

$480\ 000 \div 6000 = 80$ m

27) G.P.E. $= 200 \times 50 = 10\ 000$ J

$v^2 = (10\ 000 \times 2) \div 20 = 1000$

$v = 31.6$ m/s (to 1 d.p.)

Revision Summary for Module C5 (page 49)

5)

```
    H H
    | |
H - C - C - H
    | |
    H H
```

19) Percentage mass of aluminium $= [(27 \times 2) \div 102] \times 100$

$= 53\%$

Mass of aluminium $= (53 \div 100) \times 400 = 212$ g

Revision Summary for Module P5 (page 60)

11) $12 \div 2.5 = 4.8\ \Omega$

13) $A_1 = 0.2$ A, $V_1 = 1.4$ V, $V_2 = 0.4$ V, $V_3 = 10.2$ V,

$R_1 = 51\ \Omega$

18) 0.4 A

24) $V_s/V_p = N_s/N_p$ so $V_s = (600/20) \times 9 = 30 \times 9 = 270$ V

27) $2100 \times (1.5 \times 60) = 189\ 000$ J

28) $0.1 \times (1 + 50 \div 60) \times 8 = 1.5$p (to 1 d.p.)

30) $(70 \div 100) \times 100 = 70\%$

Bottom of page 74

1) Cu = 63.5, K = 39, Kr = 84, Cl = 35.5

2) NaOH = 40, HNO_3 = 63, KCl = 74.5, $CaCO_3$ = 100

Bottom of page 75

1) 21.4 g

2) 38 g

Revision Summary for Module C6 (page 82)

14) a) 40

b) 108

c) 44

d) 84

e) 78

f) 81

g) 106

h) 58.5

15) a)

$2Mg$	+	O_2	$\rightarrow$	$2MgO$
48				80
1 g				1.6667 g
112.1 g				186.8 g

b)

$2Na$	+	O_2	$\rightarrow$	Na_2O
46				62
0.742 g				1 g
80.3 g				108.2 g

22) $(0.479 \div 0.5) \times 100 = 95.8\%$

25) Faster, because the acid is more concentrated.

Bottom of page 83

1) speed $= (1.9 \times 10^4) \times 0.125 = 2375$ m/s

Revision Summary for Module P6 (page 91)

4) $50\ 000 \times 0.003 = 150$ m/s

10) A and D

Extract Questions (page 93)

1 a) The car is accelerating.

b) It travels at a constant speed (125 km/h) for just under two seconds, then decelerates/slows down.

2 a) 1000 m $\div 60$ m/s $= 16.\dot{6} = 16.7$ s (to 1 d.p.)

b) $200\ 000$ W $\times 16.\dot{6}$ s $= 3\ 333\ 333$ J (≈ 3.3 MJ)

(assuming no energy is lost between the battery and the motor)

3 a) G.P.E. $= 9800 \times 10 = 98\ 000$ J

$v^2 = (98\ 000 \times 2) \div 980 = 200$

$v = 14.1$ m/s (to 1 d.p.)

b)

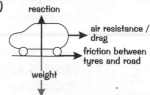

Note: Vertical forces: weight and reaction of ground are equal and opposite.

GCSE AQA

German

German revision can feel like a Black Forest, but with this brilliant CGP book you'll be out of the woods in no time! It's packed with all the study notes and practice questions you'll need for the Grade 9-1 exams in 2018 and beyond!

We've also included **free audio files** to go with the listening questions. You'll find them on the CD-ROM — or you can download them from this page:

www.cgpbooks.co.uk/GCSEGermanAudio

How to access your free Online Edition

You can read this entire book on your PC, Mac or tablet, with handy links to all the online audio files. Just go to **cgpbooks.co.uk/extras** and enter this code:

0376 4644 0105 3855

By the way, this code only works for one person. If somebody else has used this book before you, they might have already claimed the Online Edition.

Complete
Revision & Practice
<u>Everything</u> you need to pass the exams!

Contents

Contents

Published by CGP

Editors:
Izzy Bowen
Lucy Forsyth
Rose Jones
Cathy Lear
Heather McClelland
Ali Palin

Contributors:
Angela Blacklock-Brown
Miriam Mentel
Ben Merritt
Gaynor Tilley

With thanks to Glenn Rogers, Rachael Rogers, Pat Dunn, Margit Grassick and Peter Tyson for the proofreading.
With thanks to Ana Pungartnik for the copyright research.

Acknowledgements:

Audio produced by Naomi Laredo of Small Print.

Recorded, edited and mastered by Graham Williams of The Speech Recording Studio,
with the assistance of Andy Le Vien at RMS Studios.

Voice Artists:
Bernd Bauermeister
Oliver Janesh Christiansen
Lena Lohmann
Indira Varma

CD-ROM edited and mastered by Neil Hastings.

AQA material is reproduced by permission of AQA.

With thanks to iStock.com for permission to use the images on pages 35, 52, 73, 93, 100, 168 & 177.

Abridged and adapted extract from 'Effi Briest', on page 21, by Theodor Fontane.

Abridged and adapted extract from 'Der Wolf und die sieben jungen Geißlein', on page 56, by the Brothers Grimm.

Abridged and adapted extract from 'Der geduldige Mann', on page 180, by Johann Peter Hebel.

Abridged and adapted extract from 'Weihnachtszauber', on page 181, by Adolf Schwayer.

Abridged and adapted extract from 'Kasperle auf Reisen', on page 218 and in audio tracks, by Josephine Siebe.

ISBN: 978 1 78294 554 3
Printed by Elanders Ltd, Newcastle upon Tyne.
Clipart from Corel®

Numbers and Quantities

There are no two ways about it, you've got to know the numbers — so get cracking.

Eins, zwei, drei — One, two, three

0	null	13	dreizehn		
1	eins	14	vierzehn		
2	zwei	15	fünfzehn		
3	drei	16	sechzehn		
4	vier	17	siebzehn	21	einundzwanzig
5	fünf	18	achtzehn	22	zweiundzwanzig
6	sechs	19	neunzehn	23	dreiundzwanzig
7	sieben				
8	acht				
9	neun				
10	zehn				
11	elf				
12	zwölf				

The teens use numbers three to nine with 'ten' on the end — so thirteen is 'three' and 'ten' stuck together ('drei' + 'zehn'). But watch out — 16 and 17 are a bit different.

You say the in-between numbers backwards — 'one and twenty' for 'twenty-one'.

20	zwanzig	60	sechzig	100	hundert
30	dreißig	70	siebzig	1000	tausend
40	vierzig	80	achtzig	2000	zweitausend
50	fünfzig	90	neunzig	1 000 000	eine Million

For years before 2000, you say, e.g. 'neunzehnhundert...' (*nineteen hundred...*). For a 'normal' number, not a year, you say 'tausendneunhundert...' (*one thousand, nine hundred...*).

1967 neunzehnhundertsiebenundsechzig
2005 zweitausendfünf

Erste, zweite, dritte — First, second, third

1) For most numbers between 1 and 19, add '-te'. The exceptions are in blue.

2) From 20 onwards, just add '-ste'.

The article won't always be 'das'

1st	das erste	8th	das achte
2nd	das zweite	9th	das neunte
3rd	das dritte	10th	das zehnte
4th	das vierte	20th	das zwanzigste
5th	das fünfte	21st	das einundzwanzigste
6th	das sechste	70th	das siebzigste
7th	das siebte	100th	das hundertste

In German, '1st' is written '1.'.

Grammar — number endings

The endings of number words change depending on the case of the noun. See p.108-109 for more on cases.

Ich möchte den ersten Hund.
I would like the first dog.

Wie viele? — How many?

einige	*some / a few*	eine Menge	*a lot of / lots of*
mehrere	*several*	ein Dutzend	*a dozen*
viele	*many*	ein paar	*a few*

Ich habe genug Äpfel.
I have enough apples.

Der Bäcker hat anderthalb Brötchen.
The baker has one-and-a-half rolls.

In German, you say the small number first, e.g. 'one and forty'...

Read this text and then answer the questions in German — write the numbers out in full.

Heinrich ist neunzehn Jahre alt. Er hat zwei Schwestern, die siebzehn und fünfundzwanzig Jahre alt sind. Ihre Großmutter ist achtundneunzig Jahre alt — fast ein Jahrhundert!

e.g. Wie alt ist Heinrich? **Er ist neunzehn Jahre alt.**
1. Wie alt sind Heinrichs Schwestern? [1]
2. Wie alt ist ihre Großmutter? [1]
3. Wie viel älter ist ihre Großmutter als Heinrich? [1]

Times and Dates

You have to know how to say the time, as well as the days and months — examiners just love this stuff.

Wie viel Uhr ist es? — What time is it?

1) There are lots of ways to <u>ask the time</u> and <u>say the time</u> in German. You'll need to get the hang of them.

Wie viel Uhr ist es?	*What time is it?*		Wie spät ist es?	*What time is it?*

2) Here are some <u>responses</u> to questions about the time. Learn to understand and use them yourself.

Something <u>o'clock</u>

Es ist ein Uhr.	*It's 1 o'clock.*
Es ist zwei Uhr.	*It's 2 o'clock.*
Es ist zwanzig Uhr.	*It's 8pm.*

'<u>Quarter to</u>' and '<u>past</u>', '<u>half past</u>'

Viertel nach zwei	*quarter past two*
halb drei	*half past two*
Viertel vor drei	*quarter to three*

Be careful — 'halb drei' means 'half to three' (i.e. half past two), not 'half past three'.

'<u>... past</u>' and '<u>... to</u>'

zwanzig nach sieben	*twenty past seven*
fünf nach acht	*five past eight*
zehn vor zwei	*ten to two*

The <u>24-hour</u> clock

drei Uhr vierzehn	*03:14*
zwanzig Uhr zweiunddreißig	*20:32*
neunzehn Uhr fünfundfünfzig	*19:55*

Die Woche — The week

Montag	*Monday*
Dienstag	*Tuesday*
Mittwoch	*Wednesday*
Donnerstag	*Thursday*
Freitag	*Friday*
Samstag	*Saturday*
Sonntag	*Sunday*

Grammar — on Mondays

To say '<u>on Monday</u>', use '<u>Montag</u>' or '<u>am Montag</u>'.

To talk about something that happens regularly '<u>on Mondays</u>', use '<u>montags</u>'. Use the other days in the same way.

heute	*today*
morgen	*tomorrow*
gestern	*yesterday*
übermorgen	*the day after tomorrow*
vorgestern	*the day before yesterday*
die Woche	*week*
das Wochenende	*weekend*

Januar, Februar, März, April...

Januar	*January*	Juli	*July*
Februar	*February*	August	*August*
März	*March*	September	*September*
April	*April*	Oktober	*October*
Mai	*May*	November	*November*
Juni	*June*	Dezember	*December*

die Jahreszeit	*season*
der Frühling	*spring*
der Sommer	*summer*
der Herbst	*autumn*
der Winter	*winter*

Ich fahre im August mit meiner Familie nach Köln.	*I'm going to Cologne in August with my family.*
Es gab letzten Winter viel Eis und Schnee.	*There was lots of ice and snow last winter.*

in March — im März
this summer — diesen Sommer

on Wednesday — am Mittwoch
the day before yesterday — vorgestern

Times and Dates

You can put it all together to say the date. You can also say how often you do things.

Der Wievielte ist heute? — What's the date today?

Watch out for dates in German — make sure you use the correct case. See p.108-109 for more on cases.

In German, a date is written as a number with a dot after it. Der 4. April is said 'der vierte April'.

Es ist der 4. April. — It's the 4th April. — the 8th June — der 8. Juni

Ich komme am 20. Oktober. — I'm coming on the 20th October. — on the 14th August — am 14. August

You say this as 'am vierzehnten August'. This ending is used because it's in the dative case.

Morgen — Tomorrow... Gestern — Yesterday...

heute Morgen	this morning
heute Abend	this evening
morgen früh	tomorrow morning
diese Woche	this week
letzte Woche	last week
alle zwei Wochen	every two weeks
jeden Tag	every day
am Wochenende	at the weekend
neulich	recently
selten	rarely, seldom

Carolina ging letzte Woche in die Bibliothek.
Carolina went to the library last week.

Question

Wie oft fährst du mit dem Bus?
How often do you travel by bus?

Simple Answer

Ich fahre jeden Tag mit dem Bus.
I travel by bus every day.

Extended Answer

Ich fahre jeden Tag mit dem Bus zur Schule. Wenn das Wetter aber schön ist, fahre ich lieber mit dem Fahrrad.
I travel by bus every day to get to school. But when the weather's nice, I prefer to cycle.

Sentences can start with a time phrase...

...but if they do, remember to switch the word order.

Um Viertel nach zwei habe ich eine Prüfung.
At quarter past two, I have an exam. — At half past ten — Um halb elf

Montags besuchen wir unsere Großmutter.
On Mondays, we visit our grandmother. — Every two weeks — Alle zwei Wochen

Am 12. Juni zweitausendsiebzehn werde ich nach Irland fahren.
On the 12th of June 2017, I will go to Ireland. — At the weekend — Am Wochenende

See p.1 for help with writing numbers.

If you start a sentence with a time phrase, put the verb second...

Helena, Jan and Lisa are catching up on what they've been doing. Listen to what they have to say and answer the questions in **English**.

e.g. When did Helena go to the museum? on Saturday
1. Who did she go to the museum with? [1]
2. What did she think of the exhibits? [1]
3. What did Helena do the day before yesterday? [1]
4. What did Jan do at the weekend? [1]
5. How often does he play with his team? [1]
6. When is Jan's birthday? [1]
7. Where will they go for the party? [1]

4

Questions

You've got to be able to understand questions. You'll have to ask them too.

Wann? Wo? Warum — When? Where? Why?

wann?	*when?*	wohin?	*where (to)?*	wie viele?	*how many?*
warum?	*why?*	woher?	*where (from)?*	was?	*what?*
wieso?	*why?*	wie?	*how?*	wer / wen / wem?	*who / whom?*
wo?	*where?*	wie viel?	*how much?*	welche/r/s?	*which (one)?*

See p.129 for when to use 'wer / wen / wem' and p.120 for more about 'welche'.

Wohin fährst du in Urlaub?
Where are you going on holiday?

Wie viel Geld hast du?
How much money do you have?

Warum kommt Hannelore nicht?
Why isn't Hannelore coming?

Mit wem sprichst du?
With whom are you talking?

Reverse word order to ask a question

To ask a question, just <u>change the word order</u>.

Ich kann mitkommen.
I can come along.
→
Kann ich mitkommen?
Can I come along?

Dein Bruder kommt auch.
Your brother is coming too.
→
Kommt dein Bruder auch?
Is your brother coming too?

Grammar — questions

In English, you change '<u>I can go</u>' to '<u>Can I go?</u>' to make it into a question — you can in German too.
Put the <u>verb first</u> and then the <u>verb's subject</u> to show it's a question.

'Wo' can mean 'where', but it sometimes means 'what'

You can write '<u>wo</u>' in front of some <u>prepositions</u> to make lots of handy question words.

<u>Womit</u> schreibst du?
<u>Worauf</u> läuft er?
<u>Worüber</u> sprechen Sie?
<u>Wozu</u> brauche ich es?

<u>What</u> are you writing <u>with</u>?
<u>What</u> is he walking <u>on</u>?
<u>What</u> are you talking <u>about</u>?
<u>What</u> do I need it <u>for</u>?

P.130-131 has more on prepositions.

Grammar — prepositions

If the preposition starts with a <u>vowel</u> — like '<u>über</u>' or '<u>auf</u>' — you need to add an '<u>r</u>' <u>between</u> it and the '<u>wo</u>'.

Learn how to say 'isn't it?'

The most common words used for this are '<u>nicht (wahr)?</u>', '<u>ja?</u>' and '<u>oder?</u>'. Just stick them on the end of a statement with a comma first and put a question mark on the end.

Gut, nicht?
Good, isn't it?

Es ging gut, ja?
It went well, didn't it?

Du schlugst die Fliege, oder?
You hit the fly, didn't you?

Questions

In the speaking exam, you'll have to ask a question — a chance to quiz your teacher, finally.

Darf ich eine Frage stellen? — May I ask a question?

It's time to put the question words from page 4 into practice.

Wann kommt Emilie?
When is Emilie coming?

Warum bist du müde?
Why are you tired?

Wo ist unser Lehrer?
Where is our teacher?

Wie sagt man das auf Deutsch?
How do you say that in German?

Wie viel kostet es?
How much does it cost?

Verkaufen Sie Briefmarken?
Do you sell postage stamps?

Weißt du die Antwort?
Do you know the answer?

Hast du ein Fahrrad?
Do you have a bicycle?

Spielt ihr Tennis?
Are you playing tennis?

Woher kommen sie?
Where do they come from?

Möchten Sie eine Tüte?
Would you like a bag?

Müssen wir tanzen?
Do we have to dance?

Darf ich mehr Milch haben?
May I have more milk?

Soll sie das machen?
Should she do that?

Willst du Spanisch lernen?
Do you want to learn Spanish?

Question

Wie viele Schüler gibt es in deiner Klasse?

How many pupils are there in your class?

Simple Answer

Es gibt fünfundzwanzig Schüler.
There are twenty-five pupils.

Extended Answer

Es gibt fünfundzwanzig Schüler in meiner Klasse.
Es gibt zehn Mädchen und fünfzehn Jungen.

There are twenty-five pupils in my class.
There are ten girls and fifteen boys.

In meiner Klasse gibt es nur vierzehn Schüler.
Meine Klasse ist ziemlich klein, nicht wahr?

In my class there are only fourteen pupils.
My class is quite small, isn't it?

You need to be able to understand and ask questions...

Here's a role-play that Finn did with his teacher.

Teacher: Was ist dein Lieblingssport, Finn?

Finn: Ich mag Eishockey.

Teacher: Das ist **ungewöhnlich**[1]. Spielst du das oft?

Finn: Ich spiele Eishockey jeden Samstag.

Teacher: Du musst sehr gut sein. Was denkst du über Sport?

Finn: Meiner Meinung nach ist Sport sehr gut für die **Gesundheit**[2]. Es macht auch viel Spaß. Und Sie, mögen Sie Sport?

Teacher: Nicht so sehr — ich bin nicht sportlich.

Finn: Was machen Sie in Ihrer **Freizeit**[3]?

Teacher: Ich koche sehr gern für meine Freunde.

Grade 6-7

[1]unusual
[2]health
[3]free-time

See p.152 for more tips on the role-play.

Tick list:
✓ tenses: present
✓ opinion phrase
✓ correct time phrase
✓ correctly formed question

To improve:
+ add a few more complex structures, e.g. weil, dass

Use the instructions below to prepare your own role-play. Address your teacher as 'Sie' and speak for about two minutes. *[15 marks]*

Du sprichst mit deinem Lehrer über Sport.
• *Lieblingssport — was*
• *wie oft*
• *!*
• *? Meinung über Sport*
• *Freizeit verbringen — wie*

'!' means you'll need to answer a question you haven't prepared. When you see '?', you need to ask a question.

Being Polite

Being polite helps you make friends and get marks. It's a win-win situation, so it's time to turn on the charm.

Learn how to start and end a conversation

To <u>reply</u> to a greeting, just <u>say it back</u>. If someone says 'Guten Tag' to you, say 'Guten Tag' to them.

Guten Morgen	*Good morning*	Auf Wiedersehen	*Goodbye*
Guten Tag	*Good day*	Bis bald	*See you later*
Guten Abend	*Good evening*	Tschüss	*Bye (informal)*
Grüß dich	*Hello (informal)*	Auf Wiederhören	*Goodbye*

'Auf Wiederhören' is used for ending telephone conversations.

Wie geht's? — How are you?

Grammar — formal and informal 'you'

There are <u>four</u> different ways to say '<u>you</u>' in German:

Informal 'you'

① Use '<u>du</u>' for a person who's a member of your <u>family</u>, a <u>friend</u>, or someone <u>your own age</u>.

② Use '<u>ihr</u>' for <u>two or more</u> people that you <u>know</u> well.

Formal 'you'

③ Use '<u>Sie</u>' for someone you <u>don't know</u>, or someone <u>important</u>, or someone <u>older</u> than you.

④ '<u>Sie</u>' is also used for a group of <u>two or more</u> people you <u>don't know</u>.

'Wie geht es (dir)?' is often shortened to 'Wie geht's?'.

Wie geht es dir?	*How are you? (inf.)*
Wie geht es Ihnen?	*How are you? (frml.)*
Wie geht es euch?	*How are you? (inf. plu.)*

Mir geht's...	*I'm...*
...(sehr) gut.	*...(very) well.*
...klasse / super.	*...great.*
...nicht so gut.	*...not so well.*
...(sehr) schlecht.	*...(very) ill.*

Here's what these short forms mean:
inf. — informal
frml. — formal
plu. — plural
If you see 'sing.', it means 'singular'.

Ich hätte gern — I would like

1) It's more polite to say '<u>ich hätte gern</u>' (*I would like*) than '<u>ich will</u>' (*I want*).

2) Here's how to say you would like <u>a thing</u>:

Ich hätte gern das Salz.
I would like the salt.

a coffee — einen Kaffee
a book — ein Buch

See p.147 for more info on the grammar behind these phrases.

3) Here's how to say you would like <u>to do</u> something:

Sie würden gern lesen.
They would like to read.

to chat — plaudern
to travel — reisen

Ich würde gern singen.
I would like to sing.

to fly — fliegen
to paint — malen

Darf ich — May I

Use '<u>darf ich</u>' rather than '<u>kann ich</u>' to ask for something. It's a <u>bit more polite</u>.

Darf ich die Milch haben?   *May I have the milk?*
Darf ich mich hinsetzen?   *May I sit down?*

the newspaper — die Zeitung
the scissors — die Schere
play with you — mitspielen
have something to drink — etwas zu trinken haben

Being Polite

Introducing yourself properly is really important. Apologising is too, so learn these polite phrases.

Darf ich Petra vorstellen? — May I introduce Petra?

Dies ist Petra.	*This is Petra.*
Herzlich willkommen!	*Welcome!*
Schön, es freut mich, Sie kennen zu lernen.	*Pleased to meet you. (frml.)*
Kommen Sie herein. Setzen Sie sich.	*Come in. Sit down. (frml.)*

Bitte und danke — Please and thank you

1) When someone says '<u>danke</u>', it's polite to say '<u>bitte</u>' or '<u>bitte schön</u>'.

bitte	*please*
danke / danke schön	*thank you*
bitte schön / bitte sehr	*you're welcome*
nichts zu danken	*it was nothing*

2) Learn these <u>phrases</u> too:

Alles Gute!	*All the best!*
Prost!	*Cheers!*
Viel Glück!	*Good luck!*

Es tut mir leid — I'm sorry

If you find yourself lost or you make a disastrous gaffe, don't worry — we've got some phrases for you.

Es tut mir leid.	*I'm sorry. (when you've done something wrong)*
Entschuldigung / Entschuldigen Sie!	*Excuse me. (when you want to ask someone something)*

Herzlich willkommen, Jens. Kommen Sie herein. Es tut mir leid, dass ich nicht da war.

Welcome, Jens. Come in. I'm sorry that I wasn't there. ← If you're using the informal 'you', say 'Komm herein' instead.

Kein Problem. Es freut mich, Sie kennen zu lernen. Danke für die Einladung. Das war nett von Ihnen.

No problem. Pleased to meet you. And thank you for the invitation. That was nice of you. ← To say 'that was nice of you' to a friend, use 'dir' instead of 'Ihnen'.

 ## Use 'du' for people your own age, your friends and your family...

Lisa has asked Josef to play in a football match on Sunday. Josef sends this email reply.

Liebe Lisa,

wie geht's? Danke, dass du mich gefragt hast, am Sonntag in der Fußballmannschaft zu spielen.

Ich würde sehr gern Fußball spielen, aber ich habe meinen Fuß **verletzt**[1]. Er ist nicht **schwer**[2] verletzt, aber ich darf keinen Sport machen.

Ich möchte aber die Mannschaft **unterstützen**[3]. Wie viel kosten die Tickets? Darf ich am Sonntag mit dir zum Fußballplatz fahren?

Es tut mir leid, dass ich nicht mitspielen kann.

Bis bald,

Josef

Grade 6-7

[1] injured
[2] badly
[3] support

Tick list:
- ✓ variety of polite phrases
- ✓ correct forms of address
- ✓ correctly formed questions
- ✓ correct word order

To improve:
- + develop each idea a bit further
- + vary sentence structure more

Josef feiert seinen Geburtstag. Du schreibst ihm eine E-Mail. Schreib, dass du zu seiner Geburtstagsfeier nicht kommen kannst. Du musst ungefähr **40** Wörter auf **Deutsch** schreiben. *[8 marks]*

Opinions

To get a decent mark, you've got to say what you think about things — anything from football to food.

Magst du...? — Do you like...?

> The verb comes straight after 'Meiner Meinung nach' (see p.114), and it goes to the end after 'dass' (see p.116).

Was hältst du von...?	*What do you think of...?*
Wie findest du...?	*How do you find...?*
Was denkst du über...?	*What do you think about...?*
Denkst du das auch?	*Do you agree?*
Was meinst du?	*What do you think?*

Meiner Meinung nach...	*In my opinion...*
Ich denke, dass...	*I think that...*
Ich halte ... für...	*I think... is...*
Ich bin für...	*I am in favour of...*

Wie findest du Fußball?	*How do you find football?*
Ich meine, dass Fußball spannend ist.	*I think that football's exciting.*

What do you think of — Was hältst du von

I believe that — Ich glaube, dass

Deine Meinung — Your opinion

Ich mag... (nicht)	*I (don't) like...*
Ich liebe...	*I love...*
Ich interessiere mich für...	*I'm interested in...*
Ich finde... toll.	*I find... great.*
Ich stimme zu.	*I agree.*

...interessiert mich nicht.	*...doesn't interest me.*
Ich hasse...	*I hate...*
Ich bin gegen...	*I am against...*
Ich bin (nicht) für...	*I am (not) in favour of...*
Das stimmt (nicht).	*That's (not) right.*

Grammar — ...gefällt mir (nicht)

'Das gefällt mir' means 'I like that'.
'Gefallen' is a dative verb, so you need to use the dative case for articles and pronouns.

Fußball gefällt mir.	***I like football.***
Putzen gefällt mir nicht.	***I don't like cleaning.***

Diese Zeitschrift interessiert mich nicht.	
This magazine doesn't interest me.	

Ich halte sie für langweilig.	
I think it is boring.	

If you've got a masculine or a neuter noun, you need 'ihn' or 'es' instead.

You might **not** have an opinion on something, so use one of these phrases to sit on the fence:

Ich bin mir nicht sicher.	*I'm not sure.*	Es geht.	*It's all right.*
Ich bin dafür und dagegen.	*I'm for and against it.*	Es ist mir egal.	*I don't mind / care.*

Ich spiele lieber Tennis — I prefer to play tennis

You can add more detail by saying what you prefer. Just put in 'lieber'.

Fisch schmeckt mir nicht.	*I don't like fish.*
Ich esse lieber Fleisch.	*I'd rather eat meat.*

cheese — Käse

Ulrich spielt gern Schach.	*Ulrich likes playing chess.*
Aber er treibt lieber Sport.	*But he prefers to do sport.*

he prefers to listen to music — er hört lieber Musik

Wir hassen Hausaufgaben.	*We hate homework.*
Wir sehen lieber fern.	*We prefer to watch TV.*

We prefer to go to the cinema — Wir gehen lieber ins Kino

Opinions

This is your chance to rant about that band you hate or that film you really can't stand.

Common opinion topics

dieses Buch	*this book*
diese Zeitschrift	*this magazine*
diese Zeitung	*this newspaper*
diese Fernsehsendung	*this TV programme*
dieser Film	*this film*
dieser Schauspieler / diese Schauspielerin	*this actor / this actress*
diese Musik	*this music*
diese Band	*this band*
dieser Sänger / diese Sängerin	*this male / female singer*
diese Mannschaft	*this team*
dieses Café	*this cafe*
dieses Restaurant	*this restaurant*

Question

Was hältst du von diesem Film?
What do you think of this film?

Simple Answer

Dieser Film ist prima.
This film is great.

Extended Answer

Dieser Film ist prima, weil die Schauspieler gut sind.
This film is great because the actors are good.

Toll — Great... Furchtbar — Terrible...

Use lots of different, interesting <u>adjectives</u> to say what you think about things and pick up plenty of marks.

toll / prima	*great*	amüsant / lustig	*amusing / funny*	anstrengend	*strenuous*
gut	*good*	wunderbar	*wonderful*	kompliziert	*complicated*
schön	*lovely*	spannend	*exciting*	furchtbar / schlimm	*terrible*
wunderschön	*beautiful*	interessant	*interesting*	schlecht / schlimm	*bad*
freundlich	*friendly*	nett	*nice (person)*	entsetzlich	*terrible*
ausgezeichnet	*excellent*	(un)sympathisch	*(not) likeable (person)*	langweilig	*boring*
fantastisch	*fantastic*	billig	*cheap*	schwierig	*difficult*
fabelhaft	*fabulous*	entspannend	*relaxing*	teuer	*expensive*

Ich mag diese Band. Ich finde sie toll.
I like this band. I find it great.

Der Rock gefällt mir. Er ist sehr schick.
I like the skirt. It's very smart.

Learn positive and negative adjectives to give your opinions...

Katrin and Julia are talking about the theatre. Read the text and answer the questions in **English**.

Katrin: Am Samstag gehe ich ins Theater, um ein Theaterstück **anzusehen**[1]. Gehst du gern ins Theater?

Julia: Nein, ich finde es sehr langweilig. Ich bekomme nie einen guten Sitzplatz und sehe also nicht, was die Schauspieler machen.

Katrin: Ja, wenn man aber die **Bühne**[2] gut sehen kann, ist das Theater interessant. Man lernt viel über das Leben.

Julia: Das ist wahr, aber ich gehe lieber ins Kino. Ich liebe Liebesfilme. Du auch?

Katrin: Liebesfilme interessieren mich nicht. Ich halte sie für unrealistisch.

[1] to watch
[2] stage

e.g. When is Katrin going to the theatre?
on Saturday

1. Why does Julia dislike the theatre? [1]
2. What problem does Julia often have at the theatre? [1]
3. Why does Katrin like to watch plays? [1]
4. What would Julia prefer to see? [1]
5. What does Katrin think of romantic films? [1]

Opinions

You've got to explain your views for the best marks. Add one of these nifty words to extend your sentences.

'Weil' — Because

'Weil' means '<u>because</u>'. When you use '<u>weil</u>', the <u>verb</u> in that part of the sentence gets shoved to the <u>end</u>.

Der Film gefällt mir. Er ist interessant.
I like the film. It is interesting.

➡ Der Film gefällt mir, weil er interessant ist.
I like the film because it is interesting.

Ich finde sie sehr nett. Sie ist freundlich.
I find her very nice. She is friendly.

➡ Ich finde sie sehr nett, weil sie freundlich ist.
I find her very nice because she is friendly.

'Denn' — Because

> You've always got to put a comma before 'weil' and 'denn'.

'Denn' means '<u>because</u>' too, but it <u>doesn't</u> change the word order.

Ich mag ihn, denn er ist wirklich nett.
I like him because he is really nice.

Ich liebe dieses Buch, denn es ist sehr spannend.
I love this book because it is very exciting.

lively — lebhaft
generous — großzügig

funny — lustig
entertaining — unterhaltsam

Don't confuse 'denn' with 'dann', which means 'then'.

Putting it all together

Include an <u>opinion phrase</u> and a super <u>adjective</u> or two — then <u>justify your view</u>.

Meiner Meinung nach ist er der beste Schauspieler, weil er talentiert ist.
In my opinion, he's the best actor because he is talented.

Ich mag Kohl nicht, weil er geschmacklos ist. Ich esse lieber Tomaten.
I don't like cabbage because it is tasteless. I prefer eating tomatoes.

Question	Simple Answer	Extended Answer
Was ist deine Meinung zu dieser Zeitung? *What's your opinion of this newspaper?*	Ich mag diese Zeitung. *I like this newspaper.*	Ich mag diese Zeitung, weil sie sehr interessant ist. *I like this newspaper because it's very interesting.*

Use a 'weil' or 'denn' phrase to justify your opinions...

Anja and Christian are discussing the things they like to do.
Listen to their conversation and decide whether the statements are true or false.

e.g. Christian likes swimming. **true**

1. Anja hates shopping because it takes too much time. *[1]*
2. Christian likes going to shopping centres. *[1]*
3. Anja hates pop concerts, even when her favourite band is playing. *[1]*
4. Christian would rather do exercise than watch TV. *[1]*
5. Anja buys newspapers every day. *[1]*

Listening Questions

Coming up are four pages of exam-style practice questions on the topics you've just revised. They're a great way to get ready for the real thing, so spend plenty of time working through them carefully.

1 Max spricht über seine Pläne für das kommende Jahr.
Ergänze die Tabelle auf **Deutsch** mit den richtigen Daten.

	Aktivität	Datum
Example:	Ausflug nach Berlin	3. Januar

	Aktivität	Datum
1 a	Geburtstagsfeier	
1 b	Besuch von seinem Bruder	
1 c	Urlaub in der Schweiz	
1 d	Konzert in Leipzig	

[4 marks]

2 Rory and Priya are making plans for the weekend. Listen to their phone conversation and answer the questions in **English**.

2 a Why doesn't Rory want to play badminton?

.... [1 mark]

2 b What does Priya think of swimming?

.... [1 mark]

2 c What did Priya's sister think of the new film?

.... [1 mark]

2 d What does Rory say about the previous film?

.... [1 mark]

Speaking Question

Get a friend or family member to read the teacher's role so you can pretend it's a real exam.
Read through the candidate's role before you start, and have a think about what you're going to say.

Candidate's Role

- Your teacher will play the role of your German friend. They will speak first.

- You should use *du* to address your friend.

- – ! – means you will have to respond to something you have not prepared.

- – ? – means you will have to ask your friend a question.

> Du willst mit einem deutschen Freund / einer deutschen Freundin in die Stadt gehen.
>
> - In die Stadt gehen — wann.
>
> - Sich treffen — um wie viel Uhr.
>
> - ? Einkaufen — Meinung.
>
> - Eine andere Aktivität in der Stadt (**ein** Detail).
>
> - !

Teacher's Role

- You begin the role-play using the introductory text below.

- You should address the candidate as *du*.

- You may alter the wording of the questions in response to the candidate's previous answers.

- Do not supply the candidate with key vocabulary.

> Introductory text: *Du willst mit einem deutschen Freund / einer deutschen Freundin in die Stadt gehen. Ich bin dein Freund / deine Freundin.*
>
> - Wann möchtest du in die Stadt gehen?
>
> - Um wie viel Uhr treffen wir uns?
>
> - ? Allow the candidate to ask you a question about shopping.
>
> - Was willst du sonst in der Stadt tun?
>
> - ! Wann warst du zum letzten Mal in der Stadt?

Reading Questions

1 Read what these two people wrote in a forum about holidays. Identify the people. Write **A (Anka)**, **B (Ben)** or **A + B (Anka and Ben)**.

Wann fährst du in Urlaub?			
Anka	Jeden März gehe ich in den Alpen mit meiner Familie wandern. Ich finde es schön, im Frühling im Urlaub zu sein, weil es nicht so viele Touristen gibt. Im Sommer würde ich nie Ferien machen. Ein Freund von mir macht jeden Winter Urlaub, das finde ich auch schrecklich!	Ben	Es kommt darauf an. Letztes Jahr bin ich im August nach Spanien geflogen. Das war super, weil ich das Sommerwetter liebe. Dieses Jahr werde ich vielleicht im April nach Frankreich fahren. Ein Frühlingsurlaub macht immer Spaß. Ich würde gern im Dezember Ski fahren — das wäre wirklich toll!

1 a Who likes going on holiday in summer? ☐ *[1 mark]*

1 b Who goes on holiday at the same time of year every year? ☐ *[1 mark]*

1 c Who enjoys spring holidays? ☐ *[1 mark]*

1 d Who would like to go on holiday in winter? ☐ *[1 mark]*

2 Read the directions provided on a theatre's website. Answer the questions in **English**.

> Von der Stadtmitte aus kann man das Theater in fünfzehn Minuten zu Fuß erreichen. Man nimmt die zweite Straße links nach dem Rathaus. Dann geht man ungefähr dreißig Meter die Straße entlang, bis man zum Kino kommt. Man muss danach die dritte Straße rechts nehmen. Das Theater befindet sich auf der linken Seite.
>
> Man kann auch mit dem Auto dahin fahren. Es gibt einen großen Parkplatz, der nur fünfundfünfzig Meter vom Theater entfernt ist. Das ist sehr praktisch. Man muss aber über zehn Euro pro Stunde für das Parken zahlen.

2 a How long does it take to walk from the town centre to the theatre? .... *[1 mark]*

2 b Which street do you take after the cinema? .... *[1 mark]*

2 c How far is the car park from the theatre? .... *[1 mark]*

2 d How much does parking cost per hour? .... *[1 mark]*

Writing Questions

1 Translate the following passage into **German**.

> I go to the cinema on Saturdays. Last week I watched a comedy. At the weekend I go swimming. The day after tomorrow I will go shopping.

....

....

....

....

[6 marks]

2 Translate the following passage into **German**.

> When I was younger I liked rock music, but now I like pop music. My favourite singer is called Anja Lan. I think that she is great because her music is fantastic. I believe that she is a nice person and in my opinion she is beautiful. I would like to go to her concert next year.

....

....

....

....

....

....

....

[12 marks]

Revision Summary for Section One

Congratulations, you've made it to the end of the first section. Here are some questions to check you know it all. Give them a go, then look back at any topics you found tricky. When you're sure you can answer a question, tick it off, and tick off the page title when you've done all the questions for it.

Numbers and Quantities (p.1) ☑

1) Count out loud from 1 to 20 in German. ☑
2) Write out the following numbers in words, in German: ☑
   a) 7   b) 17   c) 23   d) 34   e) 396   f) 1472
3) How would you say the following in German? ☑
   a) the first   b) the third   c) the eighth   d) the twenty-ninth

Times and Dates (p.2-3) ☑

4) Write out the following times in full, in German: ☑
   a) 3 o'clock   b) half past nine   c) quarter to seven   d) twenty-two minutes past six
5) Say all of the days of the week in German, from Monday to Sunday. ☑
6) How do you say these in German? ☑
   a) today   b) yesterday   c) the day after tomorrow   d) the day before yesterday
7) Write down the months of the year in German, from January to December. ☑
8) Your German friend Lars tells you: „Mittwochs spiele ich Fußball und am Wochenende gehe ich in die Stadt. Ich lese jeden Tag und alle drei Wochen gehe ich schwimmen." When does he...? ☑
   a) read   b) play football   c) go swimming   d) go into town

Questions (p.4-5) ☑

9) Translate the following questions into English: ☑
   a) Wann spielst du Tennis?   b) Wie viele Äpfel möchten Sie?   c) Was machst du?
10) Change the word order in these German sentences to form a question: ☑
   a) Steve kann mitkommen.   b) Sie können kochen.   c) Hannah spielt Klavier.
   d) Du möchtest eine Tasse Tee.   e) Du gehst aus.
11) Jens asks you: „Woher kommst du?" What does he want to know? ☑

Being Polite (p.6-7) ☑

12) You're at a party in Germany. How would you say the following? ☑
   a) Good evening   b) Thank you   c) How are you? (formal)   d) How are you? (informal)
13) In German, ask politely for a cup of tea. ☑
14) You are meeting your German exchange partner's brother. He says „Es freut mich, dich kennen zu lernen. Es tut mir leid, dass ich gestern Abend nicht da war." What has he said? ☑

Opinions (p.8-10) ☑

15) Translate these phrases into English: ☑
   a) Was hältst du von...?   b) Meiner Meinung nach   c) Denkst du das auch?
16) Say in German that you like cheese but you prefer to eat chocolate. ☑
17) Think of a film you like. Write down four German adjectives to describe it. ☑
18) Your German friend Julia has lent you a book. In German, tell her that you like the book because it is very entertaining, but in your opinion it is quite complicated. ☑

About Yourself

You never get a second chance at a first impression. So when introducing yourself in German, make sure you do it correctly. And also that the other person understands German...

Über Dich — About Yourself

sich vorstellen	*to introduce oneself*	buchstabieren	*to spell*
der Vorname	*first name*	geboren (am)	*born (on)*
der Familienname	*last name*	der Geburtstag	*birthday*
der Spitzname	*nickname*	das Geburtsdatum	*date of birth*
der Buchstabe	*letter (of the alphabet)*	der Geburtsort	*birthplace*

Wie heißt du?
Ich heiße Abi.

What are you called?
I am called Abi.

My first name is... —
Mein Vorname ist...

My nickname is...—
Mein Spitzname ist...

Wie alt bist du?
Ich bin fünfzehn Jahre alt.

How old are you?
I am fifteen years old.

Wann hast du Geburtstag?
Ich habe am 1. Mai Geburtstag.

When is your birthday?
My birthday is on 1st May.

in a town —
in einer Stadt

in the countryside
— auf dem Land

Wo wohnst du?
Ich wohne in Leicester.

Where do you live?
I live in Leicester.

near to... —
in der Nähe von...

You might be asked to <u>spell</u> your name or another word. So here's how to pronounce the <u>alphabet</u>.

A — *aah*	H — *haah*	O — *ohh*	T — *tey*
B — *bay*	I — *ee*	P — *pay*	U — *ooh*
C — *tsay*	J — *yot*	Q — *kooh*	V — *fow*
D — *day*	K — *kaah*	R — *air*	W — *vey*
E — *ay*	L — *ell*	S — *ess*	X — *iks*
F — *eff*	M — *em*	ß — *ess tsett / scharfes ess*	Y — *oohpsilon*
G — *gay*	N — *en*		Z — *tsett*

Grammar — umlauts

An <u>umlaut</u> is <u>two dots</u> above a <u>vowel</u> — it's a type of <u>accent</u>. It's only used above <u>three</u> of the vowels ('<u>a</u>', '<u>o</u>' and '<u>u</u>'). It changes their sound:

a — *aah* → ä — *ay*
o — *ohh* → ö — *urr*
u — *ooh* → ü — *ew*

Words can <u>change</u> their <u>meaning</u> if they have an umlaut, for example:

sch<u>o</u>n *already*   sch<u>ö</u>n *beautiful*

Umlauts change the way you pronounce letters...

Read the question and Frank's response.
Kannst du dich der Klasse vorstellen?

[1] on the coast
[2] the beach

Guten Tag, die Klasse! Ich möchte mich vorstellen. Ich heiße Frank. Das buchstabiert man eff - air – aah - en - kaah. Ich bin jetzt sechzehn Jahre alt und ich habe am ersten Februar Geburtstag. Ich bin in Cardiff geboren. Früher habe ich in Bangor in Wales gewohnt, was schön war, weil es **an der Küste**[1] *liegt und ich* **den Strand**[2] *liebe! Es freut mich aber sehr jetzt in Österreich zu wohnen.*

Grade 6-7

Tick list:
✓ tenses: present, simple past, perfect, conditional
✓ good, clear answer

To improve:
+ use more tenses, e.g. the future
+ give reasons for all opinions

Now answer the question yourself.
You should try to talk for about two minutes. *[10 marks]*

My Family

It's a wonder examiners don't get bored hearing about people's siblings — family's a common exam topic...

Meine Familie — My Family

die Eltern	*parents*	der Bruder	*brother*	der Enkel	*grandson*
der / die Verwandte	*relative*	die Schwester	*sister*	die Enkelin	*granddaughter*
der Vater	*father*	Stief...	*step...*	der Onkel	*uncle*
die Mutter	*mother*	Halb...	*half...*	die Tante	*aunt*
der Sohn	*son*	der Großvater	*grandfather*	der Cousin	*male cousin*
die Tochter	*daughter*	die Großmutter	*grandmother*	die Cousine	*female cousin*

Grammar — compound words

In German, you can put words <u>together</u> to make <u>new</u> ones — these are called <u>compound words</u>. The <u>gender</u> of the new word is <u>determined</u> by the gender of the <u>last</u> noun.

'Stief' + 'Vater' = 'Stiefvater' *stepfather*
'<u>Vater</u>' is <u>masculine</u>, so it's '<u>der</u> Stiefvater'.

Sie hat zwei Brüder und eine Schwester.	*She has two brothers and a sister.*
Meine Familie ist groß. Ich habe fünfzehn Cousins!	*My family is big. I have fifteen cousins!*
Ich mag meinen Stiefvater. Er ist sehr nett.	*I like my stepfather. He's very nice.*

Wie ist deine Familie? — What's your family like?

You don't need to list every family member — just say something interesting about <u>a few</u> of them.

Question	Simple Answer	Extended Answer
Beschreib deine Familie.	Ich wohne bei meinen Eltern. Ich bin ein Einzelkind.	Ich habe einen Bruder. Er und seine Freundin haben eine Tochter, also bin ich Tante. Ich besuche oft meine Nichte.
Describe your family.	*I live with my parents. I'm an only child.*	*I have one brother. He and his girlfriend have a daughter, so I am an auntie. I often visit my niece.*

> The German words for 'boyfriend' and 'girlfriend' are the same as for 'friend': 'Freund' and 'Freundin'. See p.20 for how to differentiate them.

Ich wohne bei meinem Vater und meiner Stiefmutter. Jedes zweite Wochenende besuche ich meine Mutter.	*I live with my dad and my stepmum. Every other weekend, I visit my mum.*	my stepdad — meinen Stiefvater my half-sister — meine Halbschwester
Meine Großeltern wohnen im Ausland, deswegen kann ich sie nur selten besuchen.	*My grandparents live abroad, so I can't visit them very often.*	siblings — Geschwister
Ich habe zwei Nichten. Die sind die Kinder meiner Schwester.	*I have two nieces. They are my sister's children.*	nephews — Neffen

Think of interesting ways to describe your family...

Joachim has written about himself and his family. Translate the passage into **English**. *[9 marks]*

Hallo, ich bin Joachim und ich bin in Leipzig geboren. Ich wohne mit meiner Frau, ihren zwei Töchtern und meinem Sohn. Er studiert Medizin und er will in der Zukunft Arzt werden. Eine meiner Stieftöchter hat ein Kind, das Georg heißt. Wir werden bald seinen zweiten Geburtstag feiern.

> You don't need to change the names — Georg stays as Georg, not George. Look out for false friends too, e.g. 'will'.

Describing People

People come in all shapes and sizes. So here's how to describe what they look like...

Beschreiben — To describe

klein	*small / short*	blau	*blue*	rot	*red / ginger*
groß	*big / tall*	grau	*grey*	die Augen	*eyes*
dünn	*thin*	grün	*green*	die Haare	*hair*
dick	*fat*	braun	*brown*	aussehen	*to look like*
lang	*long*	hell	*light*	der Bart	*beard*
kurz	*short*	dunkel	*dark*	der Schnurrbart	*moustache*
glatt	*straight (hair)*	blond	*blonde*	die Brille	*glasses*

Question

Wie sehen deine Familienmitglieder aus?
What do your family members look like?

Simple Answer

Meine Eltern sind groß, aber mein Bruder ist klein.
Wir alle haben rote Haare und braune Augen.

My parents are tall, but my brother is short.
We all have red hair and brown eyes.

Grammar — plurals

Some words that are <u>plural</u> in English are singular in German...

    Sie <u>trägt</u> eine Brille. *She <u>wears</u> glasses.*
    Meine Hose <u>ist</u> rot. *My trousers <u>are</u> red.*

...and some are <u>singular</u> in English but <u>plural</u> in German.

    Seine Haare <u>sind</u> braun.   *His hair <u>is</u> brown.*

Extended Answer

Meine Mutter hat lange glatte Haare und ihre Augen sind hellblau.
Mein Vater ist dünn und er hat einen Schnurrbart. Er trägt eine Brille.

My mum has long straight hair and her eyes are light blue.
My dad is thin and he has a moustache. He wears glasses.

> Adjectives have to agree if they come before a noun, but they don't have to if they're after one — look at the first sentence in the extended answer. See p.119 for more.

Das Aussehen — Appearance

> See p.121 for how to compare things.

You can extend your descriptions by <u>comparing</u> two people or saying what someone <u>doesn't have</u>.

Deine Schwester ist größer als mein Bruder.	*Your sister is taller than my brother.*	shorter — kleiner
Meine beste Freundin Sina hat kurze blonde Haare. Sie hat auch eine Tätowierung.	*My best friend Sina has short blond hair. She also has a tattoo.*	freckles — Sommersprossen
Unser Großvater hat keinen Bart, aber er hat einen grauen Schnurrbart.	*Our grandad doesn't have a beard, but he has a grey moustache.*	thick — dicken black — schwarzen

TRACK LISTENING 05 — Adjectives in front of a noun have to agree...

Your exchange partner Jamal is talking about his siblings. Answer the questions in **English**.

1. How many brothers does Jamal have? [1]
2. What is his sister's hair like? [1]
3. What does Jamal's half-sister look like? Give **two** details. [2]
4. What does he think of his brother's moustache and why? [2]

Personalities

Read on for how to tell your examiner you're a hard-working, confident, helpful and generous person...

Die Persönlichkeit — Personality

frech	*cheeky*	schüchtern	*shy*	selbstbewusst	*self-confident*
höflich	*polite*	streng	*strict*	selbstständig	*independent*
witzig	*funny*	zuverlässig	*reliable*	unternehmungslustig	*adventurous*
lebhaft	*lively*	egoistisch	*selfish*	großzügig	*generous*
lästig	*annoying*	hilfsbereit	*helpful*	gut gelaunt	*good-tempered*

Question	Simple Answer	Extended Answer	Grammar — adverbs
Wie würdest du dich selbst beschreiben? *How would you describe yourself?*	Ich bin nett und großzügig, aber manchmal egoistisch. *I'm nice and generous but sometimes selfish.*	Ich weiß, dass ich manchmal gemein sein kann. Ich versuche aber, höflich und gut gelaunt zu sein. *I know that I can sometimes be mean. But I try to be polite and good-tempered.*	Using adverbs is a good way to make your sentences more interesting. They're words like 'sehr' (very) and 'ziemlich' (quite). See p.123 for how to use them.

Der Mensch — Person

Meine Halbschwester ist absolut zuverlässig.

My half-sister is completely reliable.

Obwohl meine Großmutter manchmal ziemlich schüchtern ist, ist sie auch lebhaft.

Although my grandmother is sometimes quite shy, she is also lively.

Mein Vater ist oft streng, also versuche ich immer höflich und hilfsbereit zu sein.

My dad is often strict, so I try to always be polite and helpful.

Meiner Meinung nach bin ich selbstbewusst und großzügig. Mein Bruder meint aber, dass ich egoistisch bin.

In my opinion, I'm self-confident and generous. But my brother thinks that I'm selfish.

hard-working — fleißig
serious — ernst
quiet — ruhig
impatient — ungeduldig
honest — ehrlich
conceited — eingebildet

Give more detail by adding adverbs like 'oft' and 'manchmal'...

Dagmar has written an email to her British exchange partner describing her family.

Hallo,

ich dachte, dass ich dir eine kurze E-Mail schreiben würde, um dir Informationen über meine wirklich liebe Familie zu geben! Meine Mutter ist immer **äußerst**[1] gut gelaunt und geduldig, was wichtig ist, weil mein Vater echt faul ist. Ich war früher oft frech. Ich bin aber höflicher geworden. Zwei Geschwister habe ich auch — einen älteren Halbbruder, der Max heißt, und eine kleinere Schwester namens Julia. Beide sind ziemlich hilfsbereit und nett. Und bei dir? Wie ist deine Familie?

Liebe Grüße,

Dagmar

Grade 8-9

[1] extremely

Tick list:
✓ tenses: present, perfect, simple past, conditional
✓ good use of intensifiers
✓ complex sentences

To improve:
+ use the future tense

Du schreibst eine E-Mail über deine Familie an deine Freundin aus Deutschland. Schreib:
- wie viele Familienmitglieder du hast
- etwas über ihre Persönlichkeiten
- was deine Meinungen über ihre Persönlichkeiten sind
- wie deine Persönlichkeit war, als du jünger warst

Du musst ungefähr **90** Wörter auf **Deutsch** schreiben. Schreib etwas über alle Punkte der Aufgabe. *[16 marks]*

Relationships

You need reflexive verbs like 'sich verstehen' (*to get on with*) and 'sich streiten' (*to argue*) for this topic.

Die Beziehung — Relationship

das Verhältnis	*relationship*
die Freundschaft	*friendship*
kennen lernen	*to get to know*
sich verstehen (mit)	*to get on (with)*
auskommen (mit)	*to get on (with)*
unterstützen	*to support*
sich kümmern (um)	*to look after*
sorgen (für)	*to care (for)*
sich fühlen	*to feel*
das Gefühl	*feeling*
sich streiten (mit)	*to argue (with)*
der Streit	*argument*
sich ärgern (über)	*to be annoyed (about)*
auf die Nerven gehen	*to get on one's nerves*

Grammar — reflexives (sich + verb)

Reflexives use 'sich'. 'Sich' changes for different people.

ich — mich	wir — uns
du — dich	ihr — euch
er / sie / es — sich	Sie — sich

Ich verstehe mich gut mit Finn. *I get on well with Finn.*

See p.128 and 136 for more on reflexive verbs.

Grammar — Freund / Freundin

'Freund/in' can mean 'friend' or 'boyfriend / girlfriend'. It's usually obvious which, but if you want to make it clear:

- say 'mein Freund / meine Freundin' for boyfriend / girlfriend
- use 'ein Freund / eine Freundin von mir' for a friend

Eng befreundet sein — To be close friends

Sie verstehen sich ganz gut mit ihren Stiefgeschwistern.	*They get on very well with their step-siblings.*	argue — streiten sich
Obwohl ich normalerweise gut mit meinen Eltern auskomme, ärgere ich mich manchmal über ihre strengen Regeln.	*Although I usually get on well with my parents, I sometimes get annoyed about their strict rules.*	I sometimes just want to be alone — möchte ich manchmal einfach allein sein
Ich bin der Meinung, dass Freundschaften sehr wichtig sind. Ich fühle mich glücklich, wenn ich mit Freunden zusammen bin.	*In my opinion, friendships are very important. I feel happy when I'm with friends.*	good / comfortable — wohl
		relaxed — entspannt

The reflexive pronoun follows the verb...

Read the questions and the sample answers.

1. Was kannst du auf dem Foto sehen?

Ich sehe zwei Mädchen auf dem Foto. Sie sehen sehr glücklich aus, da sie viel lachen. Vielleicht hat eins einen Witz erzählt.

2. Verstehst du dich gut mit deinen Freunden? Warum (nicht)?

Ab und zu geht meine beste Freundin mir auf die Nerven, weil sie oft ärgerlich ist. Letzte Woche haben wir uns gestritten. Normalerweise verstehen wir uns aber sehr gut.

3. Ist es wichtig, gute Freundschaften zu haben? Warum (nicht)?

Ja, es ist wichtig, weil meine Freunde mich unterstützen. Aber es ist mir noch wichtiger, ein gutes Verhältnis mit meiner Familie zu haben. Sie werden immer für mich sorgen.

Grade 8-9

Tick list:
✓ tenses: present, perfect, future
✓ opinions justified

To improve:
+ use the subjunctive
+ use more connectives, e.g. 'obwohl'

Now try responding to questions 2 and 3 yourself. Speak for about 2 minutes. *[10 marks]*

Partnership

Marriage might seem a long way off, but it's not long till you might have to talk about it in the exam...

Die Partnerschaft — Partnership

in einem Verhältnis sein	*to be in a relationship*	heiraten	*to marry*
ledig	*single*	verheiratet	*married*
sich verloben	*to get engaged*	die Hochzeit	*wedding*
der / die Verlobte	*fiancé(e)*	sich trennen	*to separate*
die Ehe	*marriage*	getrennt	*separated*
die gleichgeschlechtliche Ehe	*same-sex marriage*	sich scheiden lassen	*to get divorced*
die zivile Partnerschaft	*civil partnership*	geschieden	*divorced*

Das Eheleben — Married life

Question	Simple Answer	Extended Answer
Möchtest du heiraten? *Do you want to get married?*	Ich glaube, dass ich heiraten will. Ich bin aber noch jung. *I think that I want to get married. But I'm still young.*	Ich bin noch nicht sicher, ob ich heiraten will. Meiner Meinung nach kann man jemandem treu bleiben, ohne verheiratet zu sein. *I'm still not sure if I want to get married. In my opinion, you can stay faithful to someone without being married.*

Grammar — future

The <u>future</u> tense can be made with a form of '<u>werden</u>' and an <u>infinitive</u> verb.

Ich <u>werde</u> ihn <u>heiraten</u>.
I <u>will marry</u> him.

Wir <u>werden</u> ledig <u>bleiben</u>.
We <u>will stay</u> single.

See p.142 for more.

Ich denke, dass ich wahrscheinlich in der Zukunft ledig bleiben werde.

I think that I will probably remain single in the future.

Ich bin geteilter Meinung über die Ehescheidung.

I have mixed opinions about divorce.

Es ist mir wichtig, dass homosexuelle Leute auch heiraten dürfen.

It's important to me that homosexual people are also allowed to marry.

unmarried — unverheiratet

same-sex partnership — die gleichgeschlechtliche Partnerschaft

single parenthood — alleinstehende Elternschaft

READING

Use the future tense with 'werden' to say what you will do...

Lies diesen Ausschnitt aus dem Buch ,Effi Briest', geschrieben von Theodor Fontane.
Sag, ob die Aussagen **richtig (R)**, **falsch (F)** oder **nicht im Text (NT)** sind.

Danach ging Effi zu ihren Freundinnen; die Zwillinge warteten schon auf sie im Garten.

„Nun, Effi", sagte Hertha, während alle drei zwischen den blühenden Blumen spazierten, „nun, Effi, wie geht es dir eigentlich?"

„Oh, ganz gut. Wir nennen uns schon du und beim Vornamen. Er heißt Geert."

„Ich mache mir aber Sorgen um dich. Ist er denn **der Richtige**[1]?"

„Natürlich ist er der Richtige. Das verstehst du nicht, Hertha. Jeder ist der Richtige. Natürlich muss er **von Adel**[2] sein und gut aussehen."

„Bist du wirklich ganz glücklich?"

„Wenn man zwei Stunden verlobt ist, ist man immer ganz glücklich. Wenigstens denk ich es mir so."

[1]'the one'
[2]noble

e.g. Die Zwillinge sitzen im Wohnzimmer. **F**

1. Effi kennt Geert seit einem Jahr. *[1]*

2. Effis Freundin Hertha ist ängstlich um sie. *[1]*

3. Die Liebe ist das Wichtigste für Effi. *[1]*

4. Effi freut sich auf die Hochzeit. *[1]*

Listening Questions

You've made it through another section but don't give up yet — here are some more practice questions to test what you've learnt. Working through these will highlight things you still need to work on.

1 Bruno is introducing himself. Answer the questions in **English**.

TRACK LISTENING 06

1 a What is Bruno's last name?

.... *[1 mark]*

1 b Where does Bruno's mother come from?

.... *[1 mark]*

1 c When is Bruno's birthday?

.... *[1 mark]*

1 d What does Bruno like about where he lives? Give **one** detail.

.... *[1 mark]*

2 Listen to the following podcast about what people look for in a friend. Answer the questions in **English**.

TRACK LISTENING 07

2 a According to the report, what is the most important characteristic that people seek?

.... *[1 mark]*

2 b What percentage of those surveyed find humour important?

.... *[1 mark]*

2 c Which quality is said to be more important than being hard-working?

.... *[1 mark]*

Speaking Question

Candidate's Role

- Your teacher will play the role of your German friend. They will speak first.

- You should use *du* to address your friend.

- – ! – means you will have to respond to something you have not prepared.

- – ? – means you will have to ask your friend a question.

> Du sprichst mit einem deutschen Freund / einer deutschen Freundin über deine Familie.
>
> - Dein Verhältnis mit deiner Familie.
>
> - Familie wichtig für dich — warum.
>
> - !
>
> - Familienaktivität diese Woche.
>
> - ? Großeltern sehen — wie oft.

Teacher's Role

- You begin the role-play using the introductory text below.

- You should address the candidate as *du*.

- You may alter the wording of the questions in response to the candidate's previous answers.

- Do not supply the candidate with key vocabulary.

> Introductory text: *Du sprichst mit einem deutschen Freund / einer deutschen Freundin über deine Familie. Ich bin dein Freund / deine Freundin.*
>
> - Verstehst du dich gut mit deiner Familie?
>
> - Ist Familie wichtig für dich? ... Warum?
>
> - ! Hast du dich mit deiner Familie gut verstanden, als du jünger warst?
>
> - Was wirst du diese Woche mit deiner Familie machen?
>
> - ? Allow the candidate to ask you how often you see your grandparents.

Reading Questions

1   Read the conversation in a chatroom between three young people
    about their relationships with different family members.

Elyas:	Als ich jünger war, habe ich mit meinen Eltern fast jeden Tag gestritten. Jetzt ist alles nicht immer besser, aber ich verstehe mich sehr gut mit meinem Cousin.
Birgit:	Im Moment habe ich ein schlechtes Verhältnis mit meiner Großmutter, weil sie oft gemein ist. Glücklicherweise ist meine Stiefschwester immer für mich da.
Noah:	Ich habe einen Sohn und wir streiten uns nie, weil er immer noch sehr jung und süß ist. Ich finde meinen Halbbruder ziemlich ärgerlich und ich hoffe, dass wir in Zukunft miteinander besser auskommen werden.

Fill in the **four** gaps in the grid in **English** to show
which relationships are **positive** and which are **negative**.

		Positive	Negative
Example:	Elyas	cousin	parents
	Birgit		
	Noah		

[4 marks]

2   Translate the following passage into **English**.

> Wir wohnen in einem Dorf in der Nähe von Swansea. Meine Frau, die
> Saskia heißt, ist sechsunddreißig Jahre alt und hat kurze, lockige, schwarze
> Haare. Sie hat auch große, braune Augen und ich glaube, dass sie sehr
> hübsch ist. Wir streiten uns nie und sie wird immer für mich sorgen.

....

....

....

....

....

....

[9 marks]

Writing Questions

1 Deine Austauschpartnerin, Franziska, hat dich über deine Freunde gefragt.
Du schreibst Franziska eine E-Mail, in der du ihr von deinen Freundschaften erzählst.

Schreib:

- etwas über deine Freunde

- ob du ein guter Freund / eine gute Freundin bist und warum

- was du in letzter Zeit mit deinen Freunden gemacht hast

- ob du lieber Zeit mit Familie oder mit Freunden verbringst und warum

Du musst ungefähr **90** Wörter auf **Deutsch** schreiben.
Schreib etwas über alle Punkte der Aufgabe.   *[16 marks]*

2 Translate the following passage into **German**.

> Unfortunately, my parents separated two years ago. At the moment,
> I am single. In the future, I would like to be in a relationship and not
> alone. However, I am not sure whether I will marry because you can
> have a family without being married. Also, lots of couples get divorced.

....

....

....

....

....

....

[12 marks]

Revision Summary for Section Two

You should now be clued up on talking about yourself, your friends and your family. Have a go at these questions and if you get stuck on something, just go back through the section and check it. Don't forget to use the tick boxes to keep track of your progress.

About Yourself (p.16) ☑

1) Introduce yourself to someone in German. Tell them your name, age and when your birthday is. ☑
2) Spell out your surname in German. ☑
3) Tabea tells you: „Mein Familienname ist Brandt. Ich bin achtzehn Jahre alt und habe am neunten Juni Geburtstag. Ich wohne in Rinteln in der Nähe von Hannover." What do you know about her? ☑

My Family (p.17) ☑

4) How do you say the following in German?
   a) relative   b) daughter   c) stepbrother   d) half-sister   e) grandson ☑
5) In German, say who you live with. ☑
6) Timo is talking about his family: „Leider bin ich ein Einzelkind, aber ich habe viele Cousins und Cousinen. Ich wohne bei meiner Mutter und meinem Stiefvater". What has he said? ☑

Describing People (p.18) ☑

7) Malaika's friend is describing her: „Malaika ist groß und hat lange, dunkelbraune Haare. Sie ist ziemlich dünn und trägt eine Brille. Sie hat auch eine Tätowierung." What does she look like? ☑
8) Choose a member of your family and describe what they look like in German. ☑
9) In German, say that your friend has red hair and green eyes, and that he / she is taller than you. ☑

Personalities (p.19) ☑

10) What's the German for...?
   a) generous   b) selfish   c) strict   d) lively   e) cheeky   f) adventurous ☑
11) In German, describe the personality of your best friend. ☑
12) Lena tells you about her boyfriend: „Normalerweise ist er gut gelaunt, aber manchmal ist er sehr lästig. Obwohl er nicht besonders zuverlässig ist, ist er oft hilfsbereit." What is he like? ☑

Relationships (p.20) ☑

13) What do the following words and phrases mean?
   a) die Beziehung   b) sich streiten   c) sich ärgern   d) kennen lernen   e) sorgen für ☑
14) Serge asks you: „Kommst du mit deinen Geschwistern gut aus oder streitet ihr euch die ganze Zeit?" What does he want to know? ☑
15) Saskia tells you: „Ich muss mich um meinen jüngeren Bruder kümmern, aber er geht mir immer auf die Nerven. Wir verstehen uns nicht gut." What do you know about her brother? ☑

Partnership (p.21) ☑

16) How would you say the following in German?
   a) civil partnership   b) marriage   c) same-sex marriage   d) single   e) to separate ☑
17) In the future, you would like to get married, but you think that weddings are too expensive. Say this in German. ☑

Music

Music's a great topic to talk about, so make sure you get this page stuck in your head like a catchy tune — known as 'ein Ohrwurm' *(an earworm)* in German.

Die Musik — Music

spielen	*to play*
singen	*to sing*
hören	*to listen to*
das Instrument	*instrument*
der Musiker / die Musikerin	*musician*
der Sänger / die Sängerin	*singer*
bevorzugen	*to prefer*
teilnehmen an	*to take part in*
die Band	*band*
der Chor	*choir*
das Orchester	*orchestra*
das Konzert	*concert*
abonnieren	*to subscribe to*

In German, you don't need a definite article ('the') when talking about playing an instrument.

Grammar — 'used to...'

You can use the simple past and 'früher' *(before, earlier)* to say what you used to do.

Früher spielte ich Klavier.
I used to play the piano.

See p.139 for more on the simple past.

Ich spiele Geige in einem Orchester. — *I play the violin in an orchestra.*

Ich singe oft in einem Chor. — *I often sing in a choir.*

Wir nehmen an einem Konzert teil. — *We're taking part in a concert.*

Question
Spielst du ein Instrument?
Do you play a musical instrument?

Simple Answer
Ja, ich spiele Gitarre und Trompete.
Yes, I play the guitar and the trumpet.

Extended Answer
Ja, ich spiele Querflöte seit vier Jahren. Als ich jünger war, spielte ich Klarinette und ich sang in einer Band.
Yes, I've been playing the flute for four years. When I was younger, I played the clarinet and I sang in a band.

Der Musikgeschmack — Taste in music

Here are a few sentences for talking about your taste in music:

Ich höre am liebsten Rockmusik. — *I like listening to rock music the most.*

Er hörte früher Popmusik, aber jetzt mag er Volksmusik. — *He used to listen to pop music, but now he likes folk music.*

Am allerliebsten höre ich Musik auf meinem Handy. — *More than anything else, I like listening to music on my mobile.*

Je öfter ich in einem Orchester spiele, desto mehr mag ich klassische Musik. — *The more often I play in an orchestra, the more I like classical music.*

pop music — Popmusik
rap — Rapmusik
classical music — klassische Musik
streams — überträgt / streamt
CD player — CD-Spieler
in a brass band — in einer Blaskapelle

You can talk about instruments you'd like to learn too...

A group of music pupils are introducing themselves and talking about their tastes in music. Match each of them with one of the statements below.

e.g. Johanna... *G*
1. Johanna... [1]
2. Preethi... [1]
3. Jürgen... [1]

A. ...has a sister who likes pop music.
B. ...hates listening to rock music.
C. ...thinks classical music is relaxing.
D. ...finds rock concerts too loud.
E. ...likes classical music for ballet.
F. ...found a rap song terrible.
G. ...went to a rock concert.
H. ...enjoys playing the same songs.

Cinema

Give your German some Hollywood glamour by learning this page so you can talk about your favourite films.

Das Kino — Cinema

die Eintrittskarte	*ticket*	die Werbung	*advert(s)*
die Leinwand	*screen*	der Actionfilm	*action film*
der Schauspieler / die Schauspielerin	*actor / actress*	der Horrorfilm	*horror film*
der Trailer	*trailer*	der Liebesfilm	*romantic film*
die Handlung	*plot*	der Krimi	*crime film*

Question

Was für Filme siehst du gern?

What kind of films do you like watching?

Simple Answer

Liebesfilme gefallen mir am besten, weil sie immer ein Happy End haben.

I like romantic films best because they always have a happy ending.

Extended Answer

Ich sehe gern Krimis, weil die Handlungen immer spannend sind. Actionfilme mag ich auch. Ich würde aber keinen Horrorfilm sehen, da ich zu viel Angst davor habe.

I like watching crime films because the plots are always exciting. I also like action films. But I wouldn't watch a horror film because I'm too scared of them.

Obwohl die Werbung mich ärgert, gehe ich gern ins Kino.

Although the adverts annoy me, I like going to the cinema.

Die Trickeffekte sind immer beeindruckend.

The special effects are always impressive.

Grammar — ins / im Kino

'In' is a preposition. It can take the accusative or the dative case. If there's movement, use the accusative. 'Ins' is short for 'in das'.

Wir gehen ins Kino. *We're going to the cinema.*

If there's no movement, use the dative. 'Im' is short for 'in dem'.

Wir sind im Kino. *We're in the cinema.*

See p.131 for more on cases and prepositions.

Gehst du gern ins Kino? — Do you like going to the cinema?

Adjectives are useful when you're giving your opinion of a film. Luckily, we've written a few below...

Ich habe einen Horrorfilm gesehen.

I have watched a horror film.

Den Film fand ich sehr bewegend.

I found the film very moving.

Ich gehe gern ins Kino, da ich es besser finde, Filme auf der Kinoleinwand zu sehen. Die Eintrittskarten sind aber teuer.

I like going to the cinema because I find it better to watch films on the big screen. But the tickets are expensive.

a sci-fi film — einen Science-Fiction-Film
a comedy — eine Komödie
a romcom — eine romantische Komödie

boring — langweilig
fascinating — faszinierend
scary — gruselig
entertaining — unterhaltsam

Use 'gern' to say what you like watching...

Translate the following passage into **German**. *[12 marks]*

I like going to the cinema. Last weekend, I went to the cinema with my friend and we watched an action film. I found the film really exciting although it was a little bit scary. Next week, I will watch a comedy with my sister because she prefers funny films. In the future, I would like to be an actor.

TV

From the big screen to the small... TV is another good topic for giving opinions so have some adjectives ready.

Das Fernsehen — Television

fernsehen	*to watch television*	die Nachrichten	*news*
der Sender	*TV channel*	der Dokumentarfilm	*documentary*
die Sendung	*TV programme*	der / die Promi	*celebrity*
die Serie	*series*	umschalten	*to switch channels*
die Seifenoper	*soap opera*	senden	*to broadcast*

Mein Bruder sieht gern die Nachrichten, aber ich würde lieber einen Krimi sehen.

My brother likes watching the news, but I would rather watch a crime show.

a quiz show — eine Quizsendung

Man kann viel von Dokumentarfilmen lernen.

You can learn a lot from documentaries.

a reality show — eine Reality-Show

Ich sehe lieber Serien ohne Werbung, deswegen bevorzuge ich die Sender, die keine Werbung zeigen.

I prefer watching series without adverts, so I prefer the TV channels that don't show adverts.

You can also use 'anschauen' for 'to watch'. It's a separable verb — see below.

Was kommt im Fernsehen? — What's on TV?

Question

Was hast du neulich im Fernsehen angeschaut?

What have you watched recently on TV?

Simple Answer

Ich schaute gestern einen interessanten Dokumentarfilm an.

I watched an interesting documentary yesterday.

Extended Answer

Die Nachrichten schaue ich jeden Tag an, da es wichtig ist zu wissen, was in der Welt passiert.

I watch the news every day because it's important to know what's happening in the world.

fern ⚡ sehen

Grammar — fernsehen

'Fernsehen' *(to watch TV)* is a separable verb. It splits into two parts — 'fern' and 'sehen'.

Ich sehe fern. *I watch TV.*

In the perfect tense, the 'ge-' prefix is added to the start of the second part to make the past participle. The verb is written as one word.

Ich habe ferngesehen. *I have watched TV.*

If it's used in the infinitive form, it's not separated.

Ich will fernsehen. *I want to watch TV.*

See p.145 for more on separable verbs.

 You'll have 'Quadrataugen'* after all that...

Read Marlene's opinions about TV, then decide if each statement is true, false or not in the text.

Ich sehe regelmäßig fern, meistens abends oder am Wochenende. Am liebsten sehe ich Musiksendungen oder Quizsendungen, weil ich sie unterhaltsam finde. Leider gibt es auch viele langweilige Sendungen im Fernsehen, wie zum Beispiel die Nachrichten oder Sportsendungen. Die interessieren mich überhaupt nicht. Auch finde ich die Werbung im Fernsehen furchtbar. Ich schalte dann schnell auf eine andere Sendung um. Meine Schwester sitzt stundenlang vor dem Fernseher, obwohl meine Mutter dann **schimpft**[1], weil es nicht gut für die Augen ist. Aber das ist ihr egal. Ich glaube, dass sie **fernsehsüchtig**[2] ist.

[1]complains [2]addicted to television

e.g. Marlene rarely watches TV. **false**

1. She doesn't like news or sports programmes. [1]

2. Marlene finds adverts on TV very interesting. [1]

3. Her sister doesn't spend much time watching TV. [1]

4. Marlene never watches TV with her sister. [1]

---

*'Quadrataugen' means 'square eyes'.

Food

This page is pretty heavy on vocab. But it's all about food, so that makes it more palatable...

Das Essen — Food

das Gemüse	vegetables	das Fleisch	meat	die Wurst	sausage
die Tomate	tomato	das Rindfleisch	beef	die Bratwurst	fried sausage
die Karotte	carrot	das Schweinefleisch	pork	das Hähnchen	chicken
der Pilz	mushroom	der Schinken	ham	das (Wiener) Schnitzel	veal / pork cutlet
die Zwiebel	onion				
die Kartoffel	potato	der Fisch	fish	das Brot	bread
die Erbsen	peas	der Lachs	salmon	das Brötchen	bread roll
das Obst	fruit	der Thunfisch	tuna	der Reis	rice
der Apfel	apple	die Meeresfrüchte	seafood	die Nudeln	pasta
die Birne	pear			die Pommes frites	chips
die Banane	banana	lecker	tasty	die Suppe	soup
die Apfelsine	orange	ekelhaft	disgusting		
die Ananas	pineapple	scharf	hot / spicy	die Milch	milk
die Nuss	nut	süß	sweet	der Käse	cheese

die Butter — butter
das Ei — egg

Was isst du gern? — What do you like eating?

Question

Was isst du am liebsten?

What do you like eating the most?

Simple Answer

Ich esse sehr gern Fisch, allerdings mag ich keinen Lachs.

I really like eating fish. However, I don't like salmon.

Extended Answer

Mein Lieblingsgericht ist Reis mit Tomatensoße und Erbsen. Ich finde es lecker. Da ich Vegetarier bin, esse ich kein Fleisch.

My favourite meal is rice with tomato sauce and peas. I find it tasty. Because I'm a vegetarian, I don't eat meat.

Grammar — essen (to eat)

'Essen' is irregular. Here are its forms in the present tense:

ich esse	wir essen
du isst	ihr esst
er / sie / es isst	Sie / sie essen

In the simple past, the stem is 'aß'. The past participle in the perfect tense is 'gegessen'.

Ich finde, dass Rindfleisch ekelhaft schmeckt.	*I find that beef tastes disgusting.*
Ich mag kein scharfes Essen.	*I don't like hot / spicy food.*
Ich esse gern Bananen, aber Ananasse sind zu süß für meinen Geschmack.	*I like eating bananas, but pineapples are too sweet for my taste.*
Ich habe Hunger und ich habe Durst.	*I'm hungry and I'm thirsty.*

delicious — köstlich
salty — salziges
sweet — süßes
fatty — fettiges

You can also say 'ich bin hungrig / durstig'.

TRACK LISTENING 09

'Essen' is an irregular verb, so learn the different forms...

Elsa, Sonja and Moritz are discussing their food preferences. Complete the sentences.

		A.	B.	C.	
e.g.	Elsa has decided not to eat...	A. fatty food.	B. vegetables.	C. meat and fish.	**C**
1.	Elsa particularly likes...	A. apples.	B. pineapples.	C. bananas.	[1]
2.	Sonja's favourite food is...	A. sausages.	B. pork.	C. roast potatoes.	[1]
3.	Sonja doesn't usually like...	A. red meat.	B. fried food.	C. pork.	[1]
4.	Moritz enjoys...	A. cooking.	B. eating out.	C. eating healthily.	[1]

Eating Out

And for dessert, a page on eating out. Restaurants are a popular topic for the role-play, so get learning...

Das Restaurant — Restaurant

reservieren	*to book*
die Kneipe / das Gasthaus	*pub*
das Café	*café*
die Karte	*menu*
die Vorspeise	*starter*
das Hauptgericht	*main course*
die Nachspeise	*dessert*
bestellen	*to order*
der Kellner / die Kellnerin	*waiter / waitress*
die Selbstbedienung	*self-service*
bezahlen	*to pay*
die Rechnung	*bill*
Bedienung inbegriffen	*service included*
das Trinkgeld	*tip*

Grammar — asking questions

To ask questions, reverse the order of the verb and the subject.
Du hast den Lachs bestellt. *You ordered the salmon.*
Hast du den Lachs bestellt? *Did you order the salmon?*
Question words like 'wie viel' *(how much)* are also handy:
Wie viel kostet das Bier? *How much does the beer cost?*
See p.4-5 for more on asking questions.

Ich hätte gern die Suppe.	*I would like the soup.*
Könnte ich bitte die Rechnung haben?	*Could I please have the bill?*
Ich würde gern bezahlen.	*I would like to pay.*

Was möchten Sie essen? — What would you like to eat?

Zum Hauptgericht hätte ich gern das Tagesgericht.

For the main course, I would like the dish of the day.

— the steak — das Steak

Ich esse gern im Restaurant, weil man Speisen probieren kann, die man zu Hause nie kochen würde. Letzte Woche habe ich chinesisches Essen probiert.

I like eating in restaurants because you can try dishes that you would never cook at home. Last week, I tried Chinese food.

Indian — indisches
Thai — thailändisches

Ich will mich beschweren. Die Suppe ist kalt.

I want to complain. The soup is cold.

burnt — angebrannt

'Ich hätte gern' is more polite than 'Ich will'...

Here's an example role-play. Ciara is ordering food in a restaurant.

Kellner: Guten Abend. Haben Sie eine Reservierung?

Grade 6-7

Ciara: Leider habe ich keine Reservierung. Haben Sie einen Tisch frei? Ich würde gern am Fenster sitzen.

Kellner: Natürlich. Was nehmen Sie?

Ciara: Ich hätte gern ein großes Glas stilles Mineralwasser und eine Bratwurst mit Pommes frites. Das finde ich immer sehr lecker.

Kellner: Sonst noch etwas?

Ciara: Ja, ich nehme auch dazu eine Portion Erbsen.

Kellner: Möchten Sie auch gleich die Nachspeise bestellen?

Ciara: Nein. Das werde ich später machen. Vielen Dank.

Tick list:
✓ variety of tenses
✓ correct question

To improve:
+ use the past tense
+ use a subordinate clause

Prepare the role-play card below. Use 'Sie' and speak for about two minutes. *[15 marks]*

Sie sind in einem Restaurant.
- *Tisch reserviert — für wie viele Personen*
- *Schon hier gegessen — wann*
- *Etwas zu trinken (ein Detail)*
- *? Tagesgericht*
- *!*

Sport

Whether you're sporty or not, you need to know some sporty vocab. Ready? On your marks, get set, GO!

Der Sport — Sport

spielen	to play	der Fußball	football	der Basketball	basketball
gewinnen	to win	das Rugby	rugby	Fahrrad fahren	to cycle
verlieren	to lose	das Tennis	tennis	segeln	to sail
trainieren	to train	der Federball	badminton	Ski fahren	to ski
joggen / laufen	to run	das Hockey	hockey	spazieren gehen	to go for a walk
schwimmen	to swim	der Korbball	netball	wandern	to hike

Question

Wie oft treibst du Sport?

How often do you do sport?

Simple Answer

Ich treibe ziemlich selten Sport. Ich wandere aber gern — ich wandere jedes Wochenende.

I don't do sport very often. I like hiking though — I go hiking every weekend.

Extended Answer

Ich bin Mitglied einer Fußballmannschaft. Wir trainieren dreimal pro Woche und jeden zweiten Samstag spielen wir ein Match. Letztes Mal haben wir gewonnen und ich habe ein Tor geschossen.

I'm a member of a football team. We train three times a week, and every other Saturday, we play a match. Last time, we won and I scored a goal.

Welche Sportarten treibst du? — What sports do you do?

It's useful to talk about <u>where</u> and <u>how often</u> you do sport, as well as what you <u>think</u> of different sports.

das Schwimmbad	swimming pool
das Stadion	stadium
der Sportplatz	sports field
das Sportzentrum	sports centre
das Fitnessstudio	gym
der Verein	club
die Mannschaft	team
das Training	training
das Rennen	race
der Wettbewerb	competition

Grammar — adverbs of time

<u>Adverbs of time</u> are words like '<u>now</u>' and '<u>rarely</u>'. You use them to say <u>when</u> and <u>how often</u> you do something. They usually go <u>after</u> the <u>first verb</u> in a German sentence.

Ich spiele <u>regelmäßig</u> Hockey.   *I play hockey <u>regularly</u>.*
Wir haben <u>immer</u> verloren.   *We <u>always</u> lost.*

You can also put them at the <u>beginning</u> of a sentence to emphasise <u>when</u> something happens.

<u>Gestern</u> bin ich geschwommen.   *<u>Yesterday</u>, I swam.*

For more about adverbs of time, see p.124.

Ich bin Mitglied eines Fahrradvereins.	*I'm a member of a cycling club.*	of a gymnastics club — eines Turnvereins
Auf dem Sportplatz treibe ich Leichtathletik. Wir trainieren zweimal pro Woche.	*On the sports field, I do athletics. We train twice a week.*	I play cricket — spiele ich Kricket
Ich spiele Hockey, weil ich es mag, Mitglied einer Mannschaft zu sein.	*I play hockey because I like being a member of a team.*	I prefer training with other people — ich lieber mit anderen Leuten trainiere
Wenn wir ein Match im Stadion spielen, bin ich immer nervös.	*When we play a match in the stadium, I'm always nervous.*	I'm usually excited — bin ich normalerweise begeistert
Ich bevorzuge es, Sport draußen zu treiben. Deswegen gehe ich nie ins Fitnessstudio.	*I prefer to do sport outside. Therefore, I never go to the gym.*	in the fresh air — an der frischen Luft

Sport

Here's another page on sport — get stuck in so you can win a gold medal in your exam...

Was hältst du von Sport? — What do you think about sport?

Meiner Meinung nach ist Sport super, weil er mich nach dem Schulstress entspannt.

In my opinion, sport is great because it relaxes me after the stress of school.

Ich halte Sport für fantastisch, da ich ihn mit meinen Freunden treiben kann.

I think sport is fantastic because I can do it with my friends.

Sport treiben interessiert mich überhaupt nicht, obwohl ich gern Fußball im Fernsehen sehe.

Doing sport doesn't interest me at all although I like watching football on TV.

it helps me to stay healthy — er mir hilft, gesund zu bleiben

the Olympics — die Olympischen Spiele

Grammar — word order

Think about <u>word order</u> when you use <u>conjunctions</u>.

The order stays the <u>same</u> with <u>coordinating conjunctions</u>, e.g. '<u>aber</u>' *(but)*.

Ich mag Hockey, <u>aber</u> ich <u>finde</u> Rugby langweilig.
I like hockey, <u>but</u> I <u>find</u> rugby boring.

The order <u>changes</u> with <u>subordinating conjunctions</u>, e.g. '<u>weil</u>' *(because)*. The <u>verb</u> moves to the <u>end</u>.

Ich mag Hockey, <u>weil</u> es spannend <u>ist</u>.
I like hockey <u>because</u> it <u>is</u> exciting.

For more on word order, see p.114.

Question

Schaust du Sport im Fernsehen an?
Do you watch sport on TV?

Simple Answer

Ja, ich finde ihn total spannend!
Yes, I find it really exciting!

Extended Answer

Ich schaue Sport fast nie im Fernsehen an, da ich es ein bisschen langweilig finde. Ich denke aber, dass es nützlich ist, weil man viel von den Profis lernen kann.
I hardly ever watch sport on TV because I find it a bit boring. But I think it's useful because you can learn a lot from the pros.

Using conjunctions makes your sentences more interesting...

Your exchange partner Martin has sent an email discussing which sports he does and why.

Hallo,

wie geht's? Ich treibe im Moment ziemlich viel Sport, weil er mich entspannt und mir total Spaß macht. Ich spiele jeden Mittwoch mit meinen Freunden Fußball auf dem Sportplatz und **außerdem**[1] gehe ich regelmäßig Rad fahren und schwimmen. Früher war ich Mitglied in einem Tennisverein, aber jetzt interessiere ich mich mehr für Mannschaftssport, da ich sehr **kontaktfreudig**[2] bin. In der Zukunft möchte ich öfter Ski fahren gehen, weil ich nur zweimal in meinem Leben Ski gefahren bin. Und du? Treibst du oft Sport?

Liebe Grüße,

Martin

Grade 8-9

Du schreibst eine E-Mail über Sport. Schreib:

- welche Sportarten du machst
- wie oft du Sport treibst
- was deine Meinungen über diese Sportarten sind
- ob es einen Sport gibt, den du in der Zukunft ausprobieren möchtest

Du musst ungefähr **90** Wörter auf **Deutsch** schreiben. Schreib etwas über alle Punkte der Aufgabe. *[16 marks]*

[1] in addition
[2] sociable

Tick list:
✓ tenses: present, perfect, simple past, conditional
✓ adverbs
✓ opinions justified

To improve:
+ use more adjectives

Listening Questions

That's right — you've finished the section so it's time for some more exam-style questions.
Doing these is really great practice for the real thing, so give it your best shot.

1   Listen to the following conversation between three people at a restaurant.
     Answer the questions in **English**.

TRACK LISTENING 10

1 a   Why has Herr Hoffmann come back to the restaurant?

     ....   *[1 mark]*

1 b   Give **two** details about the table Herr Hoffmann asks for.

     ....   *[2 marks]*

1 c   Which dish does the waitress recommend?

     ....   *[1 mark]*

1 d   What is Herr Hoffmann's colleague allergic to?

     ....   *[1 mark]*

2   Listen to this news report about the actor Franz von Oberfranz.
     Which **three** statements are true? Write the correct letters in the boxes.

TRACK LISTENING 11

A	Franz has given up acting.
B	He only acts in action films.
C	He was born in a city in Austria.
D	He went to America before the age of ten.
E	His first major success was an action film.
F	He has won a lot of prizes.

☐ ☐ ☐

[3 marks]

Speaking Question

Candidate's Material

- Spend a couple of minutes looking at the photo and the questions below it.

- You can make notes on a separate piece of paper.

© iStock.com/FlairImages

You will be asked the following **three** questions, and **two** questions you haven't prepared:

- Was gibt es auf dem Foto?

- Siehst du gern fern? Warum?

- Was hast du diese Woche im Fernsehen gesehen?

Teacher's Material

- Allow the student to develop his / her answers as much as possible.

- You need to ask the student the following questions **in order**:

  - Was gibt es auf dem Foto?

  - Siehst du gern fern? Warum?

  - Was hast du diese Woche im Fernsehen gesehen?

  - Wirst du in Zukunft mehr oder weniger fernsehen? Warum?

  - Würdest du lieber fernsehen oder Sport treiben?

Reading Questions

1   Translate the following passage into **English**.

> Letzte Woche gab es ein großes Konzert in Berlin und ich bin mit meinen Freunden
> dorthin gefahren. Unsere Lieblingsband hat gespielt — das war sehr spannend.
> Ich finde Livemusik ganz toll, deswegen besuche ich oft Konzerte. Am besten
> gefällt mir Rockmusik und in der Zukunft möchte ich Elektrogitarre spielen lernen.

....

....

....

....

....

....

....

[9 marks]

2   Du liest diese Beiträge in einem Forum zum Thema „Essen". Wähle die richtige Person.
Schreib **A (Alina)**, **B (Berndt)** oder **A + B (Alina und Berndt)**.

Ist gesundes Essen wichtig für Sie?			
Alina	Ich versuche immer, gesund zu essen. Mein ganzes Leben lang bin ich Vegetarierin gewesen. Ich finde das gesünder, als viel Fleisch zu essen.	Berndt	Theoretisch würde ich gern gesund essen, aber leider habe ich oft nicht genug Zeit. Ich arbeite lange Schichten und nachher habe ich keine Lust mehr, etwas zu kochen.

2 a   Wer ist zu beschäftigt, um gesund zu essen? ☐

2 b   Wer isst kein Fleisch? ☐

Essen Sie gern mit anderen Leuten?			
Alina	Für mich können Mahlzeiten eine wichtige soziale Aktivität sein. Ich esse oft mit meinen Freundinnen in der Stadt, was immer schön ist.	Berndt	Meiner Meinung nach macht es mehr Spaß, wenn man mit anderen isst. Dann kann man plaudern und etwas zusammen genießen. Ich esse gern in Restaurants.

2 c   Wem gefällt es, mit anderen zu essen? ☐

[3 marks]

Writing Questions

1 Du schreibst einen Artikel über das Kino für eine Zeitschrift für Jugendliche.

• Schreib etwas über das letzte Mal, als du im Kino warst.

• Vergleich einen Film im Kino mit einem Film zu Hause.

Du musst ungefähr **150** Wörter auf **Deutsch** schreiben.
Schreib etwas über beide Punkte der Aufgabe.

[32 marks]

2 Translate the following passage into **German**.

> I don't enjoy doing sport, but my brother is sporty. The leisure centre is near our house, and he goes there almost every day. Yesterday he went swimming there with his friends. Tomorrow he will go there to play badminton. I prefer to watch television.

....

....

....

....

....

....

....

[12 marks]

Revision Summary for Section Three

Now you've done lots of work on hobbies, here's another fun activity for you: some more revision questions. Don't worry if you can't answer something — just go back over the section and try again.

Music (p.27) ☑

1) What's the German for the following?
   a) choir   b) concert   c) (female) musician   d) (male) singer   e) to play ☑

2) Kira says: „Ich spiele Querflöte in einem Orchester." What does she play? ☑

3) You have been learning the guitar for five years and you would like to learn the trumpet. Say this in German. ☑

4) In German, say what kind of music you like and how you listen to it. ☑

Cinema (p.28) ☑

5) Your friend says „Ich kann nicht oft ins Kino gehen, weil die Eintrittskarten so teuer sind." Explain what the problem is in English. ☑

6) You read an online film review: „Die Trickeffekte waren sehr beeindruckend, aber leider war die Handlung langweilig." What did the reviewer find positive and negative about the film? Answer in English. ☑

7) In German, describe a film you watched recently. Say whether or not you liked it, and why. ☑

TV (p.29) ☑

8) Raphael wants to watch a drama. Which of the following would NOT be suitable for him?
   a) die Nachrichten   b) ein Krimi   c) eine Seifenoper ☑

9) Was für Sendungen siehst du gern? Beantworte die Frage auf Deutsch. ☑

10) You like watching TV but the adverts annoy you. How would you say this in German? ☑

Food and Eating Out (p.30-31) ☑

11) In German, list three types of... a) vegetable   b) fruit   c) meat ☑

12) Gunther says: „Ich mag scharfes Essen, aber ich finde Meeresfrüchte ekelhaft." What does he like / dislike? Answer in English. ☑

13) You're planning your birthday meal. In German, say what you'll eat for each course. ☑

14) You're at a restaurant in Germany. Say that you would like to pay and ask if service is included. ☑

15) Dein Freund isst weder Fleisch noch Fisch. Was kann er im Restaurant bestellen?
    a) Bratwurst mit Pommes   b) Lachs mit Kartoffeln   c) Nudeln mit Pilzen und Käse ☑

Sport (p.32-33) ☑

16) Translate these phrases into English:
    a) spazieren gehen   b) Fahrrad fahren   c) Federball spielen ☑

17) Welche Sportarten treibst du gern? Beantworte die Frage auf Deutsch. ☑

18) Your friend Maike sends you a message: „Hast du Lust, heute Abend mit mir ins Fitnessstudio oder zum Schwimmbad zu gehen?" What does she ask you if you'd like to do? ☑

19) Martin tells you: „Letzte Woche habe ich an einem Wettbewerb teilgenommen." What did he do? ☑

20) In German, say that you are a member of a hockey team, and it helps you to relax after school. ☑

Technology

Technology is a hot topic — it's always changing. Examiners love talking about it, so revise this section carefully. There's a lot of specific vocab, and you need to be able to talk about the pros and cons.

Die Technologie — Technology

der Computer	computer	die Kamera	camera	hochladen (sep.)	to upload
der Laptop	laptop	schicken	to send	herunterladen (sep.)	to download
der Tablet-PC	tablet	simsen	to text	löschen	to delete
das Handy	mobile phone	empfangen	to receive	(aus)drucken	to print (out)
das Smartphone	smartphone	anrufen	to call	der Drucker	printer

Mir ist es wichtig, mein Handy immer dabei zu haben.

It's important to me to always have my phone with me.

Ich simse, um mit meinen Freunden in Kontakt zu bleiben.

I text in order to stay in contact with my friends.

Grammar — um... zu...

You can use the 'um...zu...' construction to say 'in order to...' or 'to...' something. 'Zu' goes near the end of the sentence, just before the infinitive.

Ich benutze mein Handy, um mit meinen Freunden zu chatten.
I use my mobile phone to chat with my friends.

Question	**Simple Answer**	**Extended Answer**
Ist es dir wichtig, das neueste Smartphone zu haben?	Ja. Heutzutage entwickelt sich die Technologie so schnell. Man braucht das Neueste, um aktuell zu bleiben.	Nein. Ich habe schon ein Smartphone. Es hat keinen Sinn, ein neues mit einer Kamera zu kaufen, die nur ein kleines bisschen besser ist oder womit man schneller das Internet surfen kann.
Is it important to you to have the latest smartphone?	*Yes. These days technology develops so fast. You need the latest one to stay up to date.*	*No. I already have a smartphone. It doesn't make sense to buy a new one with a camera that's only slightly better or one that you can surf the Internet faster with.*

Auf meinem Laptop — On my laptop

Ich mache meine Hausaufgaben auf meinem Laptop.

I do my homework on my laptop.

I play video games —
Ich spiele Videospiele

Meiner Meinung nach sind Tablet-PCs viel praktischer als Laptops, denn sie sind so viel kleiner.

In my opinion, tablets are much more practical than laptops because they're so much smaller.

they have touchscreens —
sie haben Touchscreens

they're not as heavy —
sie sind nicht so schwer

Ich lade Fotos auf meinen Laptop hoch, die ich mit meiner Kamera gemacht habe.

I upload photos onto my laptop that I've taken with my camera.

my tablet —
meinem Tablet-PC

my smartphone —
meinem Smartphone

Ich lösche die Fotos, die ich nicht mag, und ich drucke den Rest aus.

I delete the photos that I don't like and I print out the rest.

save — speichere

Question	**Simple Answer**	**Extended Answer**
Verbringst du zu viel Zeit auf deinem Laptop?	Ja vielleicht, aber ich brauche ihn für meine Hausaufgaben.	Ja, ich verbringe ungefähr drei Stunden pro Tag auf meinem Laptop. Ich sollte mich mehr bewegen.
Do you spend too much time on your laptop?	*Yes, perhaps, but I need it for my homework.*	*Yes, I spend around three hours a day on my laptop. I should get more exercise.*

Technology

As for the Internet... who can imagine life without it now? Make sure you learn the technical vocab below so you can give accurate opinions. You're just one click away from mastering this page...

Das Internet — Internet

die Website	*website*
die Startseite	*homepage*
online	*online*
die (E-)Mail	*email*
die E-Mail-Adresse	*email address*
das Konto	*account*
erforschen	*to research*
streamen	*to stream*
das Netzwerk	*network*
das WLAN	*Wi-Fi*
das Passwort	*password*
schützen	*to protect*
die Sicherheit	*security*

der Punkt	*full stop*
der Bindestrich	*hyphen*
der Schrägstrich	*forward slash*
der Unterstrich	*underscore*

Punctuation is useful for spelling out an email or webpage address.

Es geht mir auf die Nerven, wenn das Netzwerk nicht funktioniert.

It gets on my nerves when the network doesn't work.

Die Sicherheit online ist sehr wichtig. Man braucht ein Passwort, um sein Postfach zu schützen.

Security online is very important. You need a password to protect your mailbox.

Wofür benutzt du das Internet? — What do you use the Internet for?

Question	Simple Answer	Extended Answer
Könntest du ohne das Internet leben?	Nein, ich benutze das Internet für alles, zum Beispiel Einkaufen.	Schon als Kind habe ich das Internet benutzt, also finde ich es schwer, mir das Leben ohne Internet vorzustellen. Aber ich könnte es schaffen.
Could you live without the Internet?	*No, I use the Internet for everything, for example shopping.*	*Even as a child, I used the Internet, so I find it hard to imagine life without it. But I could do it.*

Ich benutze Suchmaschinen, um Informationen zu finden.

I use search engines in order to find information.

→ visit lots of web pages — besuche viele Webseiten

Ich verbringe viel Zeit beim Internetsurfen.

I spend a lot of time on the Internet.

→ waste — verschwende

Ich spiele Videospiele online. Das kann ich mit Leuten auf der ganzen Welt tun.

I play video games online. I can do this with people all over the world.

→ chat in forums — chatte in Foren

Man kann im Internet viel erforschen. Das finde ich nützlich, wenn ich meine Hausaufgaben mache.

You can research a lot on the Internet. I find that useful when I do my homework.

→ find out — herausfinden

Ich streame Musik.

I stream music.

→ read the news online — lese die Nachrichten online

Use the present tense to talk about what you usually do...

Translate the text into **German**. *[12 marks]*   Have a look at the grammar box on p.41 for help.

I have a mobile and a tablet. I use the Internet every day. I use it to do my homework. I recently downloaded lots of films. I text twenty or thirty times per day. In future, I will try to use my phone less often and to do more sport.

Social Media

Social media might be wonderful for procrastination, but unfortunately, you do have to revise it as well...

Das soziale Netzwerk — Social network

das Konto	account
chatten	to chat online
die Nachricht	message
das Postfach	mailbox
teilen	to share
das Video	video
das Foto	photo
gehören zu	to belong to
die Gruppe	group
bloggen	to blog

Grammar — hochladen, herunterladen

'Laden' (to load) is an irregular verb, so 'hochladen' (to upload) and 'herunterladen' (to download) are irregular too. You can put 'hoch' or 'herunter' in front of 'laden'. Learn the forms of 'laden'.

ich lade	I load	wir laden	we load
du lädst	you load	ihr ladet	you load
er / sie / es lädt	he / she / it loads	Sie / sie laden	you / they load

Make sure you can use it in the past tense too:

Ich lud die Fotos hoch. *I uploaded the photos.*
Wir haben es heruntergeladen. *We have downloaded it.*

So oft wie möglich chatte ich mit meinen Freunden. *As often as possible, I chat online with my friends.*

Ich bin Blogger(in) und gehöre zu mehreren sozialen Netzwerken. Ich teile Fotos von meinen Ferienreisen. *I am a blogger and I belong to several social networks. I share photos of my travels.*

Die Vorteile sind... — The advantages are...

You need to be able to discuss the pros of social networks. Think about your own opinion.

Ich bin der Meinung, dass soziale Netzwerke nützlich sind, weil man ganz einfach mit Freunden und Familie in Kontakt bleiben kann. *In my opinion, social networks are useful because you can really easily stay in contact with friends and family.*

Es gefällt mir, dass man zu verschiedenen Gruppen gehören kann. *I like that you can belong to different groups.*

Ich schicke fast keine E-Mails mehr, weil ich mit meinen Freunden chatte. *I hardly send emails any more because I chat online with my friends.*

organise an event — eine Veranstaltung organisieren

meet people who share the same interests — Leute, die die gleichen Interessen teilen, kennen lernen

keep up to date with important news — auf dem Laufenden über wichtige Neuigkeiten bleiben

Watch out for separable verbs like 'hochladen'...

Read Brigitte's email about her use of social media and then answer the questions below.

Hallo,

ich wollte dir meine Meinungen über soziale Netzwerke geben. Meiner Meinung nach sind soziale Netzwerke sehr nützlich, um in Kontakt mit Familie und Freunden zu bleiben. Obwohl ich nur mit fünfzig Leuten auf einem sozialen Netzwerk befreundet bin, ist das genug. Ich chatte nur mit Leuten, die ich persönlich kenne. Ich genieße es sehr und bin abends immer online. Meine Eltern denken aber, dass ich zu viel Zeit auf dem Computer verbringe.

Und wie ist es bei dir? Bist du oft online?

Brigitte

e.g. Why does Brigitte think social networks are useful?
Because they help her to stay in contact with family and friends.

1. How many friends does she have on a social network? [1]
2. Whom does she chat to? [1]
3. When is she online? [1]
4. What do her parents think? [1]

The Problems with Social Media

This page is going to sound a bit like your parents going on about how dangerous social media is — sorry!

Soziale Medien — Social media

der Vorteil	*advantage*	die Einstellung	*setting*	gefährlich	*dangerous*
der Nachteil	*disadvantage*	das Privatleben	*private life*	missbrauchen	*to abuse / misuse*
die App	*app*	das Risiko	*risk*	das Cyber-Mobbing	*cyber-bullying*

Question	Simple Answer	Extended Answer
Denkst du, dass soziale Netzwerke gefährlich sein können?	Ich glaube, dass man vorsichtig sein muss. Im Allgemeinen sind sie allerdings nicht gefährlich.	Solange man die Einstellungen vorsichtig verändert, muss man nicht alles teilen. Daher kann man sicher sein. Aber es ist nicht möglich, das Cyber-Mobbing zu kontrollieren.
Do you think that social networks can be dangerous?	*I think that you have to be careful. In general, however, they're not dangerous.*	*As long as you carefully change the settings, you don't have to share everything. Therefore, you can be safe. But it's not possible to control cyber-bullying.*

Die Nachteile sind... — The disadvantages are...

Ein Nachteil von sozialen Netzwerken ist, dass es schwierig ist, das Privatleben zu schützen.	*A disadvantage of social networks is that it's difficult to protect your private life.*
Allerdings ist es möglich, die Einstellungen zu verändern, sodass niemand auf persönliche Informationen zugreifen kann.	*However, it's possible to change the settings so no one can access personal information.*
Es gibt immer ein Risiko, dass jemand ein soziales Netzwerk missbrauchen könnte. Manche Leute benutzen sie für Cyber-Mobbing.	*There's always a risk that someone could misuse a social network. Some people use them for cyber-bullying.*

Try to give a balanced answer by discussing the pros and cons...

Read Rohan's answer to this question.

Was sind für dich die Vor- und Nachteile sozialer Medien?

Wie viele Leute meiner Generation bin ich **abhängig**[1] vom Internet und ich benutze jeden Tag soziale Netzwerke. Für Jugendliche sind soziale Netzwerke wichtiger als E-Mail. Meine Freunde und ich teilen viele Fotos und Neuigkeiten, was ich sehr mag, weil ich immer auf dem Laufenden über ihre Leben bin. Wenn ich von zu Hause wegziehe, wird es noch nützlicher sein.

Allerdings weiß ich, dass ich immer vorsichtig sein muss, da es ein Risiko gibt, dass **Fremde**[2] meine Fotos sehen könnten. Ich versuche, mein Konto sicher zu halten, indem ich regelmäßig die Einstellungen kontrolliere. Ein Freund von mir war letztes Jahr **Opfer**[3] des Cyber-Mobbings. Es war furchtbar.

[1]dependent
[2]strangers
[3]victim

Tick list:
✓ varied word order
✓ good relevant vocab
✓ complex structures, e.g. 'indem...'

To improve:
+ use more adjectives if relevant

Now try answering these questions. Try to talk for about two minutes. *[10 marks]*

- Wie benutzt du soziale Netzwerke?
- Was sind deiner Meinung nach die Vorteile sozialer Netzwerke?
- Und was sind die Nachteile?

Listening Questions

There's a lot of tricky vocab in this section so you need to check it's all gone in. Here's your chance —
we've got another four pages of exam-style questions for you.

1   Young people were interviewed about their use of mobile technology as part of
     a government research programme. Complete the sentences in **English**.

Example: Benedikt uses his laptop to...

    play video games every night
    .... · *[1 mark]*

1 a   Sümeyye uses her phone to...

    .... · *[1 mark]*

1 b   Asli enjoys...

    .... · *[1 mark]*

1 c   Dimitri thinks the Internet is great because...

    .... · *[1 mark]*

2   Hör diesen Podcast, in dem Lina über ihre Familie spricht.
     Wähle dic richtige Antwort.

2 a   Welchen Kurs hat ihre Mutter neulich gemacht?

A	einen Kamerakurs
B	einen Computerkurs
C	einen Handykurs

□   *[1 mark]*

2 b   Was möchte ihre Mutter gern als Nächstes lernen?

A	wie man Fotos herunterlädt
B	wie man Nachrichten verschickt und bekommt
C	wie man soziale Medien benutzt

□   *[1 mark]*

2 c   Was hält ihr Bruder vom Kurs ihrer Mutter?

A	Er denkt, dass es unnötig und teuer ist.
B	Er findet es klasse und ist stolz auf seine Mutter.
C	Er glaubt, dass der Kurs im Beruf weiterhelfen wird.

□   *[1 mark]*

Speaking Question

Candidate's Role

- Your teacher will play the role of the shop assistant. They will speak first.

- You should use *Sie* to address the shop assistant.

- – ! – means you will have to respond to something you have not prepared.

- – ? – means you will have to ask the shop assistant a question.

> Sie kaufen einen neuen Laptop in einem Computerladen in Deutschland.
> Sie sprechen mit dem Verkäufer / der Verkäuferin.
>
> - Suchen — was.
>
> - Den alten Laptop gekauft — wann.
>
> - !
>
> - Tablet-PCs — Ihre Meinung.
>
> - ? Empfehlung — Laptop oder Tablet-PC.

Teacher's Role

- You begin the role-play using the introductory text below.

- You should address the candidate as *Sie*.

- You may alter the wording of the questions in response to the candidate's previous answers.

- Do not supply the candidate with key vocabulary.

> Introductory text: *Sie kaufen einen neuen Laptop in einem Computerladen in Deutschland. Sie sprechen mit dem Verkäufer / der Verkäuferin. Ich bin der Verkäufer / die Verkäuferin.*
>
> - Kann ich Ihnen helfen? Was suchen Sie?
>
> - Wann haben Sie den alten Laptop gekauft?
>
> - ! Wofür werden Sie den neuen Laptop benutzen?
>
> - Was halten Sie von Tablet-PCs?
>
> - ? Allow the candidate to ask you if you recommend a laptop or a tablet.

Reading Questions

1   Translate the following passage into **English**.

> Soziale Medien können nützlich sein. Jedoch muss man aufpassen, wen man im Internet kennenlernt. Auch schadet man der Gesundheit, wenn man zu viel Zeit vor Bildschirmen verbringt. Früher gab es keine sozialen Medien, deshalb haben Jugendliche mehr Sport getrieben. In der Zukunft werden Jugendliche wahrscheinlich soziale Medien noch häufiger verwenden.

....

....

....

....

....

....

[9 marks]

2   Lies die Kommentare zu mobiler Technologie in einem Forum.

> **Tanya:**   Ich weiß nicht, was ich ohne mein Handy machen würde, weil es mich und meine Familie beruhigt, wenn ich alleine unterwegs bin. Allerdings nervt es auch manchmal, weil meine Eltern immer wissen wollen, wo ich bin.
>
> **Nina:**   Ich finde mein Handy äußerst praktisch — man kann schnell etwas im Internet nachschauen und sich informieren. Aber das Herunterladen von Informationen ist leider auch ziemlich teuer.
>
> **Paul:**   Jeder hat heutzutage ein Handy und es ist klasse, dass man überall mit seinen Freunden kommunizieren kann. Doof finde ich es aber, wenn man sich vom Handy abhängig macht, weil man immer erreichbar sein möchte.

Füll die Tabelle auf **Deutsch** aus, um die Vor- und Nachteile mobiler Technologie zu zeigen.

		Vorteil	Nachteil
Example:	Tanya	bietet Sicherheit	Eltern wollen ständig informiert werden.
	Nina		
	Paul		

[4 marks]

Writing Questions

1   Dein österreichischer Freund Tim macht ein Schulprojekt zum Thema Internet.
Er möchte wissen, was du vom Internet hältst.

Schreib:

• etwas über deine Meinung zum Internet

• was du gern online machst

• wofür du diese Woche das Internet benutzt hast

• ob du in der Zukunft das Internet oft benutzen wirst

Du musst ungefähr **90** Wörter auf **Deutsch** schreiben.
Schreib etwas über alle Punkte der Aufgabe.   *[16 marks]*

2   Translate the following passage into **German**.

> Social media is very popular with young people. At school we learnt that you should always be careful online. You should not share too much personal information, particularly with strangers. Also, you should never meet up with someone you don't know. I will never do that.

....

....

....

....

....

....

....

[12 marks]

Revision Summary for Section Four

You've nearly got another section under your belt, you just need to have a bash at these revision questions. Don't go skipping them — they're great at highlighting things you're a bit shaky on. Make sure you tick off the questions as you complete them.

Technology (p.39-40) ☑

1) What's the German for...?
   a) to text   b) to call   c) to download   d) to delete   e) to print ☑

2) Dieter tells you: „Ich muss mein Handy immer dabei haben, damit ich mit meinen Freunden in Kontakt bleiben kann." Translate this into English. ☑

3) You got a new smartphone for your birthday. In German, say two things you use it for, using the 'um...zu' construction. ☑

4) Your German friend Anna is talking about technology: „Es ist sehr wichtig, einen Laptop zu haben." In German, say whether or not you agree with her, and why. ☑

5) In German, give one reason why tablets are more practical than laptops. ☑

6) Your German exchange partner is trying to use his laptop in a café. He says „Wie ärgerlich — das WLAN funktioniert hier nicht. Ich muss eine wichtige E-Mail schicken." Say what the problem is in English. ☑

7) Könntest du ohne das Internet leben? Beantworte die Frage auf Deutsch. ☑

8) Daniel wrote an article on the Internet as part of a school project. Read this extract: „Meiner Meinung nach ist das Internet sehr wichtig für Schüler. Man kann Suchmaschinen benutzen, um verschiedene Themen zu erforschen, und das geht immer sehr schnell. Man findet immer etwas Neues heraus." What is his opinion of the Internet? Answer in English. ☑

9) In German, say that you think the Internet is useful, but some young people waste time online. ☑

Social Media (p.41-42) ☑

10) What do the following words and phrases mean in English?
    a) das Postfach   b) teilen   c) die Nachricht   d) das Konto ☑

11) Justin sends you a message: „Ich habe gerade die Fotos von meinem Urlaub hochgeladen. Sie sehen wirklich toll aus." What has he just done? Answer in English. ☑

12) Gehörst du zu sozialen Netzwerken? Beantworte die Frage auf Deutsch. ☑

13) In German, write down three advantages of social networks. ☑

14) Niko uses social media to meet people who share the same interests. How would you say this in German? ☑

15) How would you say the following in German?
    a) disadvantage   b) settings   c) to abuse / misuse   d) risk ☑

16) Yasmin is worried about social media. She tells you: „Ich meine, dass soziale Medien sehr gefährlich sein können. Man hat kein Privatleben mehr." Do you agree with her? Explain why in German. ☑

17) What does 'Cyber-Mobbing' mean in English? ☑

18) In German, write down one way that you can stay safer online. ☑

Festivals in German-Speaking Countries

You might not feel too festive with all this revision, but read on and you'll find out how to jazz up your next celebration with some traditions from the German-speaking world.

Frohe Weihnachten! — Merry Christmas!

Heiliger Abend	*Christmas Eve*	schmücken	*to decorate*
Weihnachten	*Christmas*	der Weihnachtsbaum	*Christmas tree*
Heilige Drei Könige	*Epiphany*	der Adventskranz	*advent wreath*
feiern	*to celebrate*	anzünden	*to light*
bekommen	*to receive*	die Kerze	*candle*
das Geschenk	*present*	die Weihnachtslieder	*Christmas carols*
sich freuen auf	*to look forward to*	die Weihnachtskarte	*Christmas card*

Viele Familien gehen am Heiligen Abend in die Kirche. — *Lots of families go to church on Christmas Eve.*

have a big festive meal — haben [...] ein großes Festessen

Ich singe gerne Weihnachtslieder. — *I like singing Christmas carols.*

decorate the Christmas tree — schmücken den Weihnachtsbaum

Meine Eltern stellen die Geschenke unter den Weihnachtsbaum. — *My parents put the presents under the Christmas tree.*

invite the whole family — laden die ganze Familie ein

Weihnachten in Deutschland — Christmas in Germany

Christmas is a bit <u>different</u> in Germany. On 6th December, <u>Sankt Nikolaus Tag</u> (*St Nicholas' Day*) is celebrated. Children leave their shoes at the door, and if they've been good, they are filled with <u>treats</u>.

Deutsche Kinder stellen ihre Schuhe vor die Tür, damit Sankt Nikolaus ihnen Süßigkeiten und Nüsse schenken kann. — *German children put their shoes at the door so that St Nicholas can give them presents of sweets and nuts.*

In Deutschland packt man die Geschenke am Heiligen Abend aus. — *In Germany, people unwrap the presents on Christmas Eve.*

> **Grammar** — sich freuen auf
>
> Use '<u>sich freuen auf</u>' + <u>accusative</u> to say you're <u>looking forward to</u> something. Don't forget to choose the right <u>reflexive pronoun</u>.
>
> **Ich <u>freue mich auf</u> den Lebkuchen.**
> ***I <u>am looking forward to</u> the gingerbread.***
> **Er <u>freut sich auf</u> den Weihnachtsmarkt.**
> ***He's <u>looking forward to</u> the Christmas market.***

 READING

6th December is an important day in Germany...

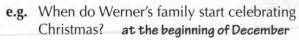

Read the passage about Werner's Christmas and answer the questions in **English**.

Bei uns beginnt die Weihnachtsfeier am Anfang Dezember. Jedes Jahr macht meine Mutter einen Adventskranz mit vier Kerzen. Jede Woche zünde ich eine Kerze an und die Letzte zündet meine Schwester am Heilgen Abend an. Mein Vater kauft uns immer einen großen Weihnachtsbaum und wir alle helfen, den Baum zu schmücken. Meine Oma backt Lebkuchen und Kekse mit Sternen und Herzen aus Schokolade darauf.

e.g. When do Werner's family start celebrating Christmas? ***at the beginning of December***

1. What does his mother do every year? [1]
2. Who lights the last candle and when does this happen? [2]
3. What does Werner's father do? [1]
4. Who decorates the tree? [1]
5. Describe what Werner's grandmother bakes. [2]

Festivals in German-Speaking Countries

Now you're getting into the party mood, here are some other festivals to talk about. It's my gift to you...

Ostern — Easter

Karfreitag	*Good Friday*	die Auferstehung	*resurrection*	das Osterei	*Easter egg*
Ostersonntag	*Easter Sunday*	die Christen	*Christians*	verstecken	*to hide*
Jesu Tod	*Christ's death*	religiös	*religious*	der Osterhase	*Easter bunny*

Christen feiern Jesu Auferstehung. — *Christians celebrate the resurrection of Christ.*

Der Osterhase bringt die Ostereier. — *The Easter bunny brings the Easter eggs.*

Die Eltern verstecken die Schokoladeneier. — *Parents hide the chocolate eggs.*

Andere religiöse Feste — Other religious festivals

islamisch	*Muslim*	christlich	*Christian*
jüdisch	*Jewish*	hinduistisch	*Hindu*

Ich bin Jude / Jüdin. — *I am Jewish.* → Sikh — Sikh / Hindu — Hindu

Ich feiere Chanukka. — *I celebrate Hanukkah.* ← the festival of lights — das Lichterfest

Grammar — religions

In German, you need a different word for <u>Christian</u>, <u>Muslim</u>, <u>Jewish</u> etc. depending on whether it describes a <u>person</u> or a <u>thing</u>.

Ich bin Moslem(in). *(I am Muslim.)*
ein islamistisches Fest *(a Muslim festival)*

Question	**Simple Answer**	**Extended Answer**
Welche Feste feierst du?	Ich feiere das Fest des Fastenbrechens.	Zu Hause feiern wir das Fest des Fastenbrechens. Es kommt nach Ramadan, einer Fastenzeit, die einen Monat dauert. Wir laden unsere Verwandten zu einem Festessen ein.
Which festivals do you celebrate?	*I celebrate Eid.*	*At home we celebrate Eid. It follows Ramadan, a period of fasting, which lasts a month. We invite our relatives to a festive meal.*

Karneval / Fasching — Carnival

<u>Karneval</u> (or <u>Fasching</u>) is a celebration <u>before Lent</u>. There are <u>carnival parades</u> and <u>parties</u>. Some of the biggest events take place on <u>Rosenmontag</u> (*Rose Monday*), which is the Monday before <u>Ash Wednesday</u>.

Es gibt einen Umzug. — *There is a procession.*

Die Leute verkleiden sich. — *People put on fancy dress.*

TRACK LISTENING 14

You can talk about any religious festivals you celebrate...

Listen to this podcast about Karneval and answer the questions in **English**.

e.g. What other German names are there for Karneval? **Fasching / Fastnachtszeit**

1. In which countries is Karneval celebrated? [3]
2. How is Karneval described? [2]
3. Where are the biggest parties? [1]
4. What do most people do? [1]

Festivals in German-Speaking Countries

The German Bundesländer (Federal States) have a lot of say in which days are public holidays.

Der Tag der Deutschen Einheit — The Day of German Unity

Am 3. Oktober feiert man die Wiedervereinigung Deutschlands.

Der Tag der Deutschen Einheit ist ein Feiertag.

Es gibt ein großes Feuerwerk.

On the 3rd October, people celebrate the reunification of Germany.

The Day of German Unity is a public holiday.

There is a big fireworks display.

Germany was divided into East and West Germany after the Second World War.

Official reunification took place in 1990, creating the Bundesrepublik Deutschland (*Federal Republic of Germany*).

Weitere Feste — More festivals

Silvester	*New Year's Eve*
der Neujahrstag	*New Year's Day*
der Valentinstag	*Valentine's Day*
das Pfingsten	*Whitsuntide*
der Maifeiertag	*May Day*

Grammar — use 'zu...' for 'at...' or 'on...'

With <u>single</u> words like 'Pfingsten' (*Whitsuntide*), German uses '<u>zu</u>' to say '<u>at</u>' or '<u>on</u>':

<u>zu</u> Silvester — ***on New Year's Eve***

If the word ends in '<u>Tag</u>' or a <u>day of the week</u>, use '<u>am</u>':

<u>am</u> Neujahrstag — ***on New Year's Day***

Der erste Januar ist ein Feiertag. Die meisten Leute arbeiten nicht.

Ich habe eine Einladung zu einer Party bei einem Freund bekommen.

The first of January is a public holiday. Most people don't work.

I have received an invitation to a party at a friend's house.

Many shops are shut — Viele Geschäfte haben zu

at my neighbour's house — bei meinem Nachbarn

Question	**Simple Answer**	**Extended Answer**
Was hältst du vom Valentinstag?	Ich finde ihn blöd und sinnlos.	Meiner Meinung nach ist Valentinstag zu kommerziell. Die Geschäfte wollen einfach Geld machen. Es ist völlig unnötig.
What do you think of Valentine's Day?	*I think it's stupid and pointless.*	*In my opinion, Valentine's Day is too commercial. The shops just want to make money. It's completely unnecessary.*

 SPEAKING

Learn how to say 'at' and 'on' with festivals...

Laura is talking to her teacher about festivals.

Teacher: Was ist dein Lieblingsfest?

Laura: Ich mag den Maifeiertag, weil alles schön bunt und laut ist. In meinem Dorf gab es dieses Jahr viele Feierlichkeiten.

Teacher: Kannst du mir ein deutsches Fest beschreiben?

Laura: Am 6. Dezember feiern die Deutschen den Sankt Nikolaus Tag. Die Kinder stellen ihre Schuhe vor die Tür und bekommen Süßigkeiten.

Teacher: Was hältst du von Karneval?

Laura: Es klingt sehr spannend. Ich würde gern daran teilnehmen. Welche Feste feiern Sie?

Teacher: Ich feiere immer das Lichterfest. Feierst du auch ein religiöses Fest?

Laura: Ich bin zwar nicht religiös, aber ich feiere Ostern mit meiner Familie.

 Grade 6-7

Tick list:
✓ range of adjectives
✓ tenses: present, simple past, conditional

To improve:
+ use more subject-specific vocab
+ use more complex sentences

Now answer the questions yourself. Address your teacher as 'Sie' and talk for about 2 minutes. [15 marks]

Listening Questions

That was a pretty short section so you should have plenty of energy left for some exam-style questions.

1 Einige Jugendliche sprechen über Ostern für ein Schulprojekt.
Beantworte die Fragen auf **Deutsch**.

(TRACK LISTENING 15)

1 a Was macht Tina mit ihrer Schwester zu Ostern? Gib **zwei** Punkte.

.... *[2 marks]*

1 b Was macht Jakobs Opa jedes Jahr zu Ostern?

.... *[1 mark]*

1 c Was würde Laura nicht gut finden?

.... *[1 mark]*

1 d Was gefällt Jan nicht so sehr zu Ostern? Gib **einen** Punkt.

.... *[1 mark]*

2 Listen to Antje talking about how she celebrates Christmas in Germany.
Answer the questions in **English**.

(TRACK LISTENING 16)

2 a How does Antje celebrate Christmas? Give **two** details.

.... *[2 marks]*

2 b What is she looking forward to most at Christmas?

.... *[1 mark]*

2 c What was different last year?

.... *[1 mark]*

2 d Does Antje prefer the German or the English tradition?

.... *[1 mark]*

Speaking Question

Candidate's Material

- Spend a couple of minutes looking at the photo and the questions below it.

- You can make notes on a separate piece of paper.

© iStock.com/monkeybusinessimages

You will be asked the following **three** questions, and **two** questions you haven't prepared:

- Was gibt es auf dem Foto?

- Feierst du gern Feste mit deiner Familie?   Warum (nicht)?

- Welche Feste hast du dieses Jahr schon gefeiert?

Teacher's Material

- Allow the student to develop his / her answers as much as possible.

- You need to ask the student the following questions **in order**:

  - Was gibt es auf dem Foto?

  - Feierst du gern Feste mit deiner Familie?   Warum (nicht)?

  - Welche Feste hast du dieses Jahr schon gefeiert?

  - Denkst du, dass manche Feste zu kommerziell sind?

  - Was wirst du dieses Jahr zu Silvester machen?

Reading Questions

1 Translate the following message into **English**.

> Freust du dich schon auf Weihnachten? Ich bin schon total aufgeregt, weil ich Weihnachten so sehr liebe. Am meisten freue ich mich darauf, Geschenke einzupacken. Das hat mir letztes Jahr großen Spaß gemacht. Was wünschst du dir zu Weihnachten? Ich hoffe, dass es an Weihnachten schneien wird. Das wäre toll.

....

....

....

....

....

....

[9 marks]

2 Read this email Lukas sent to his friend. Answer the questions in **English**.

> Hallo Ali,
> im Moment ist es sehr lustig bei uns hier in Köln, da es Karnevalszeit ist. Jedes Jahr im Februar verwandelt sich Köln für ein paar Tage in ein buntes Meer von Kostümen und die Straßen sind voller Prinzessinnen, Piraten und gruseligen Gespenstern.
>
> Es gibt auch den Rosenmontagsumzug — das ist eine Prozession durch die Straßen, wo verkleidete Leute Süßigkeiten und Blumen von dekorierten Wagen in die Menschenmenge werfen. Das gefällt mir sehr gut. Das Beste ist aber, dass wir an Karneval schulfrei bekommen, damit alle mitfeiern können.
>
> Bis bald,
> Lukas

2 a What do people dress up as? Give **two** examples.

.... *[2 marks]*

2 b What gets thrown into the crowd? Give **two** details.

.... *[2 marks]*

2 c What does Lukas find particularly great about Karneval?

.... *[1 mark]*

Writing Questions

1 Du warst neulich in Deutschland und hast ein deutsches Fest gefeiert. Du schreibst ein Blog darüber.

- Schreib etwas über das Fest — welches Fest es war und was passiert ist.

- Vergleich deutsche Feste mit den Festen, die du zu Hause feierst.

Du musst ungefähr **150** Wörter auf **Deutsch** schreiben.
Schreib etwas über beide Punkte der Aufgabe.

[32 marks]

2 Translate the following passage into **German**.

I am not religious, but I like Easter. It is nice to spend time with the family. My father bakes a cake, and we decorate the house. Last year, I ate too much chocolate, and I was ill. I will not do that this year. I hope it will be sunny so we can be outside.

....

....

....

....

....

....

[12 marks]

Revision Summary for Section Five

And for my next trick... some more revision summary questions. There are lots of festivals and traditions to get your head round, so work your way through these questions carefully. If you can't remember something, just have a gander back through the section. You might learn something else too.

Festivals in German-Speaking Countries (p.48-50) ☑

1) What's the German for...?
   a) Merry Christmas!   b) Christmas Eve   c) Epiphany ☑

2) Jo tells you: „Ich freue mich sehr darauf, den Weihnachtsbaum zu schmücken." What is she looking forward to? ☑

3) Was machst du am Heiligen Abend? Beantworte die Frage auf Deutsch. ☑

4) Your German exchange partner Fabian has written to you about Christmas in Germany: „Sankt Nikolaus Tag ist sehr wichtig für uns hier in Deutschland. Die Kinder stellen ihre Schuhe vor die Tür und bekommen Süßigkeiten, Nüsse und andere kleine Geschenke vom Sankt Nikolaus." Translate what he has told you into English, so you can share it with your family. ☑

5) How would you say "I'm looking forward to the presents" in German? ☑

6) In German, write down three things people might do on Christmas day. ☑

7) Laura tells you: „Mein jüngerer Bruder glaubt immer noch an den Osterhasen, also verstecken wir jedes Jahr zu Ostern viele Schokoladeneier." What does her family do at Easter, and why? ☑

8) How do you say the following in German? a) I am Jewish (give the male and female form)
   b) a Christian celebration   c) a Hindu festival ☑

9) In German, describe a festival you celebrate with your family. Say what you do together, and whether or not you enjoy it. ☑

10) Your cousin doesn't speak any German but has heard someone mention Karneval. Give her a brief explanation of what it is. ☑

11) One of your Bavarian friends has just been celebrating Fasching. She tells you: „Es war wirklich prima — alles war so laut und bunt. Ich habe mich als Prinzessin verkleidet." What does she think about Fasching? Answer in English. ☑

12) Was macht man am dritten Oktober in Deutschland? Gib zumindest zwei Details auf Deutsch. ☑

13) During your school exchange in Switzerland, your exchange partner tells you: „Pass mal auf — morgen ist ein Feiertag. Das heißt, dass die Geschäfte zuhaben. Wenn du etwas brauchst, solltest du heute einkaufen gehen." What has he warned you about? Answer in English. ☑

14) What do the following mean in English?
   a) der Maifeiertag   b) der Neujahrstag   c) das Pfingsten ☑

15) You receive a message from one of your German friends: „Ich habe jedes Jahr zu Silvester eine große Party. Ich möchte dich einladen." Translate this into English. ☑

16) Verbringst du Silvester lieber mit Freunden oder mit deiner Familie? Beantworte die Frage auf Deutsch. ☑

17) Tobias has written to you about Valentine's Day: „Ich finde den Valentinstag schön. Viele sagen, dass er zu kommerziell ist, aber ich stimme diesen Leuten nicht zu. Ich schenke meiner Freundin immer Blumen und wir gehen zusammen essen — das ist prima." Do you share Tobias's view? In German, write a response to Tobias, saying whether or not you agree with him. ☑

The Home

Home sweet home; home is where the heart is; there's no place like home... you might not agree with the clichés, but you do need to be able to talk about your abode (humble or otherwise).

Wie ist dein Haus? — What's your house like?

das Haus	*house*	der Wohnblock	*block of flats*
die Wohnung	*flat*	das Einfamilienhaus	*detached house*
das Doppelhaus	*semi-detached house*	am Stadtrand	*on the outskirts*
das Reihenhaus	*terraced house*	im Stadtzentrum	*in the town centre*

Ich wohne in einem alten Haus.	*I live in an old house.*
Wir ziehen in ein Reihenhaus um.	*We're moving into a terraced house.*
Meine Wohnung liegt in der Nähe von einem Park und den Geschäften.	*My flat is near a park and the shops.*

modern — modernen   *new* — neuen
big — großen   *small* — kleinen

farm house — Bauernhaus

the motorway — der Autobahn
a train station — einem Bahnhof

Wie sehen die Zimmer aus? — What do the rooms look like?

das Wohnzimmer	*living room*	die Vorhänge	*curtains*
das Badezimmer	*bathroom*	die Möbel	*furniture*
das Esszimmer	*dining room*	das Bett	*bed*
das Schlafzimmer	*bedroom*	das Etagenbett	*bunk bed*
die Küche	*kitchen*	der Schrank	*cupboard*
die Wände	*walls*	der Stuhl	*chair*
der Teppich	*carpet*	der Garten	*garden*

> **Grammar** — identifying plurals
>
> You can use grammatical <u>markers</u> like <u>articles</u> and <u>verb forms</u> to tell whether a noun is <u>plural</u> or not.
>
> **<u>Die</u> Zimmer <u>sind</u> schön.**
> *The rooms <u>are</u> nice.*
>
> **<u>Das</u> Zimmer <u>ist</u> schön.**
> *The room <u>is</u> nice.*

Die Küche ist hell und geräumig.	*The kitchen is bright and spacious.*
Im Schlafzimmer habe ich einen riesigen Kleiderschrank.	*In the bedroom, I have a huge wardrobe.*
Mein Haus hat einen Garten.	*My house has a garden.*

on the ground floor — im Erdgeschoss

a double bed — ein Doppelbett

a conservatory — einen Wintergarten

Don't just list the rooms in your house — use adjectives too...

Read this extract from 'Der Wolf und die sieben jungen Geißlein' by the Brothers Grimm. Answer the questions in **English**.

Wer aber hereinkam, war der Wolf. Die **Geißlein**[1] hatten Angst und wollten sich verstecken. Das erste sprang unter den Tisch, das zweite ins Bett, das dritte in den Ofen, das vierte in die Küche, das fünfte in den Schrank, das sechste unter die Waschschüssel, das siebente in den **Kasten**[2] der Wanduhr. Aber der Wolf fand sie und **verschluckte**[3] eins nach dem andern. Nur das jüngste in dem Uhrkasten fand er nicht.

[1](goat) kids
[2]case
[3]swallowed

e.g. What did the goat kids want to do?
  They wanted to hide from the wolf.

1. Where did the first kid go? *[1]*
2. List three other hiding places mentioned. *[3]*
3. Which kid did the wolf **not** find? *[1]*

What You Do at Home

Whether you spring out of bed as soon as the alarm clock sounds, or huddle under the duvet for as long as possible, you need to be able to talk about your daily routine.

Mein Tagesablauf — My Daily Routine

aufwachen	*to wake up*	sich waschen	*to have a wash*	sich anziehen	*to get dressed*
aufstehen	*to get up*	sich rasieren	*to shave*	frühstücken	*to have breakfast*
sich duschen	*to have a shower*	sich schminken	*to put on make-up*	verlassen	*to leave (house)*

Ich stehe um acht Uhr auf.   *I get up at 8 o'clock.*

Oft esse ich mit meiner   *I often have lunch*
Familie zu Mittag.   *with my family.*

Nach dem Essen mache   *After the meal,*
ich meine Hausaufgaben.   *I do my homework.*

Grammar — reflexive verbs

Verbs like 'sich anziehen' are <u>reflexive</u> — they need a <u>pronoun</u> (mich, dich etc.). The pronoun needs to agree with the subject. See p.128 for more.

ich wasche <u>mich</u>	*I wash <u>myself</u>*
du wäschst <u>dich</u>	*you wash <u>yourself</u>*
wir waschen <u>uns</u>	*we wash <u>ourselves</u>*

Was machst du zu Hause? — What do you do at home?

putzen / sauber machen	*to clean*	den Tisch decken	*to lay the table*
vorbereiten	*to prepare*	kochen	*to cook*
aufräumen	*to tidy up*	die Mahlzeit	*meal / mealtime*
Staub saugen	*to vacuum*	abwaschen	*to wash up*
Staub wischen	*to dust*	(sich) kümmern (um)	*to look after*

Jeden Tag decke ich den Tisch.   *Everyday, I set the table.* ← ⌐ *I look after my brother* — kümmere ich mich um meinen Bruder

Am Wochenende putze ich das   *At the weekend, I clean* ←
Badezimmer und sauge Staub.   *the bathroom and vacuum.* ⌐ *I cook dinner* — koche ich das Abendessen

Question

Musst du zu Hause helfen?

Do you have to help at home?

Simple Answer

Ja, ich wische Staub und manchmal räume ich mein Zimmer auf.

Yes, I dust and sometimes, I tidy my room.

Extended Answer

Nachdem ich aufgestanden bin, muss ich an Schultagen das Frühstück für meinen Halbbruder vorbereiten. Ich dusche mich kurz danach, wasche ab und mache die Küche sauber. Abends koche ich für meine Familie. Ich Ärmster!

After I have got up, I have to prepare breakfast for my half-brother on schooldays. I have a shower shortly afterwards, wash up and clean the kitchen. In the evening, I cook for my family. Poor me!

You need lots of reflexive verbs to describe your daily routine...

Translate this blog post into **English**. *[9 marks]*

Ich wohne bei meinen Eltern in einer Wohnung in Berlin. Ich muss jeden Tag zu Hause helfen. Das nervt mich. Nach der Schule putze ich die Wohnung. Ich muss auch für meine Eltern kochen, weil sie spät nach Hause kommen. Gestern räumte ich mein Zimmer auf. Ich hoffe, dass ich am Wochenende mehr Freizeit haben werde.

Talking About Where You Live

You need to be able to describe the area you live in, and talk about what you can do there.

Wo wohnst du? — Where do you live?

Don't forget to give an <u>opinion</u> about where you live — it'll help you impress the examiner.

auf dem Land	*in the countryside*	am Meer	*by the sea*	im Norden	*in the north*
an der Küste	*on the coast*	in den Bergen	*in the mountains*	die Großstadt	*city*
die Gegend	*region*	in der Nähe von	*near (to...)*	die Stadt	*town*

Ich wohne in einem Dorf im Süden.	*I live in a village in the south.*	*in a town* — in einer Stadt
Meine Heimatstadt liegt in Nordwales.	*My home town is in north Wales.*	*in north-east England* — in Nordostengland
Die Landschaft um mein Haus ist schön und grün.	*The landscape around my home is beautiful and green.*	*mountainous* — bergig *flat* — flach
Ich finde meine Stadt sehr lebendig und interessant.	*I think my town is very lively and interesting.*	*boring* — langweilig *peaceful* — ruhig

Was gibt es in deiner Stadt? — What is there in your town?

Es gibt viele Geschäfte, darunter eine Bäckerei und eine Metzgerei.	*There are lots of shops, including a bakery and a butcher's.*	*a chemist's* — eine Drogerie
Der Hafen ist einen Besuch wert.	*The harbour is worth a visit.*	*The cathedral* — Der Dom
Es ist immer was los.	*There's always something going on.*	*never* — nie
Ich gehe oft zum Markt.	*I often go to the market.*	*to the library* — in die Bibliothek
Es gibt ein paar historische Gebäude.	*There are a few historic buildings.*	*green spaces* — Grünanlagen

---

Don't forget to use the dative case with 'wohnen'...

Ein Freund hat dir eine E-Mail geschickt, in der er seine Stadt beschreibt.

Grüß dich! Ich wohne in Köln, das eine schöne Großstadt in Westdeutschland ist. Es gibt hier so viel für Besucher zu tun, weil es riesig ist — wir haben über 1 000 000 Einwohner! Obwohl Köln in der Vergangenheit eine Industriestadt war, ist es jetzt viel sauberer und moderner, glaube ich. Wir haben viele Sehenswürdigkeiten, wie interessante Museen, einen beeindruckenden Dom und viele geräumige Grünanlagen, wo man spazieren gehen kann. Ich liebe das Leben hier, weil immer viel los ist. Wie ist dein Wohnort? Gibt es dort viel zu tun?

Grade 8-9

Tick list:
- ✓ tenses: present, simple past
- ✓ opinions justified using 'weil...'
- ✓ varied adjectives

To improve:
- + say what the town might be like in the future
- + use the conditional to say whether you'd recommend the town to visitors

Du schreibst eine Antwort auf die E-Mail. Schreib etwas über die folgenden Punkte:

- wo du wohnst
- deine Meinung zu der Gegend und zu den Sehenswürdigkeiten.

Schreib ungefähr **90** Wörter auf **Deutsch**. Beantworte die beiden Teile der Frage. *[16 marks]*

Clothes Shopping

You might not be interested in clothes, but you still need to learn how to talk about them in German.

Ich brauche neue Klamotten — I need new clothes

das Hemd	shirt
das T-Shirt	T-shirt
der Pullover	sweater
das Kleid	dress
der Rock	skirt
die Hose (sing.)	trousers
die Jeans (sing.)	jeans
Schuhe	shoes
die Sportschuhe	trainers
die Klamotten	clothes
anprobieren	to try on
ausgeben	to spend (money)
Schlange stehen	to queue
pleite (sein)	(to be) skint
der Kunde	(male) customer
die Kundin	(female) customer

Im Einkaufszentrum kaufe ich Röcke und T-Shirts. — *At the shopping centre, I buy skirts and T-shirts.*

Ich gebe mein Geld für Schuhe und Kleider aus. — *I spend my money on shoes and dresses.*

Ich trage gern bunte Kleidungsstücke. — *I like wearing colourful clothes.*

Kleider stehen mir nicht. Ich trage lieber Hosen. — *Dresses don't suit me. I prefer to wear trousers.*

Grammar — stehen + dative

To say that something <u>suits</u> someone, use 'stehen' with the <u>dative</u>.

Die Farbe steht <u>dir</u> sehr gut. — *The colour really suits <u>you</u>.*

Das rote Hemd steht <u>ihm</u> nicht. — *The red shirt doesn't suit <u>him</u>.*

Gehst du gern einkaufen? — Do you like going shopping?

Ja, ich gehe jedes Wochenende einkaufen. — *Yes, I go shopping every weekend.* ← *from time to time —* ab und zu

Einkaufen mit Freunden macht Spaß. — *Shopping with friends is fun.* ← *is boring —* ist langweilig

Question

Gehst du gern einkaufen?
Do you like going shopping?

Simple Answer

Ja, Einkaufen gefällt mir sehr gut. Meistens kaufe ich Sportschuhe und Jeans.
Yes, I really like shopping. I mostly buy trainers and jeans.

Extended Answer

Ja, sehr gern. Ich gebe mein ganzes Geld für Klamotten aus. Gestern war ich in der Stadt unterwegs und habe viele schöne Sachen in den Geschäften gesehen. Schließlich habe ich mich für einen blauen Rock entschieden — ich werde ihn sehr oft tragen. Meine Eltern denken, dass ich Geld verschwende, aber Einkaufen macht mir Spaß!

Yes, absolutely. I spend all my money on clothes. Yesterday, I was out and about in town and saw lots of lovely things in the shops. In the end, I decided on a blue skirt — I'll wear it a lot. My parents think that I waste money, but I find shopping fun!

'Einkaufen', 'anprobieren' and 'ausgeben' are separable verbs...

Jana spricht über Einkaufen. Beantworte die Fragen auf **Deutsch**.

e.g. In welchem Geschäft ist Jana einkaufen gegangen? **im Kaufhaus**

1. Welche zwei Kleidungsstücke hat Jana gekauft? [2]
2. Was fand sie positiv im Geschäft? [1]
3. Warum kann sie erst am Samstag einen Pullover kaufen? [1]   'Erst' can be used to mean 'not until'.
4. Was würde Jana gern kaufen, wenn sie mehr Geld hätte? [1]

Shopping

This page is positively awash with practical phrases you can use during your next German shopping spree.

Was möchten Sie? — What would you like?

das Kilo	*kilo(gram)*	die Schachtel	*box*
das Gramm	*gram*	eine Menge	*a lot of*
das Pfund	*pound*	ein paar	*a few*
die Scheibe	*slice*	ein bisschen	*a bit*
das Stück	*piece*	einige	*some*
die Flasche	*bottle*	mehrere	*several*
die Dose	*can / tin*	ungefähr	*about*
das Gewicht	*weight*	viel / viele	*a lot / many*

Sizes are different in some EU countries. E.g.:
<u>Women's Clothes</u>

Size	8	10	12	14	16	18
Größe	34	36	38	40	42	44

<u>Men's Shoes</u> (Rough equivalents)

Size	6	7	8	9	10	11
Größe	40	41	42	43	44	45

Ich möchte eine Hose. Meine Größe ist 36.　　*I'd like a pair of trousers. I'm a size 10.*

Ich hätte gern eine Schachtel Pralinen.　　*I'd like a box of chocolates.*

> Another way to say 'I would like...' is 'Ich hätte gern...'. See p.6 for more.

Ich hätte gern drei Kilo Käse — I would like three kilos of cheese

Question

Kann ich Ihnen helfen?

Can I help you?

Simple Answer

Ich möchte ein Kilo Orangen und eine Menge Kirschen.

I'd like a kilo of oranges and a lot of cherries.

Grammar — viel / viele

'Viel' (a lot of) is used with <u>singular</u> or <u>uncountable</u> nouns. 'Viele' (many) is used with <u>plural</u> nouns.

**Ich brauche <u>viel</u> Obst.　*I need <u>a lot of</u> fruit.*

**Ich möchte <u>viele</u> Kekse.　*I'd like <u>many</u> biscuits.*

Extended Answers

Ja, ich hätte gern ein großes Stück Käse, ein paar Eier und zwei Scheiben Schinken. Ich nehme bitte auch eine Dose Cola und eine Tüte Chips dazu.

Yes, I'd like a large piece of cheese, a few eggs and two slices of ham. I'll have a can of cola and a bag of crisps with that as well, please.

Ja, ich möchte hundert Gramm Erbsen, viermal Zwiebeln und einige Pilze, wenn Sie welche haben. Etwas Süßes wäre auch schön. Was für Kuchen haben Sie?

Yes, I'd like a hundred grams of peas, four onions and some mushrooms if you have any. Something sweet would be nice too. What sort of cake do you have?

Always use 'Sie' when you talk to shop assistants in Germany...

Lies diese Kritik eines neuen Geschäfts.

Letzte Woche besuchte ich ein Geschäft und ich hatte viele Probleme. Ich hatte schon eine neue Hose gekauft. Aber ich wollte ein blaues Hemd anprobieren. Ich trage Größe 38. Der Verkäufer brachte mir aber ein Hemd, das viel zu groß war! Zehn Minuten später gab er mir ein weißes Hemd, das ich sehr hässlich fand. Ich bin mit diesem Kleidergeschäft gar nicht zufrieden.

> Grade 6-7

Tick list:
✓ tenses: present, simple past, pluperfect
✓ variety of phrases

To improve:
+ use a 'weil' clause
+ add a future or conditional
+ use more adjectives

Schreib eine eigene Kritik eines Geschäfts. Schreib etwas über die folgenden Punkte:

- *was du gekauft hast*
- *deine Meinung dazu*

*Schreib ungefähr **90** Wörter auf **Deutsch**. Beantworte die beiden Teile der Frage. [16 marks]*

In the Shop

Once you've found that perfect outfit, you need to make sure you can actually pay for it.

Ein gutes Angebot — A good deal

Get your head around <u>euro coins</u> and <u>notes</u> in advance and avoid embarrassment at the till...

das Taschengeld	*pocket money*	die Kasse	*till*
anbieten	*to offer*	die Quittung	*receipt*
das Angebot	*offer*	wechseln	*to change (money)*
der Ausverkauf	*sale*	das Bargeld	*cash*
das Sonderangebot	*special offer*	das Kleingeld	*small change*
preiswert / günstig	*good value*	das Geldstück	*coin*
der Rabatt	*discount*	der Geldschein	*note*
kostenlos / gratis	*free of charge*	das Euro-Stück	*euro coin*
der Preis	*price*	der Euro-Schein	*euro note*

There are 100 cents in a euro.

If something costs 5,50 €, you say the price like this: fünf Euro fünfzig Cent.

Wie viel kostet das? — How much does it cost?

These phrases could come in handy if you get a <u>shopping role-play</u> in the speaking exam.

Kann ich mit Karte bezahlen oder akzeptieren Sie nur Bargeld?
Can I pay by card, or do you only accept cash?

Die Hose ist zu teuer, aber der Rock ist günstig.
The trousers are too expensive, but the skirt is good value.

Ich muss mein Geld in Euro wechseln.
I need to change my money into euros.

Ich will mein Geld zurück.
I want my money back.

Grammar — separable verbs

<u>Separable verbs</u> have <u>two</u> parts, e.g. 'anbieten' (*to offer*). See p.145 for more. In the <u>present</u> tense, the <u>separable prefix</u> goes to the <u>end</u> of the clause:
Der Laden bietet einen Rabatt an.
The shop offers a discount.
In the <u>perfect</u> tense, the 'ge' goes in the <u>middle</u> of the two parts of the verb:
Er hat es mir kostenlos angeboten.
He offered it to me free of charge.

 ## This topic could easily come up in the speaking exam...

Read the conversation below. Jonas is on holiday in Austria and wants to buy a few things.

Verkäufer: Guten Tag. Kann ich Ihnen helfen? *(Grade 6-7)*
Jonas: Ich hätte gern vier Scheiben Käse, hundert Gramm Kartoffelsalat und zwei Brötchen, bitte. Ich nehme auch eine Flasche Wasser. Wie viel kostet das?
Verkäufer: Das macht zehn Euro fünfzig. Sonst noch etwas?
Jonas: Ja, kann ich bitte ein Stück Schokoladenkuchen haben? Er sieht lecker aus. Ich würde ihn gern probieren.
Verkäufer: Ja, natürlich.
Jonas: Darf ich bitte eine Quittung haben?
Verkäufer: Ja, bitte schön. Auf Wiedersehen.

Tick list:
✓ tenses: present, conditional
✓ opinion phrase
✓ correctly formed questions

To improve:
+ use conjunctions to link the sentences

Use the instructions below to prepare your own role-play. Address the assistant as 'Sie' and speak for about two minutes. [15 marks]

Sie sind am Markt in Österreich.
- *drei Produkte*
- *Ihre Meinung (zwei Punkte)*
- *? Rabatt*
- *!*
- *kein Kleingeld*

Giving and Asking for Directions

Feeling like you could do with a little direction? Look no further, here are some useful phrases...

Wo ist...? — Where is...?

der Bahnhof	*train station*	das Kino	*cinema*	der Park	*park*
der Busbahnhof	*bus station*	die Post	*post office*	die Apotheke	*pharmacy*

liegen	*to be situated*	(nach) links	*(to the) left*	gegenüber	*opposite*
drüben	*over there*	(nach) rechts	*(to the) right*	neben	*near*
weg	*away*	geradeaus	*straight on*	bleiben	*to stay*
überqueren	*to cross (road)*	mitten in	*in the middle of*	nehmen	*to take*

Entschuldigung. Wo ist der Markt, bitte?

Excuse me. Where is the market please?

Gehen Sie hier links, gehen Sie geradeaus und der Markt ist auf der rechten Seite.

Go left here, go straight on and the market is on the right-hand side.

Ich bin hier fremd. Wie komme ich zu der Post?

I am a stranger here. How do I get to the post office?

Geh hier rechts und nimm die erste Straße links.

Go right here and take the first street on the left.

> Don't forget to use the polite form 'Sie' for people who are older than you.

Wie weit ist es? — How far is it?

nah	*near*	weit	*far*	die Ecke	*corner*
in der Nähe	*nearby*	entfernt	*(far) away*	die Meile	*mile*

Die Bank ist zwei Kilometer von hier.

The bank is two kilometres from here.

Der Supermarkt ist ganz in der Nähe.

The supermarket is really close by.

Es ist gar nicht weit von hier.

It's not at all far from here.

Es ist um die Ecke.

It's round the corner.

Der Bahnhof ist zehn Minuten von hier entfernt.

The station is ten minutes away from here.

Grammar — prepositions and cases

Some prepositions take either the accusative <u>or</u> the dative case.

If <u>movement</u> is involved, use the <u>accusative</u>:

Gehen Sie <u>in die Stadt</u>. (accusative)
Go <u>into town</u>.

If <u>no movement</u> is involved, use the <u>dative</u>:

Die Post ist <u>in der Stadt</u>. (dative)
The post office is <u>in town</u>.

TRACK LISTENING 18

Directions are tricky but they could come in handy...

Listen to the dialogue. A tourist is asking for directions. Which sentences are **true**? *[3 marks]*

A. The tourist is looking for the cinema.

B. There are two cinemas nearby.

C. The theatre is called 'Agora'.

D. The tourist is not far from his destination.

E. The destination is on the right-hand side.

Weather

Weather is an important topic for talking about where you live, and it's helpful for describing holidays too.

Wie ist das Wetter? — What's the weather like?

Es...	It is...
schneit	snowing
regnet	raining
hagelt	hailing
donnert	thundering

Es ist...	It is...
heiß	hot
warm	warm
feucht	damp
nass	wet

windig	windy
sonnig	sunny
bedeckt	overcast
trocken	dry
nebelig	foggy

die Jahreszeit	season
der Sommer	summer
der Herbst	autumn
der Winter	winter
der Frühling	spring

Question	**Simple Answer**	**Extended Answer**
Wie ist das Wetter?	Es regnet, es ist windig und bewölkt.	Heute Morgen war es ziemlich wolkig und es hat geschneit, aber jetzt regnet es und es ist windig. Es hat ungefähr sechs Grad.
What's the weather like?	*It's raining, it's windy and cloudy.*	*This morning, it was fairly cloudy and it snowed, but now it's raining and it's windy. It's about six degrees.*

Die Wettervorhersage — The weather forecast

Am Wochenende wird es schneien.
At the weekend, it will snow.

Morgen wird es warm sein.
Tomorrow, it will be warm.

Im Süden wird es bedeckt sein.
In the south, it will be overcast.

Im Osten wird die Sonne scheinen.
In the East, the sun will shine.

it will be stormy — wird es Gewitter geben
windy — windig
fine and dry — heiter und trocken
In the West — Im Westen

Grammar — the future tense

Use the future tense to say what the weather will be like. Use the correct form of 'werden' and the infinitive. (See p.142.)

Morgen wird es regnen.
Tomorrow, it will rain.

Es wird heute Abend kalt sein.
It will be cold this evening.

To say 'it's snowing' or 'it's raining' just use the present tense...

Lies die Wettervorhersage. Sind die Aussagen **richtig**, **falsch** oder **nicht im Text**?

Hier ist die Wettervorhersage für dieses Wochenende in Deutschland. Im Norden ist es im Moment sonnig, aber am Wochenende wird es wolkiger werden. Leider wird es auch in Ost- und Westdeutschland das ganze Wochenende bewölkt sein. Obwohl das Wetter im Süden des Landes wärmer sein wird, wird es auch Gewitter dort geben. Es wird regnerisch sein und wir werden einige Hagelschauer sehen.

e.g. Die Wettervorhersage ist für Samstag und Sonntag. **richtig**

1. Es wird in Norddeutschland sonnig bleiben. *[1]*
2. In Ostdeutschland wird es kälter als im Norden sein. *[1]*
3. Im Süden von Deutschland wird es nicht so kalt sein. *[1]*
4. Es wird in Süddeutschland nicht donnern und blitzen. *[1]*
5. Es wird im Süden des Landes trocken sein. *[1]*

Listening Questions

There are lots of different topics in this section, and any one of them could come up in your exam. Try these exam-style questions to help you get to grips with it all and go over anything you can't remember.

1 Dein Austauschpartner Jonas spricht über seinen Wohnort. Füll die Tabelle auf **Deutsch** aus. Erwähne **zwei** positive und **zwei** negative Aspekte.

	Aspekt 1	Aspekt 2
Positiv		
Negativ		

[4 marks]

2 Listen to Kai ordering groceries on the phone.
Fill in the table in **English** with the quantities and products he orders.

	Quantity	Product
Example:	three	oranges

	Quantity	Product
2 a		
2 b		
2 c		
2 d		

[4 marks]

Speaking Question

Candidate's Role

- Your teacher will play the role of your Austrian friend. They will speak first.

- You should use *du* to address your friend.

- – ! – means you will have to respond to something you have not prepared.

- – ? – means you will have to ask your friend a question.

> Du sprichst mit einem Freund / einer Freundin aus Österreich über deinen Tagesablauf.
>
> - Vor der Schule — was machen.
>
> - !
>
> - Zu Hause helfen — was gemacht.
>
> - Hausaufgaben machen — wann.
>
> - ? Aktivitäten heute Abend.

Teacher's Role

- You begin the role-play using the introductory text below.

- You should address the candidate as *du*.

- You may alter the wording of the questions in response to the candidate's previous answers.

- Do not supply the candidate with key vocabulary.

> Introductory text: *Du sprichst mit einem Freund / einer Freundin aus Österreich über deinen Tagesablauf. Ich bin dein Freund / deine Freundin.*
>
> - Was machst du morgens vor der Schule?
>
> - ! Um wie viel Uhr isst du zu Abend?
>
> - Was hast du diese Woche gemacht, um zu Hause zu helfen?
>
> - Wann machst du deine Hausaufgaben?
>
> - ? Allow the candidate to ask you what you will do this evening.

Reading Questions

1 Lies diese Broschüre über Linz. Welche **vier** Aussagen sind richtig?
Schreib die richtigen Buchstaben in die Kästchen.

> Hier in Linz ist immer etwas los. Im Stadtzentrum haben wir zwei Kinos und ein Theater. Ganz in der Nähe ist ein großes Einkaufszentrum, wo man alles unter einem Dach finden kann. Es gibt um die Ecke ein altes Rathaus und ein Museum, wo man mehr über Linz herausfinden kann.
>
> Wenn man sportlich ist, gibt es ein Sportzentrum — vom Verkehrsamt gehen Sie geradeaus und nehmen Sie die erste Straße links.
>
> Um die Ecke vom Verkehrsamt ist auch ein Supermarkt — nehmen Sie die dritte Straße rechts und gehen Sie bis zur Ampel. Der Supermarkt ist auf der linken Seite.

A	Es gibt viel zu tun in Linz.
B	Man kann in Linz einen Film sehen.
C	In Linz gibt es nur ein kleines Einkaufszentrum.
D	Das Einkaufszentrum ist sehr weit vom Theater entfernt.
E	Man kann nichts über die Geschichte von Linz lernen.
F	Um das Sportzentrum vom Verkehrsamt zu finden, muss man geradeaus und dann nach links gehen.
G	Wenn man vom Verkehrsamt zum Supermarkt gehen will, sollte man sofort nach links gehen.
H	Der Supermarkt ist in der Nähe von einer Ampel.

[4 marks]

2 Translate the following passage into **English**.

> Ich bin zum Sportgeschäft gegangen, weil ich für meine Tochter neue Sportschuhe kaufen musste. An der Kasse habe ich dem Assistenten einen Hunderteuroschein gegeben. Ich habe zehn Euro zurückbekommen. Die Sportschuhe sind zu groß und ich will mein Geld zurück. Leider hat der Assistent mir keine Quittung gegeben.

....

....

....

....

....

....

[9 marks]

Writing Questions

1 Letzten Monat bist du umgezogen und deine deutsche Freundin Dani möchte mehr darüber wissen. Schreib Dani eine E-Mail über die beiden Häuser.

- Schreib etwas über dein altes Haus und deine Meinung dazu.

- Vergleich das neue Haus mit dem alten Haus.

Du musst ungefähr **150** Wörter auf **Deutsch** schreiben.
Schreib etwas über beide Punkte der Aufgabe.

[32 marks]

2 Translate the following passage into **German**.

> Although it was cold in many European countries last autumn, it was hot, dry and sunny in Germany. It was rarely cloudy, but it was fairly windy. However, in winter it was extremely cold, and it snowed in northern Germany in January. We hope that it will be sunny this summer.

....

....

....

....

....

....

....

[12 marks]

Revision Summary for Section Six

Phew, that was a long section, but it's not quite over yet. Have a go at these revision summary questions to test all those things you've learnt how to say about where you live. If you get stuck on something, don't panic — just have another look through the revision pages. Don't forget to tick off the questions when you're happy you can answer them.

The Home (p.56-57) ☑

1) What do the following mean in English?
   a) die Wohnung   b) das Einfamilienhaus   c) das Doppelhaus ☑

2) Melissa says: „Ich wohne in einem Reihenhaus in der Nähe von dem Stadtzentrum."
   Where does she live? ☑

3) In German, describe your house. Say what kind of house it is and what rooms it has. ☑

4) Lars is describing his daily routine: „Ich stehe jeden Morgen um sieben Uhr auf. Ich dusche und rasiere mich und dann ziehe ich mich an. Danach frühstücke ich." Say this in English. ☑

5) Your German friend wants to know about your daily life. In German, write down a brief description of your routine. Make sure you say what time you do things. ☑

6) Was machst du, um zu Hause zu helfen? Beantworte die Frage auf Deutsch. ☑

Talking About Where You Live (p.58) ☑

7) During your German exchange, you are asked to describe your home town. In German, say which part of the country it's in, and what you think of it. ☑

8) You are on holiday in a small Austrian town. How would you tell your German-speaking friends that there is a market, a bakery and a few historic buildings, but no cathedral? ☑

9) Your brother is really interested in boats. Which of these would appeal to him?
   a) die Metzgerei   b) der Hafen   c) die Grünanlagen ☑

Shopping (p.59-61) ☑

10) You want to buy a blue sweater, a grey shirt and some jeans. Say this in German. ☑

11) Gehst du gern einkaufen? Warum / warum nicht? ☑

12) You see Nele's shopping list: „Drei Flaschen Mineralwasser, eine Schachtel Pralinen, vier Stück Kuchen und eine Menge Weintrauben." What is she going to buy? ☑

13) What's the German for...? a) small change   b) cash   c) coin ☑

14) You've bought some shoes in Berlin but they don't fit. Ask politely for your money back. ☑

Giving and Asking for Directions (p.62) ☑

15) You need to go to the post office in Munich. Ask how to get there. ☑

16) Your friend has given you directions to his house: „Vom Busbahnhof musst du nach links gehen. Nimm die zweite Straße rechts und geh geradeaus. Mein Haus liegt am Ende der Straße." How do you get there? ☑

17) You are told „Die Apotheke ist um die Ecke." What does this mean? ☑

Weather (p.63) ☑

18) In German, describe today's weather. ☑

19) „Morgen wird es im Norden heiter und trocken sein, aber im Süden wird es feucht sein." Where's the best place for a picnic? ☑

Healthy Living

You probably know what makes a healthy lifestyle, you just need to learn how to talk about it in German.

Die Gesundheit — Health

die Bewegung	*exercise*	aufgeben	*to give up*
sich bewegen	*to exercise*	aufhören	*to stop*
sich fit halten	*to keep yourself fit*	die Ernährung	*diet / nutrition*
in Form sein	*to be in good shape*	abnehmen	*to lose weight*
gesund	*healthy*	zunehmen	*to put on weight*

See p.32-33 for info on how to talk about sports.

Ich möchte in Form sein. — *I would like to be in good shape.*
→ a bit healthier — ein bisschen gesünder

Eine ausgewogene Ernährung ist wichtig für die Gesundheit. — *A balanced diet is important for your health.*
→ Regular exercise — Regelmäßige Bewegung

Question

Ist es dir wichtig, dich zu bewegen?

Is it important to you to exercise?

Simple Answer

Ich finde es wichtig, mich zu bewegen, weil es gesund ist.

I find it important to exercise because it's healthy.

Extended Answer

Es ist mir wichtig, mich fit zu halten, aber man muss sich auch entspannen, um völlig gesund zu sein.

It's important to me to keep myself fit, but you also have to relax in order to be completely healthy.

Um mich fit zu halten... — To keep myself fit...

Um mich fit zu halten, schwimme ich dreimal pro Woche. — *To keep myself fit, I swim three times a week.*
→ To stay in good shape — Um in Form zu bleiben

Ich stelle sicher, dass ich genug schlafe. — *I make sure that I sleep enough.*
→ drink — trinke

Ich versuche, mich nach der Schule zu entspannen, sodass ich nicht gestresst werde. — *I try to relax after school so that I don't get stressed.*
→ tired — müde

Ich esse gesund — ich habe aufgehört, Süßigkeiten zu essen. — *I eat healthily — I have stopped eating sweets.*
→ a balanced diet — eine ausgewogene Ernährung
→ given up chocolate — Schokolade aufgegeben

Extend your answer by saying what you could do differently...

Wadi has written a blog about how he keeps himself healthy.

Um in Form zu sein, esse ich ein gesundes Frühstück. Ich trinke ein Glas fettarme Milch und ich esse Joghurt mit Müsli. Es ist wichtig, jeden Tag zu frühstücken. Als ich jünger war, habe ich viele Süßigkeiten und Schokolade gegessen. Aber ich habe aufgehört, so viel **zuckerhaltiges**[1] Essen zu essen. Ich spiele auch Basketball und ich fahre jeden Tag mit dem Fahrrad zur Schule. Ich hoffe, dass ich immer gesund bleiben werde.

Grade 6-7

[1]sugary

Tick list:
✓ tenses: present, simple past, perfect, future
✓ good use of subordinating conjunctions, e.g. 'als'.

To improve:
+ use subjunctives like 'hätte' or 'wäre' in a 'wenn' clause.

Du schreibst ein Blog über gesundes Leben. Schreib:
* was du machst, um gesund zu essen
* wie sich deine Gewohnheiten geändert haben
* wie du dich fit hältst
* wie du in Zukunft gesund bleiben wirst

Schreib ungefähr **150** Wörter auf **Deutsch**. Schreib etwas über alle Punkte der Aufgabe. *[32 marks]*

Unhealthy Living

This page is all about obesity, drugs, smoking and binge drinking. It's not very cheerful stuff...

Gesundheitsschädlich — Bad for your health

der Alkohol	alcohol
betrunken	drunk
rauchen	to smoke
die Drogen	drugs
süchtig	addicted
die Fettleibigkeit	obesity
übergewichtig	overweight
schädlich	harmful

Grammar — modal verbs

Modal verbs are useful for discussing healthy living. P.146 has more info.

dürfen	to be allowed to	müssen	to have to
können	to be able to	sollen	to be supposed to
mögen	to like to	wollen	to want to

These verbs are usually followed by a second verb in the infinitive.

Man darf nicht rauchen.   You are not allowed to smoke.

Question

Ist Fettleibigkeit ein ernstes Problem?

Is obesity a serious problem?

Simple Answer

Ja. Ich vermeide Süßigkeiten, da ich nicht übergewichtig werden will.

Yes. I avoid sweets because I don't want to become overweight.

Extended Answer

Fettleibigkeit ist ein großes Gesundheitsproblem in unserer Gesellschaft. Mehr Leute sind übergewichtig als vorher.

Obesity is a serious health problem in our society. More people are overweight than before.

Die Sucht — Addiction

Ich habe nie geraucht. Das Rauchen ist für die Gesundheit sehr schädlich.

Ich werde Drogen immer vermeiden.

Es ist schwierig auf Partys, wenn man keinen Alkohol trinkt.

I have never smoked. Smoking is very harmful to your health.

I will always avoid drugs.

It's difficult at parties if you don't drink.

taken drugs — Drogen genommen

cigarettes — Zigaretten

you're teetotal — man abstinent ist

 Use modal verbs to say what you should and shouldn't do...

Mia is talking to her teacher about young people and their health problems.

Teacher: Denkst du, dass Jugendliche zu viel Alkohol trinken?

Mia: Ja, ich glaube, dass viele Jugendliche oft zu viel trinken. Ich bin abstinent, aber viele meiner Freunde betrinken sich regelmäßig.

Teacher: Steht man unter Gruppendruck, Alkohol zu trinken?

Mia: Ja, manchmal. Gestern war ich auf einer Party und ich war die einzige, die keinen Alkohol getrunken hat. Leider haben viele das langweilig gefunden.

Teacher: Was ist das größte Gesundheitsproblem für Jugendliche?

Mia: Ich glaube, dass Übergewichtigkeit das größte Problem ist, weil viele übergewichtig sind. Sind Sie auch dieser Meinung?

Teacher: Ja, du hast recht. Was sollte man tun, wenn man übergewichtig ist?

Mia: Wenn ich übergewichtig wäre, würde ich gesünder essen und Sport treiben.

Teacher: Gibt es auch andere Gesundheitsprobleme unter Jugendlichen?

Mia: Jugendliche stehen oft unter Stress, was sehr gesundheitsschädlich ist.

Grade 8~9

Tick list:
✓ tenses: present, perfect, simple past
✓ good range of topical vocabulary
✓ correct use of the subjunctive

To improve:
+ use the future
+ use different phrases to express opinions

Now answer the questions yourself. You should speak for around two minutes. *[15 marks]*

Illnesses

There's a mix of specific health problems and wider social health issues to think about on this page.

Die Krankheit — Illness

krank	*ill*	das Krankenhaus	*hospital*
weh tun	*to hurt*	die Krankenversicherung	*health insurance*
verletzt sein	*to be injured*	der Kopf	*head*
der Schmerz	*pain*	der Hals	*neck / throat*
das Medikament	*medicine*	der Bauch	*stomach*
der Arzt / die Ärztin	*doctor*	der Rücken	*back*

Ich habe Kopfschmerzen und eine Erkältung.

I have a headache and a cold.

Sie ist allergisch gegen Nüsse.

She's allergic to nuts.

Mein Rücken tut mir weh.

My back hurts.

Ich muss zur Apotheke gehen, weil ich ein Medikament brauche.

I need to go to the pharmacy because I need medicine.

stomach ache — Bauchschmerzen
hay fever — Heuschnupfen
a fever — Fieber
asthmatic — asthmatisch
diabetic — zuckerkrank
tablets — Tabletten
antibiotics — Antibiotika

Grammar — reflexive verbs

Some reflexive verbs use <u>reflexive pronouns</u> in the <u>dative case</u>. 'Sich weh tun' *(to hurt oneself)* does this.

Ich habe <u>mir</u> weh getan. *I have hurt <u>myself</u>.*

See p.128 for a <u>list</u> of dative reflexive pronouns.

Grammar — gegen

In German, you take medicine '<u>gegen</u>' *(against)* an illness. The noun that follows is in the <u>accusative</u>.

Ich nehme Tabletten <u>gegen</u> meine Kopfschmerzen.

I'm taking tablets <u>for</u> my headache.

Das Gesundheitsproblem — Health problem

Psychische Probleme sind immer noch stigmatisiert.

Mental health problems are still stigmatised.

Es gibt viele Krankheiten, die noch nicht heilbar sind, zum Beispiel Asthma.

There are many illnesses that aren't yet curable, for example asthma.

In Deutschland muss man Krankenversicherung haben. Jedoch gibt es in Großbritannien einen nationalen Gesundheitsdienst.

In Germany, you have to have health insurance. However, in the UK, there is a national health service.

Viele Jugendliche leiden an psychischen Problemen, da sie unter viel Druck stehen, ,cool' zu sein.

Many young people suffer from mental health problems, as they are under a lot of pressure to be 'cool'.

cancer — Krebs
dementia — Demenz
AIDS — Aids
to get good marks — gute Noten zu bekommen
to conform to stereotypes — sich an Stereotypen anzupassen

You need a dative reflexive pronoun with 'sich weh tun'...

Translate this passage into **English**. *[9 marks]*

Letzte Woche war meine Schwester krank. Sie hatte Kopfschmerzen, ihr Hals tat weh und ihre Wangen waren sehr rot. Mein Vater dachte, dass sie Fieber hatte. Jetzt fühle ich mich krank und ich habe seit ungefähr einer Woche Bauchschmerzen. Ich muss zur Apotheke gehen. Ich werde Schmerztabletten kaufen.

Listening Questions

To make sure you're really in shape for your exams, work your way through these practice questions.

1 Du hörst eine Radiosendung zum Thema Fitness.
Füll die Tabellen auf **Deutsch** aus.

TRACK LISTENING 21

		Man sollte...	Man sollte nicht...
Example:	Nada	Rad fahren	mit dem Auto fahren

		Man sollte...	Man sollte nicht...
1 a	Horst		

[2 marks]

		Man sollte...	Man sollte nicht...
1 b	Naima		

[2 marks]

2 Listen to Mario describing his lifestyle on a German radio programme about health. Complete the sentences in **English**.

TRACK LISTENING 22

Example: Until a year ago, Mario did not feel happy with his ...fitness... .

2 a In the past, Mario ate sweets and too much .... *[1 mark]*

2 b He also .... *[1 mark]*

2 c He didn't want to become .... *[1 mark]*

2 d According to his doctor he was .... *[1 mark]*

Speaking Question

Candidate's Material

- Spend a couple of minutes looking at the photo and the questions below it.

- You can make notes on a separate piece of paper.

© iStock.com/fuchs-photography

You will be asked the following **three** questions, and **two** questions you haven't prepared:

- Was gibt es auf dem Foto?

- Ist es dir wichtig, gesund zu essen? Warum (nicht)?

- Was hast du diese Woche gemacht, um gesund zu leben?

Teacher's Material

- Allow the student to develop his / her answers as much as possible.

- You need to ask the student the following questions **in order**:

  - Was gibt es auf dem Foto?

  - Ist es dir wichtig, gesund zu essen? Warum (nicht)?

  - Was hast du diese Woche gemacht, um gesund zu leben?

  - Glaubst du, dass die meisten Jugendlichen gesund leben?

  - Was könntest du anders machen, um gesünder zu sein?

Reading Questions

1   Translate the following passage into **English**.

> Ich bin im Moment traurig, da meine Stiefmutter alkoholsüchtig ist. Meiner Meinung nach trinkt sie zu oft alkoholische Getränke und ich mache mir große Sorgen, weil das sehr ungesund ist. Ich hoffe, dass sie bald aufhören wird. Eine Freundin von mir war Drogensüchtige und eine Sucht kann sehr gefährlich sein.

....

....

....

....

....

....

[9 marks]

2   Translate the following article into **English**.

> Manche Ärzte glauben, dass Studenten an Universitäten ungesund leben. Manchmal werden Studenten krank, weil sie zu viel trinken und nicht genug schlafen. Stress kann auch ein großes Problem sein, weil er Kopfschmerzen und Bauchschmerzen verursachen kann. Außerdem ist es schwierig, Erkältungen zu vermeiden, wenn man so viel Zeit mit anderen verbringt.

....

....

....

....

....

....

[9 marks]

Writing Questions

1   Du glaubst, dass ein Freund / eine Freundin von dir nicht gesund lebt und machst dir
    Sorgen. Schreib einen Brief an einen Lehrer, in dem du das Problem beschreibst.

    Schreib:

    • etwas über das Problem deines Freundes / deiner Freundin

    • wann das Problem begonnen hat

    • warum du dir Sorgen um ihn / sie machst

    • was er / sie machen sollte, um gesünder zu leben

    Du musst ungefähr **90** Wörter auf **Deutsch** schreiben.
    Schreib etwas über alle Punkte der Aufgabe.   *[16 marks]*

2   Translate the following passage into **German**.

    > Last week I played rugby with my friends, and I injured my back. I saw the doctor
    > and he thought that the problem was unfortunately quite serious. I need medicine,
    > so I must go to the pharmacy tomorrow. I hope that I won't have to go to hospital.

    ....

    ....

    ....

    ....

    ....

    ....

    ....

                                                                        [12 marks]

Revision Summary for Section Seven

Just in case you're in need of some more mental exercise, here are some revision questions for you to get your teeth into. When you've managed to tick them all off you can go and reward yourself with a nice healthy carrot and a jog.

Healthy Living (p.69) ☑

1) Michael tells you: „Ich will in Form sein, also halte ich mich fit." What has he said? ☑

2) How would you say the following in German? ☑
   a) healthy   b) to exercise   c) to put on weight   d) to stop   e) to give up

3) Sabine is talking about her new diet: „Ich esse jeden Tag nur fünf Orangen. Ich habe ganz viel abgenommen." Is this a healthy diet? Say why / why not in German. ☑

4) Bewegst du dich oft? Beantworte die Frage auf Deutsch. ☑

5) At your German partner school, you read a leaflet on healthy living: „Um nicht gestresst zu werden ist es sehr wichtig, dass du genug schläfst. Regelmäßige Bewegung kann dir auch helfen, dich zu entspannen." Translate the advice into English. ☑

6) Sami tells you proudly: „Früher habe ich sehr ungesund gegessen, aber jetzt habe ich damit aufgehört. Ich habe Süßigkeiten komplett aufgegeben." What has he done? ☑

Unhealthy Living (p.70) ☑

7) A German teacher warns you: „Alkohol ist sehr gesundheitsschädlich." What does this mean in English? ☑

8) Give the English translation of the following words. ☑
   a) übergewichtig   b) rauchen   c) betrunken

9) Your Swiss friend's grandmother says: „Heutzutage essen Leute meistens sehr ungesund. Das ist ein großes Problem." Do you agree with her? In German say why / why not. ☑

10) In Germany, you overhear someone telling her friend: „Ich bin sehr besorgt, weil mein Freund manchmal auf Partys Drogen nimmt. Ich glaube, dass er süchtig ist." What is the problem? ☑

11) In German, say that you have never smoked because you think it is very harmful. ☑

12) Halimah tells you: „Wegen meiner Religion bin ich abstinent. Meiner Meinung nach trinken die meisten Jugendlichen viel zu viel Alkohol." What has she said? ☑

Illnesses (p.71) ☑

13) Nadiya says: „Mein Bein tut mir weh. Ich glaube, ich habe mich gestern beim Sport verletzt." What is wrong? ☑

14) You've arranged to meet your Austrian friend but he sends you this message to cancel: „Leider muss ich zum Arzt, weil ich Halsschmerzen habe. Nachher muss ich wahrscheinlich zur Apotheke." Why can't he meet you? ☑

15) Rafiq has invited you to play frisbee but you don't want to. In German, tell him you can't go because you have hay fever. ☑

16) „Ich glaube, dass wir immer noch zu wenig über psychische Probleme wissen." Translate this into English. ☑

17) What does 'Krankenversicherung' mean in English? ☑

18) Warum leiden Jugendliche an psychischen Problemen? Gib zwei Gründe auf Deutsch. ☑

Environmental Problems

Unfortunately, this isn't the most fun section, but you need to learn it if you want to make waves in your exam.

Die Umwelt — The environment

umweltfreundlich	*environmentally friendly*	der Brennstoff	*fuel*
umweltfeindlich	*bad for the environment*	das Kohlendioxid	*carbon dioxide*
schützen	*to protect*	die Sonnenenergie	*solar energy*
die Verschmutzung	*pollution*	die erneuerbare Energie	*renewable energy*
der Treibhauseffekt	*greenhouse effect*	zerstören	*to destroy*
der Klimawandel	*climate change*	die Abholzung	*deforestation*
der Verbrauch	*consumption*	das Hochwasser	*flood / flooding*
das Kraftwerk	*power station*	der Orkan	*hurricane*

Grammar — compound words

You can put two or more German words <u>together</u> to make <u>new</u> ones.

die Verschmutzung *pollution*
die <u>Luft</u>verschmutzung *<u>air</u> pollution*
die <u>Wasser</u>verschmutzung *<u>water</u> pollution*

The <u>gender</u> of the <u>new</u> word is determined by the <u>last</u> word in the <u>compound</u>. See p.111 for more.

Kraftwerke verschmutzen die Umwelt.	*Power stations pollute the environment.*
Fossile Brennstoffe sind umweltfeindlich.	*Fossil fuels are bad for the environment.*
Wir sollten die Umwelt schützen.	*We should protect the environment.*

Verschmutzen — To pollute

Es gibt zu viele Autos, die Kohlendioxid produzieren.	*There are too many cars that produce carbon dioxide.*
Busse und Züge können umweltfreundlicher sein als Autos.	*Buses and trains can be more environmentally friendly than cars.*
Viele glauben, dass Abgase zum Treibhauseffekt beitragen.	*Many think that exhaust fumes contribute to the greenhouse effect.*
Manche Kraftwerke benutzen einen Brennstoff, der zu Luftverschmutzung führen kann.	*Some power stations use fuel which can lead to air pollution.*

We use many vehicles — Wir benutzen viele Fahrzeuge

exhaust fumes — Abgase

to the destruction of the ozone layer — zur Zerstörung der Ozonschicht

to climate change — zum Klimawandel

coal — Kohle

oil — Öl

Die Erderwärmung — Global warming

Die Erderwärmung ist ein erhebliches Problem.	*Global warming is a significant problem.*
Einige befürchten, dass die Erderwärmung zu extremeren Wetterbedingungen führen könnte.	*Some fear that global warming could lead to more extreme weather conditions.*
Bäume können Kohlendioxid in Sauerstoff umwandeln, deswegen wirkt die Abholzung negativ auf den Klimawandel ein.	*Trees can convert carbon dioxide to oxygen, so deforestation has a negative effect on climate change.*
Alle Länder müssen zusammenarbeiten, um den Klimawandel zu bekämpfen.	*All countries need to work together to fight climate change.*

Environmental Problems

And more problems... Luckily, we've got some solutions on this page as well to cheer you up.

Die Naturkatastrophe — Natural disaster

Wegen der Erderwärmung könnte es mehr Naturkatastrophen geben.	*Because of global warming, there could be more natural disasters.*
Erdbeben können Tsunamis verursachen.	*Earthquakes can cause tsunamis.*
Wenn die Eisschichten schmelzen, könnte Hochwasser öfter auftreten.	*If the ice caps melt, flooding could occur more often.*
Orkane sind eine mögliche Folge des Klimawandels.	*Hurricanes are one possible result of climate change.*

droughts — Dürren
landslides — Erdrutsche
destruction — Zerstörung
Tornados — Wirbelstürme
Extreme temperatures — Extreme Temperaturen

Die Lösung — Solution

You can make your answers more sophisticated by talking about a <u>problem</u> and then giving a <u>solution</u>.

Statt Kohle und Öl zu verbrauchen, sollten wir erneuerbare Energiequellen nutzen.	*Instead of consuming coal and oil, we should use renewable sources of energy.*
Die Sonnenenergie ist eine mögliche Lösung.	*Solar energy is a possible solution.*
In Deutschland stammt ein hoher Anteil des Stroms aus erneuerbaren Energiequellen.	*In Germany, a large percentage of power comes from renewable energy sources.*
Die Windparks sind umstritten.	*Wind farms are controversial.*

alternative — alternative
Hydroelectric power — Die Wasserkraft
Geothermal energy — Die Erdwärme
Solar farms — Die Solarparks
Solar panels — Die Solarzellen

Die Zukunft — The future

Question	**Simple Answer**	**Extended Answer**
Denkst du, dass die Situation sich verbessern wird? *Do you think that the situation will improve?*	Ich glaube, dass wir eine Lösung für das Problem des Klimawandels finden werden. Man kann alles mit Technologie machen. *I believe we will find a solution to the problem of climate change. You can do anything with technology.*	Es gibt ziemlich viele Lösungen, zum Beispiel erneuerbare Energiequellen. Ich bin aber nicht sicher, ob wir den Treibhauseffekt verlangsamen können. Die Regierungen müssen zusammenarbeiten, aber oft streiten sie sich. *There are quite a few solutions, for example renewable energy sources. But I'm not sure if we can slow down the greenhouse effect. Governments need to work together, but they often argue.*

You'll need to use the future tense a lot in this topic...

Translate the following passage into **German**. *[12 marks]*

I think that we have caused many environmental problems. Air pollution is very dangerous for people and animals. It can also lead to global warming. Renewable energy sources are a possible solution because they are more environmentally friendly than coal. If we do nothing, the problems will get worse in the future.

Problems in Society

From hurricanes to racism... This section isn't exactly a ray of sunshine. These are important topics though.

Soziale Probleme — Social problems

die Gesellschaft	*society*	die Gleichheit	*equality*
die Armut	*poverty*	die Menschenrechte	*human rights*
arbeitslos	*unemployed*	die Gleichberechtigung	*equal rights*
die Sozialhilfe	*income support*	die Diskriminierung	*discrimination*
die Verhältnisse	*(living) conditions*	der Rassismus	*racism*
die Einwanderung	*immigration*	das Verbrechen	*(a) crime*
der Einwanderer / die Einwanderin	*immigrant*	stehlen	*to steal*
der Flüchtling	*refugee*	die Gewalt	*violence*
die Eingliederung	*integration*	der Krieg	*war*

Ich mache mir Sorgen um den Rassismus.	*I'm worried about racism.*
Die Gleichheit ist mir wichtig.	*Equality is important to me.*
Für mich sind alle Menschen gleich.	*To me, all people are equal.*

Grammar — masculine, feminine and neuter

You can sometimes guess the <u>gender</u> of a word using its <u>ending</u>. Here are a few <u>examples</u> — for more see p.110.

Masculine	**-<u>mus</u>**	e.g. **der Sexi<u>mus</u>**	*(sexism)*
Feminine	**-<u>heit</u>**	e.g. **die Frei<u>heit</u>**	*(freedom)*
	-<u>ung</u>	e.g. **die Eingliederung**	*(integration)*
Neuter	**-<u>chen</u>**	e.g. **das Kanin<u>chen</u>**	*(rabbit)*

In Armut leben — To live in poverty

In unserer Gesellschaft leben manche Leute in Armut.	*In our society, some people live in poverty.*
Es gibt viel Diskriminierung gegen Menschen, die arbeitslos sind.	*There's a lot of discrimination against people who are unemployed.*
Man hört oft in den Medien, dass Leute zu viel Sozialhilfe bekommen.	*You often hear in the media that people get too much in benefits.*
Die Kluft zwischen Arm und Reich nimmt zu.	*The gap between poor and rich is getting bigger.*
Die Arbeitslosigkeit ist ein großes Problem.	*Unemployment is a big problem.*

Die Kriminalität — Crime

Ich bin davon überzeugt, dass wir das Problem der Gewalt lösen müssen.	*I am convinced that we must solve the problem of violence.*
Die Kriminalitätsrate ist höher in Städten.	*The crime rate is higher in towns.*
Bestimmte Bedingungen, zum Beispiel die Ungleichheit, können zu einer höheren Kriminalitätsrate führen.	*Certain conditions, for example inequality, can lead to a higher crime rate.*
Der Einbruch ist illegal.	*Burglary is illegal.*

of vandalism — des Vandalismus

to riots — zu Krawallen

to theft — zum Diebstahl

Murder — Der Mord

Problems in Society

Immigration is a complex topic, so it's important you're able to discuss the pros and cons.

Die Wanderung — Migration

Viele Ausländer ziehen nach Deutschland um, um dort zu arbeiten.

A lot of foreigners move to Germany in order to work there.

migrants — Migranten

Wir müssen viel tun, um die Einwanderer zu integrieren.

We must do a lot to integrate immigrants.

refugees — Flüchtlinge

Sie sprechen manchmal nur wenig Deutsch und haben Schwierigkeiten, eine Ausbildung zu bekommen.

They sometimes only speak a little German and have difficulty getting an education.

must attend a German course — müssen einen Deutschkurs besuchen

Die Einwanderer haben die Kultur in Deutschland bereichert.

Immigrants have enriched the culture in Germany.

the European Union — der Europäischen Union

Question	Simple Answer	Extended Answer
Sollte die Europäische Union mehr Flüchtlinge aufnehmen?	Idealerweise würde die EU jeder Person helfen, die Hilfe braucht. Es gibt aber so viele Flüchtlinge, deswegen ist es ganz schwierig.	Ja, weil die Flüchtlinge schon furchtbare Sachen erlebt haben. Es wäre menschlich, mehr Flüchtlinge aufzunehmen. Allerdings ist es schwierig, die Flüchtlinge zu integrieren, weil sie eine andere Sprache sprechen.
Should the European Union take in more refugees?	*Ideally, the EU would help every person that needs help. But there are so many refugees, so it's very hard.*	*Yes, because the refugees have already experienced horrible things. It would be humane to take in more refugees. However, it's hard to integrate the refugees because they speak another language.*

Der Konflikt — Conflict

Manchmal gibt es Konflikte zwischen verschiedenen Gemeinschaften.

Sometimes there are conflicts between different communities.

ethnic groups — ethnischen Gruppen

Wenn es Konflikt am Arbeitsplatz gibt, ist es oft wegen der Diskriminierung.

When there's conflict in the workplace, it's often because of discrimination.

of sexism — des Sexismus

Flüchtlinge fliehen aus Ländern, die im Krieg sind.

Refugees flee from countries that are at war.

in which human rights aren't protected — in denen Menschenrechte nicht geschützt sind

Wie man den Flüchtlingen helfen sollte, ist immer noch ein umstrittenes Thema.

How we should help refugees is still a controversial topic.

in which there's a lot of violence — in denen es viel Gewalt gibt

TRACK LISTENING 23

Don't forget to consider other view points and opinions...

Sofia, Peter und Lionel sprechen über soziale Probleme. Wähle das passende Thema für jede Person und schreib den richtigen Buchstaben neben den Namen.

A	der Diebstahl	D	die Armut	1. Sofia [1]
B	die Einwanderung	E	die Gleichheit	2. Peter [1]
C	die Gewalt	F	der Vandalismus	3. Lionel [1]

Contributing to Society

After all that doom and gloom, here's a more positive page on how you can make a difference.

Beitragen — To contribute

spenden	*to donate*	obdachlos	*homeless*	die Not	*need*
die Wohltätigkeit	*charity*	unterstützen	*to support*	der Müll	*rubbish*
ehrenamtlich	*voluntarily*	das Rote Kreuz	*the Red Cross*	wegwerfen	*to throw away*
die Suppenküche	*soup kitchen*	wiederverwerten	*to recycle*	verschwenden	*to waste*

Wenn ich älter bin, möchte ich für das Rote Kreuz arbeiten.

When I'm older, I would like to work for the Red Cross.

Ich habe an eine wohltätige Organisation für Obdachlose gespendet.
Die Wohltätigkeit ist mir wichtig.

I donated to a charity for homeless people. Charity is important to me.

Ich arbeite ehrenamtlich bei einer Suppenküche. *I work voluntarily for a soup kitchen.*

as a doctor
— als Arzt (Ärztin)

as a police officer
— als Polizist(in)

disabled people
— Behinderte

cancer sufferers
— Krebskranke

Anderen helfen — To help others

Question

Was könnte man machen, um anderen zu helfen?

What could you do to help others?

Simple Answer

Man könnte einem Obdachlosen etwas zu essen geben. Man könnte auch Spenden für Behinderte sammeln.

You could give a homeless person something to eat. You could also collect money for disabled people.

Extended Answer

Es gibt viel, was man tun könnte, um anderen zu helfen. Meiner Meinung nach sollte jeder regelmäßig Freiwilligenarbeit machen. Wenn ich älter bin, möchte ich bei einem Sorgentelefon ehrenamtlich arbeiten. Das wäre eine sehr erfüllende Aufgabe.

There is a lot that you could do to help others. In my opinion, everyone should regularly do voluntary work. When I'm older, I would like to volunteer with a helpline. That would be a very rewarding task.

SPEAKING If you don't do voluntary work, say if you'd like to and why...

Chao is talking to his teacher about problems in society and how he tries to help.

[1] no fixed abode

Teacher: Welches Gesellschaftsproblem ist dir wichtig?

Chao: Die Obdachlosigkeit, da die Obdachlosen **keinen festen Wohnsitz**[1] haben.

Teacher: Was machst du, um zur Lösung dieses Problems beizutragen?

Chao: Ich gebe ihnen sehr oft etwas zu essen und ich habe ab und zu ehrenamtlich bei einer Suppenküche gearbeitet.

Teacher: Wirst du etwas anderes in der Zukunft machen?

Chao: Ich werde einen Marathon laufen, um Spenden zu sammeln.

Teacher: Ist dir die Umwelt wichtig?

Chao: Ja. Wir müssen alle etwas machen, um die Umwelt zu schützen.

Teacher: Was machst du zum Umweltschutz?

Chao: Früher habe ich alles im gleichen Mülleimer weggeworfen. Jetzt trenne ich den Müll, sodass ich ihn wiederverwerten kann.

Grade 8-9

Tick list:
✓ tenses: present, perfect, future
✓ good use of 'um... zu...' construction
✓ adverbs of time

To improve:
+ ask a question
+ justify opinions

Now answer the questions yourself. Aim to talk for around 2 minutes. *[15 marks]*

Listening Questions

As you'll probably be expecting, there are four pages of handy practice questions coming up. The more you go over this stuff, the less likely you are to get caught out in the exam, so give them your full attention.

---

1   Du hörst das Gespräch zwischen Lola und Max, die über Probleme in der Gesellschaft reden. Beantworte die Fragen auf **Deutsch**.

TRACK LISTENING 24

1 a   Für wen ist Armut besonders ein Problem?

.... *[1 mark]*

1 b   Was kann man tun, um zu helfen?

.... *[1 mark]*

1 c   Was hat Lola letzte Woche gemacht?

.... *[1 mark]*

1 d   Max zufolge, wie könnte die Regierung helfen?

.... *[1 mark]*

2   While on holiday in Germany, you hear Klara talking about environmental issues on the radio. Which **three** statements are true? Write the correct letters in the boxes.

TRACK LISTENING 25

A	Klara cannot stand people who are environmentally friendly.
B	Klara finds it difficult to be environmentally friendly.
C	Klara thinks that it is important to protect our world.
D	Klara doesn't think that the environment is her problem.
E	Klara is worried about future generations.
F	Klara thinks it is unfair to make the problems worse for future generations.

☐ ☐ ☐

[3 marks]

Speaking Question

Candidate's Role

- Your teacher will play the role of your friend's grandparent. They will speak first.

- You should use *Sie* to address your friend's grandparent.

- – ! – means you will have to respond to something you have not prepared.

- – ? – means you will have to ask your friend's grandparent a question.

> Sie sprechen mit dem Opa / der Oma Ihres Freundes über die Umwelt.
> - Das größte Umweltproblem — was.
> - Ihre Familie — etwas Umweltfeindliches neulich gemacht.
> - !
> - Erneuerbare Energiequellen — Ihre Meinung.
> - ? Umwelt wichtig.

Teacher's Role

- You begin the role-play using the introductory text below.

- You should address the candidate as *Sie*.

- You may alter the wording of the questions in response to the candidate's previous answers.

- Do not supply the candidate with key vocabulary.

> Introductory text: *Sie sprechen mit dem Opa / der Oma Ihres Freundes über die Umwelt. Ich bin der Opa / die Oma Ihres Freundes.*
> - Was ist Ihrer Meinung nach das größte Umweltproblem?
> - Was hat Ihre Familie neulich gemacht, was umweltfeindlich sein könnte?
> - ! Interessieren sich Ihre Freunde für die Umwelt?
> - Was halten Sie von erneuerbaren Energiequellen?
> - ? Allow the candidate to ask you about the importance of the environment.

Reading Questions

1 Lies die Anzeige auf der Website einer deutschen Universität.
Beantworte die Fragen auf **Deutsch**.

> Hier an der Universität bieten wir Ihnen ein tolles Erlebnis an. Sie können in einem Altenheim in der Nähe — nur zwei Kilometer — von der Universität wohnen und älteren und / oder behinderten Menschen helfen. Nur ein- oder zweimal in der Woche müssen Sie arbeiten: das heißt, nur zehn Stunden pro Woche sind Pflicht.
> ***Was für Arbeit würden Sie tun?*** Hier sind einige Beispiele:
> - einige Lebensmittel kaufen
> - beim Kochen helfen
> - beim Waschen helfen
> - einfach plaudern.
>
> Als Dank für Ihre Arbeit bekommen Sie für ein ganzes Jahr kostenlose Unterkunft!

1 a Wie oft muss man im Altenheim arbeiten?

.... *[1 mark]*

1 b Was wird man im Altenheim tun, um zu helfen? Gib **zwei** Details.

.... *[2 marks]*

1 c Was bekommt man, wenn man im Altenheim arbeitet?

.... *[1 mark]*

2 Translate the following passage into **English**.

> Flüchtlinge fliehen aus gefährlichen Gebieten. Sie müssen andere Länder finden, wo sie sich eingliedern können. Sie wohnen oft in schrecklichen Verhältnissen. Obwohl Flüchtlinge manchmal Sozialhilfe bekommen, ist das meistens nicht viel Geld. Manchmal kann die Gesellschaft auch unfreundlich sein und die Armut ist für viele Flüchtlinge ein großes Problem.

....

....

....

....

....

....

[9 marks]

Writing Questions

1 Du machst oft freiwillige Arbeit. Du schreibst einen Artikel für eine deutsche Website darüber.

- Schreib etwas über die freiwillige Arbeit, die du neulich gemacht hast.

- Vergleich diese Arbeit mit freiwilliger Arbeit, die du früher gemacht hast.

Du musst ungefähr **150** Wörter auf **Deutsch** schreiben.
Schreib etwas über beide Punkte der Aufgabe.

[32 marks]

2 Translate the following passage into **German**.

> Lots of people believe that the greenhouse effect is a very big problem. In the past, some people were not so environmentally friendly, and now the world is becoming warmer and warmer. In order to solve this difficult problem, we must find alternative sources of energy.

....

....

....

....

....

....

[12 marks]

Revision Summary for Section Eight

Admittedly that wasn't the cheeriest stuff, but that's no reason not to learn it thoroughly. Speaking of which, here are some handy revision questions so you can check your knowledge of all things global. Go back over anything you find tricky and keep track of your progress using the tick boxes.

Environmental Problems (p.77-78) ☑

1) How would you say the following in German?
   a) the environment   b) pollution   c) carbon dioxide   d) fuel   ☑

2) Aarav says: „Meiner Meinung nach sind Kraftwerke sehr umweltfeindlich. Wir müssen unseren Planeten schützen." What does this mean in English?   ☑

3) You read an information leaflet written by an environmental group: „Man sollte sein Auto zu Hause lassen und mit dem Bus in die Stadt fahren. Autos produzieren Abgase, die die Luft verschmutzen." Translate this into English.   ☑

4) How would you say "we must fight climate change" in German?   ☑

5) In German, write down three possible effects of global warming ('die Erderwärmung').   ☑

6) Mahnoor says: „Ich bin für erneuerbare Energiequellen." What is she in favour of?   ☑

7) Denkst du, dass man eine Lösung für die Umweltprobleme finden wird? Beantworte die Frage auf Deutsch.   ☑

Problems in Society (p.79-80) ☑

8) Translate the following into English:
   a) die Gleichheit   b) die Flüchtlinge   c) die Gesellschaft   ☑

9) Zahid tells you: „In meiner Gegend gibt es viele Einwanderer." What is he saying?   ☑

10) How would you say "there is a lot of violence in my town" in German?   ☑

11) You hear Eloise talking about social inequality: „Es gibt zu viele Menschen, die in Armut leben. Ich glaube, dass die Kluft zwischen Arm und Reich zunimmt." Translate this into English.   ☑

12) Egon lives in a big city. He tells you: „Dieses Jahr sind viele Flüchtlinge angekommen. Wir müssen sie integrieren und den Kindern erlauben, eine Ausbildung zu bekommen." What does he think needs to be done?   ☑

13) How would you say "that's still a controversial topic" in German?   ☑

14) What's the German for...?
   a) communities   b) discrimination   c) sexism   d) human rights   ☑

Contributing to Society (p.81) ☑

15) Brenda texts you: „Dieses Wochenende werde ich ehrenamtlich bei einer wohltätigen Organisation für Obdachlose arbeiten. Hast du Lust, mitzuhelfen?" What has she invited you to do?   ☑

16) How would you say "charity is very important to me" in German?   ☑

17) Marvin tells you: „Mein jüngerer Bruder ist behindert. Wohltätige Organisationen haben uns sehr geholfen, aber meiner Meinung nach müssen wir noch mehr für Behinderte tun." What does this mean in English?   ☑

18) Wie kann man anderen helfen? Beantworte die Frage auf Deutsch.   ☑

19) You are helping out with an environmental campaign at your German partner school. In German, write down two pieces of advice to help students to be environmentally friendly.   ☑

Where to Go

It might seem like an impossible dream right now, but one day you will be free to go on holiday again...

Wohin fahren wir? — Where are we going?

When you're <u>walking</u> somewhere, use 'gehen'. When you're travelling in a <u>vehicle</u>, use '<u>fahren</u>'. '<u>Fliegen</u>' (*to fly*) and '<u>reisen</u>' (*to travel*) are handy words, too.

Deutschland	*Germany*	Belgien	*Belgium*
Frankreich	*France*	Amerika	*America*
Spanien	*Spain*	Australien	*Australia*
Russland	*Russia*	China	*China*
Italien	*Italy*	Polen	*Poland*
Österreich	*Austria*	die Schweiz	*Switzerland*

Grammar — 'in' / 'nach' + country

To say you're <u>going</u> somewhere, you use '<u>in</u>' instead of '<u>nach</u>' for countries with an <u>article</u>.

Ich fahre <u>in die</u> Türkei. *I'm going <u>to</u> Turkey.*
Ich fahre <u>nach</u> China. *I'm going <u>to</u> China.*

Question

Wohin fährst du diesen Sommer?

Where are you going this summer?

Simple Answer

Ich reise mit meiner Familie nach Spanien und Portugal.

I'm going to Spain and Portugal with my family.

Extended Answer

Im Juli fliegen meine Eltern und ich nach Frankreich, weil es letzten Sommer jede Menge Spaß gemacht hat.

In July, my parents and I are flying to France because it was so much fun last summer.

Reiseziele — Destinations

der Schwarzwald	*the Black Forest*	der Rhein	*the Rhine*	Bayern	*Bavaria*
das Mittelmeer	*the Mediterranean*	die Donau	*the Danube*	Köln	*Cologne*
der Ärmelkanal	*the English Channel*	die Ostsee	*Baltic Sea*	München	*Munich*
die Alpen	*the Alps*	der Bodensee	*Lake Constance*	Wien	*Vienna*

Ich reise lieber in Europa, besonders in den Alpen.

I prefer to travel in Europe, especially in the Alps. ← *in Asia* — in Asien
in the U.S. — in den Vereinigten Staaten

Letzten Sommer bin ich ans Mittelmeer gefahren.

Last summer, I went to the Mediterranean. ← *to the South of France* — nach Südfrankreich
to Lake Constance — an den Bodensee

READING

Remember the difference between 'gehen' and 'fahren'...

Lies das Blog, das Ian über eine Reise geschrieben hat. Beantworte die Fragen auf **Deutsch**.

Vor zehn Jahren war ich noch zu jung, um allein ins Ausland zu reisen. Ich musste also jeden Sommer mit meiner Stiefmutter und meinem Vater in Belgien zelten. Wir sind immer mit dem Auto dorthin gefahren — die Reise hat oft zwölf Stunden gedauert! Damals fand ich diese Urlaube todlangweilig und ich wollte einfach selbstständig sein.

Als ich mit den Prüfungen fertig war und nachdem ich achtzehn Jahre alt wurde, konnte ich endlich alleine fahren, deshalb bin ich mit Klamotten und Toilettensachen in einem Rucksack spontan nach Kanada geflogen! Das war zwar ganz stressig, ich fühlte mich aber befreit.

Und nächstes Jahr? Ich bin mit Nordamerika fertig. Ich will Belgien wieder besuchen, weil ich das Land eigentlich vermisse!

e.g. Warum konnte Ian vor zehn Jahren nicht allein in Urlaub fahren?
Er war zu jung.

1. Wie ist Ian nach Belgien gefahren? [1]

2. Wie beschreibt Ian die Urlaube in Belgien? [1]

3. Wie hat Ian seine Sachen nach Kanada transportiert? [1]

4. Wohin wird Ian nächstes Jahr fahren? [1]

Accommodation

Can't decide between a soggy tent and a five-star hotel? Here are some useful phrases to help you choose.

Die Unterkunft — Accommodation

der Aufenthalt	*stay*	das Hotel	*hotel*
übernachten	*to stay (overnight)*	die Pension	*small hotel*
wohnen	*to stay*	die Jugendherberge	*youth hostel*
reservieren	*to book*	der Campingplatz	*campsite*
der Wohnwagen	*caravan*	das Zelt	*tent*
das Gasthaus	*guesthouse*	zelten	*to camp*

Grammar — dative case

You use the <u>dative case</u> when saying <u>where</u> you stayed.
Wir wohnen in einem Hotel.
We are staying in a hotel.

Ich suche eine günstige Unterkunft.	I'm looking for cheap accommodation.
Gibt es ein Hotel in der Nähe?	Is there a hotel nearby?
Kann man hier zelten?	Can you camp here?

a cheap hotel — ein günstiges Hotel

in the town centre — im Stadtzentrum

stay overnight — übernachten

Question	**Simple Answer**	**Extended Answer**
Wo haben Sie gewohnt? *Where did you stay?*	Wir haben auf einem Campingplatz übernachtet. Es war unbequem, aber gesellig. Es gab sogar einen Jugendklub. *We stayed on a campsite. It was uncomfortable but sociable. There was even a youth club.*	Wir übernachteten in einem Gasthaus in Wolfsburg. Es war sehr bequem, aber teuer. Nächstes Mal werden wir in einer Jugendherberge wohnen, da es billiger ist. Da kann man selbst kochen und seine Wäsche waschen. *We stayed in a guesthouse in Wolfsburg. It was very comfortable, but expensive. Next time, we will stay in a youth hostel because it's cheaper. There, you can cook for yourself and do your washing.*

Wo werden Sie übernachten? — Where will you stay?

Describing your <u>holiday plans</u> is a good opportunity to use the <u>future</u> tense and <u>conditional</u> clauses.

In den Sommerferien wird meine Familie in einem Hotel in Wales wohnen.	*In the summer holidays, my family will stay in a hotel in Wales.*	in the countryside — auf dem Land
Im August werde ich in einer altmodischen Pension in Devon übernachten.	*In August, I will stay in an old-fashioned small hotel in Devon.*	in northern Scotland — in Nordschottland
Ich würde lieber in einem Hotel wohnen, da Zelten mir zu unbequem ist.	*I would rather stay in a hotel because I find camping too uncomfortable.*	inconvenient — umständlich
Ich würde gern mit meinen Freunden in einer Jugendherberge am Meer wohnen.	*I would like to stay with my friends in a youth hostel by the sea.*	in the mountains — in den Bergen

TRACK LISTENING 26

Think about where you'd like to stay and why...

Drei Freunde reden über Unterkunft. Was meinen sie dazu? Sag welche Meinung **positiv** ist, welche Meinung **negativ** ist und welche Meinung **positiv und negativ** ist. *[3 marks]*

1. Monika   **2.** Ben   **3.** Anton

Booking

This is the practical stuff you need for booking rooms... and for the exam role-plays...

Haben Sie Zimmer frei? — Do you have any vacancies?

das Einzelzimmer	*single room*	die Bestätigung	*confirmation*
das Zweibettzimmer	*twin room*	die Aussicht	*view*
das Doppelzimmer	*double room*	die Halbpension	*half board*
der Empfang	*reception*	die Vollpension	*full board*
die Reservierung	*reservation*	der Zuschlag	*extra charge*

Ich möchte bitte ein Einzelzimmer reservieren.
I'd like to book a single room, please.
→ a double room — ein Doppelzimmer
→ a room with a balcony — ein Zimmer mit Balkon

Ich möchte zwei Nächte hierbleiben.
I'd like to stay here for two nights.
→ for a week — eine Woche
→ for ten days — zehn Tage

Was kostet es pro Nacht für eine Person?
How much is it per night for one person?
→ two people — zwei Personen

Bieten Sie Vollpension an? — Do you offer full board?

Gibt es einen Zuschlag fürs Frühstück?
Is there an extra charge for breakfast?
→ for half board — für die Halbpension

Wenn möglich hätte ich gern ein Zimmer mit Klimaanlage.
If possible, I'd like a room with air-conditioning.
→ with a view — mit Aussicht
→ with a sea view — mit Meerblick
→ with a bath — mit Badewanne

Wir sind vom achten bis zum fünfzehnten Mai da.
We'll be there from the 8th to the 15th May.

 WRITING

This is a good opportunity to use polite phrases...

Read this conversation that Sam had with a hotel receptionist (HR).

HR: Hotel Adler, wie kann ich Ihnen helfen?

Sam: Guten Morgen, ich möchte bitte ein Zimmer reservieren.

HR: Ja, sicher! Wann kommen Sie an?

Sam: Am siebzehnten Mai für eine Nacht. Ich besuche die Gegend, um **die Berliner Mauer**[1] zu besichtigen.

HR: Schön. Und was für ein Zimmer wollen Sie?

Sam: Einmal Einzelzimmer. Bieten Sie Halbpension an?

HR: Ja, aber dafür gibt es einen Zuschlag. Auf unserer Website gibt es ein **Formular**[2]. Füllen Sie bitte das Formular aus und schicken Sie es **so bald wie möglich**[3] per E-Mail an uns.

Sam: Danke schön. Auf Wiederhören!

Grade 4-5

[1] the Berlin Wall
[2] form
[3] as soon as possible

Tick list:
✓ polite 'Sie' form

To improve:
+ use conjunctions, e.g. 'weil'
+ use the future tense with 'werden'
+ give more detail

Du schreibst eine E-Mail, um ein Zimmer in einem Hotel zu reservieren. Schreib ungefähr **90** Wörter auf **Deutsch** über die folgenden Punkte:

• was für ein Zimmer du willst
• Ankunftsdatum und Länge des Aufenthalts
• warum du die Gegend besuchst
• frag, ob das Hotel Halbpension anbietet

[16 marks]

How to Get There

Once you've got your accommodation sorted, you need to actually get there. Here's some vocab to help you.

Wie kommst du dahin? — How are you getting there?

mit dem Zug	*by train*	auf der Autobahn	*on the motorway*	das Flugzeug	*aeroplane*
mit dem Bus	*by bus*	der Bahnhof	*train station*	fliegen	*to fly*
mit dem Auto	*by car*	das Gleis	*platform*	abfahren	*to depart*
mit dem Boot	*by boat*	der Flughafen	*airport*	ankommen	*to arrive*

Ich fahre mit dem Reisebus nach Frankreich.
I'm travelling by coach to France.

by ferry — mit der Fähre
by steamer — mit dem Dampfer

Man kann mit der Straßenbahn herumfahren.
You can travel around by tram.

on the underground — mit der U-Bahn
by bike — mit dem Fahrrad

Wann kommt der Zug in Köln an?
At what time does the train arrive in Cologne?

On which platform — Auf welchem Gleis

Von welchem Gleis fährt der Zug ab?
From which platform does the train depart?

When — Wann

Man kann eine Fahrkarte am Fahrkartenautomaten kaufen.
You can by a ticket from the ticket machine.

at the ticket office — am Fahrkartenschalter
at the bus station — am Busbahnhof

Es gab Verspätungen — There were delays

unterwegs	*on the way*	die Verbindung	*connection*	der Platten	*flat tyre*
die Verspätung	*delay*	umsteigen	*to change (trains)*	der Stau	*traffic jam*
der Wartesaal	*waiting room*	verpasssen	*to miss (train / bus)*	seekrank	*seasick*

Question

Wie war die Reise?
How was the journey?

Simple Answer

Die Reise war sehr lang und langweilig. Sie hat vier Stunden gedauert.
The journey was very long and boring. It took four hours.

Extended Answer

Leider hatten wir viele Probleme unterwegs. Wir mussten umsteigen, aber der erste Zug hatte Verspätung, also haben wir die Verbindung verpasst. Wir mussten dann zwei Stunden auf den nächsten Zug warten und es war sehr kalt im Wartesaal. Am Ziel haben wir ein Auto vermietet und hatten bald einen Platten. Was für ein Albtraum!

Unfortunately, we had a lot of problems on the way. We had to change trains, but the first train was delayed, so we missed our connection. Then, we had to wait for two hours for the next train and it was very cold in the waiting room. At our destination, we rented a car and soon got a flat tyre. What a nightmare!

Make sure you can talk about problems you had...

Translate the following passage into **English**. *[9 marks]*

Letzte Woche hat mein Vater ein Zelt gekauft. Morgen fliegt die ganze Familie in die Schweiz, wo wir auf einem Campingplatz am Bodensee wohnen werden. Ich finde das sehr spannend, aber meine Stiefschwester mag Flugzeuge nicht. Wir werden hoffentlich einen schönen Blick auf die Berge haben.

What to Do

So much to do, so much to learn. It's time to think about activities you enjoy doing on holiday.

Ausflüge — Excursions

Here's some vocab for saying what a town <u>has to offer</u> and what you like to <u>do on holiday</u>.

der Ausflug	trip / excursion
besichtigen	to visit (an attraction)
die Sehenswürdigkeit	tourist attraction
die Öffnungszeiten	opening times
das Museum	museum
das Schloss	castle / palace
die Burg	castle
der Stadtbummel	stroll through town
entdecken	to discover
die Führung	guided tour
der Strand	beach
das Erlebnis	experience
beliebt	popular

Grammar — comparatives

To <u>compare</u> one thing to another in German, you usually just add 'er' to the end of the <u>adjective</u>:

klein ⇒ **kleiner**   small ⇒ smaller
Provence ist <u>schöner</u> als das Ruhrgebiet.
Provence is <u>more beautiful</u> than the Ruhr District.

If the adjective is one syllable and its vowel is 'a', 'o' or 'u', you normally add an <u>umlaut</u> as well:

lang ⇒ **länger**   long ⇒ longer
Der Strand ist <u>näher</u> als das Museum.
The beach is <u>closer</u> than the museum.

A really common exception is '<u>gut</u>' (good):

gut ⇒ **besser**   good ⇒ better

See p.121 for more info on comparing things.

Ich möchte in ein Museum gehen.	*I'd like to go to a museum.*	to visit a gallery — eine Galerie besuchen
Ich würde gern etwas Neues erleben.	*I'd like to experience something new.*	to do a sightseeing tour of the town — eine Stadtrundfahrt machen
Das Schloss ist sehenswert.	*The castle is worth seeing.*	famous — berühmt
Im Urlaub sonne ich mich gern am Strand.	*On holiday, I like to sunbathe on the beach.*	I like to hire a bicycle — miete ich gern ein Fahrrad

SPEAKING
Use a comparative to say why you prefer one thing to another...
Here's a photo question. Have a look at the sample answer to get an idea of what to say.

Was machst du gern im Urlaub?

Für mich muss der Urlaub kulturell sein. Hauptsache ist, dass ich mehr über die Stadt oder das Land lerne; ich will mich den ganzen Tag nicht nur sonnen! Ich mache immer sehr gern eine Führung — das ist interessanter als am Strand zu liegen. Letztes Jahr bin ich mit meiner Familie in die Slowakei gefahren. Das war super, weil wir viele historische Orte besichtigt haben. Nächstes Jahr werde ich nach Belgien fahren, um viele Museen dort zu besuchen.

Grade 8-9

Tick list:
✓ tenses: present, perfect, simple past, future
✓ correct use of 'um...zu' construction
✓ correct use of modals

To improve:
+ give more detailed opinions
+ use the conditional to say what you would like to do in the future

Now try answering these questions out loud. Aim to talk for two minutes.
- Was kannst du auf dem Foto sehen?
- Was ist besser: am Strand liegen oder eine Stadtrundfahrt machen? Warum?
- Wie wäre dein idealer Urlaub?   *[10 marks]*

Listening Questions

Holidays are a great topic to talk and write about in your exams, but you need to have the right vocab at your disposal. Doing these exam-style questions will help you practise what you've learnt.

1 On holiday in Austria, you overhear this conversation at a campsite.
Answer the questions in **English**.

TRACK LISTENING 27

1 a When will the campers leave the campsite?

.... *[1 mark]*

1 b How much does it cost for two people?

.... *[1 mark]*

1 c Why do they have to pay an extra €5?

.... *[1 mark]*

1 d When will they pay?

.... *[1 mark]*

2 Listen to this podcast about a holiday house.
Which **three** statements are true? Write the letters in the boxes.

TRACK LISTENING 28

A	The bathroom wasn't clean.
B	The kitchen was very dirty.
C	They couldn't use the cooker.
D	There was no water.
E	There were no restaurants nearby.
F	There was no shower.

☐ ☐ ☐

[3 marks]

Speaking Question

Candidate's Material

- Spend a couple of minutes looking at the photo and the questions below it.

- You can make notes on a separate piece of paper.

© iStock.com/monkeybusinessimages

You will be asked the following **three** questions, and **two** questions you haven't prepared:

- Was gibt es auf dem Foto?

- Magst du diese Art von Unterkunft? Warum (nicht)?

- Wo hast du während deines letzten Urlaubs übernachtet?

Teacher's Material

- Allow the student to develop his / her answers as much as possible.

- You need to ask the student the following questions **in order**:

- Was gibt es auf dem Foto?

- Magst du diese Art von Unterkunft? Warum (nicht)?

- Wo hast du während deines letzten Urlaubs übernachtet?

- Würdest du lieber in einem Hotel oder in einer Jugendherberge übernachten? Warum?

- Was ist dir lieber: ein Urlaub mit Familie oder mit Freunden? Warum?

Reading Questions

1 Read Werner's blog post. Which **four** statements are true?
Write the correct letters in the boxes.

> Mein Bruder, der Hannes heißt, wird in den Ferien für eine Woche nach Rom fahren.
> Er fährt mit der Fähre und mit dem Zug. Die Reise dauert insgesamt sechs Stunden.
>
> Er wird unsere Großeltern besuchen. Opa ist Italiener und kann kein Wort Deutsch
> sprechen. Mein Bruder lernt seit zwei Jahren Italienisch und er wird den ganzen Tag
> Italienisch sprechen. Das wird ganz schön anstrengend sein, glaube ich!
>
> Es gibt in Rom viele Sehenswürdigkeiten, die er besichtigen will, zum Beispiel das Kolosseum.
> Was er aber am liebsten sehen will, ist das Fußballstadion. Er ist verrückt nach Fußball!
>
> Es wird wahrscheinlich sonnig sein, aber wenn es regnet, wird es trotzdem viel zu tun geben.
> Leider kann ich nicht mitreisen, da ich mir vor kurzem das Bein gebrochen habe.

A	Hannes is travelling to Spain.
B	The ferry will take six hours.
C	Their grandfather cannot speak German.
D	Hannes has been learning Italian for ten years.
E	Hannes will speak Italian all day long.
F	Hannes isn't interested in sightseeing.
G	Hannes is mad about football.
H	Werner would like to travel with Hannes.

[4 marks]

2 Read these extracts from holiday brochures. Match the most
suitable holiday to each person by writing the letter in the box.

A	Das Hotel liegt am Strand und hat drei Pools. Entdecken Sie die schöne Gartenanlage mit kleinen malerischen Brücken. Entspannen Sie sich auf der Terrasse mit fantastischem Blick über die traumhaften Landschaften.
B	Möchten Sie einen Winterurlaub in einem der schönsten Skigebiete auf der Welt? Sie können Ski oder Snowboard während des Tages fahren und bei Nacht gibt es eine Menge Restaurants in der Nähe.
C	Eine Schiffsreise durch das Mittelmeer ist eine Traumreise. Besichtigen Sie die wunderschönsten Städte Europas. Fotografieren Sie die Sehenswürdigkeiten und besuchen Sie die faszinierenden Museen.

2 a Nina wants a cultural holiday visiting landmarks in different cities.

[1 mark]

2 b Alina wants a relaxing beach holiday.

[1 mark]

2 c Marlene wants an active holiday doing sports.

[1 mark]

Writing Questions

1 Du schickst eine E-Mail an deine deutsche Freundin Prisha, um ihr von deinem letzten Urlaub zu erzählen.

Schreib:

- etwas über den Urlaub

- was du dort gemacht hast

- was du am liebsten im Urlaub machst und warum

- welche Aktivitäten du nächsten Sommer ausprobieren möchtest

Du musst ungefähr **90** Wörter auf **Deutsch** schreiben.
Schreib etwas über alle Punkte der Aufgabe.

[16 marks]

2 Translate the following passage into **German**.

> I want to go to Berlin on Saturday. I don't know whether I will travel by train or by car.
> It will probably be quicker by car as you have to change trains. Also, there could be delays.
> However, you can read and eat on the train. The train goes at 11.20 from platform 4.

....

....

....

....

....

....

....

[12 marks]

Revision Summary for Section Nine

You're probably feeling ready for a holiday after all that, but before you have a well-earned break, give these revision questions a whirl. There's a lot to remember, so don't worry if you forget something — just find the right page in the section and have another look.

Where to Go (p.87) ☑

1) If you wanted to say 'I'm going to Germany', would you use 'gehen' or 'fahren'? ☑
2) In German, give the names of five countries you'd like to visit on holiday. ☑
3) Wohin bist du letztes Jahr gefahren? Beantworte die Frage auf Deutsch. ☑
4) What's the English for...?
   a) das Mittelmeer   b) Bayern   c) die Ostsee   d) der Schwarzwald   e) Wien ☑

Accommodation (p.88) ☑

5) Róisín is complaining: „Wie immer will mein Papa diesen Sommer in dem alten Wohnwagen wohnen. Das machen wir jedes Jahr, ich finde es so unbequem." What is she upset about? ☑
6) Latifa says: „Ich suche eine günstige Pension im Stadtzentrum." Where does she want to stay? ☑
7) You read a review of a hotel: „Das Hotel war schön, aber zu teuer." What was the problem? ☑
8) Wo wirst du diesen Sommer übernachten? Beantworte die Frage auf Deutsch. ☑

Booking (p.89) ☑

9) You are booking a hotel room in Austria. In German, say what kind of room you want and how long you'll be staying. ☑
10) Daphne tells you: „Wenn ich in Urlaub fahre, muss ich immer ein Zimmer mit Klimaanlage und Badewanne haben." What are her requirements? ☑
11) What does 'Vollpension' mean in English? ☑
12) How would you say "I'll be there from the fifth to the tenth of August" in German? ☑

How to Get There (p.90) ☑

13) In German, list four ways you can travel to your destination. ☑
14) On holiday in Bern, a man asks you: „Kann man hier mit der Straßenbahn herumfahren?" What does he want to know? ☑
15) You're at a train station in Bavaria. Ask which platform your train departs from and if you have to change. ☑
16) Sven tells you: „Wir sind mit dem Auto nach Frankreich gefahren. Auf der Autobahn haben wir einen Platten bekommen". What went wrong? ☑

What to Do (p.91) ☑

17) Welche Sehenswürdigkeiten hast du im Urlaub besucht? Beantworte die Frage auf Deutsch. ☑
18) Mona is talking about holidays: „Ich finde Museen wirklich langweilig. Ich liege viel lieber am Strand." What does she like / dislike doing on holiday? ☑
19) On holiday in Heidelberg, you pick up a leaflet at the tourist information centre: „Besuchen Sie unser berühmtes Schloss!" What is it advertising? ☑
20) In German, write down three things you would do on your dream holiday. ☑

School Subjects

School subjects are a familiar topic, so you should have plenty to say about them.

Schulfächer — School subjects

das Schulfach	school subject	Fremdsprachen	foreign languages
das Wahlfach	optional subject	Deutsch	German
das Pflichtfach	compulsory subject	Spanisch	Spanish
die Stunde	lesson	Französisch	French
die Klasse	class	Geschichte	history
die Prüfung	exam	Geografie / Erdkunde	geography
Mathe	maths	Religion	RE
Englisch	English	Sport	PE
Naturwissenschaften	science	Werken	design technology
Biologie	biology	Theater	drama
Chemie	chemistry	Kunst	art
Physik	physics	Musik	music

Deutsch ist mein Lieblingsfach — German is my favourite subject

You might be asked about subjects you like and dislike, so make sure you can <u>justify</u> your <u>opinions</u>.

Sport gefällt mir immer, obwohl er sehr anstrengend ist.

I always enjoy PE, although it is very strenuous.

because I prefer being outdoors — weil ich lieber an der freien Luft bin

Werken mag ich nicht, weil ich nicht sehr praktisch bin.

I don't like design technology because I'm not very practical.

I find it boring — ich es langweilig finde

Ich lerne gern Fremdsprachen, weil sie nützlich sind.

I like learning foreign languages because they are useful.

I would like to work abroad — ich im Ausland arbeiten möchte

Ich mag Naturwissenschaften, weil ich verstehen will, wie alles funktioniert.

I like science because I want to understand how everything works.

the experiments are fun — die Experimente Spaß machen

'Weil' sends the verb to the end...

Have a look at the text written by a student about the subjects offered at her school.

Hier müssen alle Schüler dreißig Stunden in der Woche lernen. Man muss einmal am Tag Spanisch oder Französisch lernen, weil eine Fremdsprache heutzutage sehr wichtig ist. Andere Pflichtfächer bei uns sind Deutsch, Mathe, Naturwissenschaften, entweder Geschichte oder Erdkunde, und Sport, weil unsere Schule eine Eliteschule des Sports ist. Wenn man kreativ ist, darf man Kunst, Musik oder Theater wählen. Die Schule bietet auch Religion und Werken an.

Grade 6-7

Tick list:
✓ relevant vocab
✓ 'weil' clauses
✓ time phrases

To improve:
+ use more adjectives
+ use more complex constructions, e.g. 'um...zu...'

Dein Lehrer hat dich über deine Schulfächer gefragt. Schreib ungefähr **90** Wörter auf **Deutsch** über die folgenden Punkte:

- was dein Lieblingsfach ist, und warum
- welche Fächer du letzte Woche hattest
- welche Fächer du nächstes Jahr lernen wirst *[16 marks]*

School Routine

You must know your school routine pretty well by now — here's how to talk about it in German.

Der Schulalltag — School routine

der Unterricht	lessons / teaching	dauern	to last	in die Schule gehen	to go to school
unterrichten	to teach	pro Tag	per day	mit dem Auto	by car
der Stundenplan	timetable				

der Unterricht — lessons / teaching
unterrichten — to teach
der Stundenplan — timetable
die (Mittags)pause — (lunch) break
anfangen — to start
aus sein — to be over / finished
plaudern — to chat / to talk
nachsitzen — to have a detention
die Versammlung — assembly
der Schultag — school day

dauern — to last
pro Tag — per day
in die Schule gehen — to go to school
mit dem Auto — by car

Grammar — verb the second idea

In German statements, the verb is always the second idea. It isn't necessarily the second word though. See p.114 for more.

Jede Woche habe ich Sport. *Every week, I have PE.*
1st idea   2nd idea

Um 11 Uhr gibt es eine Pause. *At 11 o'clock there is a break.*
1st idea   2nd idea

Montags in der ersten Stunde habe ich Deutsch. — *On Mondays, I have German in the first period.* → in the second period — in der zweiten Stunde

Am Ende des Tages habe ich Geschichte. — *At the end of the day, I have history.* → Before the lunch break — Vor der Mittagspause

Zweimal pro Woche habe ich Chemie. — *Twice a week, I have chemistry.* → Every day — Jeden Tag / Once a week — Einmal pro Woche

Question

Kannst du mir deinen Schulalltag beschreiben?
Can you describe your school routine to me?

Simple Answer

Wir haben sechs Stunden pro Tag. Die Schule ist um 16 Uhr aus.
We have six lessons a day. School finishes at 4 o'clock.

Extended Answer

Die Schule fängt um Viertel vor neun an. Wir haben jeden Tag Mathe, aber es gibt nur eine Kunststunde pro Woche. Mittwochs nehme ich in der Mittagspause an der Chorprobe teil. Das gefällt mir sehr gut.

School starts at quarter to nine. We have maths every day, but there's only one art lesson a week. On Wednesdays, I take part in choir practice during the lunch break. I really enjoy that.

Am Ende des Schultages — At the end of the school day

Oft schwatze ich im Schulhof. — *Often, I chat in the schoolyard.* → with my friends — mit meinen Freunden

Jeden Donnerstag habe ich Fußballtraining. — *Every Thursday, I have football training.* → a play rehearsal — eine Theaterprobe

Manchmal muss ich nachsitzen. — *Sometimes, I have detention.* → there's a class trip — gibt es eine Klassenfahrt

You can use lots of time phrases in this topic...

Tilly spricht über ihren Stundenplan.

1. Schreib auf **Deutsch** einen **positiven** Aspekt ihres Stundenplans. Ein positiver Aspekt ist schon für dich als Beispiel gegeben. [1]
   e.g. viermal in der Woche Geschichte

2. Schreib auf **Deutsch** zwei **negative** Aspekte ihres Stundenplans. [2]

School Life

The German school system might seem baffling at first, so go through this page carefully.

Die Schulart — Type of school

besuchen	to go to (a school)
die Grundschule	primary school
die Gesamtschule	comprehensive school
die Realschule	secondary school
die Hauptschule	(vocational) secondary school
das Gymnasium	grammar school
das Internat	boarding school
die Ganztagsschule	school that lasts all day
akademisch	academic
praktisch	vocational / practical
gemischt	mixed (sex)

Question

Welche Schulart besuchst du?
What kind of school do you go to?

Simple Answer

Ich besuche eine gemischte Realschule.
I go to a mixed secondary school.

Extended Answer

Seit vier Jahren besuche ich eine Gesamtschule in meiner Heimatstadt. Sie ist ziemlich praktisch.
For four years, I've been going to a comprehensive school in my home town. It's quite vocational.

Das Schulleben — School Life

Ich besuche eine Ganztagsschule.
Die Schule ist um 17 Uhr aus.

I go to a school that lasts all day. School finishes at 5 pm.

a mixed private school — eine gemischte Privatschule

Ich finde Gesamtschulen besser, weil sie vielfältiger sind.

I think comprehensives are better because they are more diverse.

they don't exclude anybody — sie niemanden ausschließen

Ich würde gern eine Hauptschule besuchen, weil ich sehr praktisch bin.

I'd like to go to a vocational secondary school because I'm very practical.

I'm not so academic — ich nicht so akademisch bin

Ein Gymnasium wäre zu stressig.

A grammar school would be too stressful.

very demanding — sehr anspruchsvoll

You need to know the different types of German school...

Read this email Anna wrote to her friend Nadine about German schools.

In deiner letzten E-Mail hast du über die Schularten hier gefragt. Wir haben in Deutschland mindestens drei Möglichkeiten nach der Grundschule!

Wenn man praktisch ist, ist eine Hauptschule vielleicht die beste Wahl. Schüler müssen fünf Jahre in dieser Schule bleiben. Eine Realschule ist auch eine gute Möglichkeit für praktische Jungen und Mädchen, aber sie dauert sechs Jahre. Wenn man akademischer ist und das Abitur machen will, muss man acht oder neun Jahre in einem Gymnasium lernen. Gesamtschulen, die eine Mischung von den drei Schularten sind, existieren in manchen Bundesländern auch.

According to the text, which **four** statements are true?

A   There are two different types of secondary school in Germany.

B   The Hauptschule is more vocational.

C   Pupils attend the Hauptschule for five years.

D   The Realschule is only suitable for academic students.

E   The Realschule is just for boys.

F   You can do your Abitur in the Gymnasium.

G   Gesamtschulen combine all the school types mentioned.

H   All German states offer Gesamtschulen.

[4 marks]

School Pressures

All this revision might be making you stressed, but it'll be worth it in the end.

Die Schulbelastungen — School pressures

fleißig	hard-working	bestehen	to pass	
der Druck	pressure	durchfallen	to fail	
die Note	grade	erfolgreich	successful	
der Stress	stress	das Ergebnis	result	
die Leistung	achievement	versuchen	to try	
sitzen bleiben	to repeat a year	aufpassen	to pay attention	

Grades in German are:
1 (sehr gut — *very good*)
2 (gut — *good*)
3 (befriedigend — *satisfactory*)
4 (ausreichend — *sufficient*)
5 (mangelhaft — *unsatisfactory*)
6 (ungenügend — *inadequate*)

Ich stehe unter Druck, weil ich gute Noten haben will. — *I'm under pressure because I want to get good grades.*

Man sollte versuchen, alle Prüfungen zu bestehen. — *You should try to pass all your exams.*

I am very stressed — Ich bin sehr gestresst
I always work hard — Ich arbeite immer fleißig
be successful — erfolgreich zu sein
keep calm — ruhig zu bleiben

Es gibt strenge Regeln — There are strict rules

Man muss jeden Tag anwesend sein. — *You must be present every day.*

Man soll andere Schüler und die Lehrer respektieren. — *You should respect other pupils and the teachers.*

Man darf nicht schwänzen. — *You are not allowed to play truant.*

Man muss pünktlich sein. — *You must be on time.*

> **Grammar** — modal verbs
>
> Using 'man' with a modal verb is a handy way to describe rules. You'll also need a second verb that's in the infinitive — this goes at the end of the clause. See p.146 for more info.
>
> **Man darf nicht rauchen.**
> ***You're not allowed to smoke.***

SPEAKING Use 'man' and a modal verb to talk about rules...

Here's a photo question. Read the example to get an idea of what to say.

Stehst du unter Druck im Schulleben?

Ja, ich stehe unter Druck und fühle mich die ganze Zeit äußerst gestresst. Ich will unbedingt erfolgreich sein, deswegen muss ich immer fleißig arbeiten. Letzte Woche hatten wir viele schwierige Prüfungen und ich weiß nicht, ob ich gute Noten haben werde.

In unserer Schule gibt es auch viele Regeln. Man muss eine Uniform tragen. Man darf nicht schwänzen und man muss andere respektieren. Ich finde die Schulregeln ziemlich wichtig — ohne Regeln würde das Schulleben ganz chaotisch werden. Jedoch hätte ich gern weniger Stress im Schulleben. Mehr Freizeit wäre auch schön.

Grade 8-9

Tick list:
✓ tenses: present, simple past, future, conditional, subjunctive
✓ correct use of modal verbs with 'man'

To improve:
+ use 'weil' clauses to justify statements

Now try answering these questions. Aim to talk for about 2 minutes.
- Was kannst du auf dem Foto sehen?
- Wie findest du die Regeln in deiner Schule? Warum?
- Fühlst du dich gestresst in der Schule? Warum?
- Wie kann man Schuldruck vermeiden?

[10 marks]

© iStock.com/shironosov

Education Post-16

It's time to start thinking about what you're going to do once all those GCSEs are in the bag.

Die Weiterbildung — Further education

das Abitur	*A-Level equivalent*	der Kurs	*course*
die Oberstufe	*sixth-form equivalent*	die Erfahrung	*experience*
die Universität	*university*	der Berufsberater	*careers adviser*
der Studienplatz	*university place*	die Bewerbung	*application*
die Lehre	*apprenticeship*	(sich) entscheiden	*to decide*
einstellen	*to employ*	die Gelegenheit	*opportunity*

Nach dem Abitur werde ich auf die Uni gehen, um Biologie zu studieren.
After my A-levels, I will go to uni to study biology.
study abroad — im Ausland studieren

Vor der Uni werde ich ein Jahr freinehmen, um Geld zu verdienen.
Before uni, I will take a year out in order to earn money.
to travel the world — um durch die Welt zu reisen

Der Berufsberater in der Schule denkt, dass ich etwas Praktisches machen sollte.
The school careers adviser thinks that I should do something vocational.
attend a course — einen Kurs besuchen

Die Berufserfahrung — Work experience

Ich möchte an einer Fachschule lernen, um praktische Erfahrung zu sammeln.
I'd like to study at a technical college to gain practical experience.
do voluntary work — ehrenamtlich arbeiten

Ich möchte eine Lehre machen, weil sie zu einer festen Anstellung führen kann.
I'd like to do an apprenticeship because it can lead to a permanent job.
a work placement — ein Praktikum

Berufserfahrung ist oft sehr wichtig, wenn man sich um einen Job bewirbt.
Work experience is often very important when you're applying for a job.
useful — nützlich

Question
Was wirst du nach den Prüfungen machen?
What will you do after your exams?

Simple Answer
Ich möchte ein Praktikum bei einer Bank machen.
I would like to do a work placement at a bank.

Extended Answer
Zuerst habe ich vor, ein Jahr freizunehmen, weil ich unbedingt auf Reisen gehen will. Danach werde ich wahrscheinlich auf die Uni gehen, aber ich habe mich noch nicht entschieden, was ich studieren möchte.
Firstly, I'm planning to take a year out because I really want to go travelling. After that, I will probably go to university, but I haven't yet decided what I would like to study.

'Um...zu' means 'to' or 'in order to'...

Translate the following passage into **German**. *[12 marks]*

Last year, I learned English, maths and geography. I enjoyed geography, but my maths teacher was very strict. After the exams, I will take a year out. I will find a job because I want to earn money. After that, I want to go to university to study English. I think it will be an interesting experience.

Career Choices and Ambitions

If you've got detailed future plans, great — if you haven't, make something up.

Bei der Arbeit — At work

arbeiten	*to work*
das Gehalt	*salary*
der Lohn	*wage*
der Lebenslauf	*CV*
der / die Angestellte	*employee*
berufstätig (sein)	*(to be) in work*
das Büro	*office*
die Karriere	*career*
der / die Beamte	*civil servant*
der Arzt / die Ärztin	*doctor*
der Tischler	*carpenter*

Grammar — jobs and genders

With German job titles, you have to show whether the person is a <u>man</u> or a <u>woman</u>.

For '<u>Friseur</u>' (*hairdresser*), '<u>Polizist</u>' (*police officer*) and roles ending in '<u>er</u>', you add '<u>-in</u>' for females.

der Verkäufer	**die** Verkäuferin
sales assistant (m)	*sales assistant (f)*

For roles ending in '<u>mann</u>', you change the word to '<u>frau</u>' if you're talking about a woman.

der Feuerwehr<u>mann</u>	**die** Feuerwehr<u>frau</u>
firefighter (m)	*firefighter (f)*

Question

Was willst du als Beruf machen?

What do you want to do for a living?

Simple Answer

In der Zukunft will ich in einer Bäckerei arbeiten, denn Schichtarbeit stört mich nicht.

In the future, I'd like to work in a bakery, as I don't mind shift work.

Extended Answer

Im Moment habe ich einen Teilzeitjob als Verkäuferin, aber ich werde bald Vollzeitarbeit als Klempnerin beginnen, um einen besseren Lohn zu verdienen.

At the moment, I have a part-time job as a sales assistant, but I will soon start full-time work as a plumber, in order to earn a better wage.

Warum willst du das machen? — Why do you want to do that?

Whether your plans are real or not, you need to be able to give <u>reasons</u> for them.

Ich suche eine Stelle als Gärtner, weil ich im Freien arbeiten will.	*I'm looking for a position as a gardener because I want to work in the open air.*	postman / woman — Briefträger / in
Ich möchte Maler werden, weil ich sehr kreativ bin.	*I'd like to be a painter / decorator because I'm very creative.*	actor / actress — Schauspieler / in
Es wäre toll, selbstständig zu sein, da man keinen Chef hat.	*It would be great to be self-employed because you have no boss.*	no fixed working hours — keine festen Arbeitsstunden
Ich möchte Krankenpfleger werden, weil der Beruf erfüllend ist.	*I'd like to be a (male) nurse because the profession is rewarding.*	(female) nurse — Krankenschwester

---

Most job titles have a separate feminine version in German...

Translate the following passage into **English**. *[9 marks]*

Im Moment weiß ich nicht, was ich in der Zukunft machen will. Ich habe meine Prüfungen in der Schule nicht bestanden und ich muss einen Job finden. Mein Vater ist Polizist und ich machte im Juni mit ihm mein Arbeitspraktikum, aber das möchte ich nicht als Beruf machen. Ich würde lieber selbstständig arbeiten.

Listening Questions

Congratulations, you've reached the last set of exam-style questions. As ever, have another look at the revision pages if there's anything that trips you up — you can always learn from your mistakes.

1   Listen to this report about stress at school.
    Which **three** statements are true? Write the letters in the boxes.

A	The pupils in the study were older than 16.
B	Homework is the main reason why pupils feel stressed.
C	Pupils also mentioned pressures put on them by teachers.
D	Many pupils find walking to and from school very tiring.
E	Pupils think that they don't have enough time for sport.
F	Pupils complained about doing too much independent study at school.

[3 marks]

2   Einige Schüler diskutieren über Berufe. Beantworte die Fragen auf **Deutsch**.

2 a   Wer muss kreativ und freundlich sein?

.... *[1 mark]*

2 b   Wie sollte ein Lehrer sein? Gib **zwei** Details.

.... *[2 marks]*

2 c   Welche **zwei** Eigenschaften braucht eine Bauarbeiterin?

.... *[2 marks]*

2 d   Welchen Beruf soll man vermeiden, wenn man unhöflich ist?

.... *[1 mark]*

Speaking Question

Candidate's Role

- Your teacher will play the role of the careers adviser. They will speak first.

- You should use *Sie* to address the careers adviser.

- – ! – means you will have to respond to something you have not prepared.

- – ? – means you will have to ask the careers adviser a question.

> Sie sprechen mit einem Berufsberater / einer Berufsberaterin über die Arbeit.
>
> - Traumberuf.
> - !
> - Arbeitserfahrung.
> - Arbeitszeiten.
> - ? Rat.

Teacher's Role

- You begin the role-play using the introductory text below.

- You should address the candidate as *Sie*.

- You may alter the wording of the questions in response to the candidate's previous answers.

- Do not supply the candidate with key vocabulary.

> Introductory text: *Sie sprechen mit einem Berufsberater / einer Berufsberaterin über die Arbeit. Ich bin der Berufsberater / die Berufsberaterin.*
>
> - Was ist Ihr Traumberuf?
> - ! Warum wollen Sie das machen?
> - Welche Arbeitserfahrung haben Sie schon?
> - Was für Arbeitszeiten möchten Sie haben?
> - ? Allow the candidate to ask you for advice.

Reading Questions

1 Lies das Blog von Tobias. Beantworte die Fragen auf **Deutsch**.

> Ich habe mit Englisch und Spanisch in der Grundschule angefangen, aber jetzt lerne ich auch Französisch. Englisch finde ich relativ einfach und ganz nützlich, aber für andere Fremdsprachen interessiere ich mich gar nicht. In der Zukunft will ich in den USA arbeiten und deswegen muss ich fließend Englisch sprechen. Leider finde ich Informatik doof, weil der Lehrer sehr altmodisch ist. Er hat keine Ahnung von neuer Technologie. Ich habe kein Talent für Geschichte, dennoch bin ich für Naturwissenschaften relativ begabt.

1 a Welche Fremdsprachen lernt Tobias im Moment?

.... *[1 mark]*

1 b Was wird Tobias in Amerika tun müssen?

.... *[1 mark]*

1 c Warum findet er Informatik blöd?

.... *[1 mark]*

1 d Wofür hat Tobias keine Begabung?

.... *[1 mark]*

2 Translate the following passage into **English**.

> Der Schultag fängt um halb neun an und endet um vier Uhr. Wir haben sechs Stunden pro Tag: vier am Morgen und zwei am Nachmittag. Heute gab es eine Versammlung in der Aula. Das finde ich immer langweilig. Wir haben täglich zwei Pausen. Ich hätte gern eine längere Mittagspause.

....

....

....

....

....

[9 marks]

Writing Questions

1   Du hast ein Praktikum gemacht und dein schweizerischer Freund, Lukas, möchte wissen, wie es war. Du schickst ihm eine E-Mail über das Praktikum.

- Schreib etwas über das Praktikum.

- Vergleich Praktika mit der Universität.

Du musst ungefähr **150** Wörter auf **Deutsch** schreiben.
Schreib etwas über beide Punkte der Aufgabe.

[32 marks]

2   Translate the following passage into **German**.

> At my school, there are over a thousand pupils. I go to a comprehensive school. You can choose vocational subjects. I think that is good because I am very practical. The school day lasts until four o'clock, but yesterday I played hockey after school. Next year, I would like to do A-levels.

....

....

....

....

....

....

....

[12 marks]

Revision Summary for Section Ten

You'll be well on your way to exam success after getting through all that stuff about school. What better way to round off the section than with some helpful revision questions...

School Subjects (p.97) ☑

1) Jahi tells you: „Ich habe Geschichte und Spanisch als Wahlfächer." What does this mean? ☑
2) In German, list all of the subjects you study at school. ☑
3) Was ist dein Lieblingsfach? Warum? Beantworte die Fragen auf Deutsch. ☑

School Routine (p.98) ☑

4) Choose a school day and describe your timetable in German. ☑
5) Marco says: „Gestern musste ich nach der Schule nachsitzen, weil ich in der Mathestunde zu viel geplaudert hatte." What happened? ☑
6) How would you say "I have English four times a week" in German? ☑
7) Was machst du am Ende des Schultages? Gib zwei Details auf Deutsch. ☑

School Life (p.99) ☑

8) List at least four types of German school. ☑
9) Beschreib deine Schule auf Deutsch. ☑
10) You overhear Kayla talking on the phone: „Mein Vater denkt, dass ich ein Internat besuchen sollte, aber ich würde lieber zur Gesamtschule hier in der Stadt gehen." Translate this into English. ☑

School Pressures (p.100) ☑

11) What's the German for...? a) grade b) pressure c) achievement ☑
12) Chen tells you: „Ich habe Angst, dass ich sitzen bleiben muss." What is he worried about? ☑
13) Stehst du unter Druck in deinem Schulleben? Warum? Beantworte die Fragen auf Deutsch. ☑
14) In German, write down at least three rules there are at your school. ☑

Education Post-16 (p.101) ☑

15) How would you say "before uni, I would like to travel the world" in German? ☑
16) Yannick tells you: „Ich will nicht unbedingt auf die Uni gehen. Mir ist es viel wichtiger, Arbeitserfahrung zu sammeln." What does he want to do? ☑
17) Möchtest du lieber studieren oder eine Lehre machen? Warum? ☑

Career Choices and Ambitions (p.102) ☑

18) Give the feminine forms of the following job titles:
    a) der Verkäufer b) der Feuerwehrmann c) der Arzt ☑
19) Natalie is talking about work: „Ich finde Schichtarbeit schrecklich." What doesn't she like? ☑
20) Sag auf Deutsch was du gern als Beruf machen möchtest, und gib zwei Gründe dafür. ☑

| Cases | # Cases — Nominative and Accusative |

Cases are a tricky business — but if you can get to grips with the four cases, the rest of German grammar will seem much easier, and you'll be on your way to getting a good mark.

Cases mean that you have to change words to fit

1) In German, words are written differently depending on which case they're in.

> Der kleine Hund grüßt den kleinen Hund.   *The small dog greets the small dog.*

Both these bits mean 'the small dog', but they're written differently. This is because the second bit is in a different case from the first bit.

2) This page and the next page are all about when you use the different cases.

3) Often, you have to change the words to fit the case — see p.110 for nouns, p.118 for articles and p.119-120 for adjectives.

The nominative and accusative cases

1) The nominative case and the accusative case are the cases you'll need to use the most.

2) The case of a word depends on what the word's doing in the sentence.

> Der Lehrer liest den Brief.   *The teacher reads the letter.*

The teacher is doing the action. This makes him the 'subject' of the sentence. The 'subject' is always in the nominative case.

This bit of the sentence is the verb. It tells you what's going on.

This last bit is what the verb is done to. It's in the accusative case.

> When you look a word up in a dictionary, it'll always tell you what it is in the nominative case.

So remember the golden rules...

1) Use the nominative case for who (or what) is doing the action.
Use the accusative case for who (or what) the action is done to.

> Ein Mann kauft einen Schuh. *A man buys a shoe.*

The man is doing the action, so he's in the nominative case. The shoe is being bought, so it's in the accusative case.

> Der Junge sieht den Hund. *The boy sees the dog.*

The boy is doing the action, so he's in the nominative case. The dog is being seen, so it's in the accusative case.

2) The bit in the nominative case doesn't always have to be the first bit of the sentence.

> Heute fährt Zoe nach Wales. *Today Zoe is going to Wales.*

Zoe is doing the action, so she's in the nominative case. For more on word order, see p.114.

> Möchtest du singen? *Would you like to sing?*

> Wahrscheinlich ist er krank. *He is probably ill.*

The person or thing doing the action is in the nominative case...

Read the sentences. Say which words are in the nominative case and which words are in the accusative case.

1. Der Mann spricht Deutsch.   3. Ich habe eine Schwester.   5. Meine Mutter hat ein neues Auto.
2. Die Stadt hat eine Bibliothek. 4. Er kauft Schokolade.   6. Morgen werde ich einen Rock kaufen.

Cases — Genitive and Dative

Here are some more cases — their names might sound a bit odd, but they're not as terrifying as they seem.

Use the genitive case to talk about belongings

1) When you want to say things like 'Sarah's' or 'Otto's' or 'my dad's', you need the genitive case.

Der Wagen meines Vaters.   *My father's car.* ⟵ Literally, 'the car of my father'.

Hermann isst die Suppe des Mädchens.   *Hermann eats the girl's soup.* ⟵ Literally, 'the soup of the girl'.

2) Watch out — you don't need the genitive case for phrases like 'my dad's a doctor'. This is short for 'my dad is a doctor', which is very different to saying that a doctor belongs to your dad.

Use the dative case to say 'to someone', 'from someone'...

1) Before you get going on the dative case, make sure you understand the accusative case (p.108) really well. Then have a look at these two sentences:

Accusative case

Eva schreibt einen Brief. *Eva writes a letter.*

Dative case

Eva schreibt einem Freund. *Eva writes to a friend.*

2) In the first one, Eva is writing a letter. Eva is in the nominative case because she's writing, and the letter is in the accusative case because it's being written.

3) In the second one, Eva is writing to a friend. The friend isn't being written — he's being written to. This means he can't be in the accusative case. Instead, he's in the dative case.

4) You normally need to use the dative case when you're translating these words: ⟹ on, at, from, of, in, by, with, to

5) There are some exceptions though — have a look at page 131 for situations when you need the accusative case with some of these words.

6) Sometimes you need the dative case even though you don't have one of these words. See page 135 for more.

Nouns sometimes get endings to fit the case

1) Nouns (see p.110) sometimes change depending on what case they're in.

2) Masculine and neuter nouns add 's' in the genitive case.

Das Haus meines Onkels.   *My uncle's house.*

There are some words where you have to add 'es' rather than just 's'. They usually end in '-s', '-ß', '-x' or '-z'.

3) Plural nouns add 'n' in the dative.

Ich schreibe den Kindern.   *I write to the children.*

Normally, 'children' = 'Kinder', but in the dative, it becomes 'Kindern'. If the noun already ends in '-n', you don't need to add another 'n'. 'Streets' = 'Straßen', so in the plural dative, it's still 'Straßen'.

Don't forget the noun endings...

Read these sentences. Say which words are in the genitive case and which words are in the dative case.
1. Sie ist die Schwester meiner Mutter.   3. Ich gebe meinem Bruder das Buch.   5. Wir fahren mit dem Zug.
2. Wir wohnen auf dem Land.   4. Er ist der Bruder meines Vaters.   6. Er steht in der Küche.

Nouns — Words for People, Places and Objects

Nouns (words for people, places and objects) crop up loads — so it's important to use them properly.

German nouns start with capital letters

1) In English, some <u>nouns</u> like '<u>Leeds</u>' or '<u>December</u>' always start with a capital letter.

2) In German, <u>absolutely every noun</u>, whether it's a <u>person</u>, <u>place</u> or <u>object</u>, starts with a <u>capital letter</u>.

| der Elefant | *the elephant* | | das Baby | *the baby* |

German nouns are either masculine, feminine or neuter

1) Every German noun has a gender. If a noun has '<u>der</u>' in front, it's <u>masculine</u> (in the nominative case). If it has '<u>die</u>' in front, it's <u>feminine</u> or <u>plural</u>, and if it has '<u>das</u>' in front, it's <u>neuter</u>.

2) The <u>gender of a noun</u> affects lots of things — the words for '<u>the</u>' and '<u>a</u>' change, and so do any <u>adjectives</u> (words like big, green and smelly).

| eine große Kuh | *a big cow* |

When you learn a new noun, learn whether it needs 'der', 'die' or 'das'.

Use these rules to help you recognise what gender a noun is

You can use these rules to help you recognise whether a noun is <u>masculine</u>, <u>feminine</u> or <u>neuter</u>.

Masculine → Nouns that end in... -el, -us, -ling, -ismus, -er — AND — male people, days, months, seasons

Feminine → Nouns that end in... -ie, -heit, -tion, -ung, -ei, -keit, -sion, -tät, -schaft — AND — most female people

Neuter → Nouns that end in... -chen, -um, -lein, -ment — AND — infinitives of verbs used as nouns, e.g. das Turnen — *gymnastics*

Weak nouns have strange endings

Some <u>masculine</u> nouns are called <u>weak nouns</u>, and they are mostly words for <u>people</u> and <u>animals</u>. They stay the <u>same</u> in the <u>nominative singular</u> case, but in <u>all other cases</u>, they <u>add</u> either '<u>-n</u>' (if the noun ends in '-e') or '<u>-en</u>' (for all others).

'Der Herr' is tricky. Even though it doesn't end in '-e', it only adds '-n' in the singular.

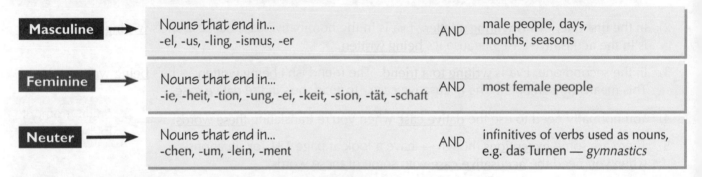

	Accusative	Genitive	Dative
der Junge (boy)	-n	-n	-n
der Mensch (person)	-en	-en	-en
der Name (name)	-n	-ns	-n
der Herr (sir / Mr)	-n	-n	-n

'der Name' is sneaky — it adds '-ns' in the genitive singular rather than just '-n'. The same happens with 'der Glaube' (*belief*), 'der Gedanke' (*thought*) and 'der Buchstabe' (*letter of the alphabet*).

| Gib dem Jungen ein Hemd. | *Give the boy a shirt.* | | die Ohren des Elefanten | *the ears of the elephant* |

You need to know a noun's gender to make your German accurate...

Look at these German nouns and use the rules on this page to fill in the gaps with 'der', 'die' or 'das'.

1. ...... Gesellschaft
2. ...... Mittwoch
3. ...... Frühling
4. ...... Mädchen
5. ...... Meinung
6. ...... Polizei
7. ...... Katrin
8. ...... Schwimmen

Words for People, Places and Objects | Nouns

Life would be boring if there were just one of everything — you need to know how to make nouns plural too.

Making nouns plural

1) When you want to make nouns plural in English, you normally just add an 's'.
German is a bit harder — there are lots of different ways to make nouns plural.

How to make the word plural	Example
No change	der Metzger (the butcher) → die Metzger (the butchers)
Add an umlaut to the stressed syllable	der Apfel (the apple) → die Äpfel (the apples)
Add an 'e'	der Tag (the day) → die Tage (the days)
Add an umlaut and an 'e'	die Hand (the hand) → die Hände (the hands)
Add 'er'	das Lied (the song) → die Lieder (the songs)
Add an umlaut and 'er'	das Haus (the house) → die Häuser (the houses)
Add an 's'	das Sofa (the sofa) → die Sofas (the sofas)
Add an 'n'	die Straße (the street) → die Straßen (the streets)
Add 'en'	die Frau (the woman) → die Frauen (the women)

When nouns are plural and are in the dative case, they add an 'n' on the end. See p.109.

Feminine nouns usually do one of these things.

2) A compound noun is a noun made of two or more words stuck together. The last word in the compound 'decides' what the noun's gender is and how the plural will be formed.

die Haustür *front door* → die Haustüren *front doors*

der Bildschirm *screen* → die Bildschirme *screens*

3) When you learn a new German noun, you should learn its plural form too. When you look for a noun in the dictionary, you'll see its plural in brackets like this... 'Bett(en)', which means 'Betten'.

You can also use adjectives as nouns

When an adjective is working as a noun in German, it needs a capital letter.

1) Sometimes in English we use adjectives as nouns — e.g. the homeless.
You can do the same with lots of adjectives in German too:

Der Deutsche ist sehr freundlich. *The German (man) is very friendly.*

The old man — Der Alte
The helpful woman — Die Hilfreiche

2) In German, you don't always need to say whether you're talking about a man or a woman. If you use 'der', it's clear you're talking about a man, and if you use 'die', it's clear you're talking about a woman.

der Deutsche *the German man*

die Deutsche *the German woman*

3) You can also use an adjective as a noun with 'ein' for males and 'eine' for females.

ein Angestellter *a male employee*

eine Angestellte *a female employee*

When an adjective is working as a noun, it has the same ending that it would have if it were still an adjective. Have a look at page 119 for the tables of endings.

Get comfortable with all these German nouns and plurals...

Translate these sentences into German. You might need to look some of the plurals up in a dictionary first.

1. There are many cars.
2. The children are small.
3. The tables are expensive.
4. The doctors are nice.
5. The old woman is called Renate.
6. The youth (male) is called Ali.

Quick Questions

Now you've made it through the first few pages of grammar it's time to see how much you can remember. Have a go at these quick questions, then go back and check anything you're not sure of.

Quick Questions

1) Underline the subject or subjects in the sentences below.
   - a) Ich gehe ins Kino.
   - b) Mein Bruder mag Tischtennis.
   - c) Wir haben einen Affen gesehen.
   - d) Mein Vater isst einen Kuchen.
   - e) Gestern habe ich Federball gespielt.
   - f) Wann besuchst du deine Tante?
   - g) Mein Freund ist sehr komisch.
   - h) Habt ihr schon gegessen?
   - i) Fußball ist langweilig.
   - j) Meine Mutter und ich gehen einkaufen.
   - k) Frankreich ist ein schönes Land.
   - l) Jeden Morgen bellt der Hund.

2) Underline the word or words in the accusative case in the sentences below.
   - a) Lara hat eine Hose gekauft.
   - b) Ich trage sehr oft einen Schal.
   - c) Das Auto da will ich haben.
   - d) Meine Eltern sprechen Spanisch.
   - e) Ich habe Schokolade mitgebracht.
   - f) Wir benutzen oft soziale Medien.
   - g) Mario hat eine E-Mail geschrieben.
   - h) Zusammen schauen wir einen Film an.
   - i) Möchten Sie eine Tasse Tee trinken?
   - j) Du musst deine Hausaufgaben machen.
   - k) Ich habe mein Handy zu Hause vergessen.
   - l) Mathe finde ich sehr langweilig.

3) Write down whether the words in **bold** are in the nominative or the accusative case.
   - a) Ich esse **den Apfel** zum Frühstück.
   - b) **Ich** esse den Apfel zum Frühstück.
   - c) Er kauft immer **Bonbons**.
   - d) **Er** kauft immer Bonbons.
   - e) **Suzi** sieht jeden Abend einen Film.
   - f) Suzi sieht jeden Abend **einen Film**.
   - g) **Die Engländerin** singt ein Lied.
   - h) Die Engländerin singt **ein Lied**.
   - i) Sie trinkt **das Mineralwasser**.
   - j) **Sie** trinkt das Mineralwasser.
   - k) Am Wochenende spielen wir **Fußball**.
   - l) Am Wochenende spielen **wir** Fußball.

4) Write down whether the words in **bold** are in the genitive or the dative case.
   - a) Ben schreibt **seinem Freund** einen Brief.
   - b) Er gibt **seiner Freundin** ein Geschenk.
   - c) Mein Vater kennt den Chef **der Bank**.
   - d) Das Auto **meiner Tante** ist blau.
   - e) Ich helfe **dem Freund** meiner Mutter.
   - f) Sie fährt den Wagen **ihres Vaters**.
   - g) Ich singe **meinem Freund** ein schönes Lied.
   - h) Ich stehle das Eis **des Mädchens**.

5) Underline the correct words in **bold** to complete the sentences.
   - a) Ich sah den Freund **meines Vaters** / **meinem Vater**.
   - b) Ich verkaufe das Haus **meines Opas** / **meinem Opa**.
   - c) Ich gehe in die Stadt mit **meines Bruders** / **meinem Bruder**.
   - d) Ich treffe die Freundin **meines Bruders** / **meinem Bruder**.
   - e) Ich schreibe **meines Freundes** / **meinem Freund** eine E-Mail.
   - f) Der Lehrer hilft **des Schülers** / **dem Schüler**.
   - g) Der Hund isst die Kekse **des Kindes** / **dem Kind**.

6) Add an '**n**' to the words in the sentences below where it is needed.
   - a) Ich gehe mit meinen Freunde....... essen.
   - b) Ich gebe meinen Brüder....... die Bücher....... .
   - c) Sie schreibt ihren Geschwister....... eine Postkarte....... .
   - d) Ich mache einen Kuchen mit Erdbeere....... darauf.
   - e) Der Lehrer hilft den Studente....... mit ihren Probleme....... .

Quick Questions

7) Underline the noun or nouns in each sentence below.
   - a) Die Blumen sind auf dem Tisch.
   - b) Ich finde Snooker langweilig.
   - c) Mein Bruder und ich lesen gern Krimis.
   - d) Meine Sportschuhe sind grün.
   - e) Das blaue Kleid steht meiner Schwester gut.
   - f) Mein Cousin kauft ein Schokoladeneis.
   - g) Es gibt keinen Dom in meiner Stadt.
   - h) Heute scheint die Sonne.
   - i) Sophie isst viel Kuchen.
   - j) Dein Freund hat ein neues Auto.
   - k) Herr Meyer fliegt nach Spanien.
   - l) Wo ist mein Regenschirm?

8) Write down whether each group of nouns is masculine, feminine or neuter.
   - a) Mädchen Liebchen Kätzchen
   - b) Metzgerei Konditorei Bäckerei
   - c) Ärztin Polizistin Lehrerin
   - d) Montag Dienstag Freitag
   - e) Sommer Winter Frühling
   - f) Lesen Schwimmen Laufen
   - g) Abteilung Buchhandlung Bedienung
   - h) Informatiker Sekretär Lehrer
   - i) Mannschaft Freundschaft Landschaft
   - j) Februar Juni Dezember
   - k) Gesundheit Vergangenheit Gewohnheit
   - l) Geburtsdatum Stadtzentrum Praktikum

9) Underline the correct form of the noun in **bold** to complete these sentences.
   - a) Der **Junge / Jungen** geht ins Kino.
   - b) Ich gebe dem **Mensch / Menschen** das Geld.
   - c) Die Dame besucht den **Herrn / Herr**.
   - d) Wir sehen die **Herrn / Herren** auf der Straße.
   - e) Das Mädchen spielt Fußball mit dem **Junge / Jungen**.
   - f) Was ist der erste Buchstabe deines **Namen / Namens**?

10) Write out the plural forms of these nouns.
   - a) die Wurst
   - b) das Lied
   - c) die Blume
   - d) der Zahn
   - e) das Kind
   - f) das Sofa
   - g) der Tag
   - h) die Einladung
   - i) die Birne
   - j) der Bruder
   - k) das Haus
   - l) das Doppelbett

11) Translate these sentences into **English**.
   - a) Der Alte ist sehr alt.
   - b) Der Obdachlose ist obdachlos.
   - c) Die Intelligente ist wirklich intelligent.

12) Complete these sentences by turning the adjectives in **bold** into nouns.
   - a) Der .... besucht England.   **deutsch**
   - b) Die .... kommen aus Deutschland.   **deutsch**
   - c) Die .... geht in die Grundschule.   **klein**
   - d) Die .... sind entsetzlich.   **klein**
   - e) Der .... rettet meinen Hund.   **nett**
   - f) Ich gebe den .... viele Geschenke.   **nett**
   - g) Ich rede mit den ....   **freundlich**
   - h) Der .... erzählt viele Witze.   **freundlich**

Word Order

German word order is a bit different. You need to learn a few rules so that you can write proper sentences.

The five commandments for German word order

> *The word order for questions and instructions is different. See p.4 and p.144 for more details.*

1) Put the verb second

The <u>verb</u> is almost <u>always</u> the <u>second</u> idea in a German sentence.

| Ich spiele Fußball. | *I play football.* |

← The word order for simple sentences like this is the same as in English. The person or thing doing the action goes first, and the verb comes second.

2) Keep the verb second

1) As long as you <u>keep</u> the verb <u>second</u>, German word order can be fairly flexible.

2) You can <u>swap</u> the information around as long as the verb is still the <u>second idea</u> in the sentence (although it might <u>not</u> be the second <u>word</u>).

3) So, if you want to say 'I play football on Mondays', you can say:

| Ich spiele montags Fußball. | | Montags spiele ich Fußball. |
| *(I play on Mondays football.)* | **OR** | *(On Mondays, I play football.)* |

3) If there are two verbs, send one to the end

If you've got two verbs, treat the <u>first</u> one as <u>normal</u> and send the <u>second</u> one to the <u>end</u> of the clause.

| Ich werde nach China fahren. | *(I will to China go).* | Ich werde viel machen. | *(I will a lot do).* |

4) Remember — When, How, Where

At school, you might have heard the phrase 'Time, Manner, Place' — it just means that if you want to describe <u>when</u>, <u>how</u> and <u>where</u> you do something, that's <u>exactly</u> the order you have to say it in.

| Ich gehe <u>heute</u> <u>mit meinen Freunden</u> <u>ins Kino</u>. | *(I am going today with my friends to the cinema).* |

WHEN (Time)   HOW (Manner)   WHERE (Place)

5) Watch out for 'joining words' — they can change the word order

Some <u>conjunctions</u> (joining words) can mess up the word order by sending the verb to the <u>end</u> of the clause. Watch out though — they <u>don't all</u> do this. See p.115-116 for more info.

| Ich schwimme, weil ich sportlich bin. | *(I swim because I sporty am.)* |

'Weil' ('because') is a joining word which sends the verb ('bin') to the end of the clause.

Check through your work using the word order rules...

Tick the sentences that use word order correctly and cross the ones that don't.

1. Ich Basketball spiele.   **3.** Ich werde in die Disco gehen.   **5.** Ich esse mit meiner Familie heute.

2. Am Montag gehe ich ins Kino.   **4.** Er lacht, weil er ist glücklich. **6.** Wir fahren am Freitag nach Berlin.

Coordinating Conjunctions

These words help you join phrases and clauses together to make interesting sentences — examiners love this.

Link sentences using coordinating conjunctions

Coordinating conjunctions <u>join</u> phrases and clauses. They <u>don't</u> affect word order — the <u>verb</u> comes <u>second</u>.

Und — And

Ich habe eine Katze.	**und**	Er hat einen Hund.
I have a cat.	***and***	*He has a dog.*

→ Ich habe eine Katze und er hat einen Hund.

I have a cat and he has a dog.

Christiane spielt gern Tennis und Rugby.   *Christiane likes playing tennis and rugby.*

Oder — Or

Ich treffe mich mit Alex.	**oder**	Ich spiele mit Ayesha Golf.
I meet up with Alex.	***or***	*I play golf with Ayesha.*

→ Ich treffe mich mit Alex oder ich spiele mit Ayesha Golf.

I meet up with Alex or I play golf with Ayesha.

Rainer spielt jeden Tag Fußball oder Rugby.   *Rainer plays football or rugby every day.*

Aber — But

You need to use a comma before 'aber'.

Ich möchte backen.	**aber**	Ich habe kein Mehl.
I would like to bake.	***but***	*I don't have any flour.*

→ Ich möchte backen, aber ich habe kein Mehl.

I would like to bake, but I don't have any flour.

Otto will Fußball spielen, aber es regnet.   *Otto wants to play football, but it's raining.*

Extend your answers using coordinating conjunctions

Using coordinating conjunctions to join phrases together will help you get the <u>best marks</u>. Here's an example using <u>denn</u> (*because, since*), which is another coordinating conjunction.

Question	Simple Answer	Extended Answer
Was ist dein Lieblingsfach?	Kunst ist mein Lieblingsfach.	Mein Lieblingsfach ist Kunst, denn ich male gern.
What's your favourite subject?	*Art is my favourite subject.*	*My favourite subject is art because I like painting.*

Coordinating conjunctions don't change the word order...

Translate these sentences into German.

1. I go by bus and you go by train.
2. We'll go to a museum or we'll play tennis.
3. I want to listen to music or watch TV.
4. He's a vegetarian, but she eats meat.
5. I love German, but hate English.

Conjunctions — Subordinating Conjunctions

Use a subordinating conjunction and get one fab German sentence. Just watch the word order.

Subordinating conjunctions send the verb to the end

A subordinating conjunction sends the <u>verb</u> to the <u>end</u> of the clause. Here are some <u>common</u> ones:

wenn	*if / when*	bevor	*before*	ob	*whether / if*	während	*while*
nachdem	*after*	bis	*until*	obwohl	*although*	weil	*because*
damit	*so that*	als	*when*	dass	*that*	da	*as, because*

Ich weiß nicht, ob er hungrig ist.
I don't know if he is hungry.

Ich frühstücke, bevor ich in die Schule gehe.
I eat breakfast before I go to school.

'Bevor' has sent 'gehe' to the end.

Make sure you can use 'weil', 'wenn', 'als' and 'obwohl'

All these conjunctions need a comma before them.

Weil — Because

Ich tanze. **weil** Ich bin froh. → Ich tanze, weil ich froh bin.
I am dancing. **because** *I am happy.* → *I am dancing because I am happy.*

Wenn — If / When

Ich werde kommen. **wenn** Ich will. → Ich werde kommen, wenn ich will.
I will come. **if** *I want to.* → *I will come if I want to.*

Ich spreche mit Faye. **wenn** Wir spielen Tennis. → Ich spreche mit Faye, wenn wir Tennis spielen.
I speak to Faye. **when** *We play tennis.* → *I speak to Faye when we play tennis.*

Als — When

'<u>Als</u>' also means '<u>when</u>', but you only use it to refer to the <u>past</u>.

Ich habe oft geweint. **als** Ich war jünger. → Ich habe oft geweint, als ich jünger war.
I often cried. **when** *I was younger.* → *I often cried when I was younger.*

Obwohl — Although

Ich werde mitspielen. **obwohl** Ich bin müde. → Ich werde mitspielen, obwohl ich müde bin.
I will play. **although** *I'm tired.* → *I will play although I'm tired.*

No 'ifs' and 'buts' — learn your German conjunctions...

Write these sentences in German — remember to put the verb in the right place.
1. I like reading because it's relaxing.
2. Come to my party if you have time (inf. sing.).
3. We were best friends when we were children.
4. I want to be a teacher although it's hard work.

Quick Questions

Learning all this grammar will help you write, speak and understand German better. So crack on with these practice questions — you know it makes sense.

Quick Questions

1) Rewrite these sentences putting the time phrase in **bold** at the beginning.
   a) Ich gehe **am Freitag** in die Stadt.
   b) Ich besuche London **im April**.
   c) Wir gehen **am Wochenende** einkaufen.
   d) Ich verlasse das Haus **um neun Uhr**.
   e) Er kommt **morgen** nicht in die Schule.
   f) Sie spielt **jeden Abend** Hockey.

2) Rewrite these groups of words to form correct sentences. There's more than one right answer for each group.
   a) ich Volleyball spiele am Freitag
   b) am Samstag ich spiele Golf
   c) ich werde besuchen Frankreich im Juli
   d) im August werde ich reisen nach Frankreich
   e) ich fahre mit dem Bus am Montag in die Schule
   f) am Dienstag fahre ich in die Schule mit dem Rad

3) Rewrite these sentences with the correct conjunction. Choose from: **und, aber, denn, oder**.
   Use each conjunction only **once**.
   a) Was magst du am liebsten — Schokolade aber Karotten?
   b) Ich möchte ein Kilo Kartoffeln denn 500 Gramm Erbsen.
   c) Wir gehen wandern, oder die Sonne scheint.
   d) Sie will ihren Freund sehen, und er ist krank.

4) Join up these sentences, using a suitable conjunction. Choose from: **und, aber, denn, oder**.
   Use each conjunction only **once**.
   a) Ich schwimme gern. Ich tanze gern.
   b) Mein Bruder möchte im Freibad schwimmen. Es ist zu kalt.
   c) Sie bleibt zu Hause. Sie hat Fieber.
   d) Kommst du mit? Gehst du nach Hause?

5) Translate these sentences into **German**.
   a) We are learning French and German.
   b) My mother would like to go to Spain or Italy.
   c) I love cake but it is unhealthy.

6) Complete the sentences using a suitable conjunction. Choose from: **weil, damit, bis, ob, obwohl, wenn**. Use each conjunction only **once**.
   a) Ich bleibe zu Hause, ... es regnet.
   b) Er fährt auf Urlaub, ... er kein Geld hat.
   c) Ich komme heute nicht ins Konzert, ... ich krank bin.
   d) Ich studiere Deutsch, ... ich in Hamburg arbeiten kann.
   e) Ich weiß nicht, ... sie mich liebt.
   f) Wir werden warten, ... du ankommst.

7) Join up each pair of sentences, using the conjunction in **bold**.
   a) Ich sonne mich. Es ist heiß. **wenn**
   b) Wir essen im chinesischen Restaurant. Wir gehen ins Theater. **bevor**
   c) Er wohnt bei seinen Eltern. Er geht an die Uni. **bis**

Articles	**'The', 'A' and 'No'**

'The' and 'a' are really tricky in German because they change to match the gender of the noun (masculine, feminine or neuter — see p.110) and the case (nominative, accusative, genitive or dative — see p.108-109).

'The' — start by learning der, die, das, die

1) In English, there's just <u>one</u> word for 'the' — simple.

2) In German, you need to know whether to use the <u>masculine</u>, <u>feminine</u> or <u>neuter</u> word for 'the' and what <u>case</u> to use (<u>nominative</u>, <u>accusative</u>, <u>genitive</u> or <u>dative</u>).

3) Start by learning the <u>first line</u> of the grid — <u>der</u>, <u>die</u>, <u>das</u>, <u>die</u>. You <u>absolutely</u> have to know those ones.

	Masculine	Feminine	Neuter	Plural
Nominative	der	die	das	die
Accusative	den	die	das	die
Genitive	des	der	des	der
Dative	dem	der	dem	den

Masculine, nominative → Der Apfel ist rot. *The apple is red.*

Plural, dative → Ich singe den Äpfeln. *I sing to the apples.*

To find out why there's an '-n' at the end of 'Äpfeln', see p.109.

'A' — start by learning ein, eine, ein

1) Like the German for 'the', the word for 'a' is different for <u>masculine</u>, <u>feminine</u> or <u>neuter</u> nouns, and for different <u>cases</u>.

2) Start by learning the <u>first line</u> of the grid — <u>ein</u>, <u>eine</u>, <u>ein</u>. Then, move on to the other ones.

	Masculine	Feminine	Neuter
Nominative	ein	eine	ein
Accusative	einen	eine	ein
Genitive	eines	einer	eines
Dative	einem	einer	einem

Masculine, nominative → Ein Hund bellt. *A dog barks.*

Feminine, accusative → Ich habe eine Katze. *I have a cat.*

'No' — kein

1) '<u>Kein</u>' means '<u>no</u>' — as in '<u>I have no potatoes</u>'.

2) It <u>changes</u> a bit like '<u>ein</u>' changes.

Plural, nominative → Keine Hunde sind lila. *No dogs are purple.*

	Masculine	Feminine	Neuter	Plural
Nominative	kein	keine	kein	keine
Accusative	keinen	keine	kein	keine
Genitive	keines	keiner	keines	keiner
Dative	keinem	keiner	keinem	keinen

Singular, neuter, accusative

Ich habe kein Buch. *I have no book.*

The article depends on the gender and case of the noun...

Fill in the gaps with the German for the word in brackets.

1. Ich mag ...... Film. *(the)*

2. Ich gebe es ...... Frau. *(the)*

3. Ich habe ...... Birne. *(a)*

4. Wer hat ...... Onkel? *(a)*

5. Ich habe ...... Bleistift. *(no)*

6. Sie wird dir ...... Geld geben. *(no)*

Words to Describe Things

Make your sentences more interesting (which means more marks) with some adjectives.

Adjectives that go after the noun don't change

When the adjective is somewhere <u>after</u> the word it's describing (e.g. apple),
it <u>doesn't change</u> at all. You just use the <u>basic</u> adjective, <u>without</u> any <u>endings</u>.

Der Apfel ist rot.   *The apple is red.*   Das Haus ist rot.   *The house is red.*

Endings for when the adjective comes before the noun

1) If the adjective comes <u>before</u> the noun, you have to give it the right <u>ending</u> from the table.

	Masculine	Feminine	Neuter	Plural
Nominative	roter	rote	rotes	rote
Accusative	roten	rote	rotes	rote
Genitive	roten	roter	roten	roter
Dative	rotem	roter	rotem	roten

Plural accusative

Ich habe rote Äpfel.
I have red apples.

2) You also use these endings if the adjective comes <u>after</u> a <u>number</u> bigger than one, or
after <u>viele</u> (*many*), <u>wenige</u> (*few*), <u>einige</u> (*some*), <u>etwas</u> (*something*) or <u>nichts</u> (*nothing*).

Ich habe viele große Äpfel.   *I have many big apples.*   etwas Neues   *something new*

> After 'etwas' and 'nichts', you need the neuter endings and a capital.

There are special endings after 'the'

You've got to add these endings if the adjective comes <u>after the</u> (der, die, das etc.),
<u>dieser</u> (*this*), <u>jeder</u> (*each / every*), <u>beide</u> (*both*), <u>welcher</u> (*which*) and <u>alle</u> (*all*).

	Masculine	Feminine	Neuter	Plural
Nominative	rote	rote	rote	roten
Accusative	roten	rote	rote	roten
Genitive	roten	roten	roten	roten
Dative	roten	roten	roten	roten

Masculine nominative

Der rote Apfel.   *The red apple.*
Dieser kleine Apfel ist gut.
This small apple is good.

There are special endings after 'a' and belonging words

You need these endings when the adjective comes <u>after</u> <u>ein</u> (*a*, or *one*)
or <u>kein</u> (*no*, or *none*), or after pronouns like <u>mein</u>, <u>dein</u>, <u>sein</u>, <u>ihr</u>...

	Masculine	Feminine	Neuter	Plural
Nominative	roter	rote	rotes	roten
Accusative	roten	rote	rotes	roten
Genitive	roten	roten	roten	roten
Dative	roten	roten	roten	roten

Masculine nominative

Mein roter Apfel ist gut.
My red apple is good.

You need to be familiar with these adjective endings...

Translate these sentences into German.

1. The horse is grey.   **3.** He has two grey horses.   **5.** Which grey horse?   **7.** I have a grey horse.

2. I see three grey horses. **4.** She likes the grey horse. **6.** The grey horse is big. **8.** This grey horse is old.

Adjectives | Words to Describe Things

Here are some adjectives to whet your appetite. You need to know how to say my, his, your... too.

Learn these adjectives

groß	*big / tall*	einfach	*easy*	neu	*new*	interessant	*interesting*
klein	*small / short*	schwierig	*difficult*	schnell	*fast*	spannend	*exciting*
lang	*long*	schön	*beautiful*	langsam	*slow*	lustig	*funny*
breit	*wide*	hässlich	*ugly*	doof	*stupid*	gut	*good*
glücklich	*happy*	alt	*old*	langweilig	*boring*	schlecht	*bad*
traurig	*sad*	jung	*young*	seltsam	*strange*	schlimm	*bad*

My, your, our — words for who it belongs to

1) You have to be able to <u>use</u> these words to say that something <u>belongs</u> to <u>you</u> ('mein') or to <u>someone else</u>.

2) But <u>watch out</u> — they need the right <u>ending</u> to go with the <u>object</u> you're talking about (they're the same as the kein / keine / kein / keine table — see p.118).

	Masculine	Feminine	Neuter	Plural
Nominative	mein	(meine)	mein	meine
Accusative	meinen	meine	(mein)	meine
Genitive	meines	meiner	meines	meiner
Dative	meinem	meiner	meinem	meinen

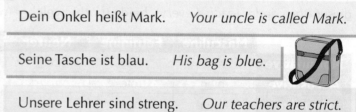

Meine Tasche ist blau.
My bag is blue.

Ich mag mein Fahrrad.
I like my bike.

3) The other possessive words are pretty neat — <u>all</u> of them use the <u>same endings</u> as 'mein' does.

The Possessive Adjectives			
mein	my	unser	our
dein	your (informal singular)	euer	your (informal plural)
sein	his	Ihr	your (formal singular & plural)
ihr	her		
sein	its	ihr	their

Dein Onkel heißt Mark.   *Your uncle is called Mark.*

Seine Tasche ist blau.   *His bag is blue.*

Unsere Lehrer sind streng.   *Our teachers are strict.*

Welcher, dieser and jeder — Which, this and every

The <u>endings</u> for these words follow the same pattern as '<u>der</u>'. Look at the <u>last letter</u> for each word in the first table on p.118 — the last line would be diese<u>m</u>, diese<u>r</u>, diese<u>m</u>, diese<u>n</u>.

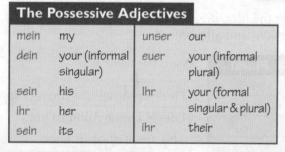

You use 'welcher' here because 'Bus' is masculine. 'Welche' is for feminine words and 'welches' is for neuter words.

Question	Simple Answer	Extended Answer
Welcher Bus fährt in die Stadt?	Dieser Bus fährt direkt in die Stadt.	Dieser Bus fährt direkt in die Stadt, aber jeder Bus fährt in diese Richtung.
Which bus goes into town?	*This bus goes directly into town.*	*This bus goes directly into town, but every bus goes in that direction.*

The happy student revised the interesting German...

Rewrite these sentences in German — use the tables on this page and p.118-119 to get the right endings.

1. My house is big. 3. Every job is boring. 5. This music is great. 7. Which coat does he want?
2. Her baby is happy. 4. Who has my new pen? 6. I bought this fast car 8. My sister's dog is funny.

Words to Compare Things

Comparatives and Superlatives

Sometimes, something isn't just big — it's the biggest, or bigger than something else...

How to say smaller, smallest, etc.

Check the top of p.120 for more adjectives.

1) In <u>English</u>, you say small, small<u>er</u>, small<u>est</u>. It's <u>almost</u> the <u>same</u> in German:

> Anna ist klein.
> *Anna is small.*

> Omar ist kleiner.
> *Omar is smaller.*

> Tina ist die Kleinste.
> *Tina is the smallest.*

Here the adjective acts as a noun, just like in English — and of course all German nouns get a capital letter.

Stem	Stem + '-er'	'der', 'die', 'das' + stem + '-(e)ste'
billig *cheap*	billig<u>er</u> *cheaper*	der / die / das Billig<u>ste</u> *the cheapest*
interessant *interesting*	interessant<u>er</u> *more interesting*	der / die / das Interessant<u>este</u> *the most interesting*

2) <u>Comparative adjectives</u> are made up of a <u>normal adjective</u> and the ending '-<u>er</u>'.
   In German, you <u>can't</u> add 'mehr' (*more*) before the adjective like you can in English.

> die wichtiger<u>en</u> Tage   *the more important days*

Comparatives work like adjectives, so you've got to use the right adjective endings — see p.119.

3) To form a <u>superlative</u>, you normally add '-<u>ste</u>' to the stem of the adjective. Sometimes you add '-<u>este</u>' instead, to make it easier to pronounce.

> Maria ist die Klugste.   *Maria is the cleverest.*
> Das Auto ist das Lauteste.   *The car is the loudest.*

4) You can add '-er' and '-(e)ste' to almost any <u>adjective</u>. A lot of <u>short</u> ones add an <u>umlaut</u>.

> Jay ist älter als Mike, aber Gavin ist der Älteste.   *Jay is older than Mike, but Gavin is the oldest.*

There are some odd ones

Just like in English, there are <u>exceptions</u> — for example, you don't say good, gooder, goodest...

Adjective			Comparative			Superlative	
gut	*good*	→	besser	*better*	→	der / die / das Beste	*the best*
groß	*big (or tall)*	→	größer	*bigger*	→	der / die / das Größte	*the biggest*
hoch	*high*	→	höher	*higher*	→	der / die / das Höchste	*the highest*
viel	*much / a lot*	→	mehr	*more*	→	der / die / das Meiste	*the most*
nah	*near*	→	näher	*nearer*	→	der / die / das Nächste	*the nearest*

> Paris ist näher als Tokio.   *Paris is nearer than Tokyo.*

> Liz ist die Größte.   *Liz is the tallest.*

Learn these four great ways of comparing things

1) Jo ist älter als Li.
   Jo is older than Li.

2) Jo ist weniger alt als Li.
   Jo is less old than Li.

3) Jo ist so alt wie Li.
   Jo is as old as Li.

4) Jo ist genauso alt wie Li.
   Jo is just as old as Li.

Never compare yourself to others — except in German...

Translate these words, phrases and sentences into German.

1. happy, happier, the happiest
2. slow, slower, the slowest
3. pretty, prettier, the prettiest
4. sad, more sad, the most sad
5. That's the bigger house.
6. Katrin is just as lazy as Klaus.

Quick Questions

The last few pages covered some really important stuff, so try these quick questions to make sure you can put it all into practice.

Quick Questions

1) Fill in the gaps with the correct German word for 'the'. The cases are given in bold.
   a) Ich mag .... Hund. **accusative**
   b) Ich singe .... Hund ein Lied. **dative**
   c) Er sieht .... Kaninchen im Garten. **accusative**
   d) Die Farbe .... Autos ist rot. **genitive**

2) Complete these sentences with the correct form of the words in brackets.
   a) Ich habe .... (a) Hund, aber .... (no) Katze.
   b) In meiner Stadt gibt es .... (no) Kino und .... (no) Dom.
   c) .... (no) Freunde haben mich besucht, als ich krank war.
   d) Ich will .... (a) Pizza essen, aber es gibt .... (no) italienisches Restaurant.

3) Complete the sentences with the correct adjective endings.
   a) Die braun...... Katze schläft auf dem grün...... Sofa neben dem weiß...... Kaninchen.
   b) Die klein...... Kinder spielen mit dem groß...... Hund in dem schön...... Park.
   c) Sie findet den schwarz...... Regenmantel und den rot...... Hut des alt...... Mannes.
   d) Ich gebe dem klein...... Mädchen die lecker...... Kekse und das frisch...... Obst.

4) Translate the following phrases into **German**, using the correct adjective endings.
   a) fresh milk   c) two red apples   e) warm water   g) lots of big dogs
   b) cold beer   d) few hot days   f) some small dogs h) ten green bottles

5) Complete these sentences with the correct articles and endings.
   a) .... (the) neu...... Haus liegt in .... (a) ruhig...... Dorf.
   b) Sie trägt immer .... (a) blau...... Rock und braun...... Stiefel.
   c) Meine älter...... Schwester hat viele sympathisch...... Freunde.
   d) Wir besuchen .... (the) historisch...... Marktplatz und .... (the) neu......
      Museum.

6) Underline the correct form of **dieser** or **welcher** to complete the sentences below.
   a) **Welcher / Welchen** Zug fährt nach Köln?
   b) Ich möchte zum Zoo fahren. **Welcher / Welchen** Bus sollte ich nehmen?
   c) **Diese / Dieser** Kuchen sind lecker.
   d) In **welcher / welche** Stadt hast du studiert?

7) Finish off these sentences with the comparative form of the adjective in **bold**.
   a) Felix ist **schnell**, aber Leonie ist ....
   b) Mein Auto ist **langsam**, aber dein Auto ist ....
   c) Dieser Film ist **gut**, aber der andere Film ist ....
   d) Meine Großmutter ist **alt**, aber mein Großvater ist ....

8) Translate these sentences into **German**.
   a) I am good, you are better, but she is the best.
   b) My house is near, your house is nearer, but his house is the nearest.
   c) The theatre is old, the church is older, but the cathedral is the oldest.

Words to Describe Actions

Adverbs

This page is about describing things you do, e.g. 'I speak German perfectly', and about adding more info, e.g. 'I speak German almost perfectly'. I'll tell you how — make yourself a nice cuppa, sit down and read on.

Make your sentences better by saying how you do things

1) In <u>English</u>, you don't say 'We speak strange' — you <u>add 'ly'</u> onto the end to say 'We speak strange<u>ly</u>'.

2) In <u>German</u>, you <u>don't</u> have to do anything — you just stick the describing word in <u>as it is</u>.

langsam	*slowly*	freiwillig	*voluntarily*
plötzlich	*suddenly*	öffentlich	*publicly*
schnell	*quickly*	mündlich	*orally*

Lou singt laut.   *Lou sings loudly.*

Sie läuft mühelos.   *She runs effortlessly.*

Wir arbeiten fleißig.   *We work hard.*

Er tanzt wunderschön.   Ich fahre langsam.
He dances beautifully.   *I drive slowly.*

happily — fröhlich   *quickly* — schnell

Use one of these words to give even more detail

1) Pop one of these words in <u>front</u> of an <u>adjective</u> or <u>adverb</u> to really impress your teacher.

sehr	*very*	etwas / ein wenig	*slightly*	zu	*too*	völlig	*completely*
ganz / ziemlich	*quite*	ein bisschen	*a bit*	viel	*a lot*	fast	*almost*

2) You can use them for sentences saying <u>how something is done</u>.

Ich spreche sehr schnell.   *I talk very quickly.*   Ute ist fast hingefallen.   *Ute almost fell over.*

3) They're also handy for sentences about <u>what something is like</u>.

Er ist ganz traurig.   *He is quite sad.*   Autos sind oft zu teuer.   *Cars are often too expensive.*

You need to know about these adverbs too

wahrscheinlich	*probably*	bestimmt	*definitely / certainly*	normalerweise	*normally / usually*
wirklich	*really*	einfach	*simply / easily*	gewöhnlich	*normally / usually*
eigentlich	*actually / really*	typisch	*typically*	leider	*unfortunately*
gewaltig	*enormously*	etwa	*about / roughly*	endlich	*finally*
kaum	*hardly*	genau	*exactly*	schließlich	*eventually / finally*

Ich esse normalerweise Eier zum Frühstück.
I normally eat eggs for breakfast.

Schließlich kamen wir am Flughafen an.
Finally, we arrived at the airport.

Use adverbs to add detail to your sentences...

Rewrite each of these sentences, adding an adverb. Use more than one adverb where you can.

1. Ich gehe.   **3.** Er hat gesprochen.   **5.** Das Auto hält.   **7.** Stephan kam spät.

2. Sie laufen.   **4.** Ich helfe Lukas.   **6.** Wir werden gewinnen.   **8.** Es kostet zwei Euro.

Adverbs	# Words to Describe Actions

Adverbs can also give details about time and place — when and where you'll be doing your German homework, for example, or something like that. Add a few to your sentences to bag loads of marks.

Use adverbs to say when you do something...

1) Adverbs can tell you <u>when</u> or <u>how often</u> something happens.

immer	*always*	täglich	*daily*	gleich	*immediately / in a minute*
oft	*often*	nie	*never*	sofort	*immediately / straightaway*
ab und zu	*now and again*	jetzt	*now*	kürzlich	*recently / lately*
manchmal	*sometimes*	früh	*early*	neulich	*recently / the other day*
selten	*seldom / rarely*	spät	*late*	schon	*already*

2) You can use an <u>adverb</u> in front of a <u>noun</u> to talk about a more <u>specific point in time</u>.

gestern Morgen	*yesterday morning*	morgen Nachmittag	*tomorrow afternoon*
gestern Abend	*yesterday evening*	morgen Abend	*tomorrow evening*

3) There are lots of other useful time phrases.

heute Vormittag	*this morning*
nächste Woche	*next week*
nächstes Jahr	*next year*
letzten Montag	*last Monday*

Wir feiern am kommenden Freitag.
We're celebrating this coming Friday.

'Nächste' and 'letzten' are adjectives, so you have to give them the right ending — see p.119.

...and where you do something

hier	*here*
dort	*there*
drüben	*over there*
überall	*everywhere*
nirgendwo	*nowhere*
irgendwo	*somewhere*

Ich wohne hier. *I live here.*

The word order changes because the verb has to be the second idea in the sentence. See p.114.

Drüben spielen wir Fußball. *Over there, we play football.*

Er wohnt irgendwo in London. *He lives somewhere in London.*

Give more detail by using when and where adverbs

Use <u>both</u> when and where adverbs <u>together</u> to really wow the examiners.

Ich gehe gleich dorthin. *I'm going there immediately.*

Ich habe schon überall gesucht.
I have already looked everywhere.

Letzten Donnerstag fuhren wir in die Stadt, aber man konnte nirgendwo parken.
Last Thursday, we went into town, but there was nowhere to park.

Adverbs go in the order 'Time, Manner, Place'...
Write these sentences in German. The adverbs are all from the boxes above.
1. I brush my teeth daily.
2. Andrea often tells jokes.
3. I never play tennis there.
4. There are birds everywhere.
5. They sometimes meet over there.
6. I'll see you here this coming Monday.

Words to Compare Actions

If you do something, and then someone else does it differently — or maybe even better — you can talk about it using comparisons. It's a lot of the same stuff from p.121, but here it's comparing actions.

You can compare how people do things

1) To say someone is doing something 'more... than' someone else, add 'er' to the adverb and use 'als'.

Ida fährt langsamer als ich. *Ida drives more slowly than me.*
Neil singt süßer als Leo. *Neil sings more sweetly than Leo.*

2) You can say someone is doing something 'less... than' someone else by using 'nicht so... wie'.

Grace arbeitet nicht so hart wie Ruth. *Grace works less hard than Ruth.*

3) If you want to say someone is doing something 'just as...' or 'just as much as...' someone else, use 'genauso... wie' and 'genauso viel wie'.

Aaron läuft genauso langsam wie Ethel. *Aaron walks just as slowly as Ethel.*
Mädchen mögen Tennis genauso viel wie Jungen. *Girls like tennis just as much as boys.*

You can say who does something the quickest, slowest...

If you want to say something's the quickest, the slowest or the craziest, you use 'am' and then add '-(e)sten' to the end of the adverb. This is the superlative.

Dani tanzt am schnellsten. *Dani dances the fastest.*
Der Vogel kräht am lautesten. *The bird crows the loudest.*

If the adverb ends in '-d' or '-t', you need to add '-esten'.

Sie läuft am langsamsten. *She runs the slowest.*
Ben kletterte auf den Baum am vorsichtigsten. *Ben climbed up the tree the most carefully.*

Watch out for these odd ones

'Gern', 'gut' and 'viele' are three strange ones that don't follow the rules.

gern	willingly	gut	good	viele	lots
lieber	preferably	besser	better	mehr	more
am liebsten	best of all	am besten	best	am meisten	the most

Ich spreche lieber Deutsch. *I prefer speaking German.*
Berlin gefällt mir am besten. *I like Berlin the best.*
Er mag die Schuhe am meisten. *He likes the shoes the most.*

Revise this well and you'll compare actions better than before...

Translate these phrases from English into German.
1. I run faster than her.
2. They play football the best.
3. We will eat more slowly.
4. He jumps the farthest.
5. The man sings the most beautifully.
6. Albert paints better than Liesl.

Quick Questions

Here are some more practice questions to jog your memory. Don't just ignore the ones you can't do — go back over the last few pages and find the information you need.

Quick Questions

1) Translate these sentences into **English**.
   a) Er singt laut und schlecht. Sie tanzt gut.
   b) Ich fahre langsam und du sprichst seltsam.
   c) Mein Bruder arbeitet fleißig und schwimmt schnell.

2) Complete the sentences using a suitable adverb. Choose from: **plötzlich**, **unglaublich**, **schlecht**, **schön**, **langsam**, **glücklich**. Use each word only once.
   a) Er spielt .... , wenn er müde ist.
   b) Ich laufe sehr .... , weil ich nicht fit bin.
   c) Das war wunderbar. Du singst ....
   d) Der Film war .... gut.
   e) Sie lächelt sehr ....
   f) .... hat es angefangen zu regnen.

3) Use a suitable adverbial phrase to complete the sentences. Choose from: **immer**, **neulich**, **manchmal**, **nächste Woche**, **gestern Abend**, **schon**. Use each phrase only once.
   a) .... scheint die Sonne, aber meistens regnet es.
   b) Ist er .... da? Ich habe ihn noch nicht gesehen.
   c) Der Zug kommt .... spät an, es ist sehr ärgerlich.
   d) Ich bin .... krank gewesen und bin noch schwach.
   e) Hast du .... etwas Schönes gemacht?
   f) Ich fahre .... nach Spanien und freue mich sehr darauf.

4) Complete the sentences with the **German** translations of the adverbial phrases given in **bold**.
   a) Die Stadt ist heute sehr belebt — es gibt .... Menschen. **everywhere**
   b) Es gibt .... ein schönes Café. Wollen wir hingehen? **over there**
   c) .... kommt mein Freund mich besuchen. **the day after tomorrow**
   d) Ich bin mir sicher, dass ich sie .... gesehen habe. **somewhere**

5) Translate the sentences below into **German**.
   a) He was there very early.   b) We always sit over there.

6) Translate these sentences into **English**.
   a) Al spricht lauter als Eoin.   c) Sami lächelt nicht so oft wie Aled.
   b) Rhys tanzt genauso gut wie Faiz.   d) Jo mag Rugby genauso viel wie Pete.

7) Complete the sentences with the **German** translations of the words given in bold.
   a) Ich mag Geschichte, aber Englisch gefällt mir .... **the best**
   b) Tanzen macht Spaß, aber ich gehe .... ins Kino. **preferably**
   c) Ich komme .... in die Stadt mit. **willingly**
   d) Du hast .... Geschenke, aber ich habe ....
   many, **more**

8) Translate the sentences below into **German**.
   a) Joanna is just as friendly as Morag.
   b) Megan runs less quickly than Anna.

I, You, He, She, We, They

Pronouns are useful little words like 'I' and 'them'. They crop up everywhere, so it's worth learning them.

You use subject pronouns in the nominative case

Check p.108 for more on the nominative case.

Words like 'I', 'you', 'he', etc. are <u>subject pronouns</u>. They replace the <u>subject</u> of a sentence.

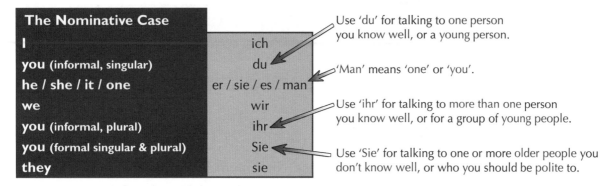

The Nominative Case	
I	ich
you (informal, singular)	du
he / she / it / one	er / sie / es / man
we	wir
you (informal, plural)	ihr
you (formal singular & plural)	Sie
they	sie

Use 'du' for talking to one person you know well, or a young person.

'Man' means 'one' or 'you'.

Use 'ihr' for talking to more than one person you know well, or for a group of young people.

Use 'Sie' for talking to one or more older people you don't know well, or who you should be polite to.

Der Hund beißt den Kamm. Er beißt den Kamm. *The dog bites the comb. He bites the comb.*

There are pronouns for the accusative case...

Words like 'me', 'you' and 'him' are for the person / thing that's <u>having the action done to it</u> (the direct object).

The Accusative Case						
me	you (inf. sing.)	him / her / it	us	you (inf. pl.)	you (frml. sing. & plu.)	them
mich	dich	ihn / sie / es	uns	euch	Sie	sie

'Anrufen' is a separable verb. See p.145.

Er ruft mich an. *He calls me.*

... and for the dative case

For things like writing <u>to someone</u>, you use the <u>dative</u> case (see p.109).

The Dative Case						
to me	to you (inf. sing.)	to him / her / it	to us	to you (inf. pl.)	to you (frml. sing. & plu.)	to them
mir	dir	ihm / ihr / ihm	uns	euch	Ihnen	ihnen

Ich schreibe ihr. *I write to her.*

Jemand, niemand — someone, no one

'<u>Jemand</u>' means '<u>someone</u>' or '<u>anyone</u>'. To say '<u>no one</u>', use '<u>niemand</u>'.

Ist jemand da? *Is someone / anyone there?*

Niemand hat mich gesehen. *No one has seen me.*

Think about which case you need for the pronoun...

Write these sentences in German, using the right case for each pronoun.

1. He sees her.
2. They see us.
3. I speak to you (inf. plu.).
4. You (frml. sing.) speak to me.
5. I know you (inf. sing.).
6. She knows them.

There are two verbs for 'to know' in German — make sure you use the right one.

Reflexive Pronouns	# Reflexive Pronouns

Some verbs don't make sense if you don't add 'myself', 'yourself', etc., so you've got to learn this stuff.

Talking about yourself — 'sich'

'Sich' means 'oneself'. It changes depending on who's doing the action.

You can tell which verbs need 'self' by checking in the dictionary. E.g. if you look up 'to get dressed', it'll say 'sich anziehen'.

Reflexive Pronouns

mich	myself	uns	ourselves
dich	yourself (inf. sing.)	euch	yourselves (inf. plu.)
sich	himself / herself / itself	sich	yourself / yourselves (frml. sing. & plu.)
		sich	themselves / each other

Ich wasche mich — I wash myself

1) Reflexive pronouns help you talk about your daily routine. They normally go after the verb.

ich wasche mich	I wash myself	wir waschen uns	we wash ourselves
du wäschst dich	you wash yourself	ihr wascht euch	you wash yourselves
er wäscht sich	he washes himself	Sie waschen sich	you wash yourself / yourselves
sie wäscht sich	she washes herself	sie waschen sich	they wash themselves
es wäscht sich	it washes itself		

2) Here are some examples of verbs that need reflexive pronouns. They're called reflexive verbs. See p.136.

sich anziehen	to get dressed	sich entschuldigen	to excuse oneself
sich fühlen	to feel	sich setzen	to sit down
sich umziehen	to get changed	sich sonnen	to sun oneself

Ich ziehe mich an. *I get dressed.*

With separable verbs (p.145), the 'sich' bit goes straight after the main verb.

Ich putze mir die Zähne — I clean my teeth

Some verbs need you to add 'to myself' and 'to yourself'. This is the dative case.

sich die Zähne putzen	to clean one's teeth
sich ... wünschen	to want / wish for...
sich ... vorstellen	to imagine...

Reflexive Pronouns in the Dative Case

mir	to myself	uns	to ourselves
dir	to yourself (inf. sing.)	euch	to yourselves (inf. plu.)
sich	to himself / herself / itself	sich	to yourself / yourselves (frml. sing. & plu.)
		sich	to themselves / each other

Ich wünsche mir ein Pferd. *I want a horse.*

Ich habe mich gewaschen — I have washed myself

The perfect tense of these verbs is pretty much the same as normal (see p.138), except they all go with 'haben', not 'sein'.

Er hat sich schlecht gefühlt.
He felt bad (ill).

Put the 'sich' straight after 'haben'.

The reflexive pronoun has to agree with the subject...

Translate these sentences into German.
1. They wash themselves. 3. He excuses himself. 5. You (inf. sing.) clean your teeth. 7. We get changed.
2. I feel happy. 4. She suns herself. 6. You (frml. plu.) want a dog. 8. I got changed.

Relative and Interrogative Pronouns

Tricky stuff this, but learn it and you'll nab yourself loads of juicy marks.

Relative pronouns — 'that', 'which', 'whom', 'whose'

1) Words like 'that', 'which', 'whom' and 'whose' are relative pronouns — they relate back to the things you're talking about.

2) In German, relative pronouns send the verb to the end of the relative clause.

The pronoun refers back to 'der Mann'.

Der Mann, der in der Ecke sitzt, ist klein.
The man who sits in the corner is small.

The verb goes to the end of the clause.

The relative clause (the bit with the relative pronoun in) is introduced by a comma.

You've got to use the right one

The relative pronoun you need depends on the noun's case (p.108-109) and its gender (p.110).

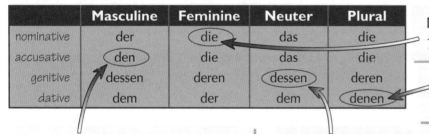

	Masculine	Feminine	Neuter	Plural
nominative	der	die	das	die
accusative	den	die	das	die
genitive	dessen	deren	dessen	deren
dative	dem	der	dem	denen

Die Katze, die mich kratzte, war weiß.
The cat which scratched me was white.

Die Hunde, denen er folgt, sind groß.
The dogs that he follows are big.

Der Mann, den ich sah, war witzig.
The man whom I saw was funny.

Das Pferd, dessen Bein gebrochen ist, ist traurig.
The horse whose leg is broken is sad.

'Was' can be used as a relative pronoun too

1) 'Was' can also be used as a relative pronoun.

2) It can be used after 'alles', 'nichts', 'etwas', 'vieles' and 'weniges'.

Alles, was der Lehrer sagte, war interessant.
Everything that the teacher said was interesting.

Wer? Was? Was für? — Who? What? What sort of?

See p.4-5 for more about questions.

1) Some pronouns can be used as question words. These are called interrogative pronouns.

Wer sitzt auf der Katze?
Who is sitting on the cat?

Was kratzt dich, Albert?
What is scratching you, Albert?

Was für eine Katze ist sie?
What sort of cat is it?

2) There are different words for 'wer'. The one you need to use depends on the case.

Nominative	Accusative	Dative
wer	wen	wem

Mit wem spreche ich?   *Whom am I talking to?*

Relative pronouns are a great way to join two sentences...

Translate these sentences into German. Use the right gender / case and remember the commas.

1. The woman who wears a hat is pretty.
2. The people to whom I write are nice.
3. The child whose coat is red laughs.
4. Whom did he see?
5. Nothing that she does is easy.

Prepositions

Prepositions are tiny little words that help make it clear what's happening in a sentence.

To — zu or nach

1) Where we use 'to', German speakers often use '<u>zu</u>'.

> When you want to say 'to go' or 'to do', you need the infinitive, not a preposition. E.g. gehen = to go, machen = to make.

| Komm zu mir. *Come to me.* | zum Bahnhof gehen *to go (by foot) to the station* |

zum = zu dem — see p.131.

2) For travelling to somewhere in a <u>vehicle</u>, it's usually '<u>nach</u>', but '<u>an</u>' and '<u>in</u>' are sometimes used too.

| nach Berlin *to Berlin* | in die USA *to the USA* | ans Meer *to the sea* |

ans = an das — see p.131.

At — an, bei, um or zu

1) Where we use 'at', in German it's usually '<u>an</u>', but sometimes '<u>bei</u>' is used:

| Ich studiere an der Universität. *I study at university.* | Er ist bei einer Party. *He is at a party.* |

2) For 'at home', it's '<u>zu</u>', and for times, it's '<u>um</u>'. zu Hause *at home*   um acht Uhr *at 8 o'clock*

On — an or auf

1) Where we use 'on', in German it tends to be '<u>an</u>'.

| an der Wand *on the wall* | am Montag *on Monday* |

am = an dem — see p.131.

2) For 'on foot', it's '<u>zu</u>' and for on top of something, it's '<u>auf</u>'. Es ist auf dem Tisch. *It is on the table.*   zu Fuß *on foot*

From — von or aus

1) When we use 'from' in English, they usually use '<u>von</u>' in German, including for where someone / something has come from <u>recently</u>.

| Der Zug ist von Paris gekommen. *The train has come from Paris.* |

> To say what something is 'made from', use 'aus'.

2) For where someone/thing is from <u>originally</u>, it's '<u>aus</u>'. Ich komme aus Wales. *I come from Wales.*

In — in or an

1) Where we use 'in', German speakers also tend to use '<u>in</u>'.

| Sina wohnt in Wien. *Sina lives in Vienna.* | Nico ist im Bett. *Nico is in bed.* |

im = in dem — see p.131.

2) For 'in the morning / evening', it's '<u>an</u>'. am Morgen *in the morning*

Learn phrases with prepositions like 'zu Hause' and 'im Bett'...

Say which German preposition should be used in each sentence. Check above for help.

1. We walk to the park. **3.** I'll find it at home. **5.** The cat is on top of the sofa. **7.** It's in the fridge.
2. The bus to Bath is slow. **4.** She goes on foot. **6.** I originally come from York. **8.** It's in the evening.

Prepositions

Yep, more prepositions. Learn which words to use where — it's not always obvious from the English.

Of — 'von', 'aus' or left out

Where we use 'of', the German is usually '<u>von</u>', but you <u>leave it out</u> of dates and it's often <u>left out</u> in <u>genitive</u> sentences too.

ein Freund von mir   *a friend of mine*

aus Holz   *made of wood*   der erste Mai   *the first of May*   einer der Besten   *one of the best*

For — für or seit

To say 'for', German speakers usually use '<u>für</u>', but for time amounts in the past, it's '<u>seit</u>'.

ein Geschenk für mich
a present for me

Ich habe sie seit zwei Jahren nicht gesehen.
I haven't seen her for two years.

Zum, am, im — short forms

Some of the words on page 130 and above get <u>shortened</u> when they go with 'dem', 'das' or 'der'.

am ersten Januar   *on the first of January*

Short forms

an dem → am	bei dem → beim
an das → ans	von dem → vom
in dem → im	zu der → zur
in das → ins	zu dem → zum

To be 100% right, you have to use the right case

See p.108-109 for more on cases.

1) These words <u>change the case</u> of the stuff <u>after</u> them. To know <u>what case</u> to use, <u>learn</u> these lists.

Accusative
bis *till, by*
durch *through*
entlang *along*
für *for*
gegen *against, about*
ohne *without*
um *round, around, at*

You might also see 'entlang' with the genitive case.

Dative
aus *from, out of*
bei *at, near*
gegenüber *opposite*
mit *with*
nach *to, after*
seit *since, for*
von *from, by, of*
zu *to, at, for*

Genitive
außerhalb *outside of*
statt *instead of*
trotz *despite*
während *during*
wegen *because of*

Dative or Accusative
an *to, on, in, at*
auf *on, to, at*
hinter *after, behind*
in *in, into, to*
neben *next to, beside*
über *via, above, over*
unter *under, among*
vor *before, ago, in front of*

2) For prepositions which use <u>either</u> the dative or accusative case, use the <u>accusative</u> when what you're talking about is <u>moving</u> and the <u>dative</u> if there's <u>no movement</u>.

Die Katze schläft hinter dem Sofa.   *The cat sleeps behind the (dative) sofa.* ← The cat <u>isn't</u> moving.

Die Katze läuft hinter das Sofa.   *The cat runs behind the (accusative) sofa.* ← The cat <u>is</u> moving.

Don't forget to use the correct case with prepositions...

Write out these phrases and sentences in German.

1. through the wood
2. without his pen
3. from her father
4. after the film
5. despite the rain
6. during the party
7. I ran along the road.
8. He stands under the bridge.

Quick Questions

You're making headway with the grammar section now, so keep up the good work and give these quick questions a whirl. It's all good practice for your exams.

Quick Questions

1) Write out these sentences again and replace the noun in **bold** with the correct pronoun.
   a) Der Hund ist schwarz. **Der Hund** heißt Max.
   b) Die Kinder gehen nicht in die Schule. **Die Kinder** spielen im Garten.
   c) Das Haus ist modern. **Das Haus** liegt am Stadtrand.
   d) Marie ist meine beste Freundin. **Marie** ist sehr sympathisch.

2) Choose the correct form of 'you' to use in the following situations when speaking **German**.
   a) Saying to your mum: 'Have you seen my mobile?'
   b) Saying to your teacher: 'Could you explain that again, please?'
   c) Asking a policeman in the street for directions.
   d) Asking a few friends: 'Would you like to come to my party?'

3) Underline the correct pronoun in **bold** to complete the sentences.
   a) Geben Sie **mich** / **mir** das Buch.
   b) Meine Katze beißt **mich** / **mir** immer.
   c) Ich werde **dich** / **dir** ein Lied singen.
   d) Ich danke **Sie** / **Ihnen** für Ihre Blumen.
   e) Er spricht mit **wir** / **uns** über **ihr** / **euch**.
   f) Ich habe **ihn** / **ihm** gesehen.
   g) Du hilfst **sie** / **ihr**.
   h) Geht **ihr** / **euch** in dieselbe Schule?

4) Translate the sentences below into **English**.
   a) Wir setzen uns schnell.
   b) Ich habe mich geduscht und dann gefrühstückt.
   c) Ich putze mir die Zähne.

5) Complete the sentences by adding the correct reflexive pronouns.
   a) Ich habe .... eine modische Uniform gewünscht.
   b) Mein Freund fühlt .... sehr kalt. Er hat .... nicht warm genug angezogen.
   c) Du hast .... heute Morgen nicht die Zähne geputzt.
   d) Ich freue .... sehr auf deinen Besuch.
   e) Ihr interessiert .... für Geschichte. Sie interessieren .... für Mathe.
   f) Ich kann .... gar nicht vorstellen, warum du .... einen Hund wünschst.

6) Underline the correct pronoun in **bold** to complete the sentences.
   a) Die Studentin, **die** / **der** Italienisch spricht, ist launisch.
   b) Der Mann, **der** / **den** ich gestern besucht habe, ist krank.
   c) Das Baby, **das** / **dessen** immer weint, ist sehr klein.
   d) Die Freundin, mit **die** / **der** ich telefoniere, ist sehr sympathisch.
   e) Das Auto, **deren** / **dessen** Fenster kaputt ist, funktioniert nicht.
   f) Die Fußballspieler, mit **deren** / **denen** ich spreche, kommen aus Frankreich.
   g) Meine Tante, **deren** / **dessen** Haus sehr klein ist, hat viele Schlangen.
   h) Der Bus, mit **der** / **dem** ich in die Stadt fahre, kommt immer spät an.

Quick Questions

7) Complete the sentences using the correct interrogative pronoun. Choose from: **wen**, **wem**, **was**, **wer**, **was für**.

a) .... wohnt in deinem Haus?

b) Mit .... sprichst du?

c) .... ein Auto hast du?

d) .... hilfst du?

e) .... hast du gemacht?

f) .... hast du besucht?

8) Underline the correct preposition in **bold** to complete the sentences.

a) Es ist fünf **vorbei** / **nach** vier und er geht **zu** / **seit** dem Café.

b) Ich studiere Informatik **an** / **zu** der Universität.

c) **Im** / **Am** Abend bleiben wir **zu** / **nach** Hause und sehen fern.

d) Ich gehe **am** / **um** vier Uhr **bei** / **nach** Hause.

e) Mein Opa wohnt **bei** / **nach** mir.

f) Das Poster ist **an** / **auf** der Wand.

g) Fährt dieser Zug **zu** / **nach** München?

h) **Im** / **Am** Sommer gehen wir immer **zu** / **auf** Fuß in die Stadt.

9) These sentences have the wrong preposition. Rewrite them, replacing the word in **bold** with the correct preposition.

a) Diese Jacke ist **von** Leder.

b) Ist diese Torte **vor** mich?

c) Ich lerne **für** zwei Jahren Deutsch.

d) Der Zug ist **nach** London gekommen.

e) Deine Tasche ist **an** dem Tisch.

10) Underline the correct word in **bold** to complete the sentences.

a) Ich gehe **ins** / **im** Kino.

b) Ich fahre über **die** / **der** Brücke.

c) Ich bleibe **ins** / **im** Hotel.

d) Das Buch liegt hinter **den** / **dem** Stuhl.

e) Wir treffen uns vor **das** / **dem** Rathaus.

f) Das Bild hängt an **die** / **der** Wand.

g) Ich sitze auf **die** / **der** Brücke.

h) Er geht hinter **das** / **dem** Sofa.

i) Die Maus läuft unter **den** / **dem** Tisch.

j) Das Haus ist neben **eine** / **einer** Bäckerei.

11) Complete the sentences using the correct prepositions. Choose from: **mit**, **gegen**, **entlang**, **während**, **trotz**, **ohne**, **über**, **zur**.

a) Er geht die Straße ....

b) .... des Wetters spielen wir Tennis.

c) West Ham spielt .... Hull.

d) .... der Woche gehe ich nicht in die Stadt.

e) Ich bin .... meine Tasche .... Schule gekommen.

f) Ich spreche .... meinen Freunden .... Politik.

12) Translate the phrases into **German**.

a) on Friday

b) on foot

c) five to three

d) twenty past four

e) to the post office

f) outside the town

g) instead of a cake

h) at three o'clock

i) at the station

j) a friend of mine

k) because of the rain

l) in front of the church *(dative)*

Present Tense

Verbs in the Present Tense

Verbs are pretty important — and the present tense is a useful place to start.

Use the present tense for what's happening now

1) Verbs in the <u>present tense</u> describe something that's occurring <u>now</u>.

2) The present tense is used to say '<u>I do</u>' and '<u>I am doing</u>' — German doesn't have a separate '<u>-ing</u>' form.

3) You have to <u>change the verb</u> for <u>different people</u>. Normally, you just change the <u>ending</u> of the word.

4) The <u>endings are the same</u> for all <u>regular verbs</u>. 'Machen' is regular, so here it is with its endings:

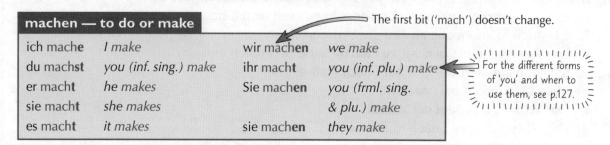

The first bit ('mach') doesn't change.

machen — to do or make			
ich mach**e**	*I make*	wir mach**en**	*we make*
du mach**st**	*you (inf. sing.) make*	ihr mach**t**	*you (inf. plu.) make*
er mach**t**	*he makes*	Sie mach**en**	*you (frml. sing.*
sie mach**t**	*she makes*		*& plu.) make*
es mach**t**	*it makes*	sie mach**en**	*they make*

For the different forms of 'you' and when to use them, see p.127.

Watch out — there's a catch

Some regular verbs don't end in '-en' — they end in '<u>-rn</u>' or '<u>-ln</u>'.

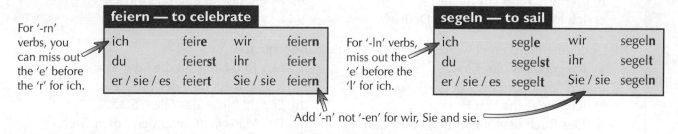

For '-rn' verbs, you can miss out the 'e' before the 'r' for ich.

feiern — to celebrate			
ich	feir**e**	wir	feier**n**
du	feier**st**	ihr	feier**t**
er / sie / es	feier**t**	Sie / sie	feier**n**

For '-ln' verbs, miss out the 'e' before the 'l' for ich.

segeln — to sail			
ich	segl**e**	wir	segel**n**
du	segel**st**	ihr	segel**t**
er / sie / es	segel**t**	Sie / sie	segel**n**

Add '-n' not '-en' for wir, Sie and sie.

Instead of 'I go swimming', say 'I go to swim'

1) You sometimes need to say '<u>I go swimming</u>' rather than just 'I swim' — so you need <u>two</u> verbs.

2) You need to put the <u>first verb</u> in the <u>right form</u> for the <u>person</u>.
The <u>second verb</u> needs to be in the <u>infinitive</u> (the form ending in '<u>-en</u>' e.g 'sehen').

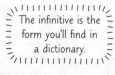

The infinitive is the form you'll find in a dictionary.

> Ich gehe + schwimmen = Ich gehe schwimmen. *I go swimming.*

Use 'seit' to say how long you've been doing something

To say things like 'I have been learning German <u>for</u> three years', use '<u>seit</u>' and the <u>present tense</u>.

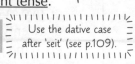

> Ich lerne seit drei Jahren Deutsch. *I have been learning German for three years.*

Use the dative case after 'seit' (see p.109).

There's no '-ing' form in German — just use the present tense...

Write these sentences in German. Use the endings for 'machen' unless the verb ends in '-rn' or '-ln'.

1. I play.
2. We believe.
3. You (inf. sing.) ask.
4. You (frml. plu.) dance.
5. I celebrate.
6. They sail.
7. I go running.
8. Jan goes camping.
9. I have been playing the piano for a year.

More About the Present Tense

You could be conned into thinking nearly all verbs are regular (see p.134). But in fact, loads aren't.

'Sein' and 'haben' are irregular

1) Verbs that <u>don't</u> follow the <u>same pattern</u> as regular verbs are called '<u>irregular verbs</u>'. Here are the <u>two</u> that you'll need most...

'Sein' means 'to be' — it's probably the most important verb... ever.

sein — to be

ich bin	*I am*	wir sind	*we are*
du bist	*you are*	ihr seid	*you are*
er / sie / es ist	*he / she / it is*	Sie / sie sind	*you / they are*

haben — to have

ich habe	*I have*	wir haben	*we have*
du hast	*you have*	ihr habt	*you have*
er / sie / es hat	*he / she / it has*	Sie / sie haben	*you / they have*

'Haben' means 'to have' — you'll need this verb loads.

2) All of these verbs are irregular too, so <u>watch out</u> for them:

lesen (er liest)	*to read (he reads)*	fahren (er fährt)	*to go (he goes)*
wissen (er weiß)	*to know (he knows)*	finden (er findet)	*to find (he finds)*
geben (er gibt)	*to give (he gives)*	tragen (er trägt)	*to wear, carry (he wears, carries)*

Er weiß viel über Sport. *He knows a lot about sport.*

Sie fährt nach Berlin. *She goes to Berlin.*

Some verbs make you use the dative case

1) You normally only need the <u>dative case</u> when you're saying '<u>to</u> something or someone'. See p.109.

2) But some German verbs <u>always</u> need the <u>dative</u> case, like '<u>helfen</u>' ('to help').

Ich helfe den Kindern. *I help the children.*

You use 'den' because 'Kinder' is plural and 'helfen' needs the dative.

3) These verbs all need the <u>dative case</u> — make sure you learn them:

danken	*to thank*	antworten	*to answer*	schreiben	*to write to*	gratulieren	*to congratulate*
folgen	*to follow*	weh tun	*to hurt*	glauben	*to believe*	empfehlen	*to recommend*

Ich gratuliere meinem Onkel. *I congratulate my uncle.*

Kannst du mir ein Café empfehlen? *Can you recommend a café to me?*

Make sure you know all the forms of 'sein' and 'haben'...

Translate these sentences into German. Watch out for any irregular verbs.

1. She has a cat.   **3.** I thank my aunt.   **5.** Do you (frml. plu.) believe me?

2. We are teachers.   **4.** You (inf. sing.) follow the man.   **6.** She wears a tie.

More About the Present Tense

The present tense just keeps getting more and more exciting — here are some different ways of using verbs.

Use negative forms to say what's not happening now

To say what <u>doesn't happen</u>, you can add a <u>negative phrase</u> to the sentence.

nicht	*not*
gar nicht	*not at all*
nicht mehr	*no longer*
noch nicht	*not yet*
nichts	*nothing*
nirgendwo	*nowhere*

Der Vogel singt nicht.   *The bird doesn't sing.*

Es ist noch nicht fertig.   *It's not ready yet.*

Der Mann sieht nichts.   *The man sees nothing.*

Use reflexive verbs to talk about 'myself', 'yourself'...

Use <u>reflexive verbs</u> when you want to talk about what people do to themselves.
See p.128 for how to say '<u>myself</u>', '<u>yourself</u>' etc. in German in the <u>accusative</u> and <u>dative</u> cases.

Er zieht sich um.
He gets changed.

Ich fühle mich krank.
I feel sick.

Wir waschen uns die Hände.
We wash our hands.

This one's in the dative case. See p.128.

Impersonal forms with 'es'

Some German phrases have 'es' as the subject. Learn these common examples:

Wie geht es dir?   *How are you?*   Es tut weh.   *It hurts.*   Es regnet.   *It's raining.*

Es gefällt mir.   *I like it.*   Es gibt viel zu tun.   *There is lots to do.*   Es tut mir Leid.   *I'm sorry.*

Using the infinitive

1) You can use the <u>infinitive</u> to say things like '<u>in order to</u>' and '<u>without</u>'.

Ich habe es gemacht, um Geld zu sparen.
I did it in order to save money.

Sie fährt nie nach Italien ohne Pizza zu essen.
She never travels to Italy without eating pizza.

2) If you want to <u>link verbs</u> in a sentence, you need to add '<u>zu</u>'.

Ich versuche ein Buch zu schreiben.   *I'm trying to write a book.*

3) <u>Leave</u> the 'zu' <u>out</u> if the first verb is a <u>modal verb</u>. See p.146.

Ich muss nach Hause gehen.   *I must go home.*

'Müssen' is a modal verb, so you don't need a 'zu'.

Show the examiner that you can use verbs in different ways...

Translate these sentences into German.

1. She does nothing.
2. It's snowing.
3. I should say something.
4. He gives it back to me.
5. I want to be famous in order to earn lots of money.
6. I can't go away without saying something.

Quick Questions

When it comes to verbs, there's a lot to get your head around, so try these quick questions for extra practice. Don't forget to watch out for irregular verbs, and ones which take the dative case.

Quick Questions

1) Write out the correct present tense form of each verb, to match the person given.
   a) hören — ich
   b) lernen — wir
   c) lieben — er
   d) sagen — ihr
   e) schicken — Sie
   f) reden — sie *(sing.)*
   g) schlagen — ich
   h) bringen — du
   i) studieren — wir
   j) trinken — ihr
   k) stellen — sie *(pl.)*
   l) suchen — du

2) Translate the sentences into **German**.
   a) I am going swimming.
   b) We are going hiking.
   c) They are going camping.
   d) I go fishing at the weekend.
   e) We go running on Wednesdays.

3) Translate the sentences into **German**.
   a) Riyam is playing football.
   b) My brother is writing an email.
   c) My dad works on Saturdays.
   d) Christopher is sailing today.
   e) I've been living here for five years.

4) Fill in the gaps with the correct form of the verb in **bold**.
   a) Ich .... fünfzehn Jahre alt. **sein**
   b) .... ihr fertig? **sein**
   c) Meine Freundin .... jeden Tag einen Apfel. **essen**
   d) Der Feuerwehrmann .... gern in seinem Feuerwehrauto. **fahren**
   e) .... deine Großmutter eine Brille? **tragen**
   f) Markus .... Lotti Blumen. **geben**
   g) Ich .... nicht. **wissen**
   h) Mein Vater .... die Zeitung. **lesen**

5) Translate the sentences into **German**.
   a) Do you *(polite)* have a dog?
   b) We are not ready yet.
   c) Katja is wearing trousers.
   d) He knows nothing.
   e) Anupa no longer travels to London.
   f) She is eating chocolate.

6) Underline the correct words in **bold** to complete the sentences.
   a) Ich helfe **die Goldfische / den Goldfischen**.
   b) Die Goldfische gehören **mich / mir**.
   c) Er trägt immer **ein weißes Hemd / einem weißen Hemd**.
   d) Sie dankt **mich / mir** sehr höflich.

7) Translate the sentences into **German** using impersonal forms with **es**.
   a) It's raining today.
   b) There is not a lot to do in my town.
   c) How is he?
   d) I like it here in Berlin.
   e) She is sorry.
   f) It hurts.

8) Rearrange the words to form sentences using infinitive constructions.
   a) um entspannen mich lese zu Ich
   b) einkaufen muss gehen Ich
   c) versucht Spanisch Er lernen zu
   d) Geld verdienen Wir um zu arbeiten

| Perfect Tense | **Talking About the Past** |

It's good to be able to talk about what's already happened. To say what you 'have done', use the perfect tense.

Use the perfect tense for things that have finished

See p.135 for all the endings for 'haben'.

1) The <u>perfect tense</u> usually starts with '<u>haben</u>' ('to have') and ends with a <u>past participle</u>.

> Ich habe einen Sessel gekauft.
> *I have bought an armchair.*

> Er hat zwei Bücher gelesen.
> *He has read two books.*

> Sie haben viel gegessen.
> *They have eaten a lot.*

2) To form the <u>past participle</u> (the past tense bit) of regular verbs, follow these steps:

kaufen *to buy*	→	kaufen - en = kauf	→	gekauft *bought*
Begin with the verb in the infinitive.		Remove '-en' from the end of the infinitive.		Add 'ge' to the start and add 't' to the end.

3) Here are some <u>more examples</u> — they all work the same way.

to do / make	machen	→	gemacht	*done / made*		*to book*	buchen	→	gebucht	*booked*
to ask	fragen	→	gefragt	*asked*		*to clean*	putzen	→	geputzt	*cleaned*

4) You don't always need the 'have' part in English.

> Ich habe mein Haus geputzt.
> *I (have) cleaned my house.*

> Sie hat ihren Flug gebucht.
> *She (has) booked her flight.*

> Wir haben es gemacht.
> *We have done / did it.*

Irregular verbs don't follow the pattern

<u>Irregular</u> verbs <u>work differently</u>. These are the <u>most important</u> ones:

to sleep	schlafen	→	geschlafen		*to see*	sehen	→	gesehen
to take	nehmen	→	genommen		*to sing*	singen	→	gesungen
to eat	essen	→	gegessen		*to break*	brechen	→	gebrochen
to drink	trinken	→	getrunken		*to receive*	bekommen	→	bekommen
to give	geben	→	gegeben		*to forget*	vergessen	→	vergessen
to bring	bringen	→	gebracht		*to understand*	verstehen	→	verstanden

Watch out — there's no 'ge' on the front.

Ist sie gegangen? — Has she gone?

See p.135 for the different forms of 'sein'.

1) Some verbs need '<u>sein</u>' ('to be') instead of '<u>haben</u>' in the <u>perfect tense</u>. | Ich bin gegangen. *I have gone.*

2) It's mostly <u>movement verbs</u> that need '<u>sein</u>'. Here's a list of some common ones:

to go / drive	fahren	→	gefahren		*to come*	kommen	→	gekommen
to run	laufen	→	gelaufen		*to stay*	bleiben	→	geblieben
to climb	steigen	→	gestiegen		*to be*	sein	→	gewesen
to follow	folgen	→	gefolgt		*to happen*	passieren	→	passiert

Verbs involving movement usually take 'sein' in the perfect tense...

Write these sentences in German. Remember to check whether you need 'haben' or 'sein'.

1. I have drunk tea.
2. We have stayed at home.
3. He has seen me.
4. You (inf. sing.) have received a letter.
5. They have asked him.
6. You (frml. plu.) have come here.

Talking About the Past
Simple Past

It's your lucky day — time for another form of the past tense. But this one's used for saying things like 'I saw'.

Regular verbs in the simple past

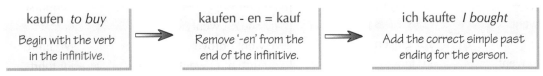
You might hear the simple past referred to as the 'imperfect', too.

1) You use the <u>simple past</u> to say what happened in the past <u>without using</u> 'haben' or 'sein'.

2) The simple past is used more in <u>written German</u>, though some forms are common in <u>speech</u> too.

3) This is how you form the simple past form of a regular verb:

kaufen *to buy*	→	kaufen - en = kauf	→	ich kaufte *I bought*
Begin with the verb in the infinitive.		Remove '-en' from the end of the infinitive.		Add the correct simple past ending for the person.

machen — to make

ich mach**te**	*I made*	wir mach**ten**	*we made*
du mach**test**	*you made*	ihr mach**tet**	*you made*
er / sie / es mach**te**	*he / she / it made*	Sie / sie mach**ten**	*you / they made*

spielen — to play

ich spiel**te**	*I played*	wir spiel**ten**	*we played*
du spiel**test**	*you played*	ihr spiel**tet**	*you played*
er / sie / es spiel**te**	*he / she / it played*	Sie / sie spiel**ten**	*you / they played*

Er hasste mich.	Wir lernten Deutsch.	Ihr kochtet zusammen.	Ich spielte Saxofon.
He hated me.	*We learned German.*	*You cooked together.*	*I played the saxophone.*

Ich hatte — I had / Ich war — I was

1) You'll use the simple past forms of '<u>haben</u>' and '<u>sein</u>' loads in writing and in speech, so it's well worth learning them.

2) You need to know the <u>simple past</u> forms of the verb for each <u>person</u>.

Ich hatte — I had

ich hat**te**	wir hat**ten**
du hat**test**	ihr hat**tet**
er / sie / es hat**te**	Sie / sie hat**ten**

Sie hatten vier Brüder.	Sie hatte ein blaues Kleid.
They had four brothers.	*She had a blue dress.*

Ich war — I was

ich war	wir war**en**
du war**st**	ihr war**t**
er / sie / es war	Sie / sie war**en**

Wir waren sehr müde.	Ich war ein komisches Kind.
We were very tired.	*I was a strange child.*

You'll pick up more marks by using the different past tenses...

Try translating these sentences into German.

1. I had a dog.
2. We were very sad.
3. I played tennis.
4. They were there.
5. You (inf. sing.) had a good idea.
6. You (frml. sing.) bought a dog.
7. He used to cook.
8. She was young.

Talking About the Past

You can use the simple past to say all kinds of things. Use it yourself to gain some juicy extra marks.

Irregular verbs in the simple past

1) Some verbs are irregular in the simple past. Here are some examples you need to learn.

gehen — to go

I went	ich ging
you (inf. sing.) went	du gingst
he / she / it went	er / sie / es ging
we went	wir gingen
you (inf. plu.) went	ihr gingt
they went	sie gingen
you (frml. sing. & plu.) went	Sie gingen

fahren — to go / drive

I went / drove	ich fuhr
you (inf. sing.) went / drove	du fuhrst
he / she / it went / drove	er / sie / es fuhr
we went / drove	wir fuhren
you (inf. plu.) went / drove	ihr fuhrt
they went / drove	sie fuhren
you (frml. sing. & plu.) went / drove	Sie fuhren

Er ging nach Hause.
He went home. — Use 'gehen' when you mean 'to go by foot'.

Wir fuhren nach Bonn.
We went / drove to Bonn. — Use 'fahren' for going somewhere in a vehicle, even if you're not the one doing the driving.

laufen — to run

I ran	ich lief
you (inf. sing.) ran	du liefst
he / she / it ran	er / sie / es lief
we ran	wir liefen
you (inf. plu.) ran	ihr lieft
they ran	sie liefen
you (frml. sing. & plu.) ran	Sie liefen

kommen — to come

I came	ich kam
you (inf. sing.) came	du kamst
he / she / it came	er / sie / es kam
we came	wir kamen
you (inf. plu.) came	ihr kamt
they came	sie kamen
you (frml. sing. & plu.) came	Sie kamen

2) Here are some other verbs which are also irregular in the simple past.

denken	ich dachte	*I thought*	trinken	ich trank	*I drank*	essen	ich aß	*I ate*
helfen	ich half	*I helped*	sehen	ich sah	*I saw*	singen	ich sang	*I sang*
schreiben	ich schrieb	*I wrote*	werden	ich wurde	*I became*	ziehen	ich zog	*I pulled*
nehmen	ich nahm	*I took*	bringen	ich brachte	*I brought*	geben	ich gab	*I gave*

Using 'seit' with the simple past

You can see more about 'seit' on p.134.

Use the simple past with 'seit' to say that something 'had been' happening 'for' or 'since' a certain time.

Ich wartete seit zwei Stunden. *I had been waiting for two hours.* — You need the dative case after 'seit', so 'hours' needs to be 'Stunden' (see p.109).

Seit 2003 brachte er Kuchen zur Schule. *Since 2003, he had been bringing cakes to school.*

Irregular simple past forms often look very different to the infinitive...

Translate the sentences below into German.

1. I drank a cup of tea.
2. I took the pen.
3. Maria wrote a book.
4. We saw him.
5. They had been helping for a year.
6. I had been eating for an hour.

Talking About the Past

Just one more form of the past tense to go — this one's called the pluperfect.

I had seen / I had bought etc...

1) The pluperfect tense is used to talk about things that happened further back in the past. You use it to say what you had done.

2) For the pluperfect tense, you need the simple past form of 'haben' (see p.139) and the past participle.

Er hatte		den Film gesehen		Er hatte den Film gesehen.
Use the simple past form of 'haben'.	+	Use the past participle of the other verb. See p.138.	=	He had seen the film. This is the pluperfect tense.

Wir hatten Rugby gespielt. *We had played rugby.*　　Ich hatte viel gelesen. *I had read a lot.*

With reflexive verbs, the 'sich' bit goes straight after 'haben'. → Mein Bruder hatte sich geduscht. *My brother had had a shower.*

Some verbs need 'sein' (to be) instead of 'haben' (to have)

1) In the perfect tense, some verbs need 'sein' instead of 'haben'. It's the same in the pluperfect tense.

2) You need the simple past form of 'sein' (see p.139) and the past participle.

Ich war		nach Ungarn gereist		Ich war nach Ungarn gereist.
Use the simple past form of 'sein'.	+	Use the past participle of the other verb.	=	I had travelled to Hungary. This is the pluperfect tense.

Er war hier geblieben. *He had stayed here.*　　Du warst schon gelandet. *You had already landed.*

3) You often need the pluperfect tense after prepositions.

Ich sprach mit ihnen, nachdem ich angekommen war. *I spoke to them after I had arrived.*

I had been playing / I had been singing etc...

You can use the pluperfect tense to say things like 'I had been playing' in German.

Es war nass. Es hatte viel geregnet. *It was wet. It had been raining a lot.* → This can also be translated like the examples above: → Es war nass. Es hatte viel geregnet. *It was wet. It had rained a lot.*

Make sure you don't confuse the pluperfect and the perfect...
Write these pluperfect sentences in German.
1. I had learnt music.
2. He had eaten an ice cream.
3. She had got dressed.
4. They had gone to the park.
5. Tim had stayed at home.
6. We had been doing our homework.

Future Tense | # Talking About the Future

You'll need to talk about things that are going to happen at some point in the future. There are two ways you can do it — and the first one's a piece of cake, so I'd learn that first if I were you.

1) You can use the present tense to talk about the future

1) Wahey — an easy bit. All you need to do to say something is <u>going</u> to happen in the <u>future</u> is to say it <u>does happen</u> and then say <u>when</u> it's going to happen. Brilliant.

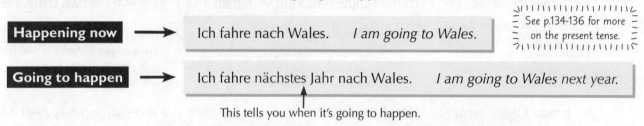

Happening now ⟶ Ich fahre nach Wales.   *I am going to Wales.*

See p.134-136 for more on the present tense.

Going to happen ⟶ Ich fahre nächstes Jahr nach Wales.   *I am going to Wales next year.*

This tells you when it's going to happen.

2) The <u>time bit</u> can go <u>anywhere</u> in the sentence, as long as you keep to the rules of <u>word order</u> — see p.114.

Nächstes Jahr fahre ich nach Wales.   *Next year, I'm going to Wales.*

nächste Woche	*next week*	am Montag	*on Monday*	im Mai	*in May*
morgen	*tomorrow*	diesen Sommer	*this summer*	in der Zukunft	*in the future*

2) You can use 'werden' to say 'will' or 'to be going to do...'

1) This part's slightly trickier. '<u>Ich werde</u>' means '<u>I will</u>' or '<u>I am going to</u>'. To form the future tense with '<u>werden</u>', you need the right form of '<u>werden</u>' and the <u>infinitive</u> of the other verb.

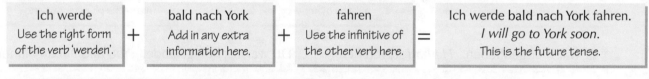

Ich werde		bald nach York		fahren		Ich werde bald nach York fahren.
Use the right form of the verb 'werden'.	+	Add in any extra information here.	+	Use the infinitive of the other verb here.	=	*I will go to York soon.* This is the future tense.

Ich werde mehr für die Umwelt tun.   *I am going to do more for the environment.*

2) '<u>Werden</u>' is an <u>irregular verb</u>, so you'll have to learn its <u>endings</u>.

Werden — will / to be going to do			
ich werde	*I will*	wir werden	*we will*
du wirst	*you (inf. sing.) will*	ihr werdet	*you (inf. plu.) will*
er / sie / es wird	*he / she / it will*	Sie / sie werden	*you (frml. sing. & plu.) / they will*

Wir werden unsere Hausaufgaben machen.   *We will do our homework.*

Eines Tages wirst du in die Schule gehen.   *One day, you will go to school.*

There are two ways to talk about the future in German...

Write these sentences in German using both the easy and the hard way of making the future tense.

1. I will go to the cinema on Monday. **3.** Angela will meet us next week. **5.** I'll eat pizza tomorrow.

2. He will explain it soon.   **4.** They will visit us next year.   **6.** Next time, we'll buy the car.

Quick Questions

You'll need to be able to use different tenses in your speaking and writing exams so it's worth going over this stuff. Adding in past and future tense phrases will make your answers much more detailed.

Quick Questions

1) Give the **German** infinitives that go with the past participles.

a)	gefahren	d)	angekommen	g)	passiert	j)	ausgegangen
b)	abgefahren	e)	geblieben	h)	gefolgt	k)	geschehen
c)	gekommen	f)	gewesen	i)	gegangen	l)	geflogen

2) Translate the sentences into **German** using the perfect tense.

a)	I went to London.	d)	He stayed in bed.	g)	We arrived at two o'clock.
b)	He ate a cake.	e)	The plane flew quickly.	h)	She drank a cup of tea.
c)	We visited an art gallery.	f)	When did the train leave?		

3) Complete the sentences by adding the correct simple past verb endings.

   a) Wir mach....... zu viel Lärm und ärger....... unsere Nachbarn.

   b) Mein Vater kauf....... ein neues Haus und ich kauf....... ein neues Auto.

   c) Mein Großvater arbeite....... als Klempner. Meine Eltern arbeite....... als Lehrer.

   d) Du spiel....... Gitarre und besuch....... viele Konzerte.

4) Give the correct simple past form of these irregular verbs. Match the person given.

a)	kommen — ich	e)	denken — sie *(pl.)*	i)	springen — wir	m)	fahren — sie *(sing.)*
b)	laufen — er	f)	nehmen — ihr	j)	werden — Sie	n)	essen — ich
c)	helfen — ich	g)	geben — ich	k)	trinken — du	o)	bringen — ihr
d)	sehen — du	h)	schreiben — er	l)	gehen — wir	p)	sein — ich

5) Translate the sentences below into **German** using the simple past.

   a) She had been working as a computer scientist for six months.

   b) I had been playing the guitar for two hours.

6) Complete the sentences in the pluperfect tense using the correct form of **haben** or **sein**.

   a) Ich .... ein Kilo Bananen gekauft.

   b) Ich .... um elf Uhr nach Hause gegangen.

   c) Du .... einen leckeren Schokoladenkuchen gemacht.

   d) Er .... ein Geburtstagsgeschenk von seinen Klassenkameraden bekommen.

   e) Wir .... in den Zug gestiegen und .... unsere Plätze gefunden.

7) Translate the sentences below into **German** using the pluperfect tense.

   a) We had driven to Bristol.   c) I had not understood what had happened.

   b) She had stayed at home for hours.

8) Translate the sentences below into **German** using the present tense.

   a) This summer, we are going to go swimming every day.

   b) I am buying a house next year.

9) Complete the sentences in the future tense using the correct form of **werden**.

   a) Du .... morgen in die Schule gehen.

   b) Susi und du, ihr .... zusammen dahin gehen.

   c) Susi .... um halb acht hier sein.

   d) Ich .... dich um halb sieben aufwecken.

   e) Wir .... Brötchen essen und Tee trinken.

   f) Deine Klassenkameraden .... in der Klasse sein.

Imperatives

Giving Orders

You're almost at the end — hurrah. Now it's your chance to boss someone about by using imperatives.

Use the imperative to give orders

1) <u>Imperatives</u> are used to give instructions. They tell people what to do, e.g. '<u>sit still</u>' or '<u>let's eat</u>'.

2) To form the <u>imperative</u>, use the <u>present tense</u> of the verb for 'du', 'ihr', 'Sie' and 'wir'. The <u>only</u> form that ends differently from the <u>normal present tense</u> is the '<u>du</u>' form. It loses its ending (the '-st').

3) Here's how to turn a verb into an imperative:

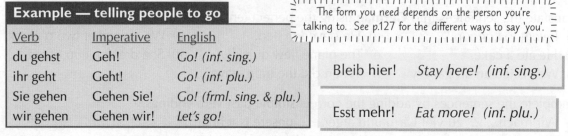

Example — telling people to go		
<u>Verb</u>	<u>Imperative</u>	<u>English</u>
du gehst	Geh!	*Go! (inf. sing.)*
ihr geht	Geht!	*Go! (inf. plu.)*
Sie gehen	Gehen Sie!	*Go! (frml. sing. & plu.)*
wir gehen	Gehen wir!	*Let's go!*

> The form you need depends on the person you're talking to. See p.127 for the different ways to say 'you'.

Bleib hier!   *Stay here! (inf. sing.)*

Esst mehr!   *Eat more! (inf. plu.)*

4) Lots of verbs have an optional '<u>e</u>' on the '<u>du</u>' form of the imperative, like 'fragen' *(to ask)*: Frag(e)! *(Ask!)*.

There are some irregular imperatives

1) Some imperatives <u>don't follow the rules</u> in the '<u>du</u>' form, e.g. '<u>lesen</u>' only loses the 't' from 'du liest'.

Lies die Zeitung!   *Read the newspaper! (inf. sing.)*

2) '<u>Haben</u>' and '<u>werden</u>' also have a different stem in the 'du' form.

<u>Verb</u>	<u>Imperative</u>	<u>English</u>
du hast	Hab!	*Have! (inf. sing.)*

<u>Verb</u>	<u>Imperative</u>	<u>English</u>
du wirst	Werde!	*Become! (inf. sing.)*

3) The stem of '<u>sein</u>' is '<u>sei</u>' in <u>all the imperative forms</u>.

<u>Verb</u>	<u>Imperative</u>	<u>English</u>
du bist	Sei!	*Be! (inf. sing.)*

Imperatives can be used with negatives and reflexive verbs

1) To form <u>negative imperatives</u>, use '<u>nicht</u>'.

Sei nicht traurig!   *Don't be sad! (inf. sing.)*

Weint nicht!   *Don't cry! (inf. plu.)*

2) For <u>reflexive verbs</u> with '<u>du</u>' or '<u>ihr</u>', the <u>reflexive pronoun</u> ('dich' or 'euch') goes after the <u>verb</u>.

Zieh dich an!   *Get yourself dressed! (inf. sing.)*

Bedient euch!   *Help yourselves! (inf. plu.)*

3) For <u>reflexive verbs</u> with '<u>wir</u>' or '<u>Sie</u>', the <u>reflexive pronoun</u> ('uns' or 'sich') goes after the '<u>wir</u>' or '<u>Sie</u>'.

Benehmen wir uns!   *Let's behave!*

Entscheiden Sie sich!   *Decide! (frml. sing. & plu.)*

Use the polite imperative for people you'd address as 'Sie'...

Translate these sentences into German. The bit in brackets tells you who you're talking to.

1. Dance! (inf. sing.)   3. Sit down! (frml. sing.)   5. Don't help us! (inf. plu.)   7. Let's go shopping!

2. Be polite! (inf. plu.)   4. Work! (inf. sing.)   6. Follow me! (frml. plu.)   8. Relax! (inf. sing.)

Separable Verbs

Dealing with separable verbs sounds like a messy business, but just follow these steps towards GCSE glory.

Separable verbs can be split up in the present tense...

1) <u>Separable verbs</u> are made up of two bits: the <u>main verb</u> and a <u>bit on the front</u> that can be taken off.

> abwaschen (*to wash up*) = ab + waschen

2) In the <u>present tense</u>, change the verb for the <u>right person</u> and send the '<u>ab</u>' bit to the <u>end of the clause</u>.

> Ich wasche gern ab.   *I like washing up.*

3) Here are some examples of <u>separable verbs</u>. The bits that can be taken off are underlined.

<u>ab</u>waschen	*to wash up*	<u>heraus</u>kommen	*to come out*
<u>an</u>kommen	*to arrive*	<u>mit</u>nehmen	*to take with you*
<u>auf</u>hören	*to stop*	<u>weg</u>gehen	*to go out / away*
<u>aus</u>gehen	*to go out*	<u>zu</u>sehen	*to watch*
<u>ein</u>treten	*to enter*	<u>zurück</u>geben	*to give back*

> Sie nimmt ihre Katze mit.
> *She takes her cat with her.*

> Ich gehe jetzt aus.
> *I'm going out now.*

> Ich trete ins Zimmer ein.
> *I enter the room.*

4) You might want to use separable verbs as <u>imperatives</u> — but you'll need to <u>split them up</u> first.

> Ruf mich an, Bernhard!   *Call me, Bernhard!*

> Passen Sie auf, bitte!   *Pay attention, please!*

...and in other tenses too

Don't forget to use the correct form of 'haben' or 'sein' as well.

1) To use a separable verb in the <u>perfect tense</u> (see p.138), keep the <u>front bit</u> the same, but put the <u>main verb</u> in the <u>perfect tense</u>.

> aufhören (*to stop*) = auf + hören ⟹ aufgehört (*stopped*) ⟹ Er hat endlich aufgehört.
> *He has finally stopped.*

2) For the <u>simple past</u> (see p.139), send the <u>front bit</u> to the <u>end</u> and put the <u>main verb</u> in the <u>simple past</u>.

> ankommen (*to arrive*) = an + kommen ⟹ kam...an (*arrived*) ⟹ Ich kam spät an.
> *I arrived late.*

3) When you use separable verbs in the <u>future tense</u> with '<u>werden</u>' (see p.142), you use them in their <u>infinitive</u> form.

> Ich werde morgen ausgehen.   *I will go out tomorrow.*

> Er wird aufräumen.   *He will tidy up.*

We're not just splitting hairs — this separating stuff's important...

Translate these sentences into German using separable verbs.

1. I arrive tomorrow.
2. She goes out.
3. He took his brother with him.
4. You (inf. sing.) have washed up.
5. I have given it back.
6. Go away, Eric!
7. Let's go out.
8. I will stop.

| # Modal Verbs

Modal verbs are words like 'should' and 'could'. They're really good for giving opinions.

Ich muss diese Verben lernen... — I must learn these verbs...

1) Here are <u>six really handy</u> modal verbs:

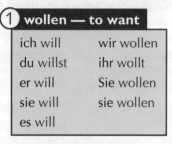

① wollen — to want

ich will	wir wollen
du willst	ihr wollt
er will	Sie wollen
sie will	sie wollen
es will	

② mögen — to like

ich mag	wir mögen
du magst	ihr mögt
er mag	Sie mögen
sie mag	sie mögen
es mag	

For 'I would like', use 'ich möchte' — see p.147.

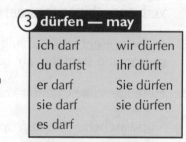

③ dürfen — may

ich darf	wir dürfen
du darfst	ihr dürft
er darf	Sie dürfen
sie darf	sie dürfen
es darf	

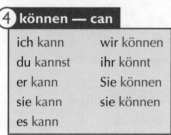

④ können — can

ich kann	wir können
du kannst	ihr könnt
er kann	Sie können
sie kann	sie können
es kann	

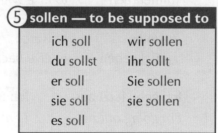

⑤ sollen — to be supposed to

ich soll	wir sollen
du sollst	ihr sollt
er soll	Sie sollen
sie soll	sie sollen
es soll	

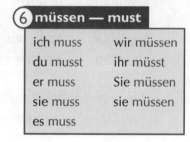

⑥ müssen — must

ich muss	wir müssen
du musst	ihr müsst
er muss	Sie müssen
sie muss	sie müssen
es muss	

2) This is how you use them:

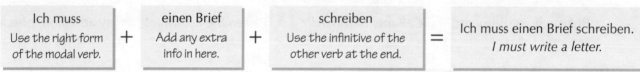

| **Ich muss** Use the right form of the modal verb. | + | **einen Brief** Add any extra info in here. | + | **schreiben** Use the infinitive of the other verb at the end. | = | **Ich muss einen Brief schreiben.** *I must write a letter.* |

Du sollst deine Hausaufgaben machen. *You are supposed to do your homework.*

You can use modal verbs in the past tense too

1) To say something like 'I wanted to wash the car', you have to use the <u>past tense</u> of the <u>modal verb</u>.

2) For the simple past, <u>take off</u> the '<u>-en</u>' and the <u>umlaut</u> if there is one, and then <u>add the endings</u> in bold.

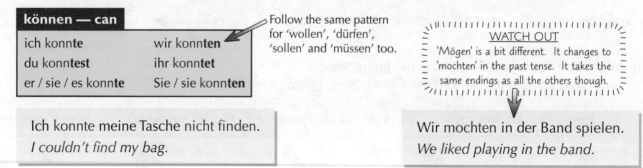

können — can

ich konn**te**	wir konn**ten**
du konn**test**	ihr konn**tet**
er / sie / es konn**te**	Sie / sie konn**ten**

Follow the same pattern for 'wollen', 'dürfen', 'sollen' and 'müssen' too.

WATCH OUT
'Mögen' is a bit different. It changes to 'mochten' in the past tense. It takes the same endings as all the others though.

Ich konnte meine Tasche nicht finden.
I couldn't find my bag.

Wir mochten in der Band spielen.
We liked playing in the band.

With modal verbs, the second verb is in the infinitive...

Write these sentences in German.

1. I want a new guitar.　**3.** You (inf. plu.) may sit down.　**5.** I'm supposed to go.　**7.** Jane had to play.

2. We like playing rugby.　**4.** He can ski very well.　**6.** She must stay.　**8.** They wanted to fly.

Would, Could and Should | Conditional

Use the conditional tense to say what you would, could and should do. You could pick up some marks too.

Ich würde Deutsch sprechen — I would speak German

1) You can say 'I would...' in German by using the conditional form of 'werden' and an infinitive.

| Ich würde
Use the right
form of 'werden' | + | Chinesisch
Add any extra
info in here. | + | lernen
Use the infinitive of the
other verb at the end. | = | Ich würde Chinesisch lernen.
I would learn Chinese.
This is the conditional tense. |

2) Make sure you learn the different conditional forms of 'werden':

Ich würde... — I would...

ich würde	wir würden
du würdest	ihr würdet
er / sie / es würde	Sie / sie würden

Was würdest du ihm sagen?
What would you say to him?

Wir würden es erlauben.
We would allow it.

Ich möchte — I would like

1) Ich möchte means 'I would like'. It's really handy for asking for things.

You can also use 'Ich hätte gern' to say what you'd like. See p.6.

Ich möchte — I would like

ich möchte	wir möchten
du möchtest	ihr möchtet
er / sie / es möchte	Sie / sie möchten

Was möchten Sie?
What would you like?

Ich möchte eine Tasse Tee, bitte.
I would like a cup of tea, please.

2) If you're adding another verb to say what you'd like to do, that verb has to go to the end.

Ich möchte das Hemd anprobieren, bitte.
I would like to try on the shirt, please.

Wir möchten in die Stadtmitte fahren, bitte.
We would like to go into the city centre, please.

Ich könnte — I could   Ich sollte — I should

1) You need to know how to use 'könnten' (*could*) and 'sollten' (*should*) too.

2) Be careful, though — 'ich könnte' means 'I could' as in 'I would be able',
as opposed to 'ich konnte', which means 'I was able' (see p.146).

Ich könnte — I could

ich könnte	wir könnten
du könntest	ihr könntet
er / sie / es könnte	Sie / sie könnten

Es könnte schlimmer sein.   *It could be worse.*

Ich sollte — I should

ich sollte	wir sollten
du solltest	ihr solltet
er / sie / es sollte	Sie / sie sollten

Ich sollte mehr essen.   *I should eat more.*

You'll impress the examiner if you can use the conditional properly...

Translate these sentences into German using the conditional tense.

1. They would not visit me.
2. Selma would like to sing.
3. We could run to the park.
4. We could ask our teacher.
5. You (inf. sing.) should wait.
6. I should eat a sandwich.

Subjunctive — I would be / I would have

You can use the subjunctive to say what you would be or what you would have if you were rich and famous. It's a tricky bit of grammar, but examiners will love it if you can use it — and that means more marks.

The subjunctive

1) The subjunctive in German is used to talk about things that could be true, but aren't.

2) Subjunctive phrases in English are things like 'if I were you'. 'Were' is in the subjunctive because it's talking about something that isn't true.

3) For your exams, you need to know the forms 'ich wäre' (I would be) and 'ich hätte' (I would have).

Ich wäre — I would be

To say 'I would be', you use 'ich wäre'. Here's how you say it for different people:

Ich wäre — I would be

ich wäre	wir wären
du wärst	ihr wärt
er / sie / es wäre	Sie / sie wären

Du wärst gut im Ballett.
You would be good at ballet.

Ich wäre ein guter Pilot
I would be a good pilot.

Ich hätte — I would have

To say 'I would have', use 'ich hätte'. Here's how you say it for different people:

Ich hätte — I would have

ich hätte	wir hätten
du hättest	ihr hättet
er / sie / es hätte	Sie / sie hätten

Er hätte ein besseres Auto.
He would have a better car.

Wir hätten mehr Zeit.
We would have more time.

Using 'wäre' and 'hätte' together

If you want to be really fancy, you can combine 'wäre' and 'hätte' together in one sentence.

Wenn ich fünf Millionen Euro hätte, wäre ich reich. *If I had five million euros, I would be rich.*

Question	Simple Answer	Extended Answer
Wie wäre dein ideales Haus?	Mein ideales Haus wäre modern und es hätte viele Zimmer.	Mein ideales Haus hätte einen großen Garten. Wenn es auch einen Balkon hätte, wäre ich sehr glücklich.
What would your ideal house be like?	*My ideal house would be modern and it would have lots of rooms.*	*My ideal house would have a big garden. If it also had a balcony, I would be very happy.*

My ideal exam would be easier and it would have fewer questions...

Translate the following sentences into German.

1. I would be a good actor.
2. He would have a dog.
3. Niklas would have a brother.
4. They would be very sad.
5. If I had a car, it would be red.
6. If I were hungry, I would eat potatoes.

Quick Questions

This stuff isn't easy, but you'll impress the examiners no end if you can use it correctly. You're on the final set of quick questions so give it your best shot, and double check anything you struggle with.

Quick Questions

1) Change these sentences into imperatives.
   a) Du stellst das Buch hin.
   b) Ihr geht in die Schule.
   c) Wir essen zusammen.
   d) Du machst deine Hausaufgaben.
   e) Sie arbeiten in Ihrem Garten.
   f) Wir bringen unseren Hund mit.
   g) Du besuchst deine Großeltern.
   h) Ihr glaubt mir.

2) Complete the sentences, using the present tense form of the separable verb in **bold**.
   a) Ich .... jeden Morgen .... **abwaschen**
   b) Normalerweise .... er abends .... **ausgehen**
   c) .... Sie bitte Ihren Koffer .... ! **mitnehmen**
   d) Am Montag .... meine Großeltern .... **ankommen**
   e) Am Mittwoch .... ich Bernd sein Buch .... **zurückgeben**
   f) Dave und Brian .... plötzlich .... zu singen. **anfangen**

3) Translate the sentences below into **German**.
   a) George will watch television tomorrow.
   b) My present arrived on Friday. *(perfect tense)*
   c) Did you *(du)* go out last night? *(simple past)*

4) Write the correct present tense form of the following modal verbs, matching the person given.
   a) wollen — ich
   b) mögen — du
   c) dürfen — er
   d) müssen — sie (sing.)
   e) sollen — Sie
   f) können — wir
   g) müssen — ich
   h) mögen — ihr
   i) wollen — wir

5) Translate the sentences below into **German**.
   a) I am supposed to stay at home, but I want to go with them.
   b) They must be very clever.
   c) You *(informal pl.)* can speak Italian very well.
   d) I had to learn Greek when I was five.
   e) We wanted to write an email, but we didn't have a computer.

6) Complete the sentences using the correct conditional form of **werden**. Choose from: **würdest**, **würden**, **würde**, **würdet**.
   a) Ich .... viel Sport treiben, aber ich bin zu faul.
   b) Du .... Musik hören, aber dein Handy funktioniert nicht mehr.
   c) Wir .... auf Urlaub fahren, aber wir haben kein Geld dafür.
   d) Ihr .... vielleicht bessere Noten bekommen, aber ihr arbeitet zu wenig.
   e) Chris .... Badminton spielen, aber es gibt keinen Klub in der Nähe.
   f) Sie .... früher ankommen, aber sie können den Flug nicht buchen.

7) Translate the sentences below into **English**.
   a) Möchtest du heute Abend eine DVD sehen?
   b) Könnten Sie mir bitte die Zahnpasta geben?
   c) Wenn ich nicht so müde wäre, würde ich heute Abend joggen gehen.
   d) Ich wäre glücklicher, wenn mein Bruder nicht so launisch wäre.

Revision Summary for Section Eleven

Congratulations, the finish line is in sight. This is your chance to see how much you can remember from the pages you've worked through. After all those quick questions, this stuff should be a doddle.

Cases and Nouns (p.108-111) ☑

1) In the sentence, "Lucas isst ein Eis", which case is 'Lucas' in? ☑
2) When do you use the genitive case? ☑
3) Which part of the following sentence is in the dative case? "Ich spreche zu meiner Schwester." ☑
4) What gender are the following nouns? a) März   b) Ärztin   c) Pickel   d) Märchen ☑
5) Give the plural form of these nouns: a) Weihnachtslied   b) Hauptstraße   c) Feuerwehrfrau ☑

Conjunctions (p.115-116) ☑

6) Is the word order correct in the sentences below? If not, write the correct version.
   a) Meine Schwester trinkt Orangensaft, denn sie hat Durst.
   b) Ich fahre gern nach Frankreich, weil ich liebe Käse.
   c) Meine Eltern denken, dass bin ich faul.
   d) Es gefällt mir hier, obwohl es regnet oft. ☑

Words to Describe and Compare (p.119-125) ☑

7) Complete the sentence with the correct adjective endings:
   Ein schwarz...... Hund spielt mit einem rot...... Ball in einem schön...... Garten. ☑
8) Translate this into German: A horse is big, a bear is bigger, but an elephant is the biggest. ☑
9) What do the following adverbs mean in English?
   a) neulich   b) täglich   c) überall   d) dort   e) irgendwo   f) ab und zu ☑

Pronouns and Prepositions (p.127-131) ☑

10) Write down the German pronouns for each person in:
    a) the nominative   b) the accusative   c) the dative ☑
11) Which case do these prepositions take? a) für   b) mit   c) wegen ☑

Verbs in Different Tenses (p.134-142) ☑

12) How do you say these sentences in German? Use the perfect tense, then the simple past.
    a) They made a cake.   b) He booked a room.   c) We drank coffee.   d) I ran. ☑
13) How do you say these sentences in German? Use the pluperfect tense.
    a) I had bought a skirt.   b) She had been shopping. ☑

Other Verb Forms (p.144-148) ☑

14) Translate these phrases into English, then rewrite them using the polite 'Sie' form:
    a) Geh!   b) Komm herein!   c) Nimm das Buch!   d) Setz dich hin! ☑
15) How do you say these phrases in German?
    a) I must eat vegetables   b) He can   c) They are supposed to go   d) I wanted ☑
16) Write these phrases in German.
    a) I would wash up   b) I would like to drive   c) I should watch TV   d) I would be tired ☑

The Listening Exam

These pages are crammed full of advice to help you tackle your exams head on, so listen up.

There are four exams for GCSE German

1) Your AQA German GCSE is assessed by four separate exams — Listening, Speaking, Reading and Writing.

2) Each exam is worth 25% of your final mark. You'll get a grade between 1 and 9 (with 9 being the highest).

3) You won't sit all of the papers at the same time — you'll probably have your speaking exam a couple of weeks before the rest of your exams.

The Listening Exam has two sections

If you're sitting foundation tier papers, the format of your exams will be slightly different, but this advice will still be useful.

1) For the listening paper, you'll listen to various recordings of people speaking in German and answer questions on what you've heard.

2) The paper is 45 minutes long (including 5 minutes' reading time) and is split into Section A and Section B.

3) Section A is the longer section — the questions are in English, and you'll write your answers in English. Section B is shorter, but the questions are in German and your answers need to be, too.

Read through the paper carefully at the start of the test

1) Before the recordings begin, you'll be given five minutes to read through the paper.

2) Use this time to read each question carefully. Some are multiple-choice, and others require you to write some short answers — make sure you know what each one is asking you to do.

3) In particular, look at the questions in Section B, which are written in German. Try to work out what the questions mean. There's a list of exam-style German question words and phrases on the inside front cover of this book to help you prepare for this.

4) Reading the question titles, and the questions themselves, will give you a good idea of the topics you'll be asked about. This should help you predict what to listen out for.

5) You can write on the exam paper, so scribble down anything that might be useful.

Make notes while listening to the recordings

1) You'll hear each audio track twice, and then there'll be a pause for you to write down your answer.

2) While you're listening, it's a good idea to jot down a few details — e.g. dates, times, names or key words. But make sure you keep listening while you're writing down any notes.

Listen to the speaker's tone, too — this will hint at their mood, e.g. angry or excited.

3) Listen right to the end, even if you think you've got the answer — sometimes the person will change their mind or add an important detail at the end.

4) Don't worry if you can't understand every word that's being said — just listen carefully both times and try to pick out the vocabulary you need to answer the question.

Don't worry if you didn't quite catch the answer...

If you've heard a track twice, and you're still not sure of the answer, scribble one down anyway — you never know, it might be the right one. You may as well write something sensible just in case — it's worth a shot.

The Speaking Exam

The Speaking Exam can seem daunting, but remember — no one is trying to catch you out.

There are three parts to the Speaking Exam

1) Your speaking exam will be conducted and recorded by your teacher.

During your preparation time, you can make notes to take in with you for the first two tasks. You can't keep the notes for the general conversation.

2) The exam is in three parts. Before you start, you'll get 12 minutes to prepare for the first two sections:

① Role-play (2 min.)	② Photo Card (3 min.)	③ Conversation (5-7 min.)
You'll get a card with a scenario on it. It'll have five bullet points — three will be notes on what to say, in German. The '!' means you'll be asked an unknown question, and '?' shows you have to ask a question about the words next to it. See, for example, p.12.	Before the exam, you'll receive a photo and three questions relating to it (see, for example, p.35). Your teacher will ask you the three questions that are on the photo card, as well as two questions you haven't seen.	You and your teacher will have a conversation. The conversation will be based on the theme that you've chosen, and the other theme that hasn't been covered on the photo card. You'll have to ask your teacher at least one question.

3) The role-play card will tell you if you should use 'du', but otherwise, use 'Sie' to talk to your teacher.

Try to be imaginative with your answers

You need to find ways to show off the full extent of your German knowledge. You should try to:

1) Use a range of tenses — e.g. for a question on daily routine, think of when something different happens.

> Morgen wird es anders sein, weil ich nach der Schule schwimmen gehen werde.
>
> *Tomorrow, it will be different because I will go swimming after school.*

Don't forget that some German words are spelt the same as in English, but are pronounced differently, like 'Religion' and 'Student'.

2) Talk about other people, not just yourself — it's fine to make people up if that helps.

> Meine Schwester liebt Eislaufen.   *My sister loves ice-skating.*

3) Give loads of opinions and reasons for your opinions.

> Meiner Meinung nach sollte man nicht rauchen, weil es sehr ungesund ist.
>
> *In my opinion, you shouldn't smoke because it is very unhealthy.*

If you're really struggling, ask for help in German

1) If you get really stuck trying to think of a word or phrase, you can ask for help — as long as it's in German.

2) For example, if you can't remember how to say 'homework' in German, ask your teacher. You won't get any marks for vocabulary your teacher's given you though.

> Wie sagt man 'homework' auf Deutsch?   *How do you say 'homework' in German?*

3) If you don't hear something clearly, just ask:

> Könnten Sie das bitte wiederholen?   *Could you repeat that, please?*

You could also ask this if you're desperately in need of time to think of an answer.

Making mistakes isn't the end of the world...

Don't panic if you make a mistake in the Speaking Exam — what's important is how you deal with it. You won't lose marks for correcting yourself, so show the examiner that you know where you went wrong.

The Reading Exam

The Reading Exam is split into three parts, so make sure you know what to do for each one.

Read the questions and texts carefully

1) The <u>higher tier</u> reading paper is <u>1 hour long</u>, and has <u>three sections</u>.

2) In Sections A and B, you'll be given a <u>variety of German texts</u> and then asked questions about them. The texts could include blog posts, emails, newspaper reports, adverts and literary texts. <u>Section A</u> has questions and answers <u>in English</u>, and <u>Section B</u> has questions and answers <u>in German</u>.

3) <u>Section C</u> is a <u>translation</u> question — you'll have to translate a short passage of text from German <u>into English</u>. See p.155 for more tips on tackling translation questions.

4) In Sections A and B, <u>scan through the text</u> first to <u>get an idea</u> of what it's about. Then read the <u>questions</u> that go with it carefully, making sure you understand <u>what information</u> you should be looking out for.

5) Next, <u>go back through the text</u>. You're not expected to understand every word, so don't get distracted by trying to work out what everything means — <u>focus</u> on finding the <u>information you need</u>.

> The inside front cover of this book has a list of common German question words, phrases and instructions.

Don't give up if you don't understand something

1) Use the <u>context</u> of the text to help you understand what it might be saying. You might be able to find some clues in the <u>title of the text</u> or the <u>type of text</u>.

2) Knowing how to spot <u>different word types</u> (e.g. nouns, verbs) can help you work out what's happening in a sentence. See the <u>grammar section</u> (p.108-150) for more.

3) You can <u>guess</u> some German words that look or sound the <u>same as English</u> words, e.g. die Schule — *school*, die Musik — *music*, der Markt — *market*.

> Look out for compound nouns: long words which contain several smaller words. E.g. 'Reisetasche' (travel bag) is made up of 'Reise' (journey, travel) and 'Tasche' (bag).

4) Be careful though — you might come across some '<u>false friends</u>'. These are German words that look like an English word, but have a <u>completely different meaning</u>:

bald	*soon*	also	*so / therefore*	der Chef	*boss*	der Rock	*skirt*	bekommen	*to get*
fast	*almost*	sensibel	*sensitive*	die Fabrik	*factory*	die Note	*grade / mark*	das Gymnasium	*grammar school*
still	*quiet*	das Handy	*mobile phone*	das Boot	*boat*	spenden	*to donate*	der Rat	*advice*

Keep an eye on the time

1) There are quite a few questions to get through in the reading exam, so you need to work at a <u>good speed</u>.

2) If you're having trouble with a particular question, you might want to <u>move on</u> and <u>come back to it later</u>.

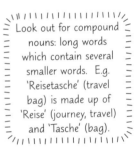

3) Don't forget that the <u>last question</u> in the paper (Section C) is a <u>translation</u> — this is worth <u>more marks</u> than any other question, so you should leave <u>plenty of time</u> to tackle it.

4) Make sure you put an answer down for <u>every question</u> — lots of the questions are multiple-choice, so even if you can't work out the answer, it's always worth putting down one of the options.

Familiarise yourself with the structure of the exam...

Don't forget, the questions in Section B will be in German. Don't panic if you don't understand them — search for any familiar vocabulary and use any answer lines or boxes to help you guess what you have to do.

The Writing Exam

The Writing Exam is a great way of showing off what you can do — try to use varied vocabulary, include a range of tenses, and pack in any clever expressions that you've learnt over the years.

There'll be three tasks in the Writing Exam

1) The <u>higher tier</u> writing paper is <u>1 hour and 15 minutes long</u> and has <u>three tasks</u>.

2) Each task is worth a <u>different number of marks</u>, so you should spend more time on the higher-mark tasks.

① Structured Task (16 marks)	② Open-ended Task (32 marks)	③ Translation (12 marks)
There will be <u>two tasks</u> to choose from. You'll be asked to write <u>about 90 words</u> in German, based on <u>four bullet points</u>. Make sure you write about each bullet point and give some <u>opinions</u>. See, for example, p.25.	There will also be <u>two tasks</u> to choose from. You'll need to write <u>about 150 words</u> in German, based on <u>two bullet points</u>. This task is more creative — make sure you include some <u>opinions</u> with <u>reasons</u>. See, for example, p.37.	You'll be given an <u>English passage</u> to translate <u>into German</u>. The passage could be on <u>any topic</u> you've studied. There's more advice for doing translations on p.155.

Read the instructions carefully, and spend some time planning

1) Read the instructions for questions 1 and 2 carefully — you'll need to make sure you cover <u>all of the bullet points</u>. You can often use <u>words from the question</u> in your answer too.

Try to use varied vocab and a range of tenses.

2) Spend a few minutes for each question <u>planning out</u> your answer. Decide <u>how</u> you're going to cover everything that's required and <u>in what order</u> you're going to write things.

3) Write the <u>best answer</u> you can, using the German <u>that you know</u> — it doesn't matter if it's not true.

Check through your work thoroughly

Checking your work is <u>really important</u> — even small mistakes can cost marks. Take a look at this checklist:

- Are all the <u>verbs</u> in the <u>right tense</u>?
  Morgen ging ich in die Stadt. ✘   Morgen werde ich in die Stadt gehen. ✓

- Does the <u>verb</u> match the <u>subject</u>?
  Du hat einen Bruder. ✘   Du hast einen Bruder. ✓

- Are the <u>adjective endings</u> correct?
  Das blaues Hemd. ✘   Das blaue Hemd. ✓

All of the points on this checklist are covered in the grammar section — see p.108-150.

- Is the <u>word order</u> correct?
  Ich mag ihn, weil er ist nett. ✘   Ich mag ihn, weil er nett ist. ✓

- Have you used the right <u>case</u> with <u>prepositions</u>?
  Ich esse mit meinen Freund. ✘   Ich esse mit meinem Freund. ✓

- Have you <u>spelt</u> everything correctly, including using the right <u>umlauts</u>?
  Eine gesunde Ernahrung ist wishtig. ✘   Eine gesunde Ernährung ist wichtig. ✓

Make sure you cover every aspect of the tasks...

When you're nervous and stressed, it's easy to miss out something the question has asked you to do. For tasks one and two, try to write about the bullet points in order, and tick them off as you go along.

The Translation Tasks

When you're studying German, you do little bits of translation in your head all the time. For the translation questions, you just need to apply those skills — one sentence at a time — to a couple of short passages.

In the Reading Exam, you'll translate from German to English

1) The final question of the reading paper will ask you to translate a <u>short German passage</u> (about 50 words) <u>into English</u>. The passage will be on a <u>topic you've studied</u>, so most of the vocabulary should be familiar.

2) Here are some <u>top tips</u> for doing your translation:

- Read the whole text <u>before you start</u>. Make some <u>notes in English</u> to remind you of the main ideas.

- Translate the text <u>one sentence at a time</u>, rather than word by word —
  this will avoid any of the German word order being carried into the English.

Er hat Fußball gespielt.	*He has football played.* ✘	*He has played football.* ✓
Ich denke, dass es prima ist.	*I think, that it great is.* ✘	*I think that it is great.* ✓

- Keep an eye out for <u>different tenses</u> — there will definitely be a variety in the passage.

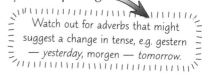

- <u>Read through</u> your translation to make sure it sounds <u>natural</u>. Some words and phrases don't translate literally, so you'll need to make sure that your sentences sound like <u>normal English</u>:

Watch out for adverbs that might suggest a change in tense, e.g. gestern — yesterday, morgen — tomorrow.

Dienstags fahre ich immer mit dem Bus.	*Tuesdays I always go with the bus.* ✘	*On Tuesdays, I always go by bus.* ✓

3) Make sure you've translated <u>everything</u> from the original text — you'll lose marks if you miss something.

In the Writing Exam, you'll translate from English to German

1) In the writing paper, you will have to translate <u>a short English passage</u> (about 50 words) <u>into German</u>.

2) Here are <u>some ideas</u> for how you could approach the translation:

- <u>Read</u> through the <u>whole text</u> before you get started so you know exactly what the text is about.

- Tackle the passage <u>one sentence at a time</u> — work carefully through each one.

- <u>Don't</u> translate things <u>literally</u> — think about what each English sentence means and try to write it in the <u>most German way</u> you know. Don't worry — the translation is likely to include similar sentences to the ones you've learnt.

Don't try to write a perfect translation first time — do it roughly first, and then write it up properly, crossing out any old drafts. Remember to keep an eye on the time.

- Work on the <u>word order</u> — remember that some conjunctions, such as 'weil' (*because*) and 'obwohl' (*although*) send the verb to the end.

3) Once you've got something that you're happy with, go back through and <u>check that you've covered everything</u> that was in the English.

4) Now <u>check</u> your German text thoroughly using the <u>list from p.154</u>.

Thankfully, none of that got lost in translation...

There's no set way of translating a text, but following these ideas is a good place to start. Now you've taken all this advice on board, it's time to test it out — have a go at tackling the practice papers.

Practice Exam

Once you've been through all the questions in this book, you should be starting to feel prepared for the final exams. As a last piece of preparation, here's a practice exam for you to have a go at. It's been designed to give you the best exam practice possible for the AQA Higher Tier papers. Good luck!

General Certificate of Secondary Education

GCSE German
Higher Tier

Listening Paper

Centre name	
Centre number	
Candidate number	

Surname	
Other names	
Candidate signature	

CGP
Practice Exam Paper
GCSE German

Time Allowed: 40 minutes approximately
+ 5 minutes of reading time before the test.

Instructions:
- Write in black ink.
- You have 5 minutes at the start of the test during which you may read through the questions and make notes. Then start the recording.
- Answer **all** questions in the spaces provided.
- Answer the questions in Section A in **English**.
- Answer the questions in Section B in **German**.
- Give all the information you are asked for, and **write neatly**.

Advice:
- Before each new question, read through all the question parts and instructions carefully.
- Listen carefully to the recording. There will be a pause to allow you to reread the question, make notes or write down your answers.
- Listen to the recording again. There will be a pause to allow you to complete or check your answers.
- You may write at any point during the exam.
- Each item on the recording is repeated once.
- You are **not** allowed to ask questions or interrupt during the exam.

Information:
- The maximum mark for this paper is **50**.
- The number of marks for each question is shown in brackets.
- You are **not** allowed to use a dictionary.

Section A   Questions and answers in **English**

Tourism

You are at a German tourist office. Jürgen, the assistant, gives you information about the town.

Answer **all** parts of the question.

Write the correct letters in the boxes.

1.1   The town is in the...

A	south of Germany.
B	west of Germany.
C	east of Germany.

[1 mark]

1.2   According to Jürgen, the mountains are...

A	very far away.
B	close by.
C	very steep.

[1 mark]

1.3   The mountain bike tours...

A	take place every day.
B	are only for the experienced cyclist.
C	are good fun.

[1 mark]

1.4   Jürgen says that the town centre...

A	is very historical.
B	has a wide range of cheap restaurants.
C	has lots to offer.

[1 mark]

Turn over

Music

Your German friend Max phones you to tell you about a concert he went to.

Answer **all** parts of the question.

Complete the following statements in **English**.

2.1 Max's favourite performer was the .... *[1 mark]*

2.2 He is thinking of starting .... *[1 mark]*

2.3 He stopped playing .... *[1 mark]*

because .... *[1 mark]*

Sport

Listen to Lars and his family discussing the sports that are on offer at a holiday club.

Complete the following statements in **English**.

3 Lars is keen to try sailing because...

.... *[1 mark]*

4 Anna likes trampolining because it is fun and...

.... *[1 mark]*

5 Their mum will stay by the pool because...

.... *[1 mark]*

6 She says that it is unhealthy to...

.... *[1 mark]*

School

Your German friend Betül is visiting your school. She talks to you at the end of the day.

7   What **two** negative aspects of your school does she mention?

Complete the table in **English**.

	Aspect 1	Aspect 2
Negative		

[2 marks]

8   What **two** positive aspects of your school does she mention?

Complete the table in **English**.

	Aspect 1	Aspect 2
Positive		

[2 marks]

Turn over

Weather

Whilst in Germany, you hear this weather forecast on the radio.

Which **three** statements are true?

Write the correct letters in the boxes.

9

A	It will snow all day in the north of Germany.
B	The temperature will be below freezing in the north.
C	It may turn cloudy in the west.
D	It's going to be warm in the west.
E	In the evening it will be wet in the east.
F	In the south it will be overcast in the afternoon.

☐ ☐ ☐

[3 marks]

Food and Eating Out

Imran is visiting a restaurant in Germany. Listen to his conversation with the waitress.

Answer **all** parts of the question in **English**.

10.1   What does Imran ask for?

.... *[1 mark]*

10.2   Which dishes does the waitress recommend? Give **two** details.

1. ....

2. .... *[2 marks]*

10.3   What does Imran order to drink?

.... *[1 mark]*

My Town

Luke is talking to his exchange partner about the advantages and disadvantages of his town.

Answer the questions in **English**.

11 What does Luke like about where he lives? Give **two** details.

1. ....

2. .... *[2 marks]*

12 Which disadvantages does Luke mention? Give **two** details.

1. ....

2. .... *[2 marks]*

13 Why does Luke want to study in a bigger town? Give **two** reasons.

1. ....

2. .... *[2 marks]*

Customs and Festivals

You are listening to a radio discussion about people's opinions of the Oktoberfest in Munich.

What is their opinion of the Oktoberfest?

Write **P** for a **positive** opinion.
Write **N** for a **negative** opinion.
Write **P + N** for a **positive and negative** opinion.

14   Naas   ☐

[1 mark]

15   Delilah   ☐

[1 mark]

16   Jerome   ☐

[1 mark]

Social Media

In a café in Germany, you hear three friends talking about their use of social media.

Answer the questions in **English**.

17   What does Lata use social media for?

....   *[1 mark]*

18   What does Shakeel find positive about social media? Give **two** details.

1. ....

2. ....   *[2 marks]*

19   What does Evie find annoying?

....   *[1 mark]*

Voluntary Work

While visiting your German exchange partner's school,
you attend an information evening about voluntary work.

Answer the questions in **English**.

20   Give **two** voluntary activities that the students can do in schools.

1. ....

2. ....   *[2 marks]*

21   What are the advantages of voluntary work? Give **two** details.

1. ....

2. ....   *[2 marks]*

Section B   Questions and answers in **German**.

Lebensstil

Eine deutsche Schulklasse diskutiert über gesundes und ungesundes Leben.

Beantworte **die beiden** Teile der Frage auf **Deutsch**.

22.1   Was ist ein gesunder Lebensstil? Erwähne **zwei** Aspekte.

	Aspekt 1	Aspekt 2
Gesund		

[2 marks]

22.2   Was ist ungesund? Erwähne **zwei** Aspekte.

	Aspekt 1	Aspekt 2
Ungesund		

[2 marks]

Berufspläne

Du hörst Tamal und Yvonne, die sich über Berufe unterhalten.

Beantworte die Fragen auf **Deutsch.**

23   Warum möchte Tamal vielleicht später Arzt werden? Gib **einen** Grund.

    ....   *[1 mark]*

24   Warum denkt Yvonne, dass sie Meeresbiologin nicht werden kann?

    ....   *[1 mark]*

25   Warum möchte Yvonne möglicherweise Lehrerin werden?

    ....   *[1 mark]*

Kasperle auf Reisen

Hör den Abschnitt aus dem Buch ‚Kasperle auf Reisen‘, geschrieben von Josephine Siebe. Kasperle ist der neue Schüler in der Klasse.

Beantworte **alle** Teile der Frage auf **Deutsch**.

26.1   Was hat Kasperle gut gefallen?

    ....   *[1 mark]*

26.2   Was machten die Kleinen, während die Großen Religion lernten?

    ....   *[1 mark]*

26.3   Warum war Herr Habermus böse mit Kasperle?

    ....   *[1 mark]*

END OF QUESTIONS

General Certificate of Secondary Education

GCSE German
Higher Tier

Centre name				
Centre number				
Candidate number				

CGP

**Practice Exam Paper
GCSE German**

Surname	
Other names	
Candidate signature	

Speaking Paper

Time Allowed: 10-12 minutes
                              + 12 minutes of supervised preparation time.

Instructions to candidates
- Find a friend or parent to read the teacher's part for you.
- You will have **12 minutes** to prepare the Role-play and Photo Card tasks.
- You may make notes on a separate piece of paper during the preparation time.
- You must not use any notes during the General Conversation.
- The General Conversation will be on the following themes: Identity and culture; Current and future study and employment.
- You must ask at least one question in the General Conversation.

Instructions to teachers
- It is essential that you give the student every opportunity to use the material they have prepared.
- You may alter the wording of the questions in response to the candidate's previous answers. However you must remember **not** to provide students with any key vocabulary.
- The candidate **must** ask you at least **one** question during the General Conversation.
- Candidates who have not yet asked you a question towards the end of the test must be prompted in **German** with the following question: 'Is there anything you want to ask me?'

Information
- The test consists of **3** tasks.
- You may only prepare the Role-play and Photo Card tasks during the preparation time.
- The Role-play task will last approximately 2 minutes.
- The Photo Card task will last approximately 3 minutes.
- The General Conversation will last between 5 and 7 minutes.
- You are **not** allowed to use a dictionary at any time during the preparation time or the test.

In the actual exam, you will nominate one theme to be asked about in the General Conversation.
This will determine your Photo Card theme and the remaining theme for the General Conversation.
For this practice paper, you don't need to nominate a theme as there's only one Photo Card,
so the General Conversation will use the two themes not covered by the Photo Card.

ROLE-PLAY
CANDIDATE'S MATERIAL

Instructions to candidate

- Your teacher will play the role of the interviewer. They will speak first.

- You should use *Sie* to address the interviewer.

- **!** – means you will have to respond to something you have not prepared.

- **?** – means you will have to ask the interviewer a question.

Sie machen ein Interview über Sport an Ihrer Schule.

- Sportunterricht — wie oft.

- Sportarten dieses Jahr an der Schule getrieben (**drei** Details).

- Ihre Meinung über Ihren Sportlehrer / Ihre Sportlehrerin.

- **!**

- **?** Seit wann Interesse an Sport.

PHOTO CARD
CANDIDATE'S MATERIAL

Instructions to candidate

- You should look carefully at the photo during the preparation time.

- You can make notes on a separate piece of paper.

- Your teacher will ask you questions about the photo and about topics related to **global issues**.

© iStock.com/Sablin

You will be asked the three questions below and then **two more questions** which you haven't seen in the preparation time.

- Was gibt es auf dem Foto?

- Ist Recyceln wichtig? Warum?

- Was hat deine Familie diesen Monat für die Umwelt gemacht?

ROLE-PLAY
TEACHER'S MATERIAL

Instructions to teacher

- You begin the role-play.

- You should use *Sie* to address the candidate.

- You may alter the wording of the questions in response to the candidate's previous answers.

- Do not supply the candidate with key vocabulary.

Begin the role-play by using the introductory text below.

Introductory text: *Sie sind an Ihrer Schule und machen ein Interview für einen Radiosender über Sportmöglichkeiten an der Schule. Ich bin der Interviewer / die Interviewerin.*

1 Ask the candidate how often he / she has PE lessons.

   Wie oft haben Sie Sportunterricht?

2 Allow the candidate to say how often he / she has PE lessons.

   Ask the candidate which sports he / she has done this year. (Elicit **three** details.)

   Welche Sportarten haben Sie dieses Jahr an der Schule getrieben?

3 Allow the candidate to name **three** sports.

   Ask the candidate his / her opinion of his / her PE teacher.

   Wie finden Sie Ihren Sportlehrer oder Ihre Sportlehrerin?

4 Allow the candidate to give an opinion about his / her PE teacher.

   ! Ask the candidate if he / she thinks that sport is important for good health. (Elicit **one** reason why / why not.)

   Glauben Sie, dass Sport treiben für die Gesundheit wichtig ist?

5 Allow the candidate to say whether he / she thinks sport is important for good health and to give one reason why / why not.

   Das ist sehr interessant.

   ? Allow the candidate to ask you how long you've been interested in sport.

   Schon seit meiner Schulzeit.

Turn over

PHOTO CARD & GENERAL CONVERSATION
TEACHER'S MATERIAL

Photo Card

Theme: Local, national, international and global areas of interest   **Topic**: Global issues

This part of the test should last for a maximum of **three minutes**. It may be less than that for some candidates. Candidates can use any notes they made during the preparation time.

Begin the conversation by asking the candidate the first question from the list below. Then ask the remaining four questions in order. You can adapt the questions, but make sure they still have the same meaning. You can repeat or reword any questions that the candidate does not understand. Allow the candidate to develop their answers as much as possible.

- Was gibt es auf dem Foto?

- Ist Recyceln wichtig? Warum?

- Was hat deine Familie diesen Monat für die Umwelt gemacht?

- Was für Umweltprobleme könnte es in der Zukunft geben?

- Welche andere Probleme gibt es in der Gesellschaft?

General Conversation

The General Conversation follows the Photo Card task. It should last between **five** and **seven minutes**, and a similar amount of time should be spent on each theme. Sample questions for a range of topics within each theme have been provided below, but these lists are not exhaustive.

Themes and sample questions for the General Conversation:

Identity and culture

1) Wie ist dein bester Freund / deine beste Freundin?

2) Ist Heiraten heute noch wichtig? Warum (nicht)?

3) Bist du abhängig von deinem Handy?

4) Wozu benutzt du deinen Computer?

5) Was hast du neulich im Kino gesehen? Wie fandest du den Film?

6) Warum soll man regelmäßig Sport treiben?

Current and future study and employment

1) Was sind deine Lieblingsfächer? Warum?

2) Was würdest du an deiner Schule gern ändern?

3) Hast du schon mal einen Schulausflug gemacht? Wohin?

4) Möchtest du gern im Ausland studieren? Warum (nicht)?

5) Ist Studieren besser als Arbeiten?

6) Welchen Beruf möchtest du später machen?

Remember — the candidate must ask you at least one question during the General Conversation. If, towards the end of the task, the candidate has not asked you a question, you must prompt them by asking, „Möchtest du mich etwas fragen?"

General Certificate of Secondary Education

GCSE German
Higher Tier

Centre name					
Centre number					
Candidate number					

CGP

Practice Exam Paper
GCSE German

Surname	
Other names	
Candidate signature	

Reading Paper

Time Allowed: 1 hour

Instructions
- Write in black ink.
- Answer **all** questions in the spaces provided.
- Answer the questions in Section A in **English**.
- Answer the questions in Section B in **German**.
- In Section C, translate the passage into **English**.
- Give all the information you are asked for, and **write neatly**.
- Cross out any rough work that you do not want to be marked.

Information
- The maximum mark for this paper is **60**.
- The number of marks for each question is shown in brackets.
- You are **not** allowed to use a dictionary.

Section A   Questions and answers in **English**

1   **Television**

Read the conversation in a chat room between four German teenagers about their TV habits.

Write the first letter of the correct name in the box.

Write **J** for Judith.
Write **T** for Thomas.
Write **I** for Ingo.
Write **Y** for Yasmin.

	Judith Ich sehe ganz selten fern, weil ich meistens keine Zeit dafür habe. Am Wochenende habe ich eigentlich immer etwas Besseres geplant. Meiner Meinung nach ist Fernsehen meistens eine Zeitverschwendung.
	Thomas Fernsehen ist total wichtig für mich, es entspannt mich nach der Schule und ich kann den ganzen Stress erstmal vergessen. Ich könnte ohne Fernsehen nicht leben!
	Ingo Ich habe früher ganz wenig ferngesehen. Im Moment gibt es aber viele spannende Serien, deshalb sehe ich fast jeden Abend nach den Hausaufgaben fern.
	Yasmin Alleine sehe ich selten fern, aber zusammen mit Freunden macht es Spaß, sich eine lustige Sendung anzuschauen. Gestern habe ich zum Beispiel mit einer Freundin eine Sitcom gesehen.

1.1   Who finds watching TV relaxing?   *[1 mark]*

1.2   Who watches more TV than they used to?   *[1 mark]*

1.3   Who prefers to watch TV with other people?   *[1 mark]*

1.4   Who is too busy to watch TV?   *[1 mark]*

2 Directions

Your German friend Klaus has invited you to a party at his house.
He has texted you some directions.

Answer the questions in **English**.

Hey,

Ich wohne in der Kirchstraße 34, in
der Nähe vom Zoo. Nimm die U-Bahn-
Linie 18 vom Hauptbahnhof und fahr
3 Stationen bis zur Haltestelle Zoo.
Dann geh links auf die Königinstraße
und geh immer geradeaus, bis du an
eine Kreuzung kommst. Geh über den
Zebrastreifen und dann nimm die erste
Straße rechts, gegenüber der Kirche.
Mein Haus ist das vierte Haus auf der
linken Straßenseite, vor dem Eingang
steht ein kleiner Apfelbaum.

Bis dann!

Klaus

< Messages   Options

2.1 Where do you take the underground from?

.... *[1 mark]*

2.2 What should you do after turning left onto Königinstraße?

.... *[1 mark]*

2.3 After the zebra crossing, what is the next direction?

.... *[1 mark]*

2.4 What will you see in front of Klaus' house?

.... *[1 mark]*

Turn over

3   **Education Post-16**

You are reading the problem page of a German magazine and see Sophia's letter.

Answer the questions in **English**.

> Ich brauche dringend Rat, weil ich keine Ahnung habe, was ich nach den Prüfungen
> machen werde. Meine Freunde wissen schon, was sie machen wollen, während ich bisher
> keine Pläne habe. Meine Eltern sind der Meinung, dass ich auf die Oberstufe gehen sollte,
> damit ich später einen Studienplatz bekommen kann. Persönlich würde ich mich lieber um
> Arbeitsstellen bewerben, aber ich habe Angst, dass ich nicht genug Erfahrung habe.
>
> Ein Arbeitspraktikum wäre auch eine Möglichkeit, aber es ist schwer, eine Stelle zu finden,
> weil meine Stadt so klein ist. Auch ist der Lohn meistens nicht besonders gut.
>
> Nächste Woche fangen die Prüfungen an. Ich glaube leider nicht, dass ich sehr erfolgreich
> sein werde und mache mir schon Sorgen.

3.1   What do Sophia's parents think she should do?

.... *[1 mark]*

3.2   Why does Sophia think she won't get a job?

.... *[1 mark]*

3.3   According to Sophia, what is the disadvantage of doing a work experience placement?

.... *[1 mark]*

3.4   How does Sophia think she will do in her exams? Write the correct letter in the box.

A	very well
B	not very well
C	better than usual

[1 mark]

4   **Mobile Technology**

You read a report about mobile phones in an Austrian newspaper.

Fill in the grid with details to show the developments in mobile phones.
Give **two** details about mobile phones for each row.

> **DIE ENTWICKLUNG DES HANDYS**
>
> Die Technik der Mobilgeräte hat sich in den letzten Jahren stark verändert. Handys waren noch vor einigen Jahren viel größer, als sie heute sind. Man konnte sie zwar schon gut zum Telefonieren und zum Simsen benutzen, aber die aktuellen Handys können noch vieles mehr. Man kann jetzt im Internet surfen und E-Mails schicken. Außerdem haben die meisten modernen Geräte ziemlich gute Kameras.
>
> Jedes Jahr kommen neue Modelle heraus und in der Zukunft wird man bestimmt noch viel schneller Filme herunterladen können. Auch wird die Batteriedauer immer besser werden und man wird mehr Daten auf dem Handy speichern können, zum Beispiel Musik.

		Detail 1	Detail 2
Example	Past	much bigger than modern phones	used for making phone calls and texting
	Present		
	Future		

[4 marks]

Turn over

5 Shopping

You are reading Marlene's blog about her recent shopping trip.

Write **T** if the statement is **true**.
Write **F** if the statement is **false**.
Write **NT** if the statement is **not in the text**.

> Gestern war ich in einem Laden in der Innenstadt, weil ich mir ein neues Kleid für eine Hochzeit kaufen wollte. Meine beste Freundin heiratet in zwei Monaten und es kostet immer viel Zeit, das richtige Kleid zu finden. Deswegen habe ich frühzeitig mit der Suche begonnen.
>
> Im Laden gab es sehr viele schöne Kleider und ich habe mindestens zehn verschiedene Stile anprobiert. Trotzdem war ich etwas genervt, weil die Kleider viel zu teuer waren. Ich bin Studentin und habe zwar einen Nebenjob, aber ich kann mir trotzdem keine teuren Klamotten leisten. Man muss immer viel Geld für langweilige Sachen wie Miete ausgeben — das finde ich total blöd!
>
> Ich war ziemlich enttäuscht, aber dann habe ich einen kleinen Laden in der Nähe entdeckt, wo es tolle Kleider im Sonderangebot gab. Das war super, ich habe mein Traumkleid gefunden und ich empfehle jedem, diesen Laden zu besuchen.

5.1 Yesterday, Marlene went shopping with her best friend. *[1 mark]*

5.2 According to Marlene, it is easy to find the right dress. *[1 mark]*

5.3 In the first shop, Marlene saw lots of dresses that she liked. *[1 mark]*

5.4 Marlene finds her job boring. *[1 mark]*

5.5 There were dresses on sale in another shop. *[1 mark]*

5.6 Marlene will go back to the shop soon. *[1 mark]*

6 Cinema

While on holiday in Berlin, you are given a leaflet advertising a new cinema.

Answer the questions in **English**.

Besuchen Sie das neueste Kino in der Berliner Stadtmitte! Wir bieten Ihnen ein ganz besonderes Kinoerlebnis an. Wir benutzen die modernste Technologie, um dafür zu sorgen, dass die Vorstellungen so spannend wie möglich sind.

Das Kino hat acht Leinwände und Sie können sich viele verschiedene Filmarten anschauen — nicht nur die beliebtesten Abenteuer- und Liebesfilme, sondern auch fremdsprachige Filme.

Wenn Sie regelmäßig ins Kino gehen, können Sie Mitglied des ,Kinoklubs' werden. Es kostet nur dreißig Euro und Sie bekommen einen zwanzigprozentigen Rabatt auf den Preis der Eintrittskarten. Als Mitglied dürfen Sie auch Privatvorstellungen buchen — perfekt für Ihre nächste Geburtstagsfeier!

© iStock.com/dolgachov

6.1 What is special about the cinema experience?

.... *[1 mark]*

6.2 What kind of films can you watch at the new cinema? Give **one** detail.

.... *[1 mark]*

6.3 What are the benefits of joining the 'Kinoklub'? Give **one** detail.

.... *[1 mark]*

178

7   Marriage and Partnership

You are reading a magazine article about marriage.

Which **four** statements are true?
Write the correct letters in the boxes.

IST HEIRATEN HEUTE NOCH ‚IN'?

Viele junge Leute denken heutzutage erstmal an die Karriere und nicht unbedingt ans Heiraten. Für die meisten Leute ist es wichtiger, im Berufsleben erfolgreich zu sein und Geld zu verdienen. Die hohen Kosten einer Hochzeit sind vielleicht auch ein Grund, warum die Jugendlichen von heute viel später als früher heiraten. Teure Hochzeiten werden immer beliebter: viele wollen ein großes, schickes Fest an einem wunderschönen Ort.

Martin Schmidt, ein Mathematikstudent aus Hamburg, kennt das Problem: „Ich weiß wirklich nicht, wie meine Freundin Silke und ich uns eine Hochzeit leisten können. Fast unser ganzes Geld müssen wir für Miete und Lebensmittel ausgeben. Wenn wir heiraten, dann soll es auch perfekt sein. Deshalb warten wir mit der Hochzeit, bis wir genug Geld gespart haben."

A	Many young people think about their career before they think about marriage.
B	For many young people, marriage is more important than a high salary.
C	Some young people cannot afford to get married until they are older.
D	All weddings are very expensive nowadays.
E	Lots of young people think that marriage is old-fashioned.
F	Martin and Silke spend nearly all their money on rent and food.
G	They think that paying for a wedding is a waste of money.
H	They will not get married straight away.

[4 marks]

8 **The environment**

In Austria, you see this flyer produced by a local environmental group.

Answer the questions in **English**.

> Manchmal denkt man, dass es sich nicht lohnt, umweltfreundlich
> zu sein, weil die Probleme schon so groß sind. Wir dürfen aber nicht
> einfach aufgeben. Es geht nicht immer um die großen Aktionen — es
> ist auch möglich, im Alltag einen Unterschied zu machen.
>
> Jeder kann mithelfen, damit die Erde, auf der wir leben, auch noch für
> unsere Kinder attraktiv ist. Zum Beispiel verbrauchen wir immer noch
> viel zu viel Plastik — jedes Jahr landen Millionen Tonnen Plastikabfälle
> im Meer.
>
> Diese Verschwendung ist leicht zu reduzieren. Hier sind ein paar Ideen:
>
> 1. Man sollte lieber keine Plastiktüten, sondern Alternativen wie
>   Stoffbeutel und Rucksäcke benutzen.
>
> 2. Man sollte auch den Müll trennen, damit man das Plastik
>   wiederverwerten kann.
>
> Machen Sie bitte mit! Zusammen werden wir viel erfolgreicher sein.

8.1 Why do some people think they can't do anything to help the environment?

.... *[1 mark]*

8.2 Why shouldn't people just give up?

.... *[1 mark]*

8.3 According to the flyer, how can people help to reduce plastic waste? Give **two** details.

1. ....

2. .... *[2 marks]*

Section B   Questions and answers in **German**

9   Der geduldige Mann

Lies diese Geschichte ‚Der geduldige Mann', geschrieben von Johann Peter Hebel.

Beantworte die Fragen.

Schreib **R**, wenn die Aussage **richtig** ist.
Schreib **F**, wenn die Aussage **falsch** ist.
Schreib **NT**, wenn die Aussage **nicht im Text** ist.

Ein Mann, der eines Nachmittags müde nach Hause kam, hätte gern ein Butterbrot mit Schnittlauch*
darauf gegessen oder etwas geräuchertes Fleisch. Aber seine Frau, die im Haus ziemlich der
Chef war, hatte den Schlüssel zum Kühlschrank in der Tasche und war bei einer Freundin.

Er schickte daher ein Mädchen und einen Jungen — seine Frau soll nach Hause kommen oder den
Schlüssel schicken.

Sie sagte, „Ich komme gleich, er soll nur ein wenig warten." Als er aber ungeduldig wurde und
sein Hunger größer wurde, trugen er und der Junge den verschlossenen Kühlschrank in das
Haus der Freundin, wo seine Frau zu Besuch war und er sagte zu seiner Frau: „Frau, sei so
gut und schließ mir den Kühlschrank auf, dass ich etwas zum Abendessen nehmen kann."

Da lachte die Frau und schnitt ihm ein kleines Stück Brot und etwas vom Fleisch.

*Schnittlauch — chives

9.1   Der Mann war müde und hatte Hunger.   *[1 mark]*

9.2   Der Mann wollte gern eine warme Mahlzeit essen.   *[1 mark]*

9.3   Seine Frau ist mit ihrer Freundin zum Essen gegangen.   *[1 mark]*

9.4   Seine Frau war seit langem bei ihrer Freundin zu Besuch.   *[1 mark]*

9.5   Seine Frau wollte, dass er wartet, bis sie nach Hause kam.   *[1 mark]*

9.6   Die Frau hat den Schlüssel vom Kühlschrank verloren.   *[1 mark]*

9.7   Der Junge war froh, dass er dem Mann helfen konnte.   *[1 mark]*

9.8   Alle lachten und aßen alle Lebensmittel aus dem Kühlschrank.   *[1 mark]*

10   Weihnachtszauber

Lies den Abschnitt aus der Geschichte ‚Weihnachtszauber‘, geschrieben von Adolf Schwayer.
Die Kinder warten auf das Christkind, das die Geschenke bringt.

Beantworte die Fragen auf **Deutsch**. Schreib vollständige Sätze.

> Jetzt schlug die Uhr vom nahen Kirchturm die Stunde. Sie hörten
> zu und zählten. „Sechs Uhr schon!" rief Klein-Elli überrascht.
> „Um die Zeit war das Christkind immer schon da bei uns."
>
> „Ja, mein Gott," meinte der fast achtjährige Otto, der Älteste, „jetzt,
> wo wir nicht in der Stadtmitte wohnen, wird es wohl noch später."
>
> „Ja", sagte Elli und ihre Augen wurden groß dabei.
>
> Und Norbert, der Jüngste, ließ sein Spielzeug fallen, starrte die
> beiden Größeren angstvoll an und sagte traurig: „Noch später."

10.1   Was findet Klein-Elli überraschend?

.... *[1 mark]*

10.2   Warum denkt Otto, dass die Kinder noch länger warten müssen?

.... *[1 mark]*

10.3   Warum ist Norbert traurig?

.... *[1 mark]*

11   Gesundheit

Du liest über Gesundheitstips bei Krankheiten in einer deutschen Zeitschrift.

Beantworte die Fragen auf **Deutsch**.

> Achtung: die Viren kommen! Der Herbst ist da und die Blätter sind bunt gefärbt, aber leider bringt der Herbst auch wieder viele Krankheiten mit sich. Wer leicht krank wird, sollte besonders gut aufpassen. Am besten schützen Sie sich, indem Sie sich warm anziehen, sich viel an der frischen Luft bewegen und Menschenmengen vermeiden.
>
> Wenn es Ihnen trotzdem schlecht geht, helfen manchmal heiße Getränke wie Tee mit Honig. Noch wichtiger ist aber viel Ruhe. Bei Schmerzen und Fieber ist das Bett der beste Platz, um sich zu erholen. Sie sollten warten, bis Sie wieder gesund sind, bevor Sie zurück zur Arbeit gehen. Danach sorgen Sie am besten mit einer gesunden Ernährung dafür, dass die Krankheit nicht wieder kommt.

11.1   Warum muss man später im Jahr aufpassen?

.... *[1 mark]*

11.2   Wie schützt man sich vor Krankheiten? Gib **zwei** Details.

1. ....

2. .... *[2 marks]*

11.3   Was hilft, wenn man krank ist? Gib **zwei** Details.

1. ....

2. .... *[2 marks]*

11.4   Was soll man bei Krankheiten nicht tun?

.... *[1 mark]*

11.5   Wie kann man in Zukunft gesünder bleiben?

.... *[1 mark]*

Section C   Translation into **English**

12   Your German penfriend is applying for a work experience placement at a veterinary practice in England. She has asked you to help her write her application.

Translate the following into **English**.

> Ich interessiere mich sehr für Tiere. Letzten Sommer habe ich in einem Tierheim gearbeitet und ich habe dort viel gelernt. Seit vier Jahren bin ich auch Mitglied einer Gruppe, die Tiere schützt. Biologie ist mein Lieblingsfach und ich möchte später Tiermedizin studieren, damit ich kranken Tieren helfen kann. Das ist mein Traumberuf.

[9 marks]

....

....

....

....

....

....

....

....

....

....

END OF QUESTIONS

General Certificate of Secondary Education

GCSE German
Higher Tier

Centre name				
Centre number				
Candidate number				

CGP
Practice Exam Paper
GCSE German

Surname	
Other names	
Candidate signature	

Writing Paper

Time Allowed: 1 hour 15 minutes

Instructions
- Write in black ink.
- Give all the information you are asked for, and **write neatly**.
- You must answer **three** questions.
- Answer **either** Question 1.1 **or** Question 1.2. Do **not** answer both questions.
- Answer **either** Question 2.1 **or** Question 2.2. Do **not** answer both questions.
- You **must** answer Question 3.
- All questions must be answered in **German**.
- In the actual exam, you must write your answers in the spaces provided. Do **not** write on blank pages.
- You may plan your answers in the exam booklet. Make sure you cross through any work you do not want to be marked.

Information
- This paper contains **3** writing tasks.
- The maximum mark for this paper is **60**.
- The number of marks for each question is shown in brackets.
- For Questions 1 and 2, the highest marks will be awarded for answers that make reference to each bullet point and include a variety of vocabulary, structures and opinions with reasons.
- You are **not** allowed to use a dictionary.

Answer **either** Question 1.1 **or** Question 1.2

1.1   Du interessierst dich sehr für Musik und schreibst ein Blog darüber.

Schreib:

- etwas über die Art von Musik, die dir am besten gefällt
- ob du dich auch früher für Musik interessiert hast
- warum du gern oder nicht gern Konzerte besuchst
- welches Instrument du in der Zukunft lernen möchtest

Du musst ungefähr **90** Wörter auf **Deutsch** schreiben. Schreib etwas über alle Punkte der Aufgabe.

[16 marks]

1.2   Du möchtest gern ein Praktikum machen und schreibst eine E-Mail an deinen deutschen Freund darüber.

Schreib:

- etwas über das Praktikum, das du machen möchtest
- warum du dich für diesen Beruf interessierst
- dass du schon relevante Erfahrung hast
- wo du in der Zukunft arbeiten möchtest

Du musst ungefähr **90** Wörter auf **Deutsch** schreiben. Schreib etwas über alle Punkte der Aufgabe.

[16 marks]

Answer **either** Question 2.1 **or** Question 2.2

2.1   Du hast einen Informationstag zum Thema Rauchen besucht und schreibst einen Artikel darüber.

• Schreib etwas über den Informationstag — was du gelernt hast und deine Meinungen dazu.

• Vergleich einen gesunden und einen ungesunden Lebensstil.

Du musst ungefähr **150** Wörter auf **Deutsch** schreiben. Schreib etwas über beide Punkte der Aufgabe.

[32 marks]

2.2   Dein Austauschpartner Gunther möchte mehr über dein Familienleben wissen. Schreib Gunther eine E-Mail über deine Familie.

• Schreib etwas über deine Beziehung zu deiner Familie.

• Vergleich deine Familie und die Familie deines besten Freundes / deiner besten Freundin.

Du musst ungefähr **150** Wörter auf **Deutsch** schreiben. Schreib etwas über beide Punkte der Aufgabe.

[32 marks]

You **must** answer Question 3

3   Translate the following passage into **German**.

I go on holiday with my family every winter. Last summer I went to Switzerland with my best friend but unfortunately it rained the whole time. Next spring we will visit Austria. We will hire bikes because we like active holidays. In the future I would like to work in a hotel abroad.

[12 marks]

....

....

....

....

....

....

....

....

....

....

....

END OF QUESTIONS

Vocabulary

Section One — General Stuff

Coordinating Conjunctions (p.115)

aber	but
denn	because
oder	or
und	and

Subordinating Conjunctions (p.116)

als	when
als ob	as if / as though
bevor	before
bis	until
damit	so that
dass	that
nachdem	after
ob	whether
obwohl	although
während	while
weil	because
wenn	if / when

Connectives

außerdem	besides / furthermore
danach	afterwards
dennoch	nevertheless
deshalb	therefore
doch	after all / on the contrary
eigentlich	actually / really
entweder... oder...	either... or...
erstens, zweitens, drittens	firstly, secondly, thirdly
jedoch	however
leider	unfortunately
natürlich	of course
nicht nur... sondern auch...	not only... but also...
ohne Zweifel	without a doubt
schließlich	eventually / finally
sowohl... als auch...	both... and...
trotzdem	nevertheless
weder... noch...	neither... nor...

Comparisons (p.121)

ähnlich	similar
anders	different(ly)
Gegenteil n (-e)	opposite
groß / größer / (der, die, das) Größte	big / bigger / the biggest
im Großen und Ganzen	by and large
gut / besser / (der, die, das) Beste	good / better / the best
hoch / höher / (der, die, das) Höchste	high / higher / the highest

Vocabulary

---

nah / näher / (der, die, das) Nächste	near / nearer / the nearest
so... wie	as... as
so viel(e)... wie	as much / many... as
Unterschied m (-e)	difference
unterschiedlich	different
Vergleich m (-e)	comparison
vergleichen	to compare
viel / mehr / (der, die, das) Meiste	much / more / the most

Prepositions (p.130-131)

ab	from
an	at / in / on / to
auf	on / onto / on top of / upon
aus	from / of / out of
bei	near / at
durch	through
entlang	along
gegen	against / at about
gegenüber	opposite
hinter	after / behind
nach	after / to / according to
neben	beside / next to
ohne	without
über	above / over / via
um	around / at
unter	among / under
von	from / by / of
vor	in front of / before / ago
vorbei	over / past / by
während	during
wegen	because of
zu	to / at / for
zwischen	between

Negatives (p.136)

gar nicht	not at all
nicht einmal	not even
nicht mehr	no longer
nichts	nothing
nie	never
niemals	never
niemand	nobody
nirgendwo	nowhere
noch nicht	not yet
überhaupt nicht	not at all

Numbers (p.1)

null	zero
eins	one
zwei	two
drei	three
vier	four
fünf	five

---

sechs	six
sieben	seven
acht	eight
neun	nine
zehn	ten
elf	eleven
zwölf	twelve
dreizehn	thirteen
vierzehn	fourteen
fünfzehn	fifteen
sechzehn	sixteen
siebzehn	seventeen
achtzehn	eighteen
neunzehn	nineteen
zwanzig	twenty
einundzwanzig	twenty-one
zweiundzwanzig	twenty-two
dreiundzwanzig	twenty-three
dreißig	thirty
vierzig	forty
fünfzig	fifty
sechzig	sixty
siebzig	seventy
achtzig	eighty
neunzig	ninety
hundert	hundred
tausend	thousand
zweitausend	two thousand
eine Million	one million
zweitausendfünf	two thousand and five
das erste	first
das zweite	second
das dritte	third
das vierte	fourth
das fünfte	fifth
das sechste	sixth
das siebte	seventh
das achte	eighth
das neunte	ninth
das zehnte	tenth
das zwanzigste	twentieth
das einundzwanzigste	twenty-first
das siebzigste	seventieth
das hundertste	hundredth
Dutzend n (-e)	dozen
einige	some / a few
genug	enough
mehrere	several
eine Menge	a lot of / lots of
Nummer f (-n)	number
Paar n (-e)	pair
viele	many
Zahl f (-en)	number / figure / digit

Times and Dates (p.2-3)

Montag	*Monday*
Dienstag	*Tuesday*
Mittwoch	*Wednesday*
Donnerstag	*Thursday*
Freitag	*Friday*
Samstag	*Saturday*
Sonntag	*Sunday*
Januar	*January*
Februar	*February*
März	*March*
April	*April*
Mai	*May*
Juni	*June*
Juli	*July*
August	*August*
September	*September*
Oktober	*October*
November	*November*
Dezember	*December*
Jahreszeit f (-en)	*season*
Frühling m (-e)	*spring*
Sommer m (-)	*summer*
Herbst m (-e)	*autumn*
Winter m (-)	*winter*
ab und zu	*now and again*
Abend m (-e)	*evening*
abends	*in the evenings*
alle zwei Wochen	*every two weeks*
Anfang m (-¨e)	*beginning / start*
Augenblick m (-e)	*moment / instant*
bald	*soon*
Datum n (Daten)	*date*
dauern	*to last*
ehemalig	*former*
einmal	*once*
endlich	*finally*
erst	*at first / only*
fast	*almost / nearly*
früh	*early*
Gegenwart f	*present (time, tense)*
genau	*exactly*
gerade	*just*
gestern	*yesterday*
gewöhnlich	*usually / normally*
gleich	*in a minute / immediately*
halb	*half past*
heute	*today*
heute Morgen	*this morning*
heute Nacht	*tonight*
heutzutage	*nowadays / these days*
immer	*always*
immer wieder	*again and again*
inzwischen	*in the meantime*
Jahr n (-e)	*year*
Jahrhundert n (-e)	*century*
jetzt	*now*
kürzlich	*recently / lately*
langsam	*slow(ly)*

Mal n (-e)	*time*
manchmal	*sometimes*
Mittag m (-e)	*midday*
Mitternacht f	*midnight*
Monat m (-e)	*month*
montags	*on Mondays*
morgen	*tomorrow*
morgen früh	*tomorrow morning*
morgens	*in the morning*
nachgehen	*to be slow*
nachher	*afterwards*
Nachmittag m (-e)	*afternoon*
Nacht f (-¨e)	*night*
neulich	*recently*
noch einmal	*once again*
normalerweise	*normally / usually*
oft	*often*
plötzlich	*suddenly*
pünktlich	*punctual / on time*
regelmäßig	*regularly*
schnell	*quick(ly)*
schon	*already*
seit	*since / for (time)*
selten	*rarely / seldom*
sofort	*immediately*
spät	*late*
Stunde f (-n)	*hour (length)*
Tag m (-e)	*day*
jeden Tag	*every day*
täglich	*daily*
übermorgen	*the day after tomorrow*
Uhr f (-en)	*clock / watch / o'clock*
Vergangenheit f	*past (time, tense)*
Viertel nach	*quarter past*
Viertel vor	*quarter to*
im Voraus	*in advance*
vorgestern	*the day before yesterday*
Vormittag m (-e)	*morning*
wieder	*again*
Woche f (-n)	*week*
diese Woche	*this week*
letze Woche	*last week*
Wochenende n (-n)	*weekend*
am Wochenende	*at the weekend*
Zeit f (-en)	*time*
Zukunft f	*future (time, tense)*

Colours and Shapes

blau	*blue*
braun	*brown*
bunt	*colourful*
dunkel	*dark*
grau	*grey*
grün	*green*
hell	*bright / light*
Farbe f (-n)	*colour*
Kreis m (-e)	*circle*
lila	*purple*

rosa	*pink*
rot	*red / ginger*
rund	*round*
schwarz	*black*
viereckig	*square*
weiß	*white*

Weights and Measures

alle (-r, -s)	*all / all the*
alle sein	*to be all gone / to have run out of*
alles	*everything*
anderer / andere / anderes	*other / different*
beide	*both*
breit	*broad / wide*
Ding n (-e)	*thing*
Dose f (-n)	*can / tin*
ein bisschen	*a little*
ein paar	*a few / a couple*
einzeln	*single*
etwa	*about / roughly*
Flasche f (-n)	*bottle*
ganz	*whole / complete / quite*
gewaltig	*enormously*
Gewicht n (-e)	*weight*
Größe f (-n)	*size*
irgend...	*some...*
Karton m (-s)	*cardboard box*
Kasten m (-¨)	*box / case / crate*
kaum	*hardly*
leer	*empty*
leicht	*light*
Maß n (-e)	*measure*
messen	*to measure*
mindestens	*at least*
mittelgroß	*medium-sized*
noch	*still*
Packung f (-en)	*packet / pack*
Paket n (-e)	*parcel*
Pfund n (-)	*pound*
pro	*per*
Schachtel f (-n)	*box / packet*
Scheibe f (-n)	*slice*
schwer	*heavy*
Stück n (-e)	*piece*
Tüte f (-n)	*bag*
ungefähr	*about*
voll	*full*
wenig	*little / not much*
wiegen	*to weigh*

Materials

Baumwolle f	cotton
bestehen aus	to consist of / to be made of
Eisen n	iron
Holz n	wood
Leder n	leather
Pappe f	cardboard
Seide f	silk
Stoff m (-e)	material
Wolle f	wool

Access

auf sein	to be open
aufmachen	to open
Ausfahrt f (-en)	exit (motorway)
Ausgang m (-̈e)	exit (building)
besetzt	occupied / engaged
Einfahrt f (-en)	entry / entrance
Eingang m (-̈e)	entrance (building)
Eintritt m (-e)	admission
frei	free
geschlossen	closed
offen	open
öffnen	to open
schließen	to close
verboten	forbidden
zu sein	to be closed
zumachen	to close

Questions (p.4-5)

Wann?	When?
Warum?	Why?
Was für...?	What sort / type of...?
Was?	What?
Welcher/e/s	Which?
Wer / Wen / Wem?	Who / Whom?
Wie lang(e)?	How long?
Wie viel(e)?	How much / many?
Wie?	How?
Wieso?	Why? / How come...?
Wo?	Where?
Woher?	Where from?
Wohin?	Where to?
Womit?	What with?
Um wie viel Uhr?	At what time? / When?
Wie viel Uhr ist es?	What's the time?
Wie spät ist es?	What's the time?

Being Polite (p.6-7)

Alles Gute!	All the best!
Auf Wiederhören!	Goodbye (on the phone)
Auf Wiedersehen!	Goodbye
Bis bald!	See you later
bitte	please
bitte schön	you're welcome
danke (schön)	thank you
Darf ich?	May I?

Darf ich Petra vorstellen?	May I introduce Petra?
Entschuldigung!	Excuse me
Es freut mich, dich kennen zu lernen	Pleased to meet you (inf.)
Es freut mich, Sie kennen zu lernen	Pleased to meet you (frml.)
Es tut mir Leid	I'm sorry
Gern geschehen!	Don't mention it
Grüß dich!	Hello (inf.)
Guten Abend!	Good evening
Guten Morgen!	Good morning
Guten Tag!	Good day
Herzlich willkommen!	Welcome!
Herzlichen Glückwunsch!	Congratulations!
Ich hätte gern...	I would like...
Ich würde gern...	I would like to...
Mir geht's gut	I'm well
nichts zu danken	it was nothing
Prost!	Cheers!
Setzen Sie sich!	Please sit down! (frml.)
Tschüss!	Bye (inf.)
Wie geht's?	How are you?
Wie geht es dir?	How are you? (inf.)
Wie geht es euch?	How are you? (inf. plu.)
Wie geht es Ihnen?	How are you? (frml.)
Viel Glück!	Good luck!

Opinions (p.8-10)

Ahnung f (-en)	idea / suspicion
im Allgemeinen	generally
amüsant	amusing / funny
angenehm	pleasant / agreeable
Angst haben	to be afraid / scared
ängstlich	anxious / apprehensive
anstrengend	strenuous
ausgezeichnet	excellent
bequem	comfortable
bestimmt	definitely / certainly
billig	cheap
blöd	stupid
Blödsinn m	nonsense / rubbish
böse	naughty / evil / angry
dafür sein	to be in favour of something
dagegen sein	to be opposed to something
das ist mir egal	it doesn't matter / it's all the same to me
das stimmt (nicht)	that's (not) right
denken	to think
Denkst du das auch?	Do you agree?

deprimiert	depressed
die Nase voll haben	to be fed up with something
doof	stupid
eindrucksvoll	impressive
entsetzlich	terrible
entspannend	relaxing
es gefällt mir	I like it
es geht	it's OK
es ist mir egal	I don't mind
es kommt darauf an, ob...	it depends whether...
es satt haben	to be fed up with something
fabelhaft	fabulous
fantastisch	fantastic
freundlich	friendly
froh	happy / glad
furchtbar	terrible
gemütlich	cosy / comfortable
genießen	to enjoy
glauben	to believe
hassen	to hate
herrlich	marvellous
hervorragend	excellent
interessant	interesting
keine Ahnung haben	to have no idea
klasse	brilliant / great
kompliziert	complicated
sich langweilen	to be bored
langweilig	boring
leicht	easy
lieb	kind / lovely / dear
lieben	to love
etwas lieber machen	to prefer to do something
lustig	amusing / funny
meinen	to think
Meiner Meinung nach...	In my opinion...
Meinung f (-en)	opinion
mies	rotten / lousy
mögen	to like
möglich	possible
mühelos	effortless
mühsam	arduous / laborious
Nachteil m (-e)	disadvantage
nett	nice (person)
nützlich	useful
nutzlos	useless
prima	great
sauer sein	to be cross / annoyed
schade	it's a shame / pity
schlecht	bad
schlimm	bad / terrible
schön	lovely
schrecklich	awful
schwierig	difficult
sensibel	sensitive

sich für etwas interessieren	*to be interested in something*
sicher	*sure / safe*
sogar	*even*
spannend	*exciting*
Spitze!	*Great!*
sympathisch	*nice (person)*
teuer	*expensive*
toll	*great*
typisch	*typical(ly)*
überrascht	*surprised*
unglaublich	*unbelievable*
unmöglich	*impossible*
unsicher	*unsure*
vielleicht	*perhaps*
völlig	*completely*
Vorteil m (-e)	*advantage*
vorziehen	*to prefer*
wahrscheinlich	*probably*
Was denkst du über...?	*What do you think of...?*
Was hältst du von...?	*What do you think of...?*

Was meinst du?	*What do you think?*
wichtig	*important*
Wie findest du...?	*How do you find...?*
wirklich	*real(ly)*
wunderbar	*wonderful*
wunderschön	*beautiful*
sich wünschen	*to wish*
zufrieden	*happy / content*
zustimmen	*to agree*

Correctness

falsch	*false / wrong / incorrect*
Fehler m (-)	*mistake / error*
Recht haben	*to be right*
richtig	*right / correct*
Unrecht haben	*to be wrong*
verbessern	*to correct / to improve*
Verbesserung f (-en)	*correction / improvement*

Abbreviations

AG (Arbeitsgruppe / Arbeitsgemeinschaft)	*work group (extra-curricular / school)*
DB (Deutsche Bahn)	*German Railways*
d.h. (das heißt)	*i.e. (that is)*
Dr (Doktor)	*doctor*
gem. (gemischt)	*mixed*
ICE (Inter-City-Express) m	*fast long-distance train*
inkl. (inklusive)	*included*
LKW (Lastkraftwagen) m (-)	*HGV / lorry*
PLZ (Postleitzahl) f	*postcode*
usw. (und so weiter)	*etc. / and so on*
z.B. (zum Beispiel)	*e.g. (for example)*

Section Two — Me, My Family and Friends

You and Your Family (p.16-17)

Alleinerziehende m/f (-n)	*single parent*
Alter n (-)	*age*
aufpassen auf	*to look after*
Bruder m (-¨)	*brother*
Buchstabe m (-n)	*letter of the alphabet*
buchstabieren	*to spell*
Cousin/e m/f (-s/-n)	*cousin*
Einzelkind n (-er)	*only child*
Eltern	*parents*
Enkel/in m/f (-/-nen)	*grandson / granddaughter*
Erwachsene m/f (-n)	*adult / grown-up*
Familienmitglied n (-er)	*family member*
Familienname m (-n)	*last name*
Freund/in m/f (-e/-nen)	*boy/girlfriend or male / female friend*
geboren (am)	*born (on)*
Geburtsdatum n (Geburtsdaten)	*date of birth*
Geburtsort m (-e)	*place of birth*
Geburtstag m (-e)	*birthday*
Geschlecht n (-er)	*sex / gender*
Geschwister (-)	*siblings*
Großeltern	*grandparents*
Großmutter f (-¨)	*grandmother*
Großvater m (-¨)	*grandfather*
Halb...	*half...*

heißen	*to be called*
Jugendliche m/f (-n)	*youth*
Junge m (-n)	*boy*
Mädchen n (-)	*girl*
Mutter f (-¨)	*mother*
Neffe m (-n)	*nephew*
nennen	*to name / call*
Nichte f (-n)	*niece*
Onkel m (-)	*uncle*
Schwester f (-n)	*sister*
Schwieger...	*...in-law*
Sohn m (-¨e)	*son*
Spielzeug n (-e)	*toy*
Spitzname m (-n)	*nickname*
Stief...	*step...*
Tante f (-n)	*aunt*
Tochter f (-¨)	*daughter*
Vater m (-¨)	*father*
Verwandte m/f (-n)	*relative*
Vorname m (-n)	*first name*
sich vorstellen	*to introduce oneself*
wohnen	*to live*
Zwillinge	*twins*

Describing People (p.18-19)

Angeber/in m/f (-/-nen)	*show-off / poser*
Augen	*eyes*
aussehen	*to look like*
Ausweis m (-e)	*identity card*
Bart m (-¨e)	*beard*
berühmt	*famous*
blond	*blonde*

Brille f (-n)	*glasses*
dick	*fat*
dünn	*thin*
egoistisch	*selfish*
ehrlich	*honest*
eifersüchtig	*jealous*
eingebildet	*conceited*
ernst	*serious*
faul	*lazy*
fleißig	*hard-working*
frech	*cheeky*
geduldig	*patient*
gemein	*mean*
glatt	*straight (hair)*
glücklich	*happy*
groß	*big / tall*
großzügig	*generous*
gut gelaunt	*good-tempered*
gute Laune haben	*to be in a good mood*
Haare (pl.)	*hair*
hässlich	*ugly*
hilfsbereit	*helpful*
höflich	*polite*
hübsch	*pretty*
humorlos	*humourless*
humorvoll	*humorous / witty*
jung	*young*
klein	*small / short*
komisch	*strange / comical*
kurz	*short*
lang	*long*
lästig	*annoying*

lebhaft	*lively*	Braut f (-¨e)	*bride*	küssen	*to kiss*
lockig	*curly*	Bräutigam m (-e)	*groom*	lachen	*to laugh*
Mensch m (-en)	*person*	Brieffreund/in m/f	*penfriend*	ledig	*single*
Ohr n (-en)	*ear*	(-e/-nen)		leiden	*to suffer*
ordentlich	*neat*	Ehe f (-n)	*marriage*	Leute f	*people*
Persönlichkeit f	*personality*	Elternschaft f	*parenting*	minderjährig	*minor / underage*
(-en)		sich entschuldigen	*to apologise*	miteinander	*with one another*
ruhig	*quiet*	entspannt	*relaxed*	nerven	*to get on someone's*
Schnurrbart m (-¨e)	*moustache*	erlauben	*to allow*		*nerves*
schüchtern	*shy*	Freundschaft f (-en)	*friendship*	Partnerschaft f (-en)	*partnership*
selbstbewusst	*confident*	sich fühlen	*to feel*	sich schämen	*to feel ashamed*
selbstständig	*independent*	Gefühl n (-e)	*feeling*	sich scheiden	*to get divorced*
Sinn für Humor m	*sense of humour*	geschieden	*divorced*	lassen	
Sommersprossen	*freckles*	getrennt	*separated*	Scheidung f (-en)	*divorce*
streng	*strict*	gleichgeschlechtlich	*same-sex (marriage*	sorgen für	*to care for*
Tätowierung f (-en)	*tattoo*		*/ partnership)*	Streit m (-e)	*argument*
traurig	*sad*	Grund m (-¨e)	*reason*	sich streiten mit	*to argue with*
unternehmungs-	*adventurous / likes*	heiraten	*to marry*	Traum m (-¨e)	*dream*
lustig	*doing lots of things*	Hochzeit f (-en)	*marriage*	Trauung f (-en)	*wedding ceremony*
verrückt	*crazy*	homosexuell	*homosexual*	sich trennen	*to separate*
witzig	*funny*	ich kann... gut	*I like... (very much)*	treu	*faithful*
Zahn m (-¨e)	*tooth*	leiden		unterstützen	*to support*
zuverlässig	*reliable*	ich kann... nicht	*I can't stand / I don't*	vergeben	*to forgive*
		leiden	*like...*	Verhältnis n (-se)	*relationship*
Relationships (p.20-21)		Junggeselle m (-n)	*bachelor*	in einem Verhältnis	*to be in a*
allein	*alone*	kennen	*to know (a person)*	sein	*relationship*
alleinstehend	*single*	kennen lernen	*to get to know*	verheiratet	*married*
ärgerlich	*annoying*	sich kümmern um	*to look after*	sich verloben	*to get engaged*
sich ärgern über	*to be annoyed about*			Verlobte m/f (-n)	*fiancé(e)*
auf die Nerven	*to get on one's*			sich verstehen mit	*to get on with*
gehen	*nerves*			verzeihen	*to forgive*
auskommen mit	*to get on with*			weinen	*to cry*
Bekannte m/f	*acquaintance /*			Witz m (-e)	*joke*
(-n/-nen)	*friend*			wohl	*good / comfortable*
Besuch m (-e)	*visit*			zivile Partnerschaft	*civil partnership*
besuchen	*to visit (person)*			f (-en)	
Beziehung f (-en)	*relationship*			zurechtkommen mit	*to cope with*
bitten	*to ask for / beg*			zusammen	*together*

Section Three — Free-Time Activities

Music, Cinema and TV		beeindruckend	*impressive*	gruselig	*scary*
(p.27-29)		bewegend	*moving*	Handlung f (-en)	*plot*
Abenteuerfilm m	*adventure film*	Bildschirm m (-e)	*screen (TV)*	hören	*to listen to*
(-e)		Blaskapelle f (-n)	*brass band*	Horrorfilm m (-e)	*horror film*
abonnieren	*to subscribe to*	Blockflöte f (-n)	*recorder*	Instrument n (-e)	*instrument*
Actionfilm m (-e)	*action film*	Chor m (-¨e)	*choir*	Interesse haben an	*to be interested in*
sich amüsieren	*to have fun*	Dirigent/in m/f	*conductor*	Kino n (-s)	*cinema*
anschauen	*to watch*	(-en/-nen)		Klarinette f (-n)	*clarinet*
aufnehmen	*to record*	Dokumentarfilm m	*documentary*	klassische Musik f	*classical music*
aufregend	*exciting*	(-e)		Klavier n (-e)	*piano*
ausschalten	*to turn off (TV)*	Eintrittsgeld n	*admission fee*	Komödie f (-n)	*comedy*
Band f (-s)	*band*	Eintrittskarte f (-n)	*ticket*	Konzert n (-e)	*concert*
		essen	*to eat*	Krimi m (-s)	*crime film*
		faszinierend	*fascinating*	langweilig	*boring*
		fernsehen	*to watch television*	Leinwand f (-¨e)	*screen (in cinema)*
		Flachbildschirm m	*flat-screen TV*	Liebesfilm m (-e)	*romantic film*
		(-e)		Lied n (-er)	*song*
		Flimmerkiste f (-n)	*TV / box / telly*	Musiker/in m/f	*musician*
		Geige f (-n)	*violin*	(-/-nen)	
				Musikgeschmack m	*taste in music*

Vocabulary

Nachrichten (pl.)	*news*	Brot n (-e)	*bread*	Magermilch f	*skimmed milk*
Orchester n (-)	*orchestra*	Brötchen n (-)	*bread roll*	Meeresfrüchte (pl.)	*seafood*
Popmusik f	*pop music*	Butter f	*butter*	Mehl n	*flour*
Promi m/f (-s)	*celebrity*	Café n (-s)	*café*	Messer n (-)	*knife*
Querflöte f (-n)	*flute*	Durst haben	*to be thirsty*	Milch f	*milk*
Quizsendung f (-en)	*quiz show*	durstig	*thirsty*	Nachspeise f (-n)	*dessert*
Rapmusik f	*rap music*	Ei n (-er)	*egg*	Nachtisch m (-e)	*dessert*
Reality-Show f (-s)	*reality show*	Eisdiele f (-n)	*ice cream parlour*	Nudeln (pl.)	*pasta / noodles*
Rockmusik f	*rock music*	ekelhaft	*disgusting*	Nuss f (-̈e)	*nut*
sammeln	*to collect*	empfehlen	*to recommend*	Obst n	*fruit*
Sänger/in m/f (-/-nen)	*singer*	Ente f (-n)	*duck*	Öl n (-e)	*oil*
		Erbsen	*peas*	Pfeffer m (-)	*pepper (spice)*
Schauspieler/in m/f (-/-nen)	*actor / actress*	Erdbeere f (-n)	*strawberry*	Pfirsich m (-e)	*peach*
		Essig m (-e)	*vinegar*	Pflaume f (-n)	*plum*
Schlagzeug n	*percussion / drums*	fettig	*fatty*	Pilz m (-e)	*mushroom*
Science-Fiction-Film m (-e)	*sci-fi film*	Fisch m (-e)	*fish*	Pommes frites	*chips*
		Fleisch n	*meat*	Praline f (-n)	*chocolate (in a box)*
Seifenoper f (-n)	*soap opera*	Forelle f (-n)	*trout*	probieren	*to try / taste*
senden	*to broadcast*	fremd	*foreign*	Pute f (-n)	*turkey*
Sender m (-)	*TV channel*	Fruchtsaft m (-̈e)	*fruit juice*	Rechnung f (-en)	*bill*
Sendung f (-en)	*TV programme*	Gabel f (-n)	*fork*	Reis m	*rice*
Serie f (-n)	*series*	Gasthaus n (-̈er)	*pub*	reservieren	*to book*
singen	*to sing*	Gemüse n	*vegetables*	Restaurant n (-s)	*restaurant*
Sitzplatz m (-̈e)	*seat*	geräuchert	*smoked*	riechen	*to smell*
Spaß machen	*to be fun*	Gericht n (-e)	*dish (food)*	Rindfleisch n	*beef*
Stimme f (-n)	*voice*	Geschmack m (-̈e)	*taste*	roh	*raw*
tcilnehmen an	*to take part in*	Gurke f (-n)	*cucumber*	Rührei n (-er)	*scrambled egg*
Trailer m (-)	*trailer*	Haferflocken	*porridge oats*	Sahne f	*cream*
Trickeffekte	*special effects*	Hähnchen n (-)	*chicken*	salzig	*salty*
Trompete f (-n)	*trumpet*	Halbfettmilch f	*semi-skimmed milk*	satt sein	*to be full up*
übertragen	*to stream*	Hauptgericht n (-e)	*main course*	scharf	*hot / spicy*
umschalten	*to switch channels*	hausgemacht	*home-made*	Schaschlik n (-s)	*kebab*
unterhaltsam	*entertaining*	Herr Ober!	*Waiter!*	Schinken m (-)	*ham*
Unterhaltung f (-en)	*entertainment*	Himbeere f (-n)	*raspberry*	schmackhaft	*tasty*
Untertitel m (-)	*subtitle*	Honig m	*honey*	schmecken	*to taste*
Vergnügen n	*fun / enjoyment*	Hunger haben	*to be hungry*	Schnellimbiss m (-e)	*snack bar*
Volksmusik f	*folk music*	Imbiss m (-e)	*snack*	(Wiener) Schnitzel n (-)	*veal / pork cutlet*
Vorstellung f (-en)	*showing / performance*	Imbissbude f (-n)	*snack bar / takeaway*		
				Schweinefleisch n	*pork*
Werbung f	*advert(s)*	Kakao m	*cocoa*	Selbstbedienung f (-en)	*self-service*
Zeichentrickfilm m (-e)	*cartoon*	Kalbfleisch n	*veal*		
		Kännchen n (-)	*pot of tea / coffee*	Senf m	*mustard*
Zeitschrift f (-en)	*magazine*	Karotte f (-n)	*carrot*	Speise f (-n)	*dish*
Zeitung f (-en)	*newspaper*	Karte f (-n)	*menu*	Speisekarte f (-n)	*menu*
Zuschauer/in m/f (-/-nen)	*spectator / member of the audience*	Kartoffel f (-n)	*potato*	Speisesaal m (Speisesäle)	*dining hall*
		Käse m	*cheese*		
		Keks m (-e)	*biscuit*	Spiegelei n (-er)	*fried egg*
Food and Eating Out (p.30-31)		Kellner/in m/f (-/-nen)	*waiter / waitress*	Spinat m	*spinach*
Ananas f (-se)	*pineapple*			Sprudelwasser n	*fizzy mineral water*
Apfel m (-̈)	*apple*	Kneipe f (-n)	*pub*	Steak n (-s)	*steak*
Apfelsine f (-n)	*orange*	Knoblauch m	*garlic*	Suppe f (-n)	*soup*
Aprikose f (-n)	*apricot*	köstlich	*delicious*	süß	*sweet*
Banane f (-n)	*banana*	Kotelett n (-s)	*pork chop*	Tagesgericht n (-e)	*dish of the day*
bedienen	*to serve*	Lachs m (-e)	*salmon*	Tagesmenü n (-s)	*menu of the day*
Bedienung inbegriffen	*service included*	Lammfleisch n	*lamb*	Teelöffel m (-)	*teaspoon*
		lecker	*tasty*	Thunfisch m (-e)	*tuna*
sich beschweren	*to complain*	Löffel m (-)	*spoon*	Tomate f (-n)	*tomato*
bestellen	*to order*			Torte f (-n)	*gateau*
bezahlen	*to pay*			Trinkgeld n (-er)	*tip*
Bier n (-e)	*beer*			Truthahn m (-̈e)	*turkey*
Birne f (-n)	*pear*			Vegetarier/in m/f (-/-nen)	*vegetarian*
Blumenkohl m (-e)	*cauliflower*				
Bratwurst f (-̈e)	*fried sausage*				

Vollmilch f	full-fat milk
vorschlagen	to suggest
Vorspeise f (-n)	starter
Weintraube f (-n)	grape
Wurst f (-¨e)	sausage
würzig	spicy
Zitrone f (-n)	lemon
Zucker m	sugar
Zwiebel f (-n)	onion

Sport (p.32-33)

angeln	to fish
Badeanzug m (-¨e)	swimsuit
Badehose f (-n)	swimming trunks
Basketball m	basketball
begeistert	excited
Bergsteigen n	mountain climbing
Eislaufen n	ice-skating
Fahrrad fahren	to cycle
fechten	to fence
Federball m	badminton
Fitnessstudio n (-s)	gym
Freibad n (-¨er)	outdoor swimming pool
Fußball m	football
gewinnen	to win
Hallenbad n (-¨er)	indoor swimming pool
Hockey n	hockey

joggen	to jog
Kegeln n	bowling (nine-pin)
klettern	to climb
Korbball m	netball
Kricket n	cricket
laufen	to run
Leichtathletik f	athletics
Lust haben, etwas zu tun	to feel like doing something
Mannschaft f (-en)	team
Match n (-es)	match
Mitglied n (-er)	member
nervös	nervous
Olympische Spiele	Olympic Games
Profi m (-s)	professional sportsperson
Rennen n (-)	race
ringen	to wrestle
rodeln	to go sledging
rudern	to row
Rollschuh laufen	to go roller skating
Rugby n	rugby
Schach n	chess
schießen	to shoot
Schlittschuh laufen	ice-skating
Schwimmbad n (-¨er)	swimming pool
schwimmen	to swim
Segelboot n (-e)	sailing boat
segeln	to sail

Ski fahren	to ski
spazieren gehen	to go for a walk
spielen	to play
Sportart f (-en)	type of sport
Sportplatz m (-¨e)	sports field
Sport treiben	to do sport
Sportzentrum n (Sportzentren)	sports centre
springen	to jump
Stadion n (Stadien)	stadium
tauchen	to dive
Tennis n	tennis
Tor n (-e)	goal
ein Tor schießen	to score a goal
trainieren	to train
Training n	training
Trainingsschuh m (-e)	sport shoe / trainer
Turnen n	gymnastics
Verein m (-e)	club
verlieren	to lose
wandern	to hike
werfen	to throw
Wettbewerb m (-e)	competition

Section Four — Technology in Everyday Life

Technology (p.39-42)

Anrufbeantworter m (-e)	answering machine
anrufen	to call
Anwendungen	applications
App f (-s)	app
(aus)drucken	to print (out)
benutzen	to use
Betriebssystem n (-e)	operating system
Bindestrich m (-e)	hyphen
bloggen	to blog
Blogger/in m/f (-/-nen)	blogger
chatten	to chat online
Computer m (-)	computer
Cyber-Mobbing n	cyber-bullying
Daten (pl.)	data
Drucker m (-)	printer
Einstellung f (-en)	setting
(E-)Mail f (-s)	email
E-Mail-Adresse f (-n)	email address
empfangen	to receive
entwickeln	to develop
erforschen	to research
Forum n (Foren)	forum
Foto n (-s)	photo

funktionieren	to work / to function
Gefahr f (-en)	danger
gefährlich	dangerous
gehören zu	to belong to
Gruppe f (-n)	group
Handy n (-s)	mobile phone
herausfinden	to find out
herunterladen	to download
hochladen	to upload
Internet n	internet
Kamera f (-s)	camera
Klingelton m (-¨e)	ringtone
in Kontakt bleiben	to stay in contact
Konto n (-s)	account
Laptop m (-s)	laptop
löschen	to delete
Medien (pl.)	media
missbrauchen	to abuse / misuse
Nachricht f (-en)	message
Netzwerk n (-e)	network
online	online
Passwort n (-¨er)	password
peinlich	embarrassing
Postfach n (-¨er)	mailbox
praktisch	practical
Privatleben n (-)	private life
Punkt m (-e)	full stop
Risiko n (Risiken)	risk

schicken	to send
Schrägstrich m (-e)	forward slash
schützen	to protect
Sicherheit f	security
simsen	to text
Smartphone n (-s)	smartphone
soziale Medien (pl.)	social media
soziales Netzwerk n (soziale Netzwerke)	social network
speichern	to save (data)
Startseite f (-n)	homepage
streamen	to stream
Suchmaschine f (-n)	search engine
surfen	to surf
Tablet-PC m (-s)	tablet
Technologie f (-n)	technology
teilen	to share
Unterstrich m (-e)	underscore
Veranstaltung f (-en)	event
Video n (-s)	video
Videospiel n (-e)	video game
Website f (-s)	website
Webseite f (-n)	web page
WLAN n	Wi-Fi
Zeit verbringen	to spend time

Section Five — Customs and Festivals

Customs and Festivals (p.48-50)

Adventskranz m (-¨e)	advent wreath
anzünden	to light
Aprilscherz m (-e)	April fool's trick
Aschermittwoch m	Ash Wednesday
Auferstehung f (-en)	resurrection
auspacken	to unwrap
bekommen	to receive
Chanukka	Hanukkah
Christen	Christians
christlich	Christian
danken	to thank
der erste Weihnachtstag	24th December
der zweite Weihnachtstag	25th December
einladen	to invite
Einladung f (-en)	invitation
Fasching m	carnival
Feier f (-n)	celebration
feiern	to celebrate
Feiertag m (-e)	public holiday
Fest n (-e)	festival / celebration
Festessen n (-)	festive meal
Feuerwerk n (-e)	fireworks display
sich freuen auf	to look forward to
sich freuen über	to be pleased about something
Frohe Weihnachten!	Merry Christmas!
Gans f (-¨e)	goose
Gast m (-¨e)	guest
Gastfreundschaft f	hospitality
Gastgeber/in m/f (-/-nen)	host
Geschenk n (-e)	present / gift
Heiliger Abend	Christmas Eve
Heilige Drei Könige	Epiphany
Hindu m/f (-s)	Hindu
hinduistisch	Hindu
islamisch	Muslim
Jesu Tod	Christ's death
Jude/Jüdin m/f (-n/-nen)	Jew
jüdisch	Jewish
Karfreitag m	Good Friday
Karneval m	carnival
Kerze f (-n)	candle
Kirche f (-n)	church
kirchlich	religious
Lebkuchen m	gingerbread
Lichterfest n (-e)	festival of lights
Maifeiertag m (-e)	May Day
Moslem/in m/f (-s/-nen)	Muslim
Muttertag m (-e)	Mother's Day
Neujahrstag m (-e)	New Year's Day
Osterei n (-er)	Easter egg
Osterhase m	Easter bunny
Ostern n	Easter
Ostersonntag m	Easter Sunday
Pfingsten n	Whitsuntide
religiös	religious
Sankt Nikolaus Tag	St Nicholas' Day
schenken	to give (as a present)
schmücken	to decorate
Sikh m (-s)	Sikh
Silvester	New Year's Eve
Tag der Arbeit	May Day
Tag der Deutschen Einheit	Day of German Unity
Umzug m (-¨e)	procession
Valentinstag m (-e)	St Valentine's Day
sich verkleiden	to dress up
verstecken	to hide
Weihnachten n	Christmas
Weihnachtsbaum m (-¨e)	Christmas tree
Weihnachtskarte f (-n)	Christmas card
Weihnachtslieder	Christmas carols
Weihnachtsmarkt m (-¨e)	Christmas market

Section Six — Where You Live

The Home (p.56)

Abstellraum m (-¨e)	storeroom
alt	old
Autobahn f (-en)	motorway
Backofen m (-¨)	oven
Badewanne f (-n)	bathtub
Badezimmer n (-)	bathroom
Bauernhaus n (-¨er)	farm house
Baum m (-¨e)	tree
Besteck n (-e)	(set of) cutlery
Bett n (-en)	bed
Bild n (-er)	picture
Blume f (-n)	flower
Dach n (-¨er)	roof
Dachboden m (-¨)	attic / loft
Diele f (-n)	hall
Doppelbett n (-en)	double bed
Doppelhaus n (-¨er)	semi-detached house
Einfamilienhaus n (-¨er)	detached house
im Erdgeschoss	on the ground floor
Esszimmer n (-)	dining room
Etage f (-n)	floor / storey
Etagenbett n (-en)	bunk bed
Flur m (-e)	corridor / hall
Fußboden m (-¨)	floor
Garten m (-¨)	garden
Gerät n (-e)	appliance
geräumig	spacious
Haus n (-¨er)	house
Haushalt m (-e)	household
Hecke f (-n)	hedge
Heizung f	heating
Hochhaus n (-¨er)	high-rise block of flats
Kleiderschrank m (-¨e)	wardrobe
Kochfeld n (-er)	hob
Kommode f (-n)	chest of drawers
Kopfkissen n (-)	pillow
Küche f (-n)	kitchen
Kühlschrank m (-¨e)	fridge
Licht n (-er)	light
Mauer f (-n)	wall (outside)
Mehrfamilienhaus n (-¨er)	house for several families
Miete f (-n)	rent
Mikrowelle f (-n)	microwave
Möbel (pl.)	furniture
Möbelstück n (-e)	piece of furniture
modern	modern
nach oben	upstairs
nach unten	downstairs
Nachbar/in m/f (-n/-nen)	neighbour
Nachttisch m (-e)	bedside table
neu	new
Rasen m (-)	lawn
Regal n (-e)	shelf
Reihenhaus n (-¨er)	terraced house
riesig	huge
Sackgasse f (-n)	cul-de-sac
Schlafzimmer n (-)	bedroom
Schlüssel m (-)	key
Schrank m (-¨e)	cupboard
Schublade f (-n)	drawer
Spiegel m (-)	mirror
am Stadtrand	on the outskirts
im Stadtzentrum	in the town centre
Stuhl m (-¨e)	chair
Tasse f (-n)	cup
Teppich m (-e)	carpet
Tiefkühlschrank m (-¨e)	freezer

Treppe f (-n)	stairs
umziehen	to move house
Vorhänge	curtains
Wand f (-¨e)	wall (inside)
Wintergarten m (-¨)	conservatory
Wohnblock m (-s)	block of flats
Wohnung f (-en)	flat
Wohnzimmer n (-)	living room
Zimmer n (-)	room

What You Do at Home (p.57)

Abendessen n	evening meal
abwaschen	to wash up
sich anziehen	to get dressed
aufräumen	to tidy up
aufstehen	to get up
aufwachen	to wake up
den Tisch decken	to lay the table
sich duschen	to have a shower
frühstücken	to have breakfast
Hausaufgaben (pl.)	homework
kochen	to cook
sich kümmern um	to look after
mähen	to mow
Mahlzeit f (-en)	meal / mealtime
putzen	to clean
sauber machen	to clean
sich rasieren	to shave
sich schminken	to put on make-up
Staub saugen	to vacuum
Staub wischen	to dust
Tagesablauf m	daily routine
verlassen	to leave (the house)
vorbereiten	to prepare
sich waschen	to have a wash

Where You Live (p.58)

am Meer	by the sea
an der Küste	on the coast
auf dem Land	in the countryside
Bäckerei f (-en)	bakery
Bahnhof m (-¨e)	train station
Bauernhof m (-¨e)	farm
bergig	mountainous
Bibliothek f (-en)	library
Brücke f (-n)	bridge
Bücherei f (-en)	library
Buchhandlung f (-en)	bookshop
Busbahnhof m (-¨e)	bus station
Denkmal n (-e)	monument
Dom m (-e)	cathedral
Dorf n (-¨er)	village
Drogerie f (-n)	chemist's
Einwohner/in m/f (-/-nen)	inhabitant
Elektrogeschäft n (-e)	shop for electrical goods
Fabrik f (-en)	factory
Feld n (-er)	field
flach	flat
Fleischerei f (-en)	butcher's

Fluss m (-¨e)	river
Friseur m (-e)	hairdresser's
Fußgängerzone f (-n)	pedestrian zone
Gebäude n (-)	building
Gegend f (-en)	region
Großstadt f (-¨e)	city
Grünanlage f (-n)	green space
Hafen m (-¨)	harbour
Hauptbahnhof m (-¨e)	main train station
historisch	historic
Hügel m (-)	hill
im Norden	in the north
in den Bergen	in the mountains
in der Nähe von	near to
Insel f (-n)	island
Juweliergeschäft n (-e)	jeweller's
Konditorei f (-en)	confectioner's
Kunstgalerie f (-n)	art gallery
Laden m (-¨)	shop
Landschaft f (-en)	landscape
lebendig	lively
Markt m (-¨e)	market
Metzgerei f (-en)	butcher's
Park m (-s)	park
Parkplatz m (-¨e)	parking place
Platz m (-¨e)	square
Post f (-en)	post office
Reinigung f (-en)	dry cleaner's
Spielplatz m (-¨e)	playground
Stadt f (-¨e)	town
Stadtviertel n (-)	district / part of town
tanken	to fill up with fuel
Tankstelle f (-n)	petrol station
Umgebung f (-en)	surrounding area
Vorort m (-e)	suburb
Wald m (-¨er)	wood / forest
Wohnort m (-e)	place of living
Wolkenkratzer m (-)	skyscraper

Shopping (p.59-61)

anbieten	to offer
Angebot n (-e)	offer
anprobieren	to try on
ausgeben	to spend (money)
Ausverkauf m (-¨e)	sale
ausverkauft	sold out
Bargeld n (-er)	cash
einkaufen gehen	to go shopping
Einkaufskorb m (-¨e)	shopping basket
Einkaufstasche f (-n)	shopping bag
Einkaufswagen m (-)	shopping trolley
Einkaufszentrum n (Einkaufszentren)	shopping centre
Euro-Schein m (-e)	euro note
Euro-Stück n (-e)	euro coin
Geld n	money
Geldschein m (-e)	note
Geldstück n (-e)	coin
Geschäft n (-e)	shop / business
Gramm n (-)	gram

gratis	free of charge
Größe f (-n)	size
günstig	good value
Hemd n (-en)	shirt
Hose f (-n)	trousers
Jeans f	jeans
kaputt	broken
mit Karte	by card
Kasse f (-n)	till
Kaufhaus n (-¨er)	department store
Kilo n (-)	kilogram
Klamotten	clothes
Kleid n (-er)	dress
Kleidergeschäft n (-e)	clothes shop
Kleingeld n	small change
kosten	to cost
kostenlos	free of charge
Kunde/Kundin m/f (-n/-nen)	customer
liefern	to deliver
Marke f (-n)	brand / make
Münze f (-n)	coin
Obst- und Gemüseladen m (-¨)	green grocer's
öffentliche Verkehrsmittel (pl.)	public transport
Pfund n	pound
pleite sein	to be skint
Preis m (-e)	price
preiswert	good value
Pullover m (-)	sweater
Quittung f (-en)	receipt
Rabatt m (-e)	discount
Rock m (-¨e)	skirt
Rolltreppe f (-n)	escalator
Schaufenster n (-)	shop window
Schlange stehen	to queue
Schuh m (-e)	shoe
Sonderangebot n (-e)	special offer
Sonst noch etwas?	Anything else?
Sportschuhe	trainers
stehen	to suit
Taschengeld n	pocket money
tragen	to wear
T-Shirt n (-s)	t-shirt
Warenhaus n (-¨er)	department store
Verkäufer/in m/f (-/-nen)	shop assistant
verschwenden	to waste
wechseln	to change (money)

Directions (p.62)

Ampel f (-n)	traffic light
auf der rechten Seite	on the right-hand side
außen	outside
außerhalb von	outside of
Bürgersteig m (-e)	pavement
draußen	outside / outdoors
drinnen	inside / indoors
(da) drüben	over there

Ecke f (-n)	corner	weg	away	nass	wet
entfernt	(far) away	weit	far	Nebel m (-)	fog
Fahrkarte f (-n)	ticket (e.g. bus)	Wo ist...?	Where is...?	nebelig	foggy
gegenüber	opposite	Zebrastreifen m (-)	zebra crossing	Niederschlag m (-̈e)	precipitation
geradeaus	straight on			Regen m (-)	rain
Haltestelle f (-n)	stop (bus / tram etc.)	**Weather (p.63)**		es regnet	it's raining
		bedeckt	overcast	Schatten m (-)	shadow
hin und zurück	return (ticket)	Blitz m	lightning	schattig	shady
Kreuzung f (-en)	crossroads	Donner m	thunder	Schauer m (-)	shower
liegen	to be situated	es donnert	it's thundering	scheinen	to shine
(nach) links	(to the) left	feucht	damp	es schneit	it's snowing
Meile f (-n)	mile	frieren	to freeze	Sturm m (-̈e)	storm
mitten in	in the middle of	frisch	fresh	stürmisch	stormy
nah	near	Gewitter n (-)	thunderstorm	trocken	dry
neben	next to	Grad m (-e)	degree	Wetterbericht m (-e)	weather report
nehmen	to take	Hagel m	hail	Wettervorhersage f (-n)	weather forecast
(nach) rechts	(to the) right	es hagelt	it's hailing		
S-Bahn f	suburban (fast) railway	heftig	heavy / severe	Wolke f (-n)	cloud
		heiter	bright / fine	wolkig	cloudy
Straße f (-n)	street	Himmel m (-)	sky		
U-Bahn f	underground train	Klima n (-s)	climate		
überqueren	to cross (road)	kühl	cool		
		Mond m (-e)	moon		

Section Seven — Lifestyle

Health (p.69-70)

abnehmen	to lose weight	Gruppendruck m	peer pressure	Erkältung f (-en)	cold
abstinent	teetotal	magersüchtig	anorexic	Erste Hilfe f	First Aid
Ader f (-n)	vein	müde	tired	Fieber n (-)	fever
Alkohol m	alcohol	Nahrung f	food / nourishment	gebrochen	broken
Atem m	breath	rauchen	to smoke	Gehirn n (-e)	brain
Atembeschwerden	breathing difficulties	Raucherhusten m	smoker's cough	Hals m (-̈e)	neck / throat
atmen	to breathe	Rauschgift n (-e)	drug / narcotic	heilbar	curable
aufgeben	to give up	regelmäßig	regular	Herz n (-en)	heart
aufhören	to stop	schaden	to damage / harm	Heuschnupfen m	hay fever
ausgewogen	balanced	schädlich	harmful	Kopf m (-̈e)	head
betrunken	drunk	schlafen	to sleep	Kopfschmerzen (pl.)	headache
Bewegung f (-en)	exercise	Sucht f (-̈e)	addiction		
sich bewegen	to exercise	süchtig	addicted	krank	ill
bewusstlos	unconscious	Süßigkeiten	sweets	Krankenhaus n (-̈er)	hospital
Drogen	drugs	Überdosis f (Überdosen)	overdose		
Drogenhändler/in m/f (-/-nen)	drug dealer			Krankenwagen m (-)	ambulance
		übergewichtig	overweight	Krankheit f (-en)	illness
Drogensüchtige m/f (-n)	drug addict	vermeiden	to avoid	Krebs m	cancer
		Zigarette f (-n)	cigarette	Leber f (-n)	liver
sich entspannen	to relax	zunehmen	to put on weight	Magen m (-)	stomach
Entziehungskur f	rehab for drug addiction / alcoholism			Medikament n (-e)	medicine
		Illnesses (p.71)		mir ist übel	I feel ill / sick
		abhängig sein von	to be addicted to	ein Mittel gegen...	a medicine for...
		Aids n	AIDS	psychische Probleme	mental health problems
Ernährung f	food / nourishment / nutrition	allergisch gegen	allergic to		
		Antibiotika	antibiotics	Rücken m (-)	back
fettarm	low in fat	Apotheke f (-n)	pharmacy	Schmerz m (-en)	pain
fettleibig	obese	Arzt/Ärztin m/f (-̈e/-nen)	doctor	Spritze f (-n)	syringe
Fettleibigkeit f	obesity			sterben	to die
sich fit halten	to keep oneself fit	asthmatisch	asthmatic	Tablette f (-n)	tablet
in Form sein	to be in good shape	Bauch m (-̈e)	stomach	tot	dead
gestresst	stressed	Bauchschmerzen (pl.)	stomach ache	Unfall m (-̈e)	accident
gesund	healthy			verletzt sein	to be injured
Gesundheit f	health	Blut n	blood	Verletzung f (-en)	injury
Gesundheits- problem n (-e)	health problem	Demenz f	dementia	weh tun	to hurt
		sich erbrechen	to be sick	zuckerkrank	diabetic

Section Eight — Social and Global Issues

Environmental Problems (p.77-78)

Abfall m (-¨e)	rubbish / waste
Abfalleimer m (-)	rubbish bin
Abgase	exhaust fumes
Abholzung f	deforestation
alternative Energiequelle f (-n)	alternative source of energy
Altpapier n (-e)	waste paper
anbauen	to grow
aussterben	to die out
bedrohen	to threaten
bekämpfen	to fight / combat
beitragen zu	to contribute to
Benzin n	petrol
Bevölkerung f (-en)	population
biologisch	biological / organic
Biomüll m	organic waste
bleifrei	lead-free
brauchen	to need
Brennstoff m (-e)	fuel
chemisch	chemical(ly)
Dürre f (-n)	drought
Energiequelle f (-n)	energy source
entsorgen	to dispose of
Erdbeben n (-)	earthquake
Erderwärmung f	global warming
Erdrutsch m (-e)	landslide
erheblich	significant
erneuerbare Energie f	renewable energy
extreme Wetterbedingungen	extreme weather conditions
Fahrradweg m (-e)	cycle lane
Fahrzeug n (-e)	vehicle
FCKWs	CFCs
Folge f (-n)	consequence / effect
fossile Brennstoffe	fossil fuels
führen zu	to lead to
Gebrauch m	usage
Hochwasser n (-)	flood / flooding
Klimawandel m	climate change
Kohle f	coal
Kohlendioxid n	carbon dioxide
Kraftwerk n (-e)	power station
Kunststoff m (-e)	man-made material
Luft f (-¨e)	air
Luftverschmutzung f	air pollution
Müll m	rubbish / waste
Mülltonne f (-n)	dustbin
Naturkatastrophe f (-n)	natural disaster
Orkan m (-e)	hurricane
Ozonloch n (-¨er)	hole in the ozone layer
Ozonschicht f (-en)	ozone layer
Pfand n (-¨er)	deposit
produzieren	to produce
reinigen	to clean
sauber	clean
Sauerstoff m	oxygen
saure Regen m	acid rain
schmutzig	dirty
Solarzelle f (-n)	solar panel
Sonnenenergie f	solar energy
sparen	to save / conserve
Spraydose f (-n)	aerosol
Statt...	Instead of...
Treibhauseffekt m	greenhouse effect
Tsunami m (-s)	tsunami
ultraviolette Strahlen	ultraviolet rays
umstritten	controversial
umwandeln	to convert
Umwelt f (-en)	environment
umweltfeindlich	bad for the environment
umweltfreundlich	environmentally friendly
sich verbessern	to get better
Verbrauch m	consumption
Verkehr m	traffic
Verkehrsmittel n (-)	means of transport
verlangsamen	to slow down
Verpackung f (-en)	packaging
verschmutzen	to pollute
Verschmutzung f	pollution
verschwinden	to disappear
Wasserkraft f (-¨e)	hydroelectric power
wegwerfen	to throw away
Windpark f (-s)	wind farm
Wirbelsturm m (-¨e)	tornado
zerstören	to destroy
zusammenarbeiten	to work together

Problems in Society (p.79-81)

arbeitslos	unemployed
Arbeitslosigkeit f	unemployment
arm	poor
Armut f	poverty
Ausländer/in m/f (-/-nen)	foreigner
Bedingung f (-en)	condition
Behinderte m/f (-n)	disabled person
belohnend	rewarding
Bettler/in m/f (-/-nen)	beggar
Deutschkurs m (-e)	German course
Dieb/in m/f (-e/-nen)	thief
Diskriminierung f	discrimination
ehrenamtlich	voluntarily
Einbruch m (-¨e)	burglary
Eingliederung f	integration
einsam	lonely
Einwanderer/in m/f (-/-nen)	immigrant
Einwanderung f	immigration
erfrieren	to freeze to death
fliehen	to flee
Flüchtling m (-e)	refugee
Gesellschaft f (-en)	society
Gewalt f	violence
gewalttätig	violent
Gleichheit f	equality
Hautfarbe f (-n)	colour of the skin
Ich mache mir Sorgen um...	I'm worried about...
integrieren	to integrate
keinen festen Wohnsitz haben	to have no fixed abode
Kluft f (-¨e)	gap
Krieg m (-e)	war
Lärm m	noise
laut	noisy
Leben n (-)	life
Lösung f (-en)	solution
Menschenrechte	human rights
menschlich	humane / human
Migrant(in) m/f (-en/-nen)	migrant
Not f	need
obdachlos	homeless
Obdachlosenheim n (-e)	hostel for homeless people
Opfer n (-)	victim
Rasse f (-n)	race
Rassismus m	racism
Rassist/in m/f (-en/-nen)	racist (person)
Regierung f (-en)	government
reich	rich
das Rote Kreuz	the Red Cross
Sexismus m	sexism
Sozialhilfe f	income support
Sozialwohnung f (-en)	council flat
spenden	to donate
stehlen	to steal
Straftat f (-en)	criminal offence
Suppenküche f (-n)	soup kitchen
Tierheim n (-e)	animal shelter
überbevölkert	over-populated
Umfrage f (-n)	survey / opinion poll
unterstützen	to support
Unterstützung f	support
Vandalismus m	vandalism
Verbrechen n (-)	crime
Verbrecher/in m/f (-/-nen)	criminal
Verhältnisse	(living) conditions
vertreiben	to drive out / expel
weltweit	worldwide
wiederverwerten	to recycle
Wiederverwertung f	recycling

Vocabulary

Wohltätigkeit f (-en)	charity	Wohltätigkeits-veranstaltung f (-en)	charity event	ziehen nach	to move to
Wohltätigkeits-konzert n (-e)	charity concert			Zuhause n	home / house

Section Nine — Travel and Tourism

Where to Go (p.87)

die Alpen	the Alps
Amerika	America
Ärmelkanal m	English Channel
Asien	Asia
Ausland n	abroad
Australien	Australia
Bayern	Bavaria
Belgien	Belgium
Bodensee m	Lake Constance
China	China
Deutschland	Germany
Donau f	River Danube
Europa	Europe
Frankreich	France
Genf	Geneva
Griechenland	Greece
Hauptstadt f (-¨e)	capital city
irgendwo	somewhere
Italien	Italy
Kanada	Canada
Köln	Cologne
Land n (-¨er)	country
Mittelmeer n	Mediterranean (Sea)
Mosel f	River Moselle
München	Munich
nirgendwo	nowhere
Österreich	Austria
Ostsee f	Baltic Sea
Polen	Poland
Portugal	Portugal
Reiseziel n (-e)	destination
Rhein m	Rhine
Russland	Russia
Schwarzwald m	Black Forest
die Schweiz	Switzerland
Spanien	Spain
die Türkei	Turkey
Vereinigte Staaten	USA
Wien	Vienna

Preparation (p.88-89)

Aufenthalt m (-e)	stay
Aussicht f (-en)	view
Autovermietung f (-en)	car rental firm
Balkon m (-s)	balcony
bequem	comfortable
Bestätigung f (-en)	confirmation
bleiben	to stay
Blick m (-e)	view / glance
Campingplatz m (-¨e)	campsite
Doppelzimmer n (-)	double room

Einzelzimmer n (-)	single room
Empfang m (-¨e)	reception
Ermäßigung f (-en)	reduction
Formular n (-e)	form
Gasthaus n (-¨er)	guesthouse
gesellig	sociable
Halbpension f	half board
Hotel n (-s)	hotel
Jugendherberge f (-n)	youth hostel
Klimaanlage f	air conditioning
Meerblick m (-e)	sea view
Pension f (-en)	small hotel
Prospekt m (-e)	brochure / leaflet
Reisebüro n (-s)	travel agency
reservieren	to book
Reservierung f (-en)	reservation
Sommerferien	summer holidays
übernachten	to stay overnight
Übernachtung mit Frühstück	B & B
umständlich	inconvenient
Unterkunft f (-¨e)	accommodation
Urlaub m (-e)	holiday
Vollpension f	full board
Wohnwagen m (-)	caravan
Zelt n (-e)	tent
zelten	to camp
Zuschlag m (-¨e)	extra charge
Zweibettzimmer n (-)	twin room

Getting There (p.90)

abfahren	to leave / depart
abholen	to collect / pick up
ankommen	to arrive
aussteigen	to alight / get off bus
Auto n (-s)	car
Bahnsteig m (-e)	platform
sich beeilen	to hurry
Boot n (-e)	boat
Bus m (-se)	bus
Dampfer m (-)	steam boat
dauern	to take (time) / last
einsteigen	to get in / on
entwerten	to stamp / validate a ticket
Fähre f (-n)	ferry
fahren	to travel (in a vehicle)
Fahrkartenautomat m (-en)	ticket machine
Fahrkartenschalter m (-)	ticket office

Fahrpreis m (-e)	fare
Fahrrad n (-¨er)	bicycle
Fahrradvermietung f	bicycle hire
Fahrt f (-en)	journey
fliegen	to fly
Flug m (-¨e)	flight
Flughafen m (-¨)	airport
Flugzeug n (-e)	aeroplane
gehen	to go / walk
Gepäck n	luggage
Gleis n (-e)	platform
herumfahren	to travel around
Koffer m (-)	suitcase
Linie f (-n)	line / number (bus)
Notausgang m (-¨e)	emergency exit
Panne f (-n)	breakdown / puncture
Passagier/in m/f (-e/-nen)	passenger
Platten m	flat tyre
Reise f (-n)	journey
Reisebus m (-se)	coach
reisen	to travel
Reisende m/f (-n)	traveller
Reisepass m (-¨e)	passport
Richtung f (-en)	direction
Rundfahrt f (-en)	round trip / tour
Schließfach n (-¨er)	locker
seekrank	seasick
Sicherheitsgurt m (-e)	safety belt / seat belt
Stau m (-s)	traffic jam
Straßenkarte f (-n)	road map
Überfahrt f (-en)	(sea) crossing
umsteigen	to change (trains)
unterwegs	on the way
Verbindung f (-en)	connection
vermieten	to hire
verpassen	to miss
Verspätung f (-en)	delay
warten auf	to wait for
Wartesaal m	waiting room
Weg m (-e)	way / path
wegfahren	to depart / go away
weiterfahren	to travel on
Zoll m	customs
Zug m (-¨e)	train

What to Do (p.91)

Andenken n (-)	souvenir
sich etwas ansehen	to have a look at something
Ausflug m (-¨e)	excursion
begleiten	to accompany

beliebt	popular		kulturell	cultural		Sonnencreme f	suntan lotion

beliebt — popular
berühmt — famous
besichtigen — to visit (an attraction)
Briefmarke f (-n) — postage stamp
Burg f (-en) — castle
entdecken — to discover
sich erinnern — to remember
Erinnerung f (-en) — memory
erleben — to experience
Erlebnis n (-se) — experience
Fotoapparat m (-e) — camera
Führung f (-en) — guided tour

kulturell — cultural
Museum n (Museen) — museum
Öffnungszeiten — opening times
örtlich — local
Schloss n (-¨er) — castle / palace
See m (-n) — lake
See f (-n) — sea
sehenswert — worth seeing
Sehenswürdigkeit f (-en) — tourist attraction
sich sonnen — to sunbathe
Sonnenbrand m — sunburn

Sonnencreme f — suntan lotion
Stadtbummel m (-) — stroll through town
Stadtrundfahrt f (-en) — sightseeing tour of the town
Strand m (-¨e) — beach
Strandkorb m (-¨e) — wicker beach chair
verbringen — to spend (time)

Section Ten — Study and Employment

School Subjects (p.97)
Biologie — biology
Chemie — chemistry
Deutsch — German
Englisch — English
Erdkunde — geography
Französisch — French
Fremdsprache f (-n) — foreign language
Geschichte — history
Geografie — geography
Hauswirtschaftslehre — home economics
Klasse f (-n) — class
Kunst — art
Lieblingsfach n (-¨er) — favourite subject
Mathe — maths
Musik — music
Naturwissenschaften — science
Pflichtfach n (-¨er) — compulsory subject
Physik — physics
Prüfung f (-en) — exam
Religion — RE
Schulfach n (-¨er) — school subject
Sozialkunde — social studies / politics
Spanisch — Spanish
Sport — PE
Stunde f (-n) — lesson
Theater — drama
Wahlfach n (-¨er) — optional subject
Werken — design technology
Wirtschaftslehre — business studies / economics

School Life (p.98-100)
1 = sehr gut — very good
2 = gut — good
3 = befriedigend — satisfactory / fair
4 = ausreichend — sufficient / pass (just)
5 = mangelhaft — poor / unsatisfactory / fail
6 = ungenügend — extremely poor / inadequate

Abschlusszeugnis n (-se) — school leaving certificate
abschreiben — to copy
akademisch — academic
Anspitzer m (-) — pencil sharpener
anspruchsvoll — demanding
Antwort f (-en) — answer
Anzug m (-¨e) — suit
aufpassen — to pay attention
Aula f (Aulen) — assembly hall
aus sein — to be over / finished
Auswahl f (-en) — choice / range
beantworten — to answer
bestehen — to pass (exam)
besuchen — to go to (a school)
blau machen — to play truant
Bluse f (-n) — blouse
Direktor/in m/f (-en/-nen) — headteacher
Druck m (-¨e) — pressure
durchfallen — to fail (a test)
Erfolg m — success
erfolgreich — successful
Ergebnis n (-se) — result
erklären — to explain
erzählen — to tell / narrate
Fachschule f (-n) — technical college
fehlen — to be absent
Ferien — holidays
Frage f (-n) — question
Ganztagsschule f (-n) — school that lasts all day
gemischt — mixed (sex)
Gesamtschule f (-n) — comprehensive school
Grundschule f (-n) — primary school
Gymnasium n (Gymnasien) — grammar school
Halle f (-n) — hall
Hauptschule f (-en) — vocational secondary school
Hausmeister/in m/f (-/-nen) — caretaker
Internat n (-e) — boarding school

Klassenarbeit f (-en) — test
Klassenfahrt f (-en) — school trip
klug — clever / intelligent
korrigieren — to correct
Krawatte f (-n) — tie
Kreide f — chalk
Labor n (-s) — laboratory
lehren — to teach
Lehrerzimmer n (-) — staff room
Leistung f (-en) — achievement
Lineal n (-e) — ruler
malen — to paint
Mittagspause f (-n) — lunch break
mündlich — orally
nachsitzen — to have a detention
Note f (-n) — grade
Notendruck m — pressure to get good marks
Pause f (-n) — break
plaudern — to chat
praktisch — vocational / practical
Privatschule f (-en) — private school
Realschule f (-n) — secondary school
rechnen — to calculate
Regel f (-n) — rule
respektieren — to respect
schaffen — to manage / create
Schere f — scissors
schriftlich — written
Schulart f (-en) — type of school
Schüler/in m/f (-/-nen) — pupil
Schulhof m (-¨e) — school yard
schwänzen — to play truant
Seite f (-n) — page
Sekretariat n (-e) — school office
sich setzen — to sit down
sitzen bleiben — to repeat a year
Sprachlabor n (-s) — language lab
Stress m — stress
Stundenplan m (-¨e) — timetable
Tafel f (-n) — black/white board
Turnhalle f (-n) — sports hall

üben	to practise
Übung f (-en)	exercise
Umkleideraum m (-̈e)	changing room
Unterricht m	lessons / teaching
unterrichten	to teach
Versammlung f (-en)	assembly
versetzt werden	to be moved up a year
versuchen	to try
wissen	to know
Wörterbuch n (-̈er)	dictionary
Zeugnis n (-se)	school report

Education Post-16 (p.101)

Azubi (Auszubildende) m/f (-s)	apprentice / trainee
Abitur n (-e)	A-level equivalent
Abiturient/in m/f (-en/-nen)	person doing the Abitur
arbeiten	to work
Arbeitspraktikum n	work experience
Ausbildungsplatz m (-̈e)	vacancy for a trainee
Berufsberater/in m/f (-/-nen)	careers adviser
Berufserfahrung f	work experience
Berufsschule f (-n)	vocational school
sich bewerben um	to apply for
Bewerbung f (-en)	application
Chef/in m/f (-s/-nen)	boss
einstellen	to employ
sich entscheiden	to decide
Erfahrung f (-en)	experience
fertig	ready / done
ein Jahr freinehmen	to take a year out
Führerschein m (-e)	driving licence
Gelegenheit f (-en)	opportunity
Kurs m (-e)	course
Lehre f (-n)	apprenticeship
Mindestlohn m (-̈e)	minimum wage
Nebenjob m (-s)	part-time job
Oberstufe f (-n)	sixth-form equivalent
Praktikum n (Praktika)	work placement
Studienplatz m (-̈e)	university place
studieren	to study
theoretisch	theoretical
auf die Uni gehen	to go to uni
Universität f (-en)	university
verdienen	to earn
Weiterbildung f	further education

Career Choices (p.102)

Angestellte m/f (-n)	employee
Apotheker/in m/f (-/-nen)	pharmacist
Arbeitgeber/in m/f (-/-nen)	employer
Arbeitszeit f	work hours
Bäcker/in m/f (-/-nen)	baker
Bauarbeiter/in m/f (-/-nen)	construction worker
bauen	to build
Bauer/Bäuerin m/f (-n/-nen)	farmer
Beamte m/f (-n)	civil servant
Beruf m (-e)	job / occupation
berufstätig sein	to be in work
beschäftigt sein	to be employed
beschließen	to decide
besitzen	to own
Besitzer/in m/f (-/-nen)	owner
Besprechung f (-en)	meeting / discussion
Bezahlung f (-en)	payment
Briefträger/in m/f (-/-nen)	postman/woman
Buchhalter/in m/f (-/-nen)	accountant
Büro n (-s)	office
Dolmetscher/in m/f (-/-nen)	interpreter
erfüllen	to fulfil
erfüllend	rewarding
Feuerwehrmann/ Feuerwehrfrau m/f (-̈er/-en)	firefighter
Fleischer/in m/f (-/-nen)	butcher
im Freien	in the open air
Friseur/in m/f (-e/-nen)	hairdresser
ganztags	all day
Gärtner/in m/f (-/-nen)	gardener
Gehalt n (-̈er)	salary
Halbtagsarbeit f	part-time work
Hausmann/Hausfrau m/f (-̈er/-en)	househusband / housewife
Informatiker/in m/f (-/-nen)	computer scientist
Ingenieur/in m/f (-e/-nen)	engineer
Journalist/in m/f (-en/-nen)	journalist
Karriere f (-n)	career
Kassierer/in m/f (-/-nen)	cashier / bank clerk
Klempner/in m/f (-/-nen)	plumber

Koch/Köchin m/f (-̈e/-nen)	cook
Krankenpfleger m (-)	(male) nurse
Krankenschwester f (-n)	(female) nurse
kündigen	to hand in one's notice / to sack someone
Lebenslauf m (-̈e)	CV
LKW-Fahrer/in m/f (-/-nen)	lorry driver
Lohn m (-̈e)	wage
Maler/in m/f (-/-nen)	painter / decorator
Metzger/in m/f (-/-nen)	butcher
Pfarrer/in m/f (-/-nen)	parish priest / vicar
Polizei f	police
Polizist/in m/f (-en/-nen)	police officer
Postbote/Postbotin m/f (-n/-nen)	postman/woman
Rechtsanwalt/ Rechtsanwältin m/f (-̈e/-nen)	lawyer
Rentner/in m/f (-/-nen)	pensioner
Schichtarbeit f	shift work
Schriftsteller/in m/f (-/-nen)	writer / author
selbstständig	self-employed / independent
Sozialarbeiter/in m/f (-/-nen)	social worker
Stelle f (-n)	position
suchen	to look for / search
Teilzeitjob m (-s)	part-time job
Termin m (-e)	appointment
Tierarzt/Tierärztin m/f (-̈e/-nen)	vet
Tischler/in m/f (-/-nen)	carpenter
Übersetzer/in m/f (-/-nen)	translator
vereinbaren	to agree / arrange
Vollzeitarbeit f	full-time work
Vorstellungsgespräch n (-e)	job interview
Werkstatt f (-̈en)	garage
Wunsch m (-̈e)	wish

Vocabulary

Answers

The answers to the translation questions are sample answers only, just to give you an idea of one way to translate them. There may be different ways to translate these passages that are also correct.

Section One — General Stuff

Page 1: Numbers and Quantities
1) Sie sind siebzehn und fünfundzwanzig Jahre alt.
2) Sie ist achtundneunzig Jahre alt.
3) Sie ist neunundsiebzig Jahre älter als Heinrich.

Page 3: Times and Dates
1) her family
2) very interesting
3) She spent time with her brother.
   or: She walked through the park with her brother.
4) Not a lot. **or:** He played handball.
5) every day
6) on Thursday
7) the cinema

Page 9: Opinions
1) She finds it (very) boring.
2) She never gets a good seat. **or:** She cannot see what the actors are doing.
3) She finds the theatre interesting. **or:** You can learn a lot about life.
4) romantic films
5) She's not interested in them. **or:** She thinks they are unrealistic.

Page 10: Opinions
1) true   3) false   5) false
2) false   4) true

Page 11: Listening Questions
1 a) 25. Februar   c) 1. Juli
  b) 10. April   d) 11. Oktober
2 a) He finds it a bit strenuous.
  b) It's (too) boring.
  c) It was fabulous.
  d) It was very exciting.

Page 13: Reading Questions
1 a) B   c) A + B
  b) A   d) B
2 a) 15 minutes
  b) the third street on the right
  c) 55 metres
  d) over 10 euros

Page 14: Writing Questions
1) Ich gehe samstags ins Kino. Letzte Woche habe ich eine Komödie gesehen / angeschaut. Am Wochenende gehe ich schwimmen. Übermorgen werde ich einkaufen / shoppen gehen.
2) Als ich jünger war, mochte ich Rockmusik, aber jetzt mag ich Popmusik. Meine Lieblingssängerin heißt Anja Lan. Ich denke, dass sie toll ist, weil ihre Musik fantastisch ist. Ich glaube, dass sie nett / ein netter Mensch ist, und meiner Meinung nach ist sie (wunder)schön. Ich möchte nächstes Jahr ihr Konzert besuchen.

Section Two — Me, My Family and Friends

Page 17: My Family
Hello, I am Joachim and I was born in Leipzig. I live with my wife, her two daughters and my son. He studies / is studying medicine and he wants to be a doctor in the future. One of my stepdaughters has a child, who is called Georg. We will soon celebrate his second birthday.

Page 18: Describing People
1) one   3) She has brown eyes and wears light blue glasses.
2) dark   4) He thinks it's dreadful because he looks ugly.

Page 21: Partnership
1) NT   2) R   3) F   4) NT

Page 22: Listening Questions
1 a) Meyer   c) 11th July
  b) Turkey   d) There's so much to do. / You can go to concerts.
2 a) reliability b) 70% c) normally being happy

Page 24: Reading Questions
1) Birgit — Positive: stepsister   Negative: grandmother
   Noah — Positive: son   Negative: half-brother
2) We live in a village near Swansea. My wife, who is called Saskia, is thirty-six years old and has short, curly, black hair. She also has big, brown eyes and I believe / think that she is very pretty. We never argue and she will always care for me.

Page 25: Writing Questions
2) Leider haben sich meine Eltern vor zwei Jahren getrennt. Im Moment bin ich ledig. In der Zukunft möchte ich in einer Beziehung und nicht allein sein. Jedoch bin ich nicht sicher, ob ich heiraten werde, weil man eine Familie haben kann, ohne verheiratet zu sein. Auch lassen sich viele Paare scheiden.

Section Three — Free-Time Activities

Page 27: Music
1) A   2) E   3) F

Page 28: Cinema
Ich gehe gern ins Kino. Letztes Wochenende bin ich mit meinem Freund / meiner Freundin ins Kino gegangen und wir haben einen Actionfilm gesehen. Ich habe den Film wirklich spannend gefunden, obwohl er ein kleines bisschen gruselig war. Nächste Woche werde ich eine Komödie mit meiner Schwester sehen, weil sie lustige Filme lieber mag. In der Zukunft möchte ich Schauspieler(in) werden.

Page 29: TV
1) true   2) false   3) false   4) not in the text

Page 30: Food
1) B   2) A   3) C   4) A

Page 34: Listening Questions
1 a) because the food was so tasty (last week)
  b) a table for two people *[1 mark]* by the window *[1 mark]*
  c) the duck
  d) nuts
2) A, E, F

Page 36: Reading Questions
1) Last week there was a big concert in Berlin and I went to it with my friends. Our favourite band played — that was very exciting. I think that live music is really great, so I often go to concerts. I like rock music best and in the future I would like to learn to play the electric guitar.
2) a) B   b) A   c) A + B

Page 37: Writing Questions
2) Ich treibe nicht gern Sport, aber mein Bruder ist sportlich / sportbegeistert. Das Freizeitzentrum ist / befindet sich in der Nähe von unserem Haus und er geht fast jeden Tag dorthin. Gestern ist er mit seinen Freunden dort schwimmen gegangen. Morgen wird er dorthin gehen, um Federball zu spielen. Ich sehe lieber fern.

Section Four — Technology in Everyday Life

Page 40: Technology

Ich habe ein Handy und einen Tablet-PC. Ich benutze jeden Tag das Internet. Ich benutze es, um meine Hausaufgaben zu machen. Ich lud vor kurzem / neulich viele Filme herunter. Ich simse zwanzig- oder dreißigmal pro Tag. In Zukunft werde ich versuchen, mein Handy weniger / nicht so oft zu benutzen und mehr Sport zu treiben.

Page 41: Social Media

1) fifty
2) people she knows personally
3) always in the evening
4) They think that she spends too much time on the computer.

Page 43: Listening Questions

1 a) make arrangements to meet up with her friends
   b) sending photos and videos to her friends
   c) you can download music and apps / downloading music is quick / downloading music is cheaper than buying CDs
2 a) B   b) C   c) B

Page 45: Reading Questions

1) Social media can be useful. However, you have to be careful who you meet / get to know online. Also, you damage your health if / when you spend too much time in front of screens. Before, there was no social media, so young people did more sport. In the future, young people will probably use social media even more often / frequently.
2) Nina Vorteil: Man kann sich schnell informieren.
          Nachteil: Das Herunterladen von Informationen ist teuer.
   Paul Vorteil: Man kann überall mit Freunden kommunizieren.
          Nachteil: Man kann vom Handy abhängig werden.

Page 46: Writing Questions

2) Soziale Medien sind unter Jugendlichen sehr beliebt. In der Schule haben wir gelernt, dass man online immer vorsichtig sein / aufpassen muss. Man soll(te) nicht zu viele persönliche Informationen teilen, insbesondere mit Fremden. Auch soll(te) man sich nie mit jemandem treffen, den man nicht kennt. Ich werde das nie machen / tun.

Section Five — Customs and Festivals

Page 48: Festivals in German-Speaking Countries

1) She makes an advent wreath with four candles.
2) his sister, on Christmas Eve
3) He always buys them a big Christmas tree.
4) everyone
5) gingerbread and biscuits **and**: with (chocolate) stars and hearts on

Page 49: Festivals in German-Speaking Countries

1) Germany, Switzerland and Austria
2) It's a very colourful and exciting festival.
3) in areas where a lot of Catholics live
4) They put on fancy dress.

Page 51: Listening Questions

1 a) Sie bemalt Eier *[1 mark]* und dekoriert das Haus *[1 mark]*.
   b) Er verkleidet sich als Osterhase.
   c) Ostern ohne Schokolade
   d) Alle Geschäfte sind geschlossen. / Seine Freunde haben keine Zeit für ihn.
2 a) Two from: She decorates the Christmas tree / sings Christmas carols / opens presents.
   b) Christmas dinner
   c) She celebrated Christmas at her English friend's house.
   d) the German tradition

Page 53: Reading Questions

1) Are you looking forward to Christmas yet? I am already really excited because I love Christmas so much. I am looking forward most of all to wrapping (up) presents. I found that really fun last year. What do you want for Christmas? I hope that it will snow at Christmas. That would be great.

2 a) Two from: princesses / pirates / ghosts
   b) sweets *[1 mark]* flowers *[1 mark]*
   c) they don't have to go to school

Page 54: Writing Questions

2) Ich bin nicht religiös, aber ich mag Ostern. Es ist schön, Zeit mit der Familie zu verbringen. Mein Vater backt einen Kuchen und wir dekorieren / schmücken das Haus. Letztes Jahr habe ich zu viel Schokolade gegessen und ich war krank. Ich werde das dieses Jahr nicht machen / tun. Ich hoffe, dass es sonnig sein wird, damit wir draußen sein können.

Section Six — Where You Live

Page 56: The Home

1) under the table
2) Any three from: the bed, the oven, the kitchen, the cupboard, (under) the basin, the clock case
3) the youngest / the one in the clock case

Page 57: What You Do at Home

I live with my parents in a flat in Berlin. I must help at home every day. That annoys me. After school, I clean the flat. I must also cook for my parents because they come home late. Yesterday, I tidied my room. I hope that I will have more free time at the weekend.

Page 59: Clothes Shopping

1) Schuhe und eine Jeans
2) Die Verkäuferinnen waren sehr freundlich und hilfsbereit.
3) Sie ist im Moment pleite.
4) ein neues Kleid

Page 62: Giving and Asking for Directions

A, D, E

Page 63: Weather

1) falsch   3) richtig   5) falsch
2) nicht im Text   4) falsch

Page 64: Listening Questions

1) Positiv: Markt (am Samstag)   schöne Kunstgalerie
   Negativ: Two from: nicht einfach, Klamotten zu kaufen / kein Kaufhaus / Stadt zu klein
2 a) quantity: one kilo   product: pears
   b) quantity: four cans   product: lemonade
   c) quantity: six slices   product: ham
   d) quantity: five pieces   product: cake

Page 66: Reading Questions

1) A, B, F, H
2) I went to the sports shop because I had to buy new trainers for my daughter. At the till I gave the assistant a 100-euro note. I got ten euros back. The trainers are too big and I want my money back. Unfortunately, the assistant didn't give me a receipt.

Page 67: Writing Questions

2) Obwohl es letzten Herbst in vielen europäischen Ländern kalt war, war es in Deutschland heiß, trocken und sonnig. Es war selten wolkig, aber es war ziemlich windig. Jedoch war es im Winter äußerst kalt und es hat im Januar in Norddeutschland geschneit. Wir hoffen, dass es im Sommer sonnig sein wird.

Section Seven — Lifestyle

Page 71: Illnesses

Last week, my sister was ill. She had a headache, her throat hurt and her cheeks were very red. My father thought that she had a fever. Now, I feel ill and I've had stomach ache for about a week. I must go to the pharmacy. I will buy painkillers.

Page 72: Listening Questions

1   a)   Man sollte: joggen gehen
         Man sollte nicht: nur zu Hause bleiben
    b)   Man sollte: jeden Tag Obst essen
         Man sollte nicht: zu viel fernsehen

2   a)   chocolate   c)   addicted / dependent
    b)   smoked cigarettes   d)   obese

Page 74: Reading Questions

1) I am sad at the moment because my stepmother is addicted to alcohol / is an alcoholic. In my opinion, she drinks alcoholic drinks too often and I am really worried because that is very unhealthy. I hope that she will stop soon. A friend of mine was a drug addict and an addiction can be very dangerous.

2) Some doctors believe that university students live unhealthily. Sometimes students become ill because they drink too much and don't sleep enough. Stress can also be a big problem because it can cause headaches and stomach ache. Furthermore, it is difficult to avoid colds if / when you spend so much time with others.

Page 75: Writing Questions

2) Letzte Woche habe ich mit meinen Freunden Rugby gespielt und ich habe mir den Rücken verletzt. Ich war beim Arzt / Ich bin zum Arzt gegangen und er dachte, dass das Problem leider ziemlich ernst war. Ich brauche ein Medikament, also muss ich morgen zur Apotheke (gehen). Ich hoffe, dass ich nicht ins Krankenhaus (gehen) muss.

Section Eight — Social and Global Issues

Page 78: Environmental Problems

Ich denke, dass wir viele Umweltprobleme verursacht haben. Die Luftverschmutzung ist sehr gefährlich für Menschen und Tiere. Sie kann auch zur Erderwärmung führen. Erneuerbare Energiequellen sind eine mögliche Lösung, weil sie umweltfreundlicher als Kohle sind. Wenn wir nichts machen, werden die Probleme in der Zukunft schlimmer werden.

Page 80: Problems in Society

1)   E   2)   C   3)   B

Page 82: Listening Questions

1   a)   für Kinder
    b)   Geld spenden
    c)   Sie hat €20 gespendet.
    d)   Sie könnte mehr für Sozialhilfe ausgeben.

2)   C, E, F

Page 84: Reading Questions

1   a)   ein- oder zweimal in der Woche
    b)   Two from: Lebensmittel kaufen / kochen / waschen / plaudern
    c)   ein Jahr kostenlose Unterkunft

2)   Refugees flee from dangerous areas. They have to find other countries where they can integrate themselves. They often live in terrible conditions. Although refugees sometimes receive income support, it mostly / usually isn't much money. Sometimes society can also be unfriendly and poverty is a big problem for many refugees.

Page 85: Writing Questions

2)   Viele (Leute) glauben, dass der Treibhauseffekt ein sehr großes Problem ist. In der Vergangenheit waren manche (Leute) nicht so umweltfreundlich und jetzt wird die Welt immer wärmer. Um dieses schwieriges Problem zu lösen, müssen wir alternative Energiequellen finden.

Section Nine — Travel and Tourism

Page 87: Where to Go

1)   mit dem Auto
2)   todlangweilig
3)   in einem Rucksack
4)   nach Belgien

Page 88: Accommodation

1)   positiv und negativ   2)   positiv   3)   negativ

Page 90: How to Get There

Last week, my father bought a tent. Tomorrow, the whole family is flying to Switzerland, where we will stay on a campsite at Lake Constance. I find that very exciting, but my step-sister doesn't like aeroplanes. We will hopefully have a lovely / beautiful view of the mountains.

Page 92: Listening Questions

1   a)   Sunday   c)   There is an extra charge for cars.
    b)   €18 per night   d)   when they leave

2)   A, C, D

Page 94: Reading Questions

1)   C, E, G, H
2   a)   C   b)   A   c)   B

Page 95: Writing Questions

2)   Ich will am Samstag nach Berlin fahren. Ich weiß nicht, ob ich mit dem Zug oder mit dem Auto fahren werde. Es wird mit dem Auto wahrscheinlich schneller sein, denn man muss umsteigen. Auch könnte es Verspätungen geben. Jedoch kann man im Zug lesen und essen. Der Zug fährt um 11.20 vom Gleis 4 ab.

Section Ten — Study and Employment

Page 98: School Routine

1)   Der Schultag endet um dreizehn Uhr.
2)   Versammlungen morgens
     and: keine Freunde beim Kunstunterricht

Page 99: School Life

B, C, F, G

Page 101: Education Post-16

Letztes Jahr habe ich Englisch, Mathe und Geografie / Erdkunde gelernt. Erdkunde hat mir gut gefallen, aber mein(e) Mathelehrer(in) war sehr streng. Nach den Prüfungen werde ich ein Jahr freinehmen. Ich werde einen Job finden, weil ich Geld verdienen will. Danach will ich an die Uni gehen, um Englisch zu studieren. Ich denke, dass es eine interessante Erfahrung / ein interessantes Erlebnis sein wird.

Page 102: Career Choices and Ambitions

At the moment, I don't know what I want to do in the future. I didn't pass my exams at school and I must find a job. My father is a police officer and in June I did my work experience with him, but I wouldn't like to do that for a living / as a job. I would prefer to be self-employed.

Page 103: Listening Questions

1)   B, C, E
2   a)   ein Friseur
    b)   gut informiert [1 mark] und geduldig [1 mark]
    c)   Man muss stark [1 mark] und fleißig [1 mark] sein
    d)   Verkäufer

Page 105: Reading Questions

1   a)   Englisch, Spanisch und Französisch
    b)   (fließend) Englisch sprechen
    c)   Der Lehrer ist sehr altmodisch.
    d)   für Geschichte

2)   The school day starts at half past eight / eight thirty and ends at four o'clock. We have six lessons a day: four in the morning and two in the afternoon. Today there was an assembly in the hall. I always find that boring. We have two breaks a day. I would like a longer lunch break.

Page 106: Writing Questions

2)   An meiner Schule gibt es über tausend Schüler. Ich besuche eine Gesamtschule. Man kann praktische Fächer wählen. Ich denke, dass das gut ist, weil ich sehr praktisch bin. Der Schultag dauert bis vier Uhr, aber gestern habe ich nach der Schule Hockey gespielt. Nächstes Jahr möchte ich das Abitur / 'A-levels' machen.

Section Eleven — Grammar

Page 108: Cases — Nominative and Accusative
1) nom. — Der Mann   acc. — Deutsch
2) nom. — Die Stadt   acc. — eine Bibliothek
3) nom. — Ich   acc. — eine Schwester
4) nom. — Er   acc. — Schokolade
5) nom. — Meine Mutter   acc. — ein neues Auto
6) nom. — ich   acc. — einen Rock

Page 109: Cases — Genitive and Dative
1) gen. — meiner Mutter   4) gen. — meines Vaters
2) dat. — dem Land   5) dat. — dem Zug
3) dat. — meinem Bruder   6) dat. — der Küche

Page 110: Words for People, Places and Objects
1) die Gesellschaft   4) das Mädchen   7) die Katrin
2) der Mittwoch   5) die Meinung   8) das Schwimmen
3) der Frühling   6) die Polizei

Page 111: Words for People, Places and Objects
1) Es gibt viele Autos / Wagen.
2) Die Kinder sind klein.
3) Die Tische sind teuer.
4) Die Ärzte / Die Ärztinnen sind nett.
5) Die alte Frau / Die Alte heißt Renate.
6) Der Jugendliche heißt Ali.

Pages 112-113: Quick Questions
1 a) Ich   g) Mein Freund
   b) Mein Bruder   h) ihr
   c) Wir   i) Fußball
   d) Mein Vater   j) Meine Mutter, ich
   e) ich   k) Frankreich
   f) du   l) der Hund
2 a) eine Hose   g) eine E-Mail
   b) einen Schal   h) einen Film
   c) Das Auto   i) eine Tasse Tee
   d) Spanisch   j) deine Hausaufgaben
   e) Schokolade   k) mein Handy
   f) soziale Medien   l) Mathe
3 a) accusative   g) nominative
   b) nominative   h) accusative
   c) accusative   i) accusative
   d) nominative   j) nominative
   e) nominative   k) accusative
   f) accusative   l) nominative
4 a) dative   e) dative
   b) dative   f) genitive
   c) genitive   g) dative
   d) genitive   h) genitive
5 a) meines Vaters   e) meinem Freund
   b) meines Opas   f) dem Schüler
   c) meinem Bruder   g) des Kindes
   d) meines Bruders
6 a) Freunden   d) Erdbeeren
   b) Brüdern   e) Studenten, Problemen
   c) Geschwistern
7 a) Blumen, Tisch   g) Dom, Stadt
   b) Snooker   h) Sonne
   c) Bruder, Krimis   i) Sophie, Kuchen
   d) Sportschuhe   j) Freund, Auto
   e) Kleid, Schwester   k) Herr Meyer, Spanien
   f) Cousin, Schokoladeneis   l) Regenschirm
8 a) N   e) M   i) F
   b) F   f) N   j) M
   c) F   g) F   k) F
   d) M   h) M   l) N

9 a) Junge   d) Herren
   b) Menschen   e) Jungen
   c) Herrn   f) Namens
10 a) die Würste   g) die Tage
   b) die Lieder   h) die Einladungen
   c) die Blumen   i) die Birnen
   d) die Zähne   j) die Brüder
   e) die Kinder   k) die Häuser
   f) die Sofas   l) die Doppelbetten
11 a) The old man is very old.
   b) The homeless person / man is homeless.
   c) The intelligent woman / girl is really intelligent.
12 a) Deutsche   e) Nette
   b) Deutschen   f) Netten
   c) Kleine   g) Freundlichen
   d) Kleinen   h) Freundliche

Page 114: Word Order
You should have ticked: 2), 3) and 6).
You should have crossed: 1), 4) and 5).

Page 115: Coordinating Conjunctions
Answers may vary, e.g.
1) Ich fahre mit dem Bus und du fährst mit dem Zug.
2) Wir werden in ein Museum gehen oder wir werden Tennis spielen.
3) Ich will Musik hören oder fernsehen.
4) Er ist Vegetarier, aber sie isst Fleisch.
5) Ich liebe Deutsch, aber ich hasse Englisch.

Page 116: Subordinating Conjunctions
Answers may vary, e.g.
1) Ich mag Lesen, weil es entspannend ist.
2) Komm zu meiner Party, wenn du Zeit hast.
3) Wir waren beste Freunde, als wir Kinder waren.
4) Ich will Lehrer(in) werden, obwohl es anstrengend ist.

Page 117: Quick Questions
1 a) Am Freitag gehe ich in die Stadt.
   b) Im April besuche ich London.
   c) Am Wochenende gehen wir einkaufen.
   d) Um neun Uhr verlasse ich das Haus.
   e) Morgen kommt er nicht in die Schule.
   f) Jeden Abend spielt sie Hockey.
2 a) Ich spiele Volleyball am Freitag.
   b) Am Samstag spiele ich Golf.
   c) Ich werde im Juli Frankreich besuchen.
   d) Im August werde ich nach Frankreich reisen.
   e) Ich fahre am Montag mit dem Bus in die Schule.
   f) Am Dienstag fahre ich mit dem Rad in die Schule.
3 a) Was magst du am liebsten — Schokolade oder Karotten?
   b) Ich möchte ein Kilo Kartoffeln und 500 Gramm Erbsen.
   c) Wir gehen wandern, denn die Sonne scheint.
   d) Sie will ihren Freund sehen, aber er ist krank.
4 a) Ich schwimme (gern) und ich tanze gern. / Ich schwimme und tanze gern.
   b) Mein Bruder möchte im Freibad schwimmen, aber es ist zu kalt.
   c) Sie bleibt zu Hause, denn sie hat Fieber.
   d) Kommst du mit oder gehst du nach Hause?
5 a) Wir lernen Französisch und Deutsch.
   b) Meine Mutter möchte nach Spanien oder (nach) Italien fahren.
   c) Ich liebe Kuchen, aber er ist ungesund.
6 a) wenn   c) weil   e) ob
   b) obwohl   d) damit   f) bis
7 a) Ich sonne mich, wenn es heiß ist.
   b) Wir essen im chinesischen Restaurant, bevor wir ins Theater gehen.
   c) Er wohnt bei seinen Eltern, bis er an die Uni geht.

Page 118: 'The', 'A' and 'No'
1) den   3) eine   5) keinen
2) der   4) einen   6) kein

Page 119: Words to Describe Things
1) Das Pferd ist grau.
2) Ich sehe drei graue Pferde.
3) Er hat zwei graue Pferde.
4) Sie mag das graue Pferd.
5) Welches graue Pferd?
6) Das graue Pferd ist groß.
7) Ich habe ein graues Pferd.
8) Dieses graue Pferd ist alt.

Page 120: Words To Describe Things
1) Mein Haus ist groß.
2) Ihr Baby ist glücklich / froh.
3) Jeder Job / Jede Stelle ist langweilig.
4) Wer hat meinen neuen Stift / Kugelschreiber?
5) Diese Musik ist toll / super / prima.
6) Ich kaufte dieses schnelle Auto / diesen schnellen Wagen.
7) Welchen Mantel will er?
8) Der Hund meiner Schwester ist lustig / komisch.

Page 121: Words to Compare Things
1) glücklich, glücklicher, der / die / das Glücklichste
2) langsam, langsamer, der / die / das Langsamste
3) hübsch, hübscher, der / die / das Hübscheste
4) traurig, trauriger, der / die / das Traurigste
5) Das ist das größere Haus.
6) Katrin ist ebenso faul wie Klaus.

Page 122: Quick Questions
1 a) den   c) das
   b) dem   d) des
2 a) einen, keine   c) Keine
   b) kein, keinen   d) eine, kein
3 a) braune, grünen, weißen
   b) kleinen, großen, schönen
   c) schwarzen, roten, alten
   d) kleinen, leckeren, frische
4 a) frische Milch   e) warmes Wasser
   b) kaltes Bier   f) einige / manche kleine Hunde
   c) zwei rote Äpfel   g) viele große Hunde
   d) wenige heiße Tage   h) zehn grüne Flaschen
5 a) Das, neue, einem, ruhigen
   b) einen, blauen, braune
   c) ältere, sympathische
   d) den, historischen, das, neue
6 a) Welcher   c) Diese
   b) Welchen   d) welcher
7 a) schneller   c) besser
   b) langsamer   d) älter
8 a) Ich bin gut, du bist besser, aber sie ist die Beste.
   b) Mein Haus ist nah, dein Haus ist näher, aber sein Haus ist das Nächste.
   c) Das Theater ist alt, die Kirche ist älter, aber der Dom ist der Älteste.

Page 123: Words to Describe Actions
1) Ich gehe sehr schnell.
2) Sie laufen leider wirklich langsam.
3) Er hat kaum gesprochen.
4) Normalerweise helfe ich Lukas viel.
5) Endlich hält das Auto.
6) Wir werden bestimmt gewinnen.
7) Leider kam Stephan etwas spät.
8) Gewöhnlich kostet es fast zwei Euro.

Page 124: Words to Describe Actions
1) Ich putze mir täglich die Zähne.
2) Andrea erzählt / macht oft Witze.
3) Ich spiele nie dort Tennis.
4) Es gibt überall Vögel.
5) Sie treffen sich manchmal (dort) drüben.
6) Ich werde dich am kommenden Montag hier sehen.

Page 125: Words to Compare Actions
1) Ich laufe schneller als sie.
2) Sie spielen am besten Fußball.
3) Wir werden langsamer essen.
4) Er springt am weitesten.
5) Der Mann singt am schönsten.
6) Albert malt besser als Liesl.

Page 126: Quick Questions
1 a) He sings loudly and badly. She dances well.
   b) I drive slowly and you speak strangely.
   c) My brother works hard and swims quickly.
2 a) schlecht   d) unglaublich
   b) langsam   e) glücklich
   c) schön   f) Plötzlich
3 a) Manchmal   d) neulich
   b) schon   e) gestern Abend
   c) immer   f) nächste Woche
4 a) überall   c) Übermorgen
   b) (da / dort) drüben   d) irgendwo
5 a) Er war sehr früh da.
   b) Wir sitzen immer (da / dort) drüben.
6 a) Al speaks louder / more loudly than Eoin.
   b) Rhys dances just as well as Faiz.
   c) Sami doesn't smile as often as / smiles less often than Aled.
   d) Jo likes rugby just as much as Pete.
7 a) am besten   c) gern
   b) lieber   d) viele, mehr
8 a) Joanna ist genauso freundlich wie Morag.
   b) Megan läuft nicht so schnell wie Anna.

Page 127: I, You, He, She, We, They
1) Er sieht sie.   4) Sie sprechen mit mir.
2) Sie sehen uns.   5) Ich kenne dich.
3) Ich spreche mit euch.   6) Sie kennt sie.

Page 128: Reflexive Pronouns
1) Sie waschen sich.   5) Du putzt dir die Zähne.
2) Ich fühle mich glücklich. 6) Sie wünschen sich einen Hund.
3) Er entschuldigt sich.   7) Wir ziehen uns um.
4) Sie sonnt sich.   8) Ich zog mich um.

Page 129: Relative and Interrogative Pronouns
1) Die Frau, die einen Hut trägt, ist hübsch.
2) Die Leute, denen ich schreibe, sind nett.
3) Das Kind, dessen Mantel rot ist, lacht.
4) Wen hat er gesehen? / Wen sah er?
5) Nichts, was sie macht, ist einfach / leicht.

Page 130: Prepositions
1) zu   4) zu   7) in (im)
2) nach   5) auf   8) an (am)
3) zu   6) aus

Page 131: Prepositions
1) durch den Wald   5) trotz des Regens
2) ohne seinen Stift   6) während der Party
3) von ihrem Vater   7) Ich lief die Straße entlang.
4) nach dem Film   8) Er steht unter der Brücke.

Pages 132-133: Quick Questions
1 a) Der Hund ist schwarz. **Er** heißt Max.
   b) Die Kinder gehen nicht in die Schule. **Sie** spielen im Garten.
   c) Das Haus ist modern. **Es** liegt am Stadtrand.
   d) Marie ist meine beste Freundin. **Sie** ist sehr sympathisch.
2 a) du   c) Sie
   b) Sie   d) ihr
3 a) mir   e) uns, euch
   b) mich   f) ihn
   c) dir   g) ihr
   d) Ihnen   h) ihr

Answers

4 a) We sit down quickly.
    b) I had a shower / showered and then had breakfast.
    c) I brush / clean my teeth.

5 a) mir   d) mich
    b) sich, sich e) euch, sich
    c) dir   f) mir, dir

6 a) die   e) dessen
    b) den   f) denen
    c) das   g) deren
    d) der   h) dem

7 a) Wer   d) Wem
    b) wem   e) Was
    c) Was für   f) Wen

8 a) nach, zu e) bei
    b) an   f) an
    c) Am, zu   g) nach
    d) um, nach h) Im, zu

9 a) Diese Jacke ist **aus** Leder.
    b) Ist diese Torte **für** mich?
    c) Ich lerne **seit** zwei Jahren Deutsch.
    d) Der Zug ist **von** London gekommen.
    e) Deine Tasche ist **auf** dem Tisch.

10 a) ins   f) der
    b) die   g) der
    c) im   h) das
    d) dem   i) den
    e) dem   j) einer

11 a) entlang   d) Während
    b) Trotz   e) ohne, zur
    c) gegen   f) mit, über

12 a) am Freitag   g) statt eines Kuchens
    b) zu Fuß   h) um drei Uhr
    c) fünf vor drei i) am Bahnhof
    d) zwanzig nach vier j) ein Freund / eine Freundin von mir
    e) zur Post / zum Postamt k) wegen des Regens
    f) außerhalb der Stadt l) vor der Kirche

Page 134: Verbs in the Present Tense
1) Ich spiele.
2) Wir glauben.
3) Du fragst.
4) Sie tanzen.
5) Ich feire.
6) Sie segeln.
7) Ich gehe laufen / joggen.
8) Jan geht zelten.
9) Ich spiele seit einem Jahr Klavier.

Page 135: More About the Present Tense
1) Sie hat eine Katze.
2) Wir sind Lehrer(innen).
3) Ich danke meiner Tante.
4) Du folgst dem Mann.
5) Glauben Sie mir?
6) Sie trägt eine Krawatte.

Page 136: More About the Present Tense
1) Sie macht nichts.
2) Es schneit.
3) Ich sollte etwas sagen.
4) Er gibt es mir zurück.
5) Ich will berühmt sein, um viel Geld zu verdienen.
6) Ich kann nicht weggehen, ohne etwas zu sagen.

Page 137: Quick Questions
1 a) ich höre   g) ich schlage
    b) wir lernen h) du bringst
    c) er liebt   i) wir studieren
    d) ihr sagt   j) ihr trinkt
    e) Sie schicken k) sie stellen
    f) sie redet   l) du suchst

2 a) Ich gehe schwimmen.
    b) Wir gehen wandern.
    c) Sie gehen zelten.
    d) Ich gehe am Wochenende fischen / angeln.
    e) Wir gehen mittwochs laufen.

3 a) Riyam spielt Fußball.
    b) Mein Bruder schreibt eine E-Mail.
    c) Mein Papa / Vater arbeitet samstags.
    d) Christopher segelt heute.
    e) Ich wohne seit fünf Jahren hier.

4 a) bin   e) Trägt
    b) Seid   f) gibt
    c) isst   g) weiß
    d) fährt   h) liest

5 a) Haben Sie einen Hund?
    b) Wir sind noch nicht fertig / bereit.
    c) Katja trägt eine Hose.
    d) Er weiß nichts.
    e) Anupa fährt nicht mehr nach London.
    f) Sie isst Schokolade.

6 a) den Goldfischen
    b) mir
    c) ein weißes Hemd
    d) mir

7 a) Es regnet heute.
    b) Es gibt in meiner Stadt nicht viel zu tun.
    c) Wie geht's / geht es ihm?
    d) Es gefällt mir hier in Berlin.
    e) Es tut ihr leid.
    f) Es tut (mir) weh.

8 a) Ich lese, um mich zu entspannen.
    b) Ich muss einkaufen gehen.
    c) Er versucht, Spanisch zu lernen.
    d) Wir arbeiten, um Geld zu verdienen.

Page 138: Talking About the Past
1) Ich habe Tee getrunken.
2) Wir sind zu Hause geblieben.
3) Er hat mich gesehen.
4) Du hast einen Brief bekommen.
5) Sie haben ihn gefragt.
6) Sie sind hier / hierher gekommen.

Page 139: Talking About the Past
1) Ich hatte einen Hund.
2) Wir waren sehr traurig.
3) Ich spielte Tennis.
4) Sie waren da.
5) Du hattest eine gute Idee.
6) Sie kauften einen Hund.
7) Er kochte.
8) Sie war jung.

Page 140: Talking About the Past
1) Ich trank eine Tasse Tee.
2) Ich nahm den Stift.
3) Maria schrieb ein Buch.
4) Wir sahen ihm.
5) Sie halfen seit einem Jahr.
6) Ich aß seit einer Stunde.

Page 141: Talking About the Past
1) Ich hatte Musik gelernt.
2) Er hatte ein Eis gegessen.
3) Sie hatte sich angezogen.
4) Sie waren zum Park gegangen.
5) Tim war zu Hause geblieben.
6) Wir hatten unsere Hausaufgaben gemacht.

Page 142: Talking About the Future
1) Ich gehe am Montag ins Kino. / Ich werde am Montag ins Kino gehen.
2) Er erklärt es bald. / Er wird es bald erklären.
3) Angela trifft sich mit uns nächste Woche. / Angela wird sich mit uns nächste Woche treffen.
4) Sie besuchen uns nächstes Jahr. / Nächstes Jahr werden sie uns besuchen.
5) Ich esse morgen Pizza. / Ich werde morgen Pizza essen.
6) Nächstes Mal kaufen wir das Auto. / Nächstes Mal werden wir das Auto kaufen.

Page 143: Quick Questions

1 a) fahren g) passieren
   b) abfahren h) folgen
   c) kommen i) gehen
   d) ankommen j) ausgehen
   e) bleiben k) geschehen
   f) sein l) fliegen

2 a) Ich bin nach London gefahren.
   b) Er hat einen Kuchen gegessen.
   c) Wir haben eine Kunstgalerie besucht.
   d) Er ist im Bett geblieben.
   e) Das Flugzeug ist schnell geflogen.
   f) Wann ist der Zug abgefahren?
   g) Wir sind um zwei Uhr angekommen.
   h) Sie hat eine Tasse Tee getrunken.

3 a) Wir mach**ten** zu viel Lärm und ärger**ten** unsere Nachbarn.
   b) Mein Vater kauf**te** ein neues Haus und ich kauf**te** ein neues Auto.
   c) Mein Großvater arbeite**te** als Klempner. Meine Eltern arbeite**ten** als Lehrer.
   d) Du spiel**test** Gitarre und besuch**test** viele Konzerte.

4 a) ich kam i) wir sprangen
   b) er lief j) Sie wurden
   c) ich half k) du trankst
   d) du sahst l) wir gingen
   e) sie dachten m) sie fuhr
   f) ihr nahmt n) ich aß
   g) ich gab o) ihr brachtet
   h) er schrieb p) ich war

5 a) Sie arbeitete seit sechs Monaten als Informatikerin.
   b) Ich spielte seit zwei Stunden Gitarre.

6 a) hatte d) hatte
   b) war e) waren, hatten
   c) hattest

7 a) Wir waren nach Bristol gefahren.
   b) Sie war stundenlang zu Hause geblieben.
   c) Ich hatte nicht verstanden, was passiert war.

8 a) Diesen Sommer gehen wir jeden Tag schwimmen.
   b) Ich kaufe nächstes Jahr ein Haus.

9 a) wirst d) werde
   b) werdet e) werden
   c) wird f) werden

Page 144: Giving Orders

1) Tanz!
2) Seid höflich!
3) Setzen Sie sich!
4) Arbeite!
5) Helft uns nicht!
6) Folgen Sie mir!
7) Gehen wir einkaufen!
8) Entspann dich!

Page 145: Separable Verbs

1) Ich komme morgen an.
2) Sie geht aus.
3) Er nahm seinen Bruder mit.
4) Du hast abgewaschen.
5) Ich habe es zurückgegeben.
6) Geh weg, Eric!
7) Gehen wir aus!
8) Ich werde aufhören.

Page 146: Modal Verbs

1) Ich will eine neue Gitarre.
2) Wir mögen Rugby spielen.
3) Ihr dürft euch setzen.
4) Er kann sehr gut Ski fahren.
5) Ich soll gehen.
6) Sie muss bleiben.
7) Jane musste spielen.
8) Sie wollten fliegen.

Page 147: Would, Could and Should

1) Sie würden mich nicht besuchen.
2) Selma möchte singen.
3) Wir könnten zum Park laufen.
4) Wir könnten unseren Lehrer / unsere Lehrerin fragen.
5) Du solltest warten.
6) Ich sollte ein Sandwich essen.

Page 148: I would be / I would have

1) Ich wäre ein guter Schauspieler / eine gute Schauspielerin.
2) Er hätte einen Hund.
3) Niklas hätte einen Bruder.
4) Sie wären sehr traurig.
5) Wenn ich ein Auto / einen Wagen hätte, wäre es / er rot.
6) Wenn ich Hunger hätte, würde ich Kartoffeln essen.

Page 149: Quick Questions

1 a) Stell(e) das Buch hin!
   b) Geht in die Schule!
   c) Essen wir zusammen!
   d) Mach(e) deine Hausaufgaben!
   e) Arbeiten Sie in Ihrem Garten!
   f) Bringen wir unseren Hund mit!
   g) Besuch(e) deine Großeltern!
   h) Glaubt mir!

2 a) Ich **wasche** jeden Morgen **ab**.
   b) Normalerweise **geht** er abends **aus**.
   c) **Nehmen** Sie bitte Ihren Koffer **mit**!
   d) Am Montag **kommen** meine Großeltern **an**.
   e) Am Mittwoch **gebe** ich Bernd sein Buch **zurück**.
   f) Dave und Brian **fangen** plötzlich **an** zu singen.

3 a) George wird morgen fernsehen.
   b) Mein Geschenk ist am Freitag angekommen.
   c) Gingst du gestern Abend aus?

4 a) ich will f) wir können
   b) du magst g) ich muss
   c) er darf h) ihr mögt
   d) sie muss i) wir wollen
   e) Sie sollen

5 a) Ich soll zu Hause bleiben, aber ich will mit ihnen (mit)gehen.
   b) Sie müssen sehr klug sein.
   c) Ihr könnt sehr gut Italienisch (sprechen).
   d) Ich musste Griechisch lernen, als ich fünf war.
   e) Wir wollten eine E-Mail schreiben, aber wir hatten keinen Computer.

6 a) würde d) würdet
   b) würdest e) würde
   c) würden f) würden

7 a) Would you like to watch a DVD this evening?
   b) Could you give me the toothpaste, please?
   c) If I wasn't so tired, I would go jogging this evening.
   d) I would be happier if my brother wasn't so moody.

Answers

Practice Exam — Listening Paper

Question Number	Answer	Marks
1.1	A	[1 mark]
1.2	B	[1 mark]
1.3	C	[1 mark]
1.4	C	[1 mark]
2.1	saxophonist / saxophone player	[1 mark]
2.2	music lessons	[1 mark]
2.3	the violin	[1 mark]
	it was too boring	[1 mark]
3	it sounds exciting	[1 mark]
4	it keeps you fit	[1 mark]
5	sport is too tiring / strenuous (for her)	[1 mark]
6	do sport when it's hot	[1 mark]
7	school uniform	[1 mark]
	longer school day	[1 mark]
8	lessons start later / school day starts later	[1 mark]
	interesting after-school / extracurricular activities	[1 mark]
9	B, C, E	[3 marks]
10.1	a vegetarian menu	[1 mark]
10.2	vegetable soup	[1 mark]
	pasta / noodles with spinach	[1 mark]
10.3	a (large) bottle of sparkling mineral water	[1 mark]
11	Two from: It's not far to the sea. / You can go surfing in summer. / The other inhabitants are mostly friendly.	[2 marks]
12	Two from: It's boring in winter. / There isn't much to do (in winter). / It's a long way to the nearest cinema.	[2 marks]
13	There would be more free-time activities.	[1 mark]
	You meet lots of interesting people.	[1 mark]
14	P	[1 mark]
15	P + N	[1 mark]
16	N	[1 mark]
17	sharing funny videos with her friends	[1 mark]
18	People share interesting articles.	[1 mark]
	You can get other people's opinions on a topic.	[1 mark]
19	when people concentrate on their phones all the time (instead of having a proper conversation)	[1 mark]
20	help younger students with reading	[1 mark]
	do sport with younger students	[1 mark]
21	Two from: You can learn another language if you volunteer abroad. / You can try out different jobs. / You can help others.	[2 marks]
22.1	viel Obst und Gemüse essen	[1 mark]
	regelmäßig Sport treiben	[1 mark]
22.2	Fast Food essen	[1 mark]
	rauchen	[1 mark]
23	Medizin interessiert ihn besonders. / Er könnte vielen Menschen helfen.	[1 mark]
24	Ihre Noten in Biologie sind (dafür) zu schlecht.	[1 mark]
25	Sie arbeitet gern mit Jugendlichen.	[1 mark]
26.1	das Lied(, das die Kinder gesungen haben)	[1 mark]
26.2	Schreiben / Sie haben geschrieben.	[1 mark]
26.3	Kasperle hat mit der linken Hand geschrieben.	[1 mark]

Total marks for Listening Paper: 50

You'll find mark schemes for the Speaking and Writing papers on p.212 & p.213.

Practice Exam — Speaking Paper

Role-play sample answer

1) Ich habe zweimal pro Woche Sportunterricht.
2) Dieses Jahr habe ich Federball, Fußball und Hockey gespielt.
3) Ich denke, dass meine Sportlehrerin sehr lustig ist.
4) Meiner Meinung nach ist Sport sehr wichtig für die Gesundheit, weil man aktiv bleiben soll.
5) Seit wann interessieren Sie sich für Sport?

Photo Card sample answer

1) Auf dem Foto sieht man viel Müll auf einem Strand. Es gibt viele Plastikflaschen und es sieht gar nicht sauber aus.
2) Ja, es ist sehr wichtig, den Müll wiederzuverwerten, weil es sonst zu viel Verschwendung gibt. Es ist sehr schlecht für die Umwelt, wenn wir alles einfach wegwerfen.
3) Diesen Monat sind meine Eltern jeden Tag mit dem Rad zur Arbeit gefahren. Normalerweise fahren sie mit dem Auto, was nicht so umweltfreundlich ist.
4) Wenn die Erde wärmer würde, könnten manche Tierarten aussterben. Es ist auch möglich, dass es in der Zukunft mehr Luftverschmutzung geben könnte.
5) In meiner Gegend gibt es viele Leute, die arbeitslos sind. Wenn man keine Arbeit hat, wird man oft auch obdachlos, weil man die Miete nicht bezahlen kann. Das ist ein großes Problem.

General Conversation sample answers

Identity and culture

1) Meine beste Freundin heißt Holly und ich habe sie in der Grundschule kennen gelernt. Meiner Meinung nach ist sie sehr witzig und wir haben viel Spaß zusammen. Sie ist auch sehr lieb und ist immer für mich da, wenn ich Probleme habe.
2) Früher haben die meisten Leute geheiratet und für manche Leute ist Heiraten immer noch sehr wichtig. Man kann aber heutzutage mit jemandem wohnen und eine Familie haben, ohne verheiratet zu sein.
3) Ich denke nicht, dass ich von meinem Handy abhängig bin. Jedoch finde ich es sehr praktisch, weil ich immer mit meinen Freunden in Kontakt bleiben kann. Ich benutze auch gern Anwendungen, um Bilder und Videos zu teilen.
4) Ich benutze meinen Computer, um E-Mails zu schicken und im Internet zu surfen. Gestern habe ich das neueste Lied von meiner Lieblingsgruppe heruntergeladen. Meine Freunde spielen oft Computerspiele, aber das interessiert mich nicht.
5) Neulich habe ich einen Abenteuerfilm im Kino gesehen. Er hat mir ziemlich gut gefallen, weil der Film sehr spannend war. Einige Szenen waren aber etwas gruselig und ich hatte ein bisschen Angst. Es gab aber auch lustige Momente, wo ich viel gelacht habe.
6) Es ist wichtig, sich regelmäßig zu bewegen, um gesund zu bleiben. Sport ist eine gute Möglichkeit, um fit zu bleiben und gleichzeitig Stress zu reduzieren. Es macht auch Spaß, wenn man mit anderen zusammen Sport treibt. Ich möchte diesen Sommer Mitglied eines Sportvereins werden.

Current and future study and employment

1) Ich gehe meistens gern in die Schule. Am besten gefällt mir Kunst, weil ich ziemlich kreativ bin. Aber Erdkunde finde ich auch gut, da ich sehr gern in fremde Länder reise und neue Städte kennen lerne. Dieses Jahr haben wir viel über Brasilien gelernt und ich habe das sehr interessant gefunden.
2) Am meisten stören mich die vielen Hausaufgaben — das würde ich auf jeden Fall ändern. Außerdem mag ich die Schuluniform gar nicht, da sie unbequem ist. Es wäre besser, wenn jeder seine eigenen Klamotten tragen dürfte.
3) Letztes Jahr sind wir mit der Schule nach Brighton gefahren. Wir haben einen Spaziergang am Meer gemacht und uns die Stadt angesehen. Der Ausflug hat mir super gefallen. Nächstes Jahr werde ich mit meiner Erdkundeklasse Island besuchen. Ich freue mich schon sehr darauf.
4) Ich würde gern im Ausland studieren, weil es Spaß macht, andere Kulturen zu erleben. Aber das ist ein bisschen schwierig, denn ich spreche nur Englisch und Deutsch. Vielleicht sollte ich auch Spanisch lernen, damit ich in Südamerika studieren könnte.
5) Ich denke, dass beides interessant sein kann. Ein Studium dauert lange und kostet viel Geld, aber man kann später einen guten Beruf haben. Wenn man arbeitet, hat man manchmal weniger Freizeit, aber man verdient sein eigenes Geld.
6) Ich weiß noch nicht, welchen Beruf ich später machen möchte. Ich interessiere mich für Sprachen, vielleicht könnte ich als Dolmetscher oder Lehrer arbeiten.

Practice Exam — Writing Paper

Q1.1 — Sample answer

Meine Freunde hören alle gern Popmusik, aber am liebsten gefällt mir Jazzmusik. Manche Jugendliche glauben, dass Jazzmusik altmodisch ist, aber eigentlich kann sie sehr modern und aufregend sein. Ich habe mich schon immer für Musik interessiert, obwohl ich früher Rockmusik bevorzugt habe. Vor allem mag ich Live-Musik, aber leider sind die Eintrittskarten oft sehr teuer. Auch gibt es in meiner Gegend nicht viele Gelegenheiten, Konzerte zu besuchen. Ich spiele schon seit zwei Jahren Saxofon, was viel Spaß macht, und in der Zukunft möchte ich Querflöte lernen. Das wäre prima.

Q1.2 — Sample answer

Ich würde gern diesen Sommer ein Praktikum bei einem Arzt machen, um mehr praktische Erfahrung zu sammeln. Ich interessiere mich sehr für Medizin, weil ich Biologie faszinierend finde, und außerdem anderen Menschen helfen möchte. Ich wollte immer schon Arzt werden, deshalb habe ich letztes Jahr ein Praktikum in einem Krankenhaus gemacht. Die Arbeit hat mir sehr gut gefallen, obwohl die Arbeitstage sehr lang waren und ich viele kranke Leute gesehen habe. Ich möchte später in einer Großstadt als Kinderarzt arbeiten, damit ich kranken Kindern helfen kann, wieder gesund zu werden.

Q2.1 — Sample answer

Letzte Woche habe ich an meiner Schule einen Informationstag über das Rauchen besucht. Wir haben viel über die Folgen des Rauchens gelernt. Meiner Meinung nach ist es entsetzlich, wie schädlich Rauchen ist. Rauchen hat viele Auswirkungen auf die Gesundheit: man kann zum Beispiel Krebs oder Atembeschwerden bekommen. Oft entwickelt man einen Raucherhusten, der sehr unangenehm ist. Rauchen ist eine Sucht und deshalb ist es nicht leicht, damit aufzuhören. Wenn man aber gesund leben will, muss man versuchen, das Rauchen aufzugeben. Jedoch ist das nicht das einzige, was man tun muss, um seine Gesundheit zu schützen. Zu einem gesunden Lebensstil gehören auch viel Bewegung und eine ausgewogene Ernährung. Im Gegensatz dazu essen viele Menschen zu viel Fett und sitzen abends lieber vor dem Bildschirm. In Zukunft möchte ich gesünder werden und deswegen werde ich versuchen, mindestens dreimal pro Woche Sport zu treiben. Wenn man fit werden will, darf man keinesfalls rauchen!

Q2.2 — Sample answer

Meistens verstehe ich mich ganz gut mit meiner Familie, obwohl wir manchmal streiten. Ich habe drei Geschwister: zwei ältere Brüder und eine jüngere Schwester. Als wir Kinder waren, habe ich sie sehr ärgerlich gefunden, aber jetzt gehen sie mir nicht mehr auf die Nerven. Ich habe ein besseres Verhältnis mit meiner Mutter als mit meinem Vater, weil er ein bisschen streng ist. Jedoch unterstützt er mich immer, wenn ich Probleme habe. Ich hatte zum Beispiel letztes Jahr viel Stress mit den Prüfungen und er hat mir sehr geholfen. Die Familie meiner besten Freundin ist kleiner als meine: sie ist ein Einzelkind. Sie kommt auch gut mit ihren Eltern aus und sie machen viel zusammen. Jedes Jahr fahren sie ins Ausland und diesen Sommer werden sie Kanada besuchen. In den Ferien bleiben wir normalerweise zu Hause, weil ein Urlaub so teuer ist, wenn man eine große Familie hat. Trotzdem ist es schön, Geschwister zu haben.

Q3 — Sample answer

Ich mache jeden Winter Urlaub mit meiner Familie. Letzten Sommer bin ich mit meinem besten Freund / mit meiner besten Freundin in die Schweiz gefahren, aber leider hat es die ganze Zeit geregnet. Nächsten Frühling werden wir Österreich besuchen. Wir werden Fahrräder mieten, weil wir aktive Urlaube mögen / weil aktive Urlaube uns gefallen. In der Zukunft möchte ich in einem Hotel im Ausland arbeiten.

Answers

Practice Exam — Reading Paper

Question Number	Answer	Marks
1.1	T	[1 mark]
1.2	I	[1 mark]
1.3	Y	[1 mark]
1.4	J	[1 mark]
2.1	the main railway station	[1 mark]
2.2	walk straight ahead (until you reach a crossroads)	[1 mark]
2.3	take the first street on the right	[1 mark]
2.4	a small apple tree	[1 mark]
3.1	go to sixth form	[1 mark]
3.2	She doesn't have enough experience.	[1 mark]
3.3	The wage isn't usually very good.	[1 mark]
3.4	B	[1 mark]
4	Present: Two from: You can surf the internet. / You can send emails. / Most of them have (quite) good cameras. Future: Two from: You'll be able to download films quicker. / The battery life will keep improving. / You'll be able to save more data / music on them.	[4 marks]
5.1	NT	[1 mark]
5.2	F	[1 mark]
5.3	T	[1 mark]
5.4	NT	[1 mark]
5.5	T	[1 mark]
5.6	NT	[1 mark]
6.1	The most modern technology is used.	[1 mark]
6.2	adventure films / romantic films / foreign films	[1 mark]
6.3	You get a 20% reduction on the ticket price. / You can book the cinema for private viewings.	[1 mark]
7	A, C, F, H	[4 marks]
8.1	The problems are already so big.	[1 mark]
8.2	It's possible to make a difference in daily life.	[1 mark]
8.3	Use fabric bags or rucksacks instead of plastic bags. Sort / separate your rubbish so the plastic can be recycled.	[2 marks]
9.1	R	[1 mark]
9.2	F	[1 mark]
9.3	F	[1 mark]
9.4	NT	[1 mark]
9.5	R	[1 mark]
9.6	F	[1 mark]
9.7	NT	[1 mark]
9.8	F	[1 mark]
10.1	Es ist schon sechs Uhr.	[1 mark]
10.2	Sie wohnen nicht mehr in der Stadtmitte.	[1 mark]
10.3	Es wird noch später werden. / Die Kinder müssen noch länger warten.	[1 mark]
11.1	Es gibt viele Krankheiten.	[1 mark]
11.2	Two from: sich warm anziehen / sich viel an der frischen Luft bewegen / Menschenmengen vermeiden	[2 marks]
11.3	Two from: heiße Getränke / viel Ruhe / im Bett bleiben	[2 marks]
11.4	zurück zur Arbeit gehen	[1 mark]
11.5	gesund essen	[1 mark]
12	I am very interested in animals. [1 mark] Last summer I worked at an animal shelter [1 mark] and I learnt a lot there [1 mark]. For four years I have also been a member [1 mark] of a group which protects animals [1 mark]. Biology is my favourite subject [1 mark] and later I would like to study veterinary medicine / science [1 mark] so that I can help sick animals [1 mark]. That is my dream job. [1 mark]	[9 marks]

Total marks for Reading Paper: 60

Speaking Exam Mark Scheme

It's difficult to mark the practice Speaking Exam yourself because there isn't one 'right' answer for most questions. To make it easier to mark, record the exam and use a dictionary, or get someone who's really good at German, to mark how well you did. Use the mark schemes below to help you, but bear in mind that they're only a rough guide. Ideally, you need a German teacher who knows the AQA mark schemes well to mark it properly.

Role-play (15 marks)

In the Role-play, you're marked separately on your communication and your use of language. There are 2 marks available for communication for each of the 5 bullet points (tasks) in the Role-play (10 marks in total), and then 5 marks are available for your use of language.

Marks	Communication (per task)
2	You complete the task clearly.
1	You complete part of the task clearly.
0	You don't complete the task correctly.

Marks	Knowledge and Use of Language (overall)
4-5	Your knowledge and use of vocabulary is good / very good.
2-3	Your knowledge and use of vocabulary is reasonable.
0-1	Your knowledge and use of vocabulary is very poor / poor.

Photo Card (15 marks)

You are scored out of 15 for the Photo Card, and the only criteria is the quality of your communication.

Marks	Communication
13-15	You reply clearly to all of the questions and develop most of your answers. You give and explain an opinion.
10-12	You reply clearly to all or most of the questions and develop some of your answers. You give and explain an opinion.
7-9	You give reasonable answers to most questions and develop one or more of your answers. You give an opinion.
4-6	You give reasonable answers to most questions, but some of your answers are short and / or a bit repetitive.
1-3	You reply to some of the questions, but your answers are short and / or repetitive.
0	You don't say anything that's relevant.

General Conversation (30 marks)

The General Conversation should last between five and seven minutes, and you are marked on four separate criteria.

Marks	Communication
9-10	You consistently give well-developed answers, present information clearly, and explain your opinions convincingly.
7-8	You regularly develop your answers, present information clearly, and give and explain your opinions.
5-6	You develop some of your answers, usually present information clearly, and often explain some of your opinions.
3-4	Your answers are generally short, but you present some information clearly and sometimes explain your opinions.
1-2	You give short answers, and there are some questions you can't answer or don't answer clearly. You give some opinions.
0	You don't say anything that's relevant to the questions.

You lose one mark for communication if you don't ask the examiner a question at some point during the General Conversation.

Marks	Range and Accuracy of Language
9-10	You use an excellent range of vocabulary and structures. You use the past, present and future tenses confidently and correctly. Any mistakes are small and only occur when you're attempting complex structures and / or vocabulary.
7-8	You use a good range of vocabulary and structures. You use past, present and future tenses correctly, with small mistakes.
5-6	Your vocabulary is good and you use some structures and tenses correctly. Your meaning is clear despite some mistakes.
3-4	You use simple vocabulary and structures well. You use some different tenses and your meaning is generally clear.
1-2	You use simple vocabulary and structures, with some repetition. Frequent mistakes can make your meaning unclear.
0	You don't say anything that makes sense or can be easily understood.

Marks	Pronunciation and Intonation
4-5	Your pronunciation and intonation are mostly / consistently good.
2-3	Your pronunciation and intonation are often good, but there are several mistakes.
1	Your pronunciation can generally be understood, and you attempt to use some intonation.
0	You don't pronounce anything clearly and you cannot be understood.

Marks	Spontaneity and Fluency
4-5	The conversation flows naturally and seems spontaneous. You answer promptly and your speech flows easily at times.
2-3	The conversation generally flows well, but at times it seems as though you're relying on pre-learnt answers. Sometimes you answer promptly, but you hesitate before answering some questions, and you may not be able to answer them all.
1	Lots of what you say seems as though it has been pre-learnt. You hesitate a lot and your answers don't flow.
0	You don't show any spontaneity and can't be easily understood.

Writing Exam Mark Scheme

Like the Speaking Exam, it's difficult to mark the writing exam yourself because there are no 'right' answers. Again, you ideally need a German teacher who knows the AQA mark schemes to mark your answers properly. Each of the writing tasks has a different mark scheme.

Question 1 (16 marks)

Marks	Content
9-10	You've completed the task fully, your meaning is always clear and you've expressed multiple opinions.
7-8	You've written a good answer covering all four bullet points. Your meaning is clear and you've used multiple opinions.
5-6	You've written a reasonable answer, covered most bullet points and given an opinion. Your meaning isn't always clear.
3-4	Your answer is quite basic, covering some of the bullet points. You've given an opinion, but your meaning can be unclear.
1-2	Your answer is limited, covering one or two bullet points. Your meaning is often unclear and you haven't given an opinion.
0	You haven't written anything relevant. If you score 0 for content, you automatically get 0 for the whole question.

Marks	Quality of Language
5-6	You've used a wide range of vocabulary, some complex sentences and structures, and at least three tenses. Errors are mostly minor, and any major errors occur only in complex sentences and structures, with the meaning remaining clear.
3-4	You've used a variety of vocabulary, some complex sentences and structures, and at least two tenses. There are frequent minor errors and some major errors, but the meaning is usually clear.
1-2	You've used a narrow range of vocabulary and your sentences are mainly short. There are frequent major errors.
0	You haven't written anything that's suitable for the task.

Question 2 (32 marks)

Marks	Content
13-15	You've written a relevant, detailed answer that clearly gives a lot of information, and you've justified your opinions.
10-12	Your answer is detailed, mostly relevant and it usually presents information clearly. You've justified your opinions.
7-9	Your answer is generally relevant and gives plenty of information. Some bits are unclear, but you have given opinions.
4-6	Your answer gives some relevant information, but at times your meaning is unclear. You have given an opinion.
1-3	Your answer is basic, contains limited relevant information and is often unclear. You may have given an opinion.
0	You haven't written anything relevant. If you score 0 for content, you automatically get 0 for the whole question.

Marks	Range of Language
10-12	You've used a wide range of vocabulary, some complex sentences and structures, and an appropriate style.
7-9	You've used a variety of vocabulary, attempted some complex sentences and structures, and used an appropriate style.
4-6	You've tried to use a variety of vocabulary and sentences. Your style of writing is not always appropriate for the task.
1-3	You've repeated some vocabulary, your sentences are mostly short and simple, and you haven't thought about your style.
0	You haven't written anything that's suitable for the task.

Marks	Accuracy
4-5	Your writing is mostly accurate and you've formed verbs and tenses correctly. There are only a few small errors.
2-3	Your writing is more accurate than inaccurate, and your verbs and tenses are mostly correct. There are some errors.
1	You have made some major errors, your verbs and tenses are often incorrect, and your meaning is not always clear.
0	You haven't written anything that makes sense or could be easily understood.

Question 3 (12 marks)

Marks	Conveying Key Messages	Marks	Use of Grammar, Language and Structures
5-6	You've conveyed nearly all / all of the key messages in your translation.	5-6	You've shown very good / excellent knowledge of vocabulary and structures, with very few mistakes.
3-4	You've conveyed most of the key messages in your translation.	3-4	You've shown a good / reasonable knowledge of vocabulary and structures, and the translation is more accurate than inaccurate.
1-2	You've conveyed very few / few of the key messages in your translation.	1-2	You've displayed limited knowledge of vocabulary and structures, and there are lots of mistakes.
0	You haven't written anything relevant. If you score 0 here, you get 0 for the whole task.	0	You haven't written anything that's suitable for the task.

Transcripts

Section One — General Stuff

Track 01 — p.3

E.g. **M1:** Hallo Lisa! Hallo Helena!
F1: Guten Tag Jan. Guten Tag Helena. Wie geht's euch?
F2: Sehr gut, danke.
M1: Mir geht's auch gut.
F1: Was hast du am Wochenende gemacht, Helena?
F2: Am Samstag habe ich das Museum besucht.

1) **F2:** Ich bin mit meiner Familie dahin gegangen.

2) **F2:** Die Antiquitäten waren sehr interessant!

3) **F2:** Und vorgestern habe ich Zeit mit meinem Bruder verbracht. Wir sind durch den Park gegangen — es hat so viel Spaß gemacht!

4) **F1:** Wie schön. Und du, Jan? Was hast du am Wochenende gemacht?
M1: Nicht viel, Lisa. Ich habe nur Handball gespielt.

5) **M1:** Ich spiele jeden Tag in einer Mannschaft.

6) **M1:** Aber am Donnerstag gehe ich nicht hin, weil ich Geburtstag habe!

7) **M1:** Kommt ihr zu meiner Party? Ich gehe ins Kino.
F2: Alles Gute zum Geburtstag, Jan. Ja, ich komme zu deiner Party, danke schön.
F1: Ja, ich gehe gern ins Kino. Bis Donnerstag, Helena.
M1: Tschüss Lisa, tschüss Helena.
F1+F2: Tschüss!

Track 02 — p.10

E.g. **M2:** Guten Tag Anja, wie geht's?
F1: Sehr gut, danke Christian. Was machst du heute Abend?
M2: Ich mag Schwimmen, also gehe ich mit Sebastian ins Schwimmbad.

1) **F1:** Das klingt schön. Heute Abend gehe ich mit meiner Schwester einkaufen, aber ich hasse einkaufen gehen! Es interessiert mich nicht, denn es kostet zu viel Zeit.

2) **M2:** Das stimmt. Einkaufszentren gefallen mir auch nicht, weil es immer so viele Leute dort gibt.

3) **M2:** Wie ist es mit Popkonzerten — magst du sie?
F1: Manchmal. Es hängt davon ab, welche Band da spielt.

4) **F1:** Wie findest du Fernsehen?
M2: Ach, ich denke, dass manche Sendungen lustig oder spannend sind, aber ich bin lieber aktiv.

5) **M2:** Was hältst du von Fernsehen?
F1: Im Fernsehen sehe ich am liebsten die Nachrichten. Früher habe ich auch Zeitungen gekauft, aber jetzt lese ich sie im Internet.

Track 03 — p.11

E.g. **M2:** Dieses Jahr habe ich viel vor. Es geht schon im Januar los. Am dritten Januar mache ich einen Ausflug nach Berlin. Das wird super sein.

1) **M2:** Ich habe am fünfundzwanzigsten Februar Geburtstag, darauf freue ich mich sehr, weil ich am selben Tag eine große Feier machen werde. Im März habe ich bisher keine Pläne, aber am zehnten April kommt mein Bruder zu Besuch.

Urlaub mache ich ab dem ersten Juli. Ich fahre mit meiner Freundin in die Schweiz. Ich möchte dieses Jahr auch mehr Konzerte besuchen. Am elften Oktober gibt meine Lieblingsband ein Konzert in Leipzig. Ich werde dorthin fahren.

Track 04 — p.11

2a) **F2:** Hallo Rory, hier ist Priya.
M1: Hey Priya, was ist los?
F2: Ich habe mich gefragt, ob du am Wochenende etwas zusammen unternehmen möchtest. Vielleicht könnten wir zusammen Federball spielen.
M1: Na ja, darauf hätte ich keine Lust, weil ich Federball ein bisschen anstrengend finde.

2b) **M1:** Ich würde lieber schwimmen gehen — das ist entspannend. Möchtest du ins Hallenbad gehen?
F2: Ich bin mir nicht sicher. Schwimmen ist mir zu langweilig. Eigentlich wäre es schön, etwas draußen im Freien zu machen. Ich gehe sehr gern wandern.
M1: Gute Idee! Ein Spaziergang wäre super.

2c) **M1:** Hast du Lust, auch nachher etwas zu tun?
F2: Ja, warum nicht? Der neue Film von Klaus Klauter läuft im Kino. Meine Schwester hat den Film schon gesehen und meint, dass er fabelhaft ist.

2d) **M1:** Einverstanden. Der letzte Film von ihm war sehr spannend.
F2: Toll. Ich freue mich schon darauf!

Section Two — Me, My Family and Friends

Track 05 — p.18

1) **M2:** Hallo! Meine Familie ist relativ groß. Ich habe drei Geschwister — einen Bruder, eine Halbschwester und eine Schwester.

2) **M2:** Obwohl meine Mutter und ich blonde Haare haben, hat meine Schwester dunkle Haare.

3) **M2:** Meine Halbschwester Lisa hat braune Augen wie ich und sie trägt eine hellblaue Brille.

4) **M2:** Mein Bruder trägt im Moment einen Schnurrbart, aber ich finde das furchtbar, weil er hässlich aussieht!

Track 06 — p.22

1) **M2:** Guten Tag! Ich möchte mich kurz vorstellen. Ich heiße Bruno und mein Nachname ist Meyer. Das buchstabiert man em – ay – oohpsilon – ay – air. Ich wohne in Salzburg, aber meine Mutter kommt aus der Türkei.

Ich bin siebzehn Jahre alt und mein Geburtstag ist am elften Juli. Obwohl es zu viele Touristen in Salzburg gibt, wohne ich sehr gern hier, weil es so viel zu tun gibt. Ich liebe Musik und man kann immer Konzerte besuchen.

Track 07 — p.22

2a) **F2:** Heute habe ich einen Bericht für unsere lieben Zuhörer über das Thema „Freundschaft". Laut einer neuen Umfrage ist die Zuverlässigkeit die wichtigste Charaktereigenschaft, die wir suchen.

2b) **F2:** An der zweiten Stelle ist nicht die Großzügigkeit oder die Geduldigkeit, sondern der Humor. Siebzig Prozent der Befragten finden also, dass ein Freund unbedingt humorvoll sein muss.

2c) **F2:** Ein Freund, der normalerweise glücklich ist, ist für viele wichtiger als ein fleißiger Freund. Es stellt sich ebenfalls heraus, dass egoistische Leute es schwierig finden, eine echte Freundschaft zu haben.

Section Three — Free-Time Activities

Track 08 — p.27

E.g. **F1:** Ich bin Johanna. Letzte Woche war ich auf einem Rockkonzert. Da hat meine Lieblingsband gespielt. Das habe ich richtig toll gefunden und ich habe laut mitgesungen. Es hat total Spaß gemacht.

1) **F1:** Meine Schwester hört aber dauernd Popmusik und zwar immer die gleichen Lieder. Das geht mir richtig auf die Nerven. Sie mag keine Rockmusik und denkt, dass ich verrückt bin.

2) **F2:** Mein Name ist Preethi. Ich finde klassische Musik manchmal langweilig, daher höre ich lieber Rockmusik. Allerdings tanze ich Ballett und dafür ist klassische Musik prima.

3) **M1:** Ich bin Jürgen. Neulich habe ich ein Musikvideo von einem Rapper gesehen, das habe ich schrecklich gefunden. Ich höre lieber Popmusik, die ist nicht so hektisch und ich finde, dass sie mich entspannt.

Track 09 — p.30

E.g. **F1:** Ich bin Elsa. Ich habe beschlossen, überhaupt kein Fleisch und keinen Fisch mehr zu essen. Mir tun die armen Tiere leid.

1) **F1:** Äpfel finde ich langweilig, aber Ananas ist total lecker. Bananen esse ich nur ab und zu.

2) **F2:** Ich heiße Sonja. Mein Lieblingsgericht ist Wurst mit Pommes.

3) **F2:** Sonst esse ich aber nicht so gern Schweinefleisch.

4) **M2:** Mein Name ist Moritz. Ich koche total gern, am liebsten für meine Freunde. Letzte Woche habe ich Fleischlasagne gekocht, die haben alle super gefunden.

Track 10 — p.34

1a) **F2:** Guten Abend, Herr Hoffmann, es ist schön, Sie wiederzusehen.

   M1: Guten Abend. Na ja, letzte Woche war das Essen so schmackhaft, dass ich jetzt mit meiner Kollegin zurückgekommen bin.

   F1: Guten Abend.

1b) **F2:** Haben Sie heute Abend eine Reservierung bei uns, Herr Hoffmann?

   M1: Nein. Könnten wir bitte einen Tisch für zwei Personen am Fenster haben?

   F2: Ja, es gibt noch einen Tisch. Sie haben Glück.

1c) **F2:** Also, die Speisekarte. Ich muss Ihnen mitteilen, dass wir heute Abend keinen Truthahn haben. Es tut mir leid, aber die Ente kann ich Ihnen empfehlen, das ist unser Tagesgericht.

1d) **F1:** Könnten Sie mir bitte sagen, ob es Nüsse in den Nudeln gibt? Ich bin gegen Nüsse allergisch und muss vorsichtig sein.

   F2: Moment mal bitte. Ich werde mit dem Chefkoch sprechen.

Track 11 — p.34

2) **M1:** Der Schauspieler Franz von Oberfranz hat es satt mit Hollywood und will nicht mehr Schauspieler sein. Er wird sich von jetzt ab um seine Familie kümmern. Viele meinen, dass er zu den besten Schauspielern gehört, die es je gegeben hat. Er hat in allerlei Filmen mitgespielt, darunter Liebesfilme, Actionfilme und sogar Horrorfilme.

   Franz von Oberfranz hat eine sehr interessante Karriere gehabt. Er ist in einem kleinen Dorf in Österreich geboren und man hat ihn schon als Kind entdeckt. Mit fünfzehn ist er dann nach Amerika umgezogen und hat kleine Rollen in eher unbekannten Filmen gespielt.

   Sein erster großer Erfolg war ein Actionfilm, in dem er den besten Freund des Helden spielte. Seitdem hat er viele Preise gewonnen. Seine zahlreichen Fans werden ihn sehr vermissen.

Section Four — Technology in Everyday Life

Track 12 — p.43

E.g. **M1:** Mein Name ist Benedikt. Also ich könnte ohne meinen Laptop nicht leben. Nachdem ich meine Hausaufgaben gemacht habe, spiele ich darauf Videospiele. Das mache ich jeden Abend und es kann schon mal Stunden dauern.

1a) **F2:** Ich heiße Sümeyye. Ich benutze mein Handy, um mich mit meinen Freunden zu verabreden. Das ist total praktisch — ich schreibe schnell eine SMS und wir treffen uns dann, um zum Beispiel ins Kino zu gehen.

1b) **F1:** Ich bin Asli. Ich schicke häufig Fotos und kurze Videos an meine Freundinnen. Das macht Spaß und so bleiben wir in Kontakt, weil wir sehen können, was die anderen so machen.

1c) **M2:** Ich heiße Dimitri. Ich weiß gar nicht, was ich ohne Internet machen würde — ich lade mir häufig Musik und Apps herunter. Das geht schnell und ist auch billiger, als CDs zu kaufen.

Track 13 — p.43

2a) **F2:** Meine Mutter hat nicht so viel Ahnung von Technik. Deshalb hat sie neulich einen Kurs gemacht, der ihr hilft, das Internet zu benutzen. Jetzt weiß sie, wie man E-Mails schreibt und verschickt und im Netz surft.

2b) **F2:** Da meine Mutter viele Freunde im Ausland hat, möchte sie als Nächstes lernen, wie man soziale Medien benutzt. So kann sie mit ihren Freunden in Kontakt bleiben und auch Fotos austauschen.

2c) **F2:** Mein Bruder war anfangs sehr überrascht, als er vom Kurs meiner Mutter gehört hat. Aber er findet es gut, dass unsere Mutter so modern ist und sich für Technologie interessiert.

Section Five — Customs and Festivals

Track 14 — p.49

E.g. **M1:** Karneval kann auch „Fasching" oder „Fastnachtszeit" heißen. Es gibt auch viele weitere regionale Namen für das Fest.

1) **M1:** Man feiert Karneval an vielen Orten in Deutschland, in der Schweiz und in Österreich.

2) **M1:** Egal wie er heißt, ist Karneval ein sehr buntes und spannendes Fest. Die Tradition ist sehr alt und man denkt, dass das Wort „Fasching" eigentlich aus dem 13. Jahrhundert stammt.

3) **M1:** Die größten Partys finden in Gegenden statt, wo viele Katholiken wohnen. Zum Beispiel ist die Bevölkerung von Bayern meist katholisch und deswegen gibt es zur Faschingszeit eine ganze Reihe von Veranstaltungen dort.

4) **M1:** Die Festivitäten sind genauso unterschiedlich wie die deutschen Regionen. Jedoch verkleiden sich die meisten Leute

Track 15 — p.51

1a) **F1:** Ich bin Tina. Ostern ist eines meiner Lieblingsfeste, weil alles so schön bunt ist. Ich bemale Eier mit meiner kleinen Schwester zusammen und wir dekorieren das Haus. Dann verstecke ich Schokoladeneier. Meine Schwester glaubt noch an den Osterhasen, das finde ich total süß.

1b) **M2:** Mein Name ist Jakob. Ich finde, dass Ostern eine schöne Tradition ist, weil sich die ganze Familie trifft und wir zusammen Eier suchen. Das macht Spaß, vor allem, weil mein Opa sich dann immer als Osterhase verkleidet und wir viel zu lachen haben. Letztes Jahr hat es leider an Ostern geschneit, so dass wir die Eier im Schnee nicht gefunden haben.

1c) **F2:** Ich heiße Laura. Ich werde Ostern dieses Jahr in Florida feiern, weil mein Vater und ich dort Urlaub machen werden. Hoffentlich gibt es da überhaupt Schokoladeneier, die schmecken mir so gut. Ostern ohne Schokolade wäre kein richtiges Fest für mich.

1d) **M1:** Ich bin Jan. An Ostern langweile ich mich ein bisschen, weil alle Geschäfte geschlossen sind und meine Freunde keine Zeit haben, sich mit mir zu treffen. Ich gehe mit meiner Familie in die Kirche und dann haben wir ein großes Festessen. Das ist in Ordnung.

Track 16 — p.51

2a) **F1:** Ich liebe Weihnachten, weil es eine schöne Tradition ist. Ich schmücke den Weihnachtsbaum mit meinem kleinen Bruder zusammen und am Heiligabend singen wir Weihnachtslieder und packen die Geschenke aus.

2b) **F1:** Am meisten freue ich mich jedes Jahr auf das Weihnachtsessen, weil es bei uns immer Truthahn gibt. Meine Großeltern und andere Verwandte kommen dann auch und mir gefällt es richtig gut, dass die ganze Familie zusammen ist.

2c) **F1:** Letztes Jahr habe ich bei meiner englischen Freundin Sophie Weihnachten gefeiert.

2d) **F1:** Es war schön, am Weihnachtsmorgen Geschenke auszupacken, aber ich liebe es besonders, wenn wir am Heiligabend bei uns zu Hause unsere Kerzen am Weihnachtsbaum anzünden.

Section Six — Where You Live

Track 17 — p.59

E.g. **F2:** Ich war gerade im Kaufhaus in der Stadtmitte, weil ich eine neue Jeans gebraucht habe.

1) **F2:** Aber an der Kasse habe ich schöne Schuhe gesehen – sie waren so süß! Neben den Schuhen waren auch tolle T-Shirts, aber es gab meine Größe leider nicht, deswegen habe ich nur die Schuhe und die Jeans gekauft.

2) **F2:** Die Musik war zu laut und es gab zu viele Kunden, aber die Verkäuferinnen waren sehr freundlich und hilfsbereit, was mir gut gefallen hat!

3) **F2:** Nächsten Samstag muss ich das Kaufhaus wieder besuchen, um einen neuen Pullover zu kaufen. Ich bin im Moment pleite! Obwohl das ein bisschen ärgerlich sein wird, wird es mir hoffentlich eine gute Chance geben, mehr preiswerte Klamotten zu kaufen.

4) **F2:** Ich hätte gern ein neues Kleid für die Geburtstagsfeier meiner besten Freundin, aber das ist momentan leider nicht möglich. Ich brauche einen Nebenjob, um Geld zu verdienen.

Track 18 — p.62

1) **M2:** Entschuldigen Sie bitte, könnten Sie mir helfen? Ich bin hier fremd und muss mich mit Freunden treffen.

F1: Ja, sicher.

M2: Ich weiß, wo das Theater ist, aber wir treffen uns vor dem Kino. Wo ist das, bitte?

F1: Es gibt drei Kinos in der Nähe von hier. Wie heißt es?

M2: Das Kino heißt „Agora", glaube ich. Ist es weit?

F1: Nein, das ist gar nicht weit – Sie sind nur einen Kilometer entfernt. Nehmen Sie da drüben die dritte Straße links, gehen Sie über die Brücke und es liegt auf der rechten Seite.

Track 19 — p.64

1) **M1:** Hier in Bad Ems haben wir jeden Samstag einen tollen Markt, wo man viel kaufen kann. Es gibt hier auch eine schöne Kunstgalerie.

Auf der anderen Seite ist es hier nicht einfach, Klamotten zu kaufen — es gibt kein Kaufhaus. Die Stadt ist einfach zu klein, was ich furchtbar finde.

Track 20 — p.64

E.g. **M2:** Guten Abend, hier spricht Kai Heibel. Darf ich bitte meine Lebensmittel bestellen?

F1: Ja sicher! Was möchten Sie heute, Herr Heibel?

M2: Zuerst möchte ich drei Orangen bestellen, bitte.

2a) **F1:** Gut, und was noch?

M2: Ein Kilo Birnen, haben Sie die?

F1: Natürlich. Frische Birnen sind heute angekommen.

2b) **M2:** Super. Ich brauche auch vier Dosen Limonade, wenn möglich.

F1: Ja, die haben wir auch.

2c) **F1:** Sonst noch etwas?

M2: Ja, ich hätte gern sechs Scheiben Schinken.

F1: Sehr gut.

2d) **F1:** Ist das alles?

M2: Heute habe ich Geburtstag, also fünf Stück Kuchen, bitte!

F1: Oh, alles Gute zum Geburtstag, Herr Heibel! Ich liefere die Lebensmittel gegen achtzehn Uhr.

M2: Toll, danke schön! Auf Wiederhören!

Section Seven — Lifestyle

Track 21 — p.72

E.g. **F1:** Ich bin Nada. Gesundes Leben ist mir äußerst wichtig, weil ich fit bleiben will. Man sollte, wenn möglich, immer Rad fahren und nie mit dem Auto fahren.

1) **F1:** Was denkst du, Horst?

M2: Ich stimme dir zu. Es ist auch gut, wenn man so oft wie möglich joggen geht. Es ist nicht gut, wenn man nur zu Hause bleibt. Bist du auch dieser Meinung, Naima?

F2: Ja, das meine ich auch. Dazu ist es eine schlechte Idee, zu viel fernzusehen. Wenn man gesund sein will, sollte man jeden Tag Obst essen.

Track 22 — p.72

E.g. **M1:** Bis vor einem Jahr war ich mit meiner Fitness nicht zufrieden.

2) **M1:** Ich war total unfit und ich habe täglich Süßigkeiten und zu viel Schokolade gegessen. Obwohl es gar nicht gesund war, habe ich die ganze Zeit auch Zigaretten geraucht.

Damals hatte ich auch große Sorgen — ich wollte nicht abhängig werden. Mein Gewicht war auch ungesund und ich habe beim Arzt herausgefunden, dass ich fettleibig war.

Section Eight — Social and Global Issues

Track 23 — p.80

1) **F2:** Ich heiße Sofia. Ich habe in der Zeitung gelesen, dass es gleichen Lohn für gleiche Arbeit jetzt gibt und ich freue mich darauf. Früher haben Frauen weniger verdient als Männer.

2) **M1:** Mein Name ist Peter. Ich mache mir Sorgen um die Gewalttätigkeit. Manchmal, wenn Menschen zu viel Alkohol trinken, kämpfen sie abends auf der Straße. Das ist sehr gefährlich.

3) **M2:** Ich bin Lionel. Es gibt so viele Menschen, die aus Syrien nach Deutschland fliehen. Sie können in Deutschland Asyl bekommen. Unser Stadtviertel ist jetzt sehr multikulturell, aber die Einwanderer sprechen nur sehr wenig Deutsch.

Track 24 — p.82

1a) **F2:** Das größte Problem in unserer Gesellschaft ist heutzutage die Armut, denke ich. Was meinst du, Max?

M2: Das meine ich auch, Lola. Die Armut ist für Kinder besonders problematisch.

1b) **F2:** Aber wie kann man dieses Problem lösen?

M2: Die deutsche Bevölkerung könnte helfen. Sie sollte Geld spenden.

1c) **F2:** Vielleicht, aber das würde nur kurzfristig helfen. Ich wollte letzte Woche hundert Euro spenden, aber ich habe nur zwanzig Euro gespendet und ich kann mir das nicht jede Woche leisten.

1d) **M2:** Ich verstehe, was du meinst. Vielleicht muss die Regierung langfristig helfen. Sie sollte mehr für Sozialhilfe ausgeben.

F2: Das stimmt.

Track 25 — p.82

2) **F1:** Ich kann Leute, die umweltfeindlich sind, gar nicht leiden. Ich finde es so einfach, umweltfreundlich zu sein und es ist wichtig, unsere Welt zu schützen.

Manche Leute sagen, dass die Umwelt nicht ihr Problem ist, aber ich mache mir große Sorgen um die zukünftigen Generationen. Es wäre nicht fair, die Probleme schlechter für sie zu machen, glaube ich.

Section Nine — Travel and Tourism

Track 26 — p.88

1) **F1:** Ich heiße Monika. Letztes Jahr haben meine Freundinnen und ich in einer Jugendherberge gewohnt. Ich hatte ein bisschen Angst, aber es war auch gleichzeitig ziemlich spannend.

2) **M1:** Ich bin Ben. Ich übernachte immer in einer Pension, weil ich sie normalerweise günstig und bequem finde.

3) **M2:** Mein Name ist Anton. Hotels kann ich nicht leiden. Sie sind für mich einfach zu groß und unpersönlich.

Track 27 — p.92

1a) **F1:** Guten Tag. Können wir bitte hier zelten? Wir möchten bis Sonntag bleiben und sind nur zu zweit.

M1: Ja natürlich, es gibt noch viele Plätze.

1b) **M1:** Für zwei Personen kostet es achtzehn Euro pro Nacht. Ist das in Ordnung für Sie?

F1: Ja klar, das ist in Ordnung.

1c) **M1:** Haben Sie ein Auto? Dafür gibt es einen Zuschlag von fünf Euro. Man muss ebenfalls einen Zuschlag von drei Euro zahlen, wenn man einen Hund mitbringen möchte.

F1: Einen Hund haben wir nicht, aber ein Auto doch. Es ist das Blaue da drüben.

M1: Kein Problem.

1d) **F1:** Müssen wir jetzt schon bezahlen?

M1: Sie können am Ende des Aufenthalts bezahlen.

F1: Schön, dann machen wir das.

Track 28 — p.92

2) **M2:** Wir haben ein Ferienhaus in der Schweiz gemietet. Leider gab es viele Probleme. Das Badezimmer war sehr schmutzig und die Toilette war kaputt. Ich habe es schrecklich gefunden. Meine Mutter ist eine wunderbare Köchin, aber der Herd hat nicht funktioniert und so mussten wir in die Stadt gehen, um zu essen. Außerdem hatten wir kein Wasser und konnten uns nicht duschen.

Section Ten — Study and Employment

Track 29 — p.98

1) **F1:** Hallo Mutti. Ich habe endlich meinen Stundenplan für das neue Schuljahr. Im Allgemeinen ist es ganz angenehm. Ich habe viermal in der Woche Geschichte, was für mich perfekt ist. Ich muss sehr fleißig arbeiten, aber das stört mich nicht. Außerdem ist die Schule sehr früh aus. Um dreizehn Uhr endet für uns der Schultag.

2) **F1:** Leider ist aber nicht alles ideal. Dieses Jahr müssen wir uns morgens zur Versammlung treffen und das finde ich eine Zeitverschwendung. Molly lernt freitags in der sechsten Stunde Musik, aber ich habe das nicht gewählt – ich habe also beim Kunstunterricht keine Freunde dabei.

Track 30 — p.103

1) **M1:** Eine Umfrage unter Schülern zwischen elf und sechzehn Jahren zeigt, dass sich viele Schüler in diesem Alter gestresst fühlen. Sie leiden unter Druck. Ihrer Meinung nach haben sie einfach zu viel Schularbeit. Der Stressfaktor Nummer eins ist Hausaufgaben. Sie nennen auch unnötigen Druck von den Lehrern.

Ein Drittel wohnt sehr weit von ihrer Schule und muss ganz früh aufstehen, um dort hinzufahren. Nach der Schule sind sie äußerst müde.

Die Kinder klagen, dass sie zu wenig Zeit für Sport und andere Freizeitaktivitäten haben. Fast die Hälfte der Kinder meint auch, dass sie mehr Zeit brauchen, um alleine in der Schule zu lernen.

Track 31 — p.103

2a) **F2:** Einige Berufe erfordern bestimmte Eigenschaften oder Fähigkeiten. Zum Beispiel soll meiner Meinung nach ein guter Friseur kreativ und freundlich sein.

2b) **M1:** Meine Mutter ist Lehrerin und sie spricht fließend Englisch. Sie muss gut informiert und geduldig sein.

2c) **F1:** Ich will Bauarbeiterin sein und ich denke, dass eine gute Bauarbeiterin stark und fleißig sein muss.

2d) **M2:** Mein Bruder ist Verkäufer und er muss immer höflich und hilfsbereit sein.

Practice Exam — Listening Paper

Track 32 — p.157-165

1) **M2:** Willkommen in unserer schönen Stadt im Süden von Deutschland. Hier gibt es jede Menge zu tun. Die Berge sind ganz in der Nähe und wenn Sie gern wandern gehen, ist das ideal.

Außerdem bieten wir wöchentlich Mountainbike-Touren an, das macht allen immer großen Spaß.

Auf jeden Fall sollten Sie sich das schöne Stadtzentrum ansehen. Dort finden Sie auch viele gute Restaurants und vieles mehr, wie zum Beispiel die berühmte Kunstgalerie und mehrere Museen.

2) **M1:** Ich war letzte Woche auf einem Konzert und die Musiker waren wirklich gut. Am besten hat mir der Saxophonspieler gefallen, er hat ganz toll gespielt. Ich würde auch gern so gut spielen können, vielleicht sollte ich Musikstunden nehmen.

Früher habe ich Geige gelernt. Das war mir aber viel zu langweilig und deswegen habe ich damit aufgehört.

3) **M2:** Also ich habe richtig Lust, segeln zu gehen. Das habe ich noch nie gemacht, aber es hört sich total spannend an.

4) **M2:** Kommst du auch segeln, Anna?

F1: Ach nee, Lars, ich möchte lieber Trampolin springen, das macht so viel Spaß und hält auch noch fit.

5) **F1:** Mama, was möchtest du machen?

F2: Sport ist mir viel zu anstrengend. Ich bleibe lieber im Schwimmbad.

6) **F2:** Außerdem ist es heute sehr heiß — da ist es ungesund, Sport zu treiben. Man wird dabei viel zu warm.

7) **F1:** Eure Schule ist wirklich ganz anders als meine. Meiner Meinung nach ist es blöd, dass man hier eine Schuluniform tragen muss. Ich finde das langweilig und trage lieber meine eigenen Klamotten. Ihr habt auch einen längeren Schultag, was sehr ermüdend ist.

8) **F1:** Dafür fängt euer Unterricht später an als unserer, was prima ist. Wir müssen schon um acht Uhr in der Schule sein. Die Schulfächer sind hier zwar die gleichen wie bei uns, aber ihr habt echt interessante Aktivitäten nach der Schule, wie zum Beispiel der internationale Filmklub.

9) **F2:** Und nun hören Sie die Wettervorhersage für heute in Deutschland. Im Norden ist es am Morgen stark bewölkt, später gibt es dann auch einige Schneeschauer. Die Temperatur liegt bei minus zwei Grad.

Im Westen ist es heute früh sonnig und trocken, am Nachmittag kann es allerdings etwas wolkig werden und es bleibt weiterhin kühl.

Im Osten bleibt es heute meistens grau und dunkel, nur selten kommt die Sonne ein bisschen hervor. Am Abend gibt es dann starken Regen.

Im Süden ist es heute freundlich und etwas milder als sonst in Deutschland. Am Nachmittag kann man sich über viel Sonne freuen.

10) **M2:** Guten Tag, ich habe eine Reservierung für einen Tisch am Fenster. Mein Name ist Imran Assaf. Ich bin Vegetarier, haben Sie denn eine vegetarische Speisekarte?

F1: Ach so, ja, wir haben keine spezielle Karte, aber ich kann Ihnen ein paar vegetarische Gerichte empfehlen. Die Gemüsesuppe ist sehr beliebt und wir haben heute auch Nudeln mit Spinat.

M2: Na gut, ich muss es mir noch überlegen. Ich bestelle erst mal etwas zu trinken. Ich hätte gern eine große Flasche Sprudelwasser, bitte.

11) **M1:** Ich wohne in einer kleinen Stadt im Süden von England. Das gefällt mir sehr gut, weil es nicht weit bis zum Meer ist und ich im Sommer immer surfen gehen kann. Außerdem sind die anderen Einwohner meistens sehr freundlich.

12) **M1:** Jedoch ist es im Winter hier manchmal langweilig, weil es nicht so viel zu tun gibt. Wir haben zwar ein Sportzentrum und es gibt auch ein Warenhaus, aber bis zum nächsten Kino ist es ziemlich weit.

13) **M1:** Ich möchte später in einer größeren Stadt studieren, wo mehr Freizeitaktivitäten angeboten werden und man viele interessante Leute trifft.

14) **M2:** Ich war neulich auf dem Oktoberfest und war beeindruckt, wie viele Leute dort waren. Jedes Jahr fahren mehr als sechs Millionen Menschen hin und feiern zwei Wochen lang. Auf dem Fest herrscht immer eine gute Atmosphäre und es ist sehr lebendig.

15) **F1:** Vor zwei Jahren bin ich aufs Oktoberfest gegangen. Es gab Bier und bayerische Speisen wie Würstchen und Brezel — die haben mir besonders gut geschmeckt. Die bayerische Musik hat mir aber nicht so gut gefallen, weil es ziemlich laut und ein bisschen nervig war.

16) **M1:** Ich war letztes Jahr mit Freunden auf dem Fest. Alles war unglaublich teuer und die Zelte waren viel zu voll. Ich habe nicht vor, wieder dahin zu fahren.

17) **F2:** Also, ich habe ein Smartphone und ich benutze ständig soziale Netzwerke. Ich teile gern lustige Videos mit meinen Freundinnen. Am besten mag ich Videos von komischen Katzen.

18) **F2:** Wie sieht es bei dir aus, Shakeel?

M1: Ich diskutiere gern mit anderen über die Nachrichten. Viele teilen interessante Artikel und schreiben Kommentare dazu. So kann man verschiedene Meinungen zu einem Thema bekommen.

19) **F2:** Was denkst du denn, Evie?

F1: Also, es nervt mich oft, wenn man sich ständig auf sein Handy konzentriert, statt sich richtig zu unterhalten. Das ist richtig doof — es ist viel besser, mit Freunden zu sprechen, anstatt über soziale Netzwerke zu kommunizieren.

20) **F2:** Jedes Jahr bietet unsere Schule freiwillige Arbeit für Schüler in verschiedenen Organisationen an. Ihr könnt bei Umweltprojekten mitmachen und zum Beispiel gefährdete Pflanzenarten schützen. Außerdem gibt es Projekte in Schulen, wo ihr den jüngeren Schülern beim Lesen helfen oder mit ihnen zusammen Sport treiben könnt.

21) **F2:** Ihr könnt übrigens im Ausland ehrenamtlich arbeiten, da lernt ihr dann auch noch eine neue Sprache. Freiwillige Arbeit ist auf jeden Fall eine tolle Idee, weil man verschiedene Berufe ausprobieren und zugleich anderen Menschen helfen kann!

22) **M2:** Um gesund zu bleiben, ist es ganz wichtig, viel Obst und Gemüse zu essen.

F2: Das stimmt. Es ist aber genauso wichtig, regelmäßig Sport zu treiben — mindestens dreimal in der Woche.

M1: Fast Food enthält zu viel Fett für den Körper, das sollte man auf keinen Fall essen.

F1: Ich finde es am schlimmsten, wenn man raucht. Das ist sehr schädlich für den ganzen Körper und für andere, die in der Nähe sind.

23) **F1:** Tamal, weißt du schon, was du später als Beruf machen möchtest?

M2: Na ja, ich habe schon viel darüber nachgedacht. Vielleicht werde ich später Arzt, da Medizin mich besonders interessiert. Dann kann ich hoffentlich vielen Menschen helfen.

24) **M2:** Und was möchtest du gern werden, Yvonne?

F1: Tja, das weiß ich noch nicht. Eigentlich wollte ich immer Meeresbiologin werden, da ich das Meer und die Tiere liebe, aber dafür braucht man sehr gute Noten in Biologie und leider sind meine Noten zu schlecht.

25) **M2:** Hast du andere Interessen oder Ideen?

F1: Ich arbeite gern mit Jugendlichen — vielleicht könnte ich später Lehrerin werden. Ich spiele auch Trompete, aber es ist sehr schwierig, eine Orchesterstelle zu kriegen.

26) **M1:** Endlich war es still und die Schule konnte beginnen. Erst sangen die Kinder ein Lied, und Kasperle hörte zu; das gefiel Kasperle gut. Danach sollten die Kleinen schreiben und die Großen biblische Geschichten erzählen.

Herr Habermus ging zu Kasperle und zeigte ihm, wie er schreiben sollte: auf, ab, und Kasperle schrieb schnell auf und ab über die ganze Tafel, dazu nahm er die linke Hand.

„Linkshänder!" schrie Herr Habermus. „Nimm die rechte Hand!" „Er nimmt wieder die Linke!" rief plötzlich jemand von hinten vor. „Die rechte Hand sollst du nehmen, Kasperle!" wiederholte Herr Habermus. „Weißt du nicht, was links und rechts ist?"

Index

Index